Critical
Security Studies
and World Politics

CRITICAL SECURITY STUDIES
KEN BOOTH, SERIES EDITOR

Critical Security Studies and World Politics

EDITED BY
Ken Booth

LYNNE
RIENNER
PUBLISHERS

BOULDER
LONDON

Published in the United States of America in 2005 by
Lynne Rienner Publishers, Inc.
1800 30th Street, Boulder, Colorado 80301
www.rienner.com

and in the United Kingdom by
Lynne Rienner Publishers, Inc.
3 Henrietta Street, Covent Garden, London WC2E 8LU

Library of Congress Cataloging-in-Publication Data
Critical security studies and world politics / Ken Booth, editor.
     p. cm.—(Critical security studies)
   Includes bibliographical references and index.
   ISBN 1-55587-825-3 (hardcover : alk. paper)
   ISBN 1-55587-826-1 (pbk. : alk. paper)
 1. Security, International. 2. World politics—1989– I. Booth, Ken, 1943–
II. Series.
JZ5588.C75   2004
355'.033—dc22

                                                    2004014979

British Cataloguing in Publication Data
A Cataloguing in Publication record for this book
is available from the British Library.

Printed and bound in the United States of America

The paper used in this publication meets the requirements
of the American National Standard for Permanence of
Paper for Printed Library Materials Z39.48-1992.

 5 4 3 2 1

Contents

PART 3   EMANCIPATION

PART 4   CONCLUSION

Preface

The search for security is primordial, and never before in history has human society faced the multidirectional challenges that will predictably develop in the coming decades. Our times demand the very best efforts from those who study security, for world politics today is hounded not only by traditional interstate conflicts but also by nuclear-armed regional threats, ever more innovative and dangerous terrorist strategies, new problems arising from the dynamics of globalization, the challenges of inflamed religious and ideological extremism, the politics of rage provoked by obscene disparities of wealth and opportunity, and all the complexities caused by the momentum of global environmental change. Intense and multilevel insecurity will be in season for the foreseeable future, and so the search for security will be at the top of the agenda in public policy making as well as dominating countless private lives.

Can academic security studies respond to this predictably dangerous future? How should we think about security in this fractious world? What is real? How reliable is our knowledge? What can we do?

We live in an era of question marks about world security, and this volume cannot attempt to give all the answers. Instead, it seeks to offer a more complex picture of the situation as a result of shifting the way security has been conceived in mainstream security studies as the subject area developed in the period since World War II. This alternative approach has been labeled critical security studies (CSS). Although self-consciously new as an academic subject area, CSS has a long and complex ancestry in terms of its social and political ideas. Its impact on the intellectual fortresses of orthodox security studies has so far been limited, but its influence is evident elsewhere, and its key ideas have to be reckoned with by anyone seriously engaging with the theory and practice of security. CSS has established an institutionalized life of its own, with courses and programs in a number of universities, as well as a steadily growing body of research. It has achieved an academic presence that exceeds what has been written in its name, being for the moment a subject without much explicit literature. This volume is one attempt to help to fill that gap.

By critically reconsidering complex global insecurities, readers will be better able to pursue their own explorations of how we—*the global we*—might learn to live together, collectively, with more success than in the past. My hope is that the book will help today's students—so many of whom feel both angry and helpless about the world they have inherited—by explaining that there are different (and more complex) ways of thinking about security than the dismal ideology of political realism. CSS is not, of course, *the* answer in itself; it is only a field of study, a starting point. It is necessary, at the least, to go beyond academic critical explorations with a more policy-focused eye, and in the concluding chapter I outline a critical theory of security that seeks to turn helplessness into a specific theoretical commitment, anger into a political orientation.

*   *   *

In completing this volume, I want to acknowledge the support of Lynne Rienner Publishers. This volume would not have been part of the Critical Security Studies Series without the backing of Lynne Rienner herself. She declined my idea of establishing a journal to promote thinking about critical approaches to security and instead suggested a book series. She had faith—and in the most concrete way. If, in years to come, CSS ceases to be seen merely as an alternative to the political realist orthodoxy of security studies, then the production of relevant literature will have been vital. Good ideas do not spread without people who will back them with material support. Others at Lynne Rienner Publishers include Sally Glover in Boulder, Colorado, and Richard Purslow, LRP's former UK editor. I want to thank them for their professionalism and patience. I wish also to thank two anonymous referees who have helped make this a better book.

The version of CSS that will be elaborated in the introductory and concluding chapters had its origins in the late 1980s in the Department of International Politics at the University of Wales, Aberystwyth. The first master's course entitled "Critical Security Studies" was taught there in 1995, and I want to thank colleagues and students not only for making such a development possible but also for contributing to the intellectual buzz that has always accompanied it. Crucial to this development, including the teaching of the first course, has been Richard Wyn Jones, whose book *Security, Strategy, and Critical Theory* was published earlier in this series; he is also a contributor to this volume. Although some of the contributors will not see themselves fully in the embrace of this Welsh School, I believe that there is an important degree of coherence throughout; this is testimony to the seriousness with which the contributors undertook their task and wrote to their brief.

For bringing the manuscript together, I want to thank Elaine Lowe once more for her technical skills and Eurwen Booth for a variety of editorial help. Don Henderson deserves thanks for helping with the bibliography. I could not have finished this volume, as departmental chair, without the best support staff in the business; our administrators and secretaries all help to make the Aber International Politics Department the unique place it is.

—Ken Booth

1

Critical Explorations

Ken Booth

One of the decisions we face, as students of security, is whether to work exclusively to increase the power of our own group against all others (be it family, tribe, nation, empire) or to seek ways by which human society as a whole might live together collectively with more harmony, tolerance, and humanity than in the past. Whatever our separate decisions, they will have to be taken in conditions in which the threats to human society are more multidirectional than ever before. We—*the global we*—stand at a world-historical crossroad, facing critical choices as individuals and even more significant ones collectively.

On a planet that is daily becoming smaller, more overcrowded, and more overheated, the local politics of world politics will be fueled by the combustible interplay of interstate conflict, globalization, population growth, extremist ideologies, apparently unstoppable technological momentum, terrorism, consumerism, tyranny, massive disparities of wealth, rage, imperialism, nuclear-biological-chemical weapons, and brute capitalism—as well as more traditional cultural threats to peoples' security as a result of patriarchy and religious bigotry. Confronted, locally and globally, by such multidirectional dangers, one understandable response would be to give way to a sense of helplessness. The approach to security outlined in this volume aims to try to counter such despair by exploring different theoretical commitments and political orientations than those that led human society into its current predicaments in the first place.

This volume cannot, of course, deal with all the world's security issues or offer a set of grand strategic prescriptions to policymakers: space alone rules out such ambition. Its aim is therefore more limited, though nonetheless fundamental, for it attempts to offer students of security a deeper perspective than is currently available within orthodox security studies. The hope is to empower those readers who are not convinced that this is the best of all possible worlds, or that political realism is the best of all possible theories of security. As gaps are opened up in the walls of orthodox security studies, students will be better able to begin their own critical explorations of this fascinating, often deadly, and primordial subject area. From these explorations, a different world politics of security might yet be constructed.

The Realities of Security

There is one world, but many realities.[1] The one world is that progressively revealed by the natural sciences; the many realities consist of "facts by human agreement" in the social world, as John Searle puts it.[2] It is these political and social realities—"nations," "war," "gender," "capitalism," "sovereignty," "human nature," and so on—that demand the primary attention of students of security. They create the structures and processes by which humankind lives—or dies. Critical explorations of the ideas that made us is part of trying to answer three fundamental questions about security: What is reality? What is reliable knowledge? What might we do?

The study of security has always been a central concern in the academic discipline of international relations (IR). This reflects the circumstances of the discipline's birth in the profound and shocking violence of World War I (1914–1918) and the concern of liberal opinion in the West that the cry "never again!" be supported by the systematic study of the causes of war and the potential foundations of lasting peace. The issue area of security subsequently dominated the intellectual preoccupations of students of international relations, particularly in the aftermath of World War II and through the nearly half-century of the Cold War.[3]

Compared with the period of the Cold War, international security ceased to be central to students of international relations in the West during the decade between the dismantling of the Soviet state and the destruction of the World Trade Center, the defining points of what we can now see as the brief interregnum of the post–Cold War era.[4] Today, however, security in all its manifestations is back at the top of the agenda and looks set to remain there for the foreseeable future. In addition to traditional insecurities (the result of interstate rivalry, ethnic conflict, patriarchy, and so on), the new threats generated by globalization together with the causes and consequences of the U.S.-led war on terrorism combine to ensure that human society will for a prolonged period live in an "Age of Anxiety," a world "on the Edge," a "runaway world."[5] Human society faces what threatens to be a "long hot century."[6]

The subject of security studies as it developed in its orthodox form during the Cold War was constructed in the image of political realism (and for the most part a rather austere version of it). The academic project of critical security studies (CSS) involves rethinking the common sense of this orthodoxy from the bottom up while exposing the extent to which political realism is part of the problem in world politics rather than being the problem-solver. Such rethinking is a daunting challenge, not least because it requires disputing orthodox assumptions about the realities of security and insecurity. Whereas security studies until the 1980s had predefined answers to predefined questions, the subject as well as the subject matter has been an area of contestation since the end of the Cold War—and indeed earlier.[7] The rethinking-security debate took on new urgency with the world's one hyperpower declaring its global war on terrorism after September 11, 2001. The whole world, in different ways and for different reasons, is pursued today by that event's clouds of destruction, terror, and incomprehension. At the same time, though not as prominently, the huge disparities in access to human well-being across the world demand urgent attention, as is evident, year by year, from the annual report of the United Nations Development Programme (UNDP).[8]

Terror comes in many forms, from states as well as extremist groups, and from economic systems as well as political ambitions. Equally varied are the ways by which terrorism can be countered, from military to legal instrumentalities, and from prioritizing war/armed forces/violence to prioritizing law/policing/intelligence. There are no easy answers, for sure, to the threat of terror, whether its modalities are small numbers of people with explosives representing extremist groups, or whole armies of advanced aircraft and tanks representing sovereign states. What is sure is that violence invariably breeds counterviolence. In this respect it remains to be seen whether the war on terror declared by U.S. president George W. Bush in 2001 has made the United States and its allies more or less safe. Did the expansion of that war into a potential confrontation with the so-called Axis of Evil in 2002, followed in 2003 by the widely-criticized U.S.-led invasion of Iraq, help or hinder the cause of taking terror out of world politics? Opinion remains greatly divided, though less so after "Europe's 9/11" in Madrid in March 2004 and the deterioration of the situation in Iraq. In the struggle against terror, as in other areas of life, the search for security has never been more difficult, more urgent, and more contested. What is at stake in this volume, when we discuss the realities of security, and its theories and practices, is a critical dimension of the way human society attempts to organize itself in a globalized and fractious world.

Critical explorations of the realities of security have to start in our heads before they can take place out in the world. The challenges to be overcome should not be underestimated, for in grappling with the most fundamental questions of security, we are also grappling with the most basic questions of philosophy as they relate to ideas about reality, beliefs about reliable knowledge, and thinking about political practice. But if the endpoint of our critical explorations of security in world politics is uncertain, there is a definite starting point, and that is the task of engaging in a critique of the political realist orthodoxy in security studies. Ulrich Beck has described Max Weber's "iron cage" (in which he believed humanity was "condemned to live for the foreseeable future") as "a prison of *categories and basic assumptions* of classical social, cultural and political sciences."9 Political realism has operated as such an iron cage in world politics; it has created a prison of categories and assumptions that have worked to create a world that does not work for most of its inhabitants. To this extent, political realism has not been in the global human interest; nor, incidentally, is it calculated to promote a more positive relationship between humans and the rest of the natural world. The critical perspectives on security offered in this volume seek some liberation from realism's iron cage, though nobody should underestimate the theoretical and political obstacles.

As the academic discipline of international relations grew, *realism*— more accurately, *political realism*—was the label that was unhelpfully given to what became the orthodoxy about the nature and dynamics of politics among nations.10 We continue to have to live with this misnomer, despite realism's blinkers when it comes to seeing the world's realities. Realist-derived security studies in the past half-century has attempted to impose just one image of reality on a world that not only consists of many sovereign states but also is multicultural, divided by gender and class, and made up of individuals, families, tribes, nations, and other collectivities; there are also some solidarities across all these (and other) subdivisions of humanity. The field of security studies, constructed out of political realism, continues to offer its students one image of reality, with predefined answers to key global questions. This makes it a serious liability in world politics, being an iron cage seeking to contain a liquid ecology. It is a textbook exemplar of a problem masquerading as the problem-solver.

The Problem of "Problem-Solving" Theory

Powerful theories constitute behavior, as has just been suggested, and political realism has been no exception. It has shaped the way governments have behaved as well as explaining that behavior. As such, the theory has been self-replicating, self-fulfilling, and literally self-explanatory. It belongs to a category Robert Cox calls *problem-solving theory*. According to Cox, a problem-solving theory accepts the world (or situation) it inherits, seeks to make it work, and in so doing contributes to replicating what exists. Cox contrasts such theories with *critical theory*, which he defines as calling into question prevailing social and power relationships and institutions.11 This section will concentrate on the problems of the problem-solving theory of political realism; the section that follows will examine the promise of critical alternatives.

Realist-derived ideas about security have been elaborated over the centuries in a classical tradition of theorizing about the struggle for power between political units. John Mearsheimer today, Hans J. Morgenthau a generation ago, Clausewitz 200 years ago, and Thucydides twenty-five centuries ago have all projected a similar image of power politics, though inevitably colored by their own historical contexts.[12] Political realism is best understood not as an unbroken idea as much as an extended family of ideas.

The realist family has "classical" and "neoclassical" branches, "structural" or "neorealist" members, and "sophisticated" and "fine-grained" cousins. The most important distinctions in these labels relate to differences over the causal dynamics in behavior. Above all, there has been the disagreement between those realists who argue that the fundamental cause of political conflict and the struggle for power and security lies with human nature, versus those realists who argue that the driver is the logic of anarchy. For classical/neoclassical realists it has been the former, whereas for structural/neorealists it is the latter.[13] Other family members have come along with new theoretical blood, offering what they consider to be more fine-grained explanations of what drives international behavior.[14] But if there are differences over causal dynamics, the family resemblances show through because all political realists share a distinctive picture of the characteristics of world politics. This picture consists of the dominating significance of sovereign states, the drive of states to survive and maximize power, the expectation of interstate struggles, crises, and war, and the sanction of military force as an instrument of policy.

While political realism has been attacked and repackaged over the years,[15] its pull has remained powerful for all those students of international relations keen to speak to government officials, the armed forces, and the media. *Realism* remains the intellectual password into the corridors of power. It therefore retains considerable leverage. Nevertheless, its flaws are multiple and overlapping. The most significant are:

1. Realism is not realistic. The most basic flaw of realism is that it falls short in terms of describing and explaining how the world works. The period of realism's greatest domination of security studies was the Cold War, when its ideas were synonymous with Western (largely U.S.) interests and outlooks. One of the reasons why political realism accurately *described* some of the reality of the time was because it had helped to *construct* some of that reality. But it offered, and offers, a far from complete picture of world affairs. "We do not see things as they are, we see them as *we* are," argued Anaïs Nin. And the *we* who made the international relations/security studies discipline in the Cold War, for the most part, were middle-class male academics from North America or Britain. This group has described a world others living in the same world have not seen, except as an ideology of domination.

2. *Realism is a misnomer.* Political realism has a powerful—indeed iconic—name. In the subject of philosophy, realism since Immanuel Kant has been taken to be the view that objects exist independently of our perceptions. When statist theorists of power politics usurped the name "realism," they helped ensure they ruled by their claim to be the source of the one true legitimate knowledge about international relations. They claimed that their perceptions corresponded with the world *as it is*, independently of our perceptions. So one of the tragedies in the history of the study of international relations has been the way in which an ideology (a theory of the powerful, by the powerful, for the powerful) has appropriated the cloak of objectivity and practicality. Being described as a realist is a label to which we all, in ordinary language, aspire, for to be thought *unrealistic* in the world of politics is to be cast into political outer space.

3. *Realism is a static theory.* Political realism lacks a conception of the future. It is one of several theories that have been prominent in academic international relations that are static and ahistorical. Nuclear deterrence is another.[16] Static theories are based on the idea of a timeless present and do not adequately address questions about the long-term future of human society. In this regard, the dynamics of international politics are seen as endlessly replicated, in different circumstances and forms, but with the same causal dynamics. As mentioned above, for classical realists (strongly influenced by Christian pessimism) conflict has been seen as a manifestation of a flawed and unchanging human nature, and for neorealists the driver has been states wanting to survive in a condition of anarchy. The resulting conception is of an endless present of international conflict. Such a belief is the inevitable outcome of believing in a constant human nature and/or a timeless structure of states in competition. Logically, this becomes the best of all possible worlds.

4. *Realism's methodology is unsophisticated.* For much of the Cold War political realism was written about and taught on the basis of a crude positivism, a *common-sense* view of the world that eschewed theorizing and assumed an unproblematic relationship between fact and value, the observer and the observed, and theory and practice. A good deal of the pervasiveness of realism has been based on methodologically unselfconscious writing about history, as well as uncritical analysis of contemporary affairs; a realist-defined truth-as-correspondence view of the world has persisted. Certainly not all political realists have been open to the criticism of being unsophisticated theoretically. Today, for example, a great deal of sophisticated thought is put into method by realist-informed rational choice theo-

rists. But a sophisticated methodology can never provide an escape from a crude set of political assumptions; method becomes smokescreen.

5. *Realism fails the test of practice.* Realist-derived security studies must be considered a failed project when judged by the high levels of insecurity in the world and the dire conditions in which many people live. Political realism only adds to the misery of those suffering as victims of economics or gender, because it leaves political, economic, and social power where it is. What is more, despite all its claims to being a practical way of dealing with the world as it is, realism does not offer its proponents a clear guide-book. Realists differed over key issues in the Cold War (nuclear weapons policy and intervention in Vietnam, for example), and they have differed over key issues ever since (notably, in 2003, they clashed over the wisdom of the U.S.-led invasion of Iraq). As a political practice, political realism has helped to construct and perpetuate a world politics that fails to provide security for the vast majority of people in the world.

6. *Realism's unspoken assumptions are regressive.* At least as significant as realism's stated agenda are its unspoken assumptions about how the world works and what is important. These include the prioritization of the victims of politics over the victims of economics, the disregard of human rights except as an instrument of foreign policy competition (propaganda), the neglect of gender and class as causes of insecurity, and the refusal to countenance the possibility of fundamental change or learning in human society (except in the technological realm). Faced by the picture of the world offered by political realism, one is struck by what is missing: Where are the poor? Where are women? Where are the voiceless? Who benefits from those who are silenced? Where is political economy and race?

7. *Realism's agenda is narrow.* Political realism offers a massive but nonetheless narrow agenda for world politics. It is an agenda based on the perceived interests of states (and therefore of their elites); this so-called national interest is concerned with maximizing state security, maximizing economic well-being, and protecting the state's way of life. A statist agenda, derived from realism, cannot today cope with the multiple dangers bearing down upon human society globally; and this will be increasingly the case in the threatening future. Realism's trinitarian assumptions—focusing on statism, strategizing, and stability—maintain anachronistic distinctions between high and low politics, state and human security, and politics and economics. Such an approach misses in particular the tensions and insecurities that fester in the human/state security nexus.[17] This is precisely because it is problem-solving in the Coxian sense, with essentially one conceptualization of what the problem—admittedly a big one—actually is.

8. *Realist ethics are hostile to the human interest.* Realism is a tribal

doctrine. This is what I have labeled the "Luttwak Simplifier." Edward Luttwak once wrote: "strategy is not a neutral pursuit and its only purpose is to strengthen one's own side in the contentions of nations."[18] Realism is sometimes said to be apolitical and amoral, but these views are seriously mistaken. Realism is profoundly political and ethical, but both rest on a collective selfishness based in what Nietzsche called the "cold monster" of the sovereign state. The ethics of realism reach to the state boundary; beyond is anarchy and necessity. Choice exists only within the polity. The basis of statist ethics is the view that there is and should be no higher decision-making body or focus of loyalty than the state. There may have been periods of history when this could have been considered rational (as in the order-seeking Europe in the aftermath of the Thirty Years' War) but not today, in a globalizing world in which many challenges can only be met, with any hope of success, through transnational decision-making structures and loyalties. Realist ethics are narrow and selfish, based on the power politics of place. This is contrary to the human interest.

9. Realism is intellectually rigid. As the hegemonial discourse in international relations during the Cold War, realism practiced in universities what it argues must happen in politics. The power politics of Athenian professors of strategy overcame those Melian dissidents in peace studies and elsewhere who pressed to bring ideas of justice and reason into the picture.[19] It has been common for realist texts to disregard, dismiss, and call for the surrender of other ways of thinking about international relations. Pluralism has not been a realist virtue. Those philosophers who have thought about peace plans, or Marx-influenced theorists who developed ideas about structural violence, or those international relations scholars with explicitly normative approaches, or peace researchers who challenged conventional wisdom—all such voices were marginalized if not totally ignored by the political realist hegemon. As a result, the work of important figures such as Immanuel Kant, Johan Galtung, Richard Falk, and Kenneth Boulding did not appear on realist-derived reading lists; or they were paraded as the unrealist Other. During the Cold War, those who did not fit the realist position were criticized as naive or fellow-travelers. It is little different today in the era of the war on terror. The bipolar mindset—what I have called the "Cold War of the mind"—is alive and well and was exhibited by President George W. Bush when he declared, infamously, that those who are not with us are against us (in other words, those who did not stand shoulder-to-shoulder with his project were in effect on the side of international terror).

If the set of flaws just indicated is valid, then the hold of political realism in its various guises must be diminished in an era in which events are more complex and confusing than ever. Old political and philosophical certainties, and even the most powerful economic beliefs, are under challenge, while the academic study of international relations is rent by divisions over theory, agenda, and method.

Despite the critique of political realism in this chapter, its ideas cannot—and should not—be ignored; its disciplinary power and influence are too considerable. What is more, the persuasiveness of its worldview and the sophistication of some of its writings (especially that of its founding figures) demands serious attention. It is therefore unfortunate that some critical perspectives do not take political realism sufficiently seriously, for it has major strengths. Above all, its exponents engage with serious questions, notably the great issues of war and peace. The events following the terror attacks on New York and Washington on September 11 confirmed for many the image of international politics being an inescapable domain of conflict, necessity, and violence in which the only way to deal with force is by more effective force.[20] The worlds of world politics are more complex than the limited realist agenda suggests, but realism performs the important function of reminding those who are apt to marginalize the issues of war and peace of the persistence and utter seriousness of that agenda.

Robert Cox, in a much-quoted phrase, wrote in the early 1980s that all theory is "*for* some one or *for* some purpose."[21] If this is the case, as I believe it is, then the political realism that created and dominated mainstream security studies was also *for* some one and *for* some purpose. It represented a certain common sense about the world, but certainly not value-free common sense. This is still the case. Realist-derived security studies continues to survive and flourish because the approach is congenial for those who prosper from the intellectual hegemony of a top-down, statist, power-centric, masculinized, ethnocentric, and militarized worldview of security. This worldview is made up of some of the most powerful and plausible "facts by human agreement" and is legitimized by some of the most powerful and plausible fact-makers.[22] The power of this way of thinking is so deeply embedded that its proponents are unable to recognize it as ideology—such a powerful ideology indeed that it is often regarded as common sense, a timeless and self-evident truth. But political realism is an ideology, and ideologies are human inventions: it is not the expression of biological destiny, or nature's law, or the will of god(s), or a Supreme Truth. Like all human inventions, the set of attitudes and behaviors constituted by political realism can be unlearned, though it is never easy to overturn theories that serve the interests of the powerful.

All students of security are, of course, interested in solving problems. In one sense this is what politics is all about. But what is the problem to be solved? From a critical perspective, realism defines what needs to be solved, but it does so in a way that replicates a particular global regime of problems. It constructs and reconstructs the problems it is supposed to solve. In contrast, critical perspectives argue that, confronted as we are by a frighteningly dangerous world political future, human society urgently needs a security studies that goes beyond problem-solving *within* the status quo and instead seeks to help engage with the problem *of* the status quo.

Critical Promises

Critical approaches to international relations and strategic studies have sought to challenge realism's conceptualizations of the world not by reject-ing *the idea of the real* but by claiming access to a more sophisticated real-ism. In this respect, Heikki Patomaki and Colin Wight were exactly right when they wrote that what is at stake among contending theories of interna-tional relations is "not whether one should be a realist, but of what kind?"[23] They continue: "for positivists, sense-experience is real; for postpositivists, discourses or intersubjectivity is real." The real is out there for everybody, but it comes in varied forms and is contested. In other words, what is real in the social universe is created by the theory conceiving it. Truth is elusive and disputed, but it is essential for the functioning of human relations at all levels, including world politics.

The general term *critical theory* has come to apply to those schools of thought that have challenged what is often generalized to be the *positivist orthodoxy* in Western social science. These critical approaches are labeled *antifoundational*, that is, theories that argue that claims about what is true in human society cannot be finally decided against any ultimately objective or perfectly neutral standard.[24] Critical approaches are also sometimes known as *postpositivist* theories to distinguish them from the flaws of posi-tivism; the term *postpositivism* is one I do not like or any more use. Positivism comes in various guises, and is understood more or less dogmat-ically, by proponents and critics alike. I prefer to consider the issue at hand in terms of *naturalism* and *postnaturalism*. *Naturalism* is the idea that since human society belongs to nature, the well-established methods of the natu-ral sciences can be transposed into the study of human society. This, for reasons that will become apparent below, is a fallacy.[25]

The defining feature of critical approaches is that they reject the idea that human social behavior can be studied with the same scientific method as the study of the behavior of glaciers. The latter is amenable to conclu-sions that might be described as "true" in a way that is not available to the former. Human social behavior can be studied systematically and with criti-cal distance, but those who claim objectivity are the furthest of all from that traditional scholarly ideal. So for me, it is *postnaturalism* that unites critical theories, not *postpositivism*. Some positivists (various peace researchers, for example) claim that their conception of positivism is compatible with value-oriented enquiry and recognize the differences between the study of the natural and the social sciences. Sophisticated positivism has a role within critical theorizing.

Critical theory attempts to stand outside the framework of analysis or action it is exploring and seeks to appraise it in terms of its origins, development, institutions, and its potentiality for change. Unlike problem-solving theory, it does not accept the inherited or given framework as its parameters. Consequently, it is not self-replicating.[26] Political realism is the classical problem-solving approach to security in world politics; in contrast, the study of security from self-consciously critical perspectives attempts to stand outside the given local or global framework, offers critiques, and then explores the immanent potentialities in order to provide ideas that might promote the emancipation of people(s) from oppressive situations and structures. To claim that critical theorists stand outside a given framework is not the same as the claim of objectivity (the ideal of traditional theorists); the aim is to achieve a position of critical distance.

Critical distance is a means of engaging in "immanent critique" with the aim of promoting emancipatory politics. *Immanent critique* is the idea that instead of trying to move forward on the basis of utopian blueprints[27] one should look for the unfulfilled potential already existing within society. This gives enormous scope for analysis and political action, because it is always possible to find some emancipatory potential, somewhere, however unpromising an existing situation might seem to be. The ideas of immanence and emancipation in critical theory were expressed pithily by Kenneth Boulding when he noted the historical and anthropological truth that "whatever exists is possible."[28] We do not have to live oppressed by human wrongs, and there is evidence to prove it.

For the most part the ideas just discussed derive from the Frankfurt School of social theorizing. In the Conclusion (Chapter 11) I will argue the case for conceiving a critical theory of security based largely on this approach.[29]

I want to conclude this section by summarizing the promises of critical approaches in comparison with the flaws of realist-derived security studies, described earlier. What follows is a summary; some of the supporting argument will be provided in Chapter 11.

• Critical theory is more self-conscious and sophisticated in its analysis than political realism and so promises to be more "realistic" in accounting for phenomena.

• Critical theorizing that is true to itself is self-reflective and therefore flexible and open to change.

• Unlike political realism, critical theory is not a misnomer. It does not promise to deliver the impossible—objectivity and reality—but rather seeks to expose the problems of contemporary social and political life from a standpoint of critical distance, and it does so with an emancipatory interest.

• Critical theory escapes the confines of privileged referents by embracing no static interest save that of the primordial human being and the species in nature.

• Critical approaches promise to be ethically progressive and inclusive in a fractious era in which people increasingly live in each other's pockets.

• The political goal of critical theory is emancipation, that is, the progressive freeing of individuals and groups from structural and contingent human wrongs.

• Critical approaches have a broader agenda than political realism because of their comprehensive conception of the drivers and referents in the multiple worlds of world politics.

• While critical theories (no more than any other exercise in political theorizing) cannot guarantee practices that always match their proponents' hopes, they can offer a better understanding of the relationship between theory and practice in this first truly global age.

• Instead of political realism's fatalism and belief in a timeless present, critical theory recognizes change, the openness of history, and the unfinished nature of the human experiment.

So how, finally, should we conceive this subject-area labeled critical security studies?

What Is CSS?

Against what was described earlier as the trinitarian security studies of the post-1945 era—preoccupied with statism, strategizing, and stability—the growth of CSS was necessary and, I believe, should be celebrated. So far, however, I have used the label "critical security studies" as a relatively unproblematic term, likely to be widely understood and fully agreed. This is premature. CSS is controversial, somewhat contested, and regularly misunderstood. The fiercest critics are realists theoretically, and positivists methodologically. Realists argue that CSS threatens disciplinary chaos in security studies and the end of international order in practice, whereas positivist social science berates critical approaches for undermining hopes for a true science in the study of human affairs.[30] There are also important differences within critical approaches, and these will also be discussed in the Conclusion. Those who are drawn to postmodernism/poststructuralism, for example, tend to argue that critical theory in the tradition of the Frankfurt School is too wedded to Enlightenment ideas such as emancipation and common humanity. Given the serious divisions within critical approaches, it is necessary to go beyond CSS (as I will do in the Conclusion) unless one is content to allow the critical challenge to orthodox security studies to remain nothing more than an area of academic enquiry.

One theme that unites critical perspectives on security is a recognition of the idea that *security is essentially a derivative concept*[31]; this means, simply, that contending theories about world politics produce different conceptualizations of what security is all about in world politics. This is a relatively simple idea, but it has enormous political and other implications. While there is a consensus on the standard definition of security—to do with *being or feeling safe from threats and danger*—security in world politics can have no final meaning. Its meanings derive from ways in which different political theories conceive the structures and processes of human society, the entities that make up social and political realities, the major threats to privileged values and groups, the agents who can change things, and so on. Although I would argue that biological drives for security are universal (to have food, water, shelter, safety, and so on) the political, economic, and social "facts by human agreement" (such as nations and capitalism) are theory-based and contextual. It is political theories that shape the political meanings of how one understands world politics. Whether or not women are invisible in the world of diplomacy, for example, is not a question of their materiality but rather of how one is taught to see.[32] All this means that—beyond basic threats to the person as a human animal— being or feeling safe is experienced and understood in terms of political theories about nations, sovereignty, class, gender, and other facts by human agreement.

The argument above does not, of course, mean that one could possibly argue one's way out of the material reality of aircraft colliding with the World Trade Center on September 11; what it does mean, however, is that one's political understanding of those collisions is navigated via one's own cultural maps and political theories. The material facts spoke that dreadful morning, but not for themselves. They were spoken for the most part by long dead political theorists and philosophers, and we who watched, in horror and amazement, were for the most part merely their mouthpieces.

By conceiving security as a derivative concept, whose features vary according to the assumptions of different political theories, it should be clearer that the ideas that shaped mainstream security studies during the half-century of the Cold War (and that are still powerful) derived from a combination of Anglo-American, statist, militarized, masculinized, top-down, methodologically positivist, and philosophically realist thinking, all shaped by the experiences and memories of the interwar years and World War II and the perceived necessities of the Cold War. The aim of critical approaches is to challenge the conceptualization of security derived from such a worldview. This requires rethinking security from the bottom up in two senses. In the first place, investigating what security might mean in theory and practice from perspectives on politics that do not start from the same political, methodological, philosophical, and historically contextual perspectives as those associated with the ideology of political realism. And second, thinking about security from the perspective of those people(s) without power—those who have been traditionally silenced by prevailing structures.

Rethinking security from the bottom up involves an analytical two-step. The first and most important move is what for a long time I have called *deepening*. This means uncovering and exploring the implications of the idea that attitudes and behavior in relation to security are derivative of underlying and contested theories about the nature of world politics. Opening up the political theory of the subject in this way will result in the construction of a critical security studies based on:

• An ontology (ideas about the "nature of being"—what really exists in the social world) embracing a more extensive set of referents for security than the sovereign state, from individuals to the whole of humanity.

• An epistemology (beliefs about what comprises "true" knowledge) that is always willing to engage with the real in world politics but that rejects naturalist approaches to knowledge that, as discussed earlier, assume we can scientifically access the social world in the same way as we do the natural world.

• An orientation toward praxis (thinking about the relationship of ideas and action) that is explicitly emancipatory (culturally-sensitive and pragmatic but also universalistic).

From *deepening* comes the second step: *broadening*. This involves expanding the agenda of security studies beyond that of the hitherto militarized and statist orthodoxy. This does not mean that CSS attempts to turn every political problem into a security issue ("securitizing" politics[33]); on the contrary, it attempts to turn every security issue into a question of political theory (what might be called *politicizing* security).

Over the years I have sometimes found people confused by the ideas of deepening and broadening. It is helpful to keep three points in mind. First, broadening is to be thought of as something secondary to deepening. Broadening security is not itself a radical move; thus broadening—what many mistake as synonymous with rethinking security—can be conservative. The inclusion onto the security agenda of issues other than military threats is not radical if the broadening is derived from a conservative political theory. A neorealist theory of international politics is able to deliver only a neorealist agenda, however broad it might seem in comparison with traditional (i.e., military) security studies. The sectoral approach of the so-called Copenhagen School, for example, identifies five issue areas for the security agenda, namely, the military, environmental, economic, societal, and political sectors.[34] This broadens the agenda, but only from within a basically neorealist perspective. The starting point for analysis must be deepening: every security agenda should be interrogated to discover the interests and assumptions that shaped it.

Second, the deepening move is sometimes mistaken for being synonymous with a *level of analysis perspective*, that is, an approach to thinking about security that looks at the ways in which different "levels" in political life (in addition to the state level) might be affected by particular policies or events. Critical perspectives do explore different levels, but the idea behind the deepening move implies much more. It is concerned with drilling down into theories and practices of security in order to discover what the underlying political and philosophical assumptions might be. It is the process by which we explicitly connect security with political theory and so reveal the implications of security as a derivative concept. An important dimension of this drilling-down, of course, is to explore the different "referents" of security, in other words, the subjects of security. But this task cannot be captured by the simple idea of levels. For one thing, referents cannot always be conceptualized in the language of vertical levels. Is the category of class, for example, above the state level or below it? Connecting politics and security goes beyond the level of analysis problem, but the study of referents (and levels where relevant) is undoubtedly a central task.[35]

Third, it should now be clear that broadening derives from deepening. The latter exposes the theoretical assumptions of a particular conception of security to discover its ideas about the dynamic forces of world politics. Having identified a theory's assumptions (about the causal forces in world politics, the main fracture zones, who is us and who is them, and so on) the agenda that derives from the theory will be revealed. Agendas can be understood as more or less broad depending on the assumptions of the political theory from which they derive. Compare, for example, a broad security agenda for world politics, as might be derived from a feminist theorist, with an agenda derived from a neorealist. A feminist's agenda would involve changes in education and society as well as in the workings of diplomacy and the priorities in defense policy; a neorealist's agenda would be limited to the interests of governments.

Following this ground-clearing, it is now time to offer an answer to the question at the head of this section: What is CSS? *Critical security studies is an issue-area study, developed within the academic discipline of international politics, concerned with the pursuit of critical knowledge about security in world politics. Security is conceived comprehensively, embracing theories and practices at multiple levels of society, from the individual to the whole human species. "Critical" implies a perspective that seeks to stand outside prevailing structures, processes, ideologies, and orthodoxies while recognizing that all conceptualizations of security derive from particular political/theoretical positions; critical perspectives do not make a claim to objective truth but rather seek to provide deeper understandings of prevailing attitudes and behavior with a view to developing more promising ideas by which to overcome structural and contingent human wrongs.*

I appreciate that this definition of CSS leaves many questions hanging in the air. Some answers will be offered in subsequent chapters. In Chapter 11, I will argue that CSS itself is only the start of rethinking security from the bottom up. It should not be the end of critical exploration, which involves moving beyond the issue area in order to develop a specific critical theory of security. The latter implies a framework of ideas that together offer a theoretical commitment and political orientation out of which can develop those emancipatory politics calculated to promote a more humane humanity.

A single volume of collected chapters such as this cannot possibly map the whole landscape of CSS. The topics have been chosen here in order to discuss the most contested concepts and to illustrate aspects of them with reference to specific cases. Instead of the predefined statist agenda of realist-derived international relations, the volume is organized in three parts in relation to the three concepts which I consider to be the core of CSS: *security*, *community*, and *emancipation*. The theoretical chapters in each of the three main subdivisions will be followed by one illustrative chapter. The scope for choice for these was, of course, enormous, but no single case could illustrate all the theoretical points that needed to be discussed. There could have been chapters on the implications of U.S. hegemony, terrorism and the war on terrorism, humanitarian intervention, AIDS in Africa, environmental threats, militarized economies—and on and on. The potential agenda—*somebody's* insecurity—is depressingly long. Engaging with these insecurities in a theoretically informed manner is the chief task for students of the subject in the years to come.[36] It is by the study of concrete examples that we can go beyond theoretical knowledge toward a more empathetic understanding of the many realities of insecurity in the world.

I deliberately avoided organizing the book around the hegemonial agenda of realist-derived security studies, as important as most of it is. Such a plan would have simply reinforced the idea that there is only one set of realities. I hope to wean students of security away from the idea that the only important items on a world security agenda are those framed by Western newspaper headlines, the pronouncements of powerful governments, or the syllabi of IR realists. Instead of taking illustrative cases from the agenda of interstate conflict and war, the chapter topics were chosen to reveal the roles played by masculinity and racism, identity and interests, and communal conflict and emancipation.

As students of security, historically embedded as we are, we should nevertheless attempt to approach the issues of security and insecurity with as much critical distance as possible. At the beginning of this chapter I stated that all students of security are confronted by a potentially critical decision: to work as exclusive agents of our own group's interests or to try to adopt perspectives committed to the concerns of common humanity. In these different ways, each of us will play a role, however large or however small, in trying to make sense of world insecurity. In choosing what we study, and how we study it, we will contribute either to replicating a world that does not work for countless millions or trying to eradicate the human wrongs that stain so much of world politics.

Notes

1. This is my one-line summary of the "Introduction" in Searle, *The Construction of Social Reality.*
2. Ibid., p. 1.
3. For brief overviews of security studies through this period see Booth, "Strategy," in Groom and Light (eds.), *Contemporary International Relations*; and Booth and Herring, *Keyguide to Information Sources.*
4. The label "interregnum," deriving from Gramsci, was the theme of a panel I organized at the joint British International Studies Association/International Studies Association annual conference in March 1989. The papers were published in Booth, *New Thinking.* See especially "Introduction—The Interregnum," pp. 1–28. The continuing appropriateness of the term was confirmed a decade later in Cox, Booth, and Dunne (eds.), *Interregnum.*
5. These are recent book titles, though the phrase "runaway world" was first used by the sociologist Edmund Leach in the 1960s: quoted by Giddens, "Affluence, Poverty, and the Idea of a Post-Scarcity Society," in Booth (ed.), *Statecraft and Security,* p. 309. See also Dunant and Porter (eds.), *The Age of Anxiety*; and Hutton and Giddens (eds.), *On the Edge.*
6. This case is elaborated in Booth, "Two Terrors, One Problem."
7. I am referring here, among others, to the work done by peace studies specialists. For a sense of the early work done in this field, see for example: Burton, *Peace Theory*; Dunn, "Peace Research," in Taylor (ed.), *Approaches and Theory in International Relations*; Galtung, "Violence, Peace, and Peace Research," pp. 167–192, and *There Are Alternatives*; and Mack, *Peace Research Around the World.* Key outlets have been the *Journal of Conflict Resolution* and the *Journal of Peace Research.*
8. UNDP, *Human Development Report* (annual).
9. Emphasis in the original. Beck, "Risk Society Revisited," in Adam, Beck, and Van Loon, *The Risk Society and Beyond,* p. 211.
10. The literature on political realism is enormous. There is no better introduction to this family of ideas than Donnelly, *Realism and International Relations.*
11. Cox, "Social Forces," pp. 128–129.
12. Mearsheimer, *The Tragedy of Great Power Politics*; Morgenthau, *Politics Among Nations*; von Clausewitz, *On War*; Thucydides, *History of the Peloponnesian War.*
13. The classical statements of each, respectively, are Morgenthau, *Politics Among Nations,* and Waltz, *Theory of International Relations.*

14. For example, van Evera, *Causes of War,* pp. 1–13. He uses the phrase "fine-grained realism" to describe his approach.

15. Van Evera, *Causes of War*, is an illustration of theoretical refinement. Examples of the updating of classical realism includes Schweller, *Deadly Imbalances*; Zakaria, *From Wealth to Power*; Mearsheimer, *Tragedy of Great Power Politics*; see also Rose, "Neoclassical Realism and Theories of Foreign Policy," pp. 144–172. For an outline of the work of mainstream security studies up to the early 1990s, see Booth, "Strategy."

16. See, for example, Nye, *Nuclear Ethics.*

17. On the human security approach, see Thomas, *Global Governance, Development, and Human Security.*

18. Luttwak, *Strategy and History*, vol. 2, p. xiii; see also Booth, "Security and Emancipation."

19. The "Melian dialogue" is a standard reference in discussions of realism. Thucydides, *Peloponnesian Wars*, pp. 360–365.

20. See, for example, Gray, "World Politics as Usual After September 11," and Waltz, "The Continuity of International Politics."

21. Cox, "Social Forces, States, and World Orders," p. 182.

22. For an introduction to realism's founding fathers—it seems to have had no mothers—see Smith, *Realist Thought from Weber to Kissinger.*

23. Patomaki and Wight, "After Postpositivism? The Promises of Critical Realism," p. 218.

24. Ibid. On the debate about positivism, see, for a start, Smith et al., *International Theory.*

25. For brief but insightful comments on the problems of naturalism, see Hollis, "The Last Post?"

26. Cox, "Social Forces, States, and World Orders."

27. For a selection, see Carey (ed.), *The Faber Book of Utopias.*

28. Quoted by Johansen, "Radical Islam and Nonviolence," p. 166.

29. On the confusing label "critical," see Brown, "'Turtles All the Way Down.'"

30. The debate about IR and its subfields as a science goes back at least to the 1930s and has been repeated by each generation. An overview is Wight, "Philosophy of the Social Sciences."

31. See Booth, "Security and Self," pp. 104–115.

32. Enloe, *Bananas*, especially chapter 5, "Diplomatic Wives."

33. This is a major theme of the Copenhagen School. See Buzan et al., *Security*, esp. pp. 23–33, and Wæver, "Securitization and Desecuritization," in Lipschutz (ed.), *On Security.*

34. Buzan et al., *Security*, chapters 2–7. The Copenhagen School is discussed in Chapter 2 and the Conclusion.

35. Buzan first gave prominence to this issue in the first edition of his *People, States, and Fear*; R. B. J. Walker expressed it nicely when he suggested "the subject of security is the *subject* of security"; p. 78 in "The Subject of Security," in Krause and Williams (eds.), *Critical Security Studies.*

36. A range of relevant articles focusing on different parts of the world is collected in *International Relations* 18, no. 1 (March 2004).

Part I

SECURITY

PART 1 FOCUSES ON SECURITY: if *critical* defines the boundary of CSS, its focus is *security*. The study of security is the territory over which students of international relations have traditionally thought themselves most familiar; students of CSS question this and ask that the landscape be explored afresh, with new eyes.

The standard dictionary definition of security is relatively straightforward: "security means, simply, the absence of threats." The word *absence* here leaves open the possibility of both *being* safe from dangers of one sort or another, as well as *feeling* safe. Being and feeling imply, respectively, an objective and subjective dimension to security; the latter, in practice, leaves open considerable space for unjustified fear and miscalculation. What might be called in this context the "objective" dimension (recognizing that this is not some absolute standard, but rather an intersubjective and transhistorical judgment) can be revealed, to a greater or lesser extent, only by historical analysis, when it can be seen whether particular threats were exaggerated, or whether people felt safe when they were not.

If the stipulative definition of security is straightforward, this is not the case when the concept is examined in the context of world politics. As was explained in Chapter 1, this is because state security policies, the rationalizations given by political actors, and the motivations of different groups derive from diverse political theories. Conceptualizations of security are therefore the product of different understandings of what politics is and should be about. Consequently, security in world politics is neither a neutral nor a simple idea. What it means *to be* or *to feel* free—or relatively free—from the absence of threats in world politics depends upon whether the security issue being considered is by a political realist, a Marxist, a feminist theorist, a racist, a liberal internationalist, or whatever. Each will have different views about the primary referent to be secured, the types of threats most feared, and the key agents for action. This is what it means to say (as in Chapter 1) that security is a *derivative* concept. Revealing the implications of this insight is the task of *deepening*, also discussed in Chapter 1.

It follows from this that there is no politics-free definition of security in world politics. There is no simple conceptualization of the stipulative definition around which everybody, from all theoretical perspectives, can agree. We must recognize, on the contrary, that all conceptualizations (and operationalizations) are necessarily theory-driven. Security in world politics must remain an arena of intense political contestation because it is both primordial and the object of conflicting theories about what is real, what constitutes reliable knowledge, and what might be done in world politics.

The best starting point for conceptualizing security lies in the real conditions of insecurity suffered by people and collectivities. Look around. What is immediately striking is that some degree of insecurity, as a life-determining condition, is universal. To the extent an individual or group is insecure, to that extent their life choices and chances are taken away; this is because of the resources and energy they need to invest in seeking safety from domineering threats—whether these are the lack of food for one's children or organizing to resist a foreign aggressor. The corollary of the relationship between insecurity and a determined life is that a degree of security creates life possibilities. Security might therefore be conceived as synonymous with opening up space in people's lives. This allows for individual and collective human becoming—the capacity to have some choice about living differently—consistent with the same but different search by others. Two interrelated conclusions follow from this. First, security can be understood as an instrumental value; it frees its possessors to a greater or lesser extent from life-determining constraints and so allows different life possibilities to be explored. Second, security is not synonymous simply with survival. One can survive without being secure (the experience of refugees in long-term camps in war-torn parts of the world, for example). Security is therefore more than mere animal survival (basic animal existence). It is survival-plus, the plus being the possibility to explore human becoming.

As an instrumental value, security is sought because it frees people(s) to some degree to do other than deal with threats to their human being. The achievement of a level of security—and security is always relative—gives to individuals and groups some time, energy, and scope *to choose to be or become, other than merely surviving as human biological organisms.* Security is an important dimension of the process by which the human species can reinvent itself beyond the merely biological.

One of the things security allows people(s) to choose, paradoxically, is danger. Elective dangers, however threatening, are to be distinguished from structural and contingent insecurities. It is important here to distinguish between security threats and bodily risks. At the level of the individual, a person might choose to engage in a dangerous (threatening) activity—such as rock climbing or skydiving—but these activities can only be pursued by a person with the time, energy, education, and resources to participate in such activities; the risks to one's life in these cases are elective, not determined. These particular bodily risks are not part of life's inexorable insecurities. Likewise, a great power choosing to attack and invade a foreign country, when it is not directly threatened itself, is engaged in elective danger; it is not acting out of insecurity, as would be the case when fighting in self-defense following an invasion of its territory. It is motivated by ambition—like the rock-climber—but for increased economic, military, or political power as opposed to individual challenge and adventure. Troops and interests are put at risk, not core values. In rock-climbing or long-distance aggression, the risks are chosen, not imposed; they are the dangers elected as a result of the possibilities created by security, not the dangers imposed by domineering threats.

Because the condition of security is of such importance to societies—because it is primordial and deeply politicized—to have something labeled *security* is to give it priority on the agenda. Security, above all, is a powerful political concept; it is the sort of word that energizes opinion and moves material power. This is because it represents instrumental and political value and demands the committing of appropriate collective resources. It is something over which people(s) have been willing to fight.

The traditional definition of security in the literature of international politics emphasizes the protection of the territory and core values of states against foreign imposition.[1] From the discussion above, and in Chapter 1, it should be clear that a critically informed definition will be much broader and deeper than any offered by the mainstream. Accordingly, my definition is as follows: *Security in world politics is an instrumental value that enables people(s) some opportunity to choose how to live. It is a means by which individuals and collectivities can invent and reinvent different ideas about being human.*

The opening chapter of Part 1 is a comprehensive review by Steve Smith of approaches to theorizing security. He begins by problematizing orthodox thinking, arguing that the word has no neutral meaning in international relations. His position is that its meaning "depends upon and in turn supports" a specific view of politics; in short, all definitions of security are theory-dependent, and all reflect normative commitments. Smith contrasts this conceptualization with those convinced that security is synonymous with "the military dimension of state security." He discusses six nonorthodox approaches: the Copenhagen School, constructivist security studies, critical security studies, feminist security studies, poststructuralist security studies, and human security. Differences between these approaches are illustrated by what he sees as their different takes on the terror attacks on the United States on September 11, 2001. Smith concludes his overview by welcoming the fact that the concept of security is now genuinely contested; at the same time, he draws attention to the worries of those who believe the concept's usefulness may have been lessened by its being stretched too far.

Chapter 3 then focuses on the central preoccupation of realist-derived security studies: military strategy. Graeme Cheeseman discusses changes in the roles of the military in the face of what are seen as new security challenges in today's rapidly changing global context. He argues that established military roles were challenged by the events of September 11, which revealed the unexpected and complex ways in which global politics are developing. He questions whether state-based defense and security planners will adjust or will instead continue to adhere to the supposed timeless wisdom of power politics. The challenges that confront orthodox thinking include the reprivatization of violence, the postmodern form of the military, the continuities of Clausewitzian warfare, and the need to respond to the new security agenda. The latter consists of a set of immediate problems: meeting the requirements of peacekeeping, upgrading human intelligence, and improving antiterrorist capabilities. This discussion raises questions about the future of conflict and the utility of existing military structures, doctrines, and mind-sets in a world in transformation. Of particular significance, Cheeseman identifies: globalization and other dynamics that are affecting the character of states; the growth of multidirectional threats that are expanding security concerns; and the tendency of military forces to be employed less for traditional defense tasks and more on broader security tasks. He points not only to the inadequacies of orthodox military thinking in meeting these challenges but also to the weaknesses of alternative approaches (associated in the past with ideas of common security). The changing context for the employment of military instrumentalities is multiplying the difficulties facing all schools of thought within security studies, as the world's dangerous political rhythms have shifted to a higher tempo.

One of the new tasks identified by Cheeseman as causing problems for today's military forces is peacekeeping. The empirical chapter that closes Part 1, by Sandra Whitworth (Chapter 4), focuses on this troubled role and at the same time illustrates a number of traditionally neglected themes in security studies. The challenges of bringing security to conflict-riddled postconflict situations—Kosovo, Sierra Leone, Afghanistan, Iraq—have become familiar features of global headlines, and peacekeeping is an activity—defined broadly—whose salience might be expected to grow with the expansion of the war on terror.

The specific situation studied by Whitworth—Somalia in the 1990s—goes back to the early years of the post–Cold War period, but this allows the author to engage it with some critical distance. Somalia offers many lessons, not least because such situations are seen today as the potential breeding grounds for terrorism: the phenomenon of failed states. In such contexts, in which sovereignty ceases to have juridical or practical meaning, massive insecurity is threatened to both the inside and outside of the formal state. This is the backdrop to Whitworth's analysis of aspects of the Canadian peacekeeping operation in Somalia; it is an account that contains important warnings for similar operations in the future.

Whitworth's study throws light on the dark side of Canadian internationalism, as well as underlining some conveniently overlooked dimensions of military life. She demonstrates that state disintegration produces not only contexts in which war crimes might be witnessed but also situations in which other peacekeeping crimes might take place. In Somalia in the early 1990s, both sets of crimes resulted from a similar source, namely, the brutal mix of masculinity, militarism, and racism. Clearly, the behavior of armed forces is not simply a continuation of politics: ingrained cultural factors also play a part. Whitworth reveals the paradoxes and problems that can arise in the attempt to use the military instrument for purposes other than its primary (i.e., war-fighting) mission. The chapter's main theme is that Canada's reputation as a country committed to the ideals of peacekeeping was seriously challenged by the way its soldiers behaved in Somalia, and she speculates whether there is any escape from the dilemma created by the differing requirements of new peacekeeping as opposed to traditional war-fighting. She believes this dilemma has been particularly perplexing since the end of the Cold War, when military organizations faced something of a legitimation crisis in parallel with what some have seen as a crisis of masculinity.

How such dilemmas will play out over the long term in the era of the war on terror remains to be seen; for one thing, it might be expected that traditional military roles and masculinist values will reassert themselves. Whatever transpires, the experiences recounted by Whitworth raise questions about peacekeeping, intervention, and military training. Somalia is an important warning that Western countries must learn to see themselves as others see them—and not be fooled by their own propaganda. Their propaganda (and capacity for self-deception) portrays their interventions as always heroic and benign, but this is not how they are necessarily seen by others. This was evident in the huge gap between the expectations of the U.S. and British governments of being greeted as liberators in Iraq in 2003, and the actual hostile reaction of many Iraqis to finding themselves under U.S.-British occupation.

Whitworth's chapter, despite its narrow focus, leaves students of security studies with a great deal to ponder: not only the explanatory significance of neglected dynamics such as gender and race but also the potential practical significance of soft dimensions of power (feminist sensibility, for example) in the toughest corners. The chapter reminds us to see ourselves as others see us and supports, by empirical example, the arguments of the previous chapters about the complex character of actions taken in the name of security. This is a suitable warning to end the discussion in Part 1.

Note

1. For a list of some widely used definitions of security in the international context, see Buzan, *Peoples, States, and Fear*, pp. 16–17.

2

The Contested Concept of Security

Steve Smith

The events of September 11, 2001, give us good reason to reassess the meaning of the concept of security. While at first glance the events seem to strengthen the traditional view of security as primarily a military domain, closer examination reveals that to explain the events requires a much wider and deeper notion of security. Both the motivations of those who undertook the attacks on September 11, and the way in which the ensuing conflict unfolded, simply do not fit within the traditional realist view of security. Indeed, they strongly support the claims of those who wish to conceive of security more broadly. Moreover, the events, and the political debate surrounding them, illustrate the main theoretical claim of this chapter, namely, that the concept of security is essentially contested.

In an influential article published in 1956, W. B. Gallie introduced the notion that certain terms used in social theory are, as he put it, essentially *contested concepts*.[1] By this phrase Gallie does not simply mean that it is difficult to agree on a definition of a concept but that there are some concepts whose meaning is *inherently* a matter of dispute because no neutral definition is possible. The classical exploration of this problem in political science is in Steven Lukes's work on power, where he offers three very different views of power, each of which is inexorably connected to a wider view of what constitutes politics.[2] So, I believe, it is with the concept of security; thus what I want to do in this chapter is to outline and assess the main schools of thought concerning the meaning of the term. The survey will obviously be informed by my view that the term is essentially contested, and the reader might want to pause and reflect on whether this view is correct: some—for example, certain realists—would argue that the term has a clear meaning (it is to do with the military dimension of state security) and that widening and/or deepening the meaning of the concept reduces its utility for an explanation of international politics. But so as to make my position explicit, I see no such neutral meaning of the concept as possible;

27

any meaning depends upon and in turn supports a specific view of politics. There is, in short, no neutral place to stand to pronounce on the meaning of the concept of security, all definitions are theory-dependent, and all definitions reflect normative commitments. Furthermore, I believe that those who claim this neutral standpoint are merely unaware of the political and normative commitments entailed by their definition. Importantly, the contributors to this volume share a broad commitment to a specific conception of security and its relation to politics, people, and processes.

The question of whether the term "security" has been contested has recently been the subject of dispute. In his pathbreaking book *People, States, and Fear,*[3] Barry Buzan refers to Gallie's notion of essentially contested concepts to explain why thinking about the concept of security has been underdeveloped: "Such concepts necessarily generate unsolvable debates about their meaning and application."[4] Buzan cites Richard Little's claim that "the debates cannot be resolved because the concepts employed contain an ideological element which renders empirical evidence irrelevant as a means of resolving the dispute. It is this ideological element that ensures that the concepts will be 'essentially contested.'"[5] This interpretation has been disputed by Bill McSweeney, who has argued that Buzan's claim has led to "a widespread myth of the 'essentially contested concept' of security."[6] McSweeney disagrees with Buzan because he thinks that Buzan wrongly singles out security as a concept that is essentially contested, implying that other concepts used in writing about social order are different: "What is contested is that other concepts, like 'state,' are not essentially contested. All concepts of the social order are contested."[7]

Additionally, McSweeney argues that words like *security* (or *justice*) have added moral significance compared with many other concepts and thus cannot be considered "factual" or "susceptible of objective measurement."[8] For McSweeney, then, Buzan misrepresents the concept of security as essentially contested in two ways: first he treats it as a special case, as being essentially contested whereas other key terms (most notably the state) are not, and then he ignores any explicit discussion of the moral content of the term. To that one might add the observation that although the term "security" might be essentially contestable, it rarely has been; by that I simply mean that the term has rarely been contested. Until the late 1980s, very few of the debates about security have questioned the meaning of the term. The paradox is that *despite* Buzan's and McSweeney's comments the term has largely remained uncontested and unexamined.

I share Ken Booth's view that security (like the other two key concepts in this volume—community and emancipation) is essentially a derivative term, in the sense that it refers to issues embedded within the deep structures of politics and economics, issues that emerge through the zones of conflict and become the components of security policies.[9] Indeed, the events of September 11 show just how intertwined these concepts are, as the debates over the right way to respond brought to the fore the contested nature of conceptions of community and emancipation. What was the community that was opposing the Taliban? Who had the right to determine what counted as emancipation for Muslim peoples, notably women? What was the link between U.S. internal security and the human security of the dispossessed of the world? Are there security issues that transcend culture and political values? Can traditional military force cope with the kinds of security threats posed by Al-Qaida? All of these questions, which were central to the debate over how to respond, illustrate the contested nature of the concepts of security, community, and emancipation.

This chapter will examine and contest the meaning of the concept of security by looking at the main debates about broadening and deepening the concept. It is difficult to organize all the many debates about the meaning of the concept of security, and any labeling of the positions carries with it the danger of falsely grouping distinct positions together under one label. A common way of dividing up the literature is into traditional approaches that seek to broaden the meaning of the concept to areas other than the military dimension, versus those that want to deepen the definition of the concept so as to recognize that the term is derivative. The consequence of deepening the term is to open up the issue of who the referent objects are, and this leads to a discussion of actors other than the state. The problem with this categorization is that many writers want to broaden and deepen the concept, while others want to stress the importance of the military dimension but broaden it to focus on individuals or social groups. Therefore I have opted to look at six main schools of thought in the debates about the meaning of the concept of security.[10] These six schools are those involved in broadening and deepening the concept, and therefore I am going to concentrate on these; this means that I do not have the space to spend much time on traditional approaches. This does not mean that I am dismissing them, only that my focus is on those approaches that want to stretch the traditional conception of security (I have also recently written extensively about traditional approaches).[11] In the conclusion I return to the relationship between broadening and deepening the definition of the concept of security and its utility in explaining world politics. I want to do this because there has been a powerful new research project within traditional strategic studies. This has reinvigorated the mainstream and means that there is a major research program based on the traditional view of the meaning of security. In the conclusion I want to discuss whether widening and deepening the term might undermine it and reduce its utility as a key concept for the analysis of international politics.

The Traditional Literature and the Meaning of Security

Before I turn to look at these six areas, I want to note that I will not be considering the work within the mainstream that has proposed extending the traditional security agenda, since this does not fundamentally challenge the definition of the concept of security. Nor will I be dealing with the work of those who want to extend the concept to a focus on common security. Again, I have written about this elsewhere.[12] However, I do want to say something about two areas of the contemporary mainstream literature.

The first concerns the relevance for security studies of what is becoming the dominant methodological tool in the U.S. social sciences, namely, rational choice theory. *Rational choice theory* is an approach based on looking at the behavior of actors (states, individuals, companies, and so on) by assuming that these actors are rational, self-interested, and value-maximizing. The approach is very successful, especially in economics, where these assumptions have allowed for the development of enormously successful predictive theories. Unfortunately, the approach omits any consideration of the interests and identities of the actors and thus is criticized for fitting the world into its assumptions. This approach dominates the political science and international relations literature in the United States, and in a 1999 paper in *International Security* Stephen Walt evaluated its application to security studies.[13] For Walt, this was important because: "To put it bluntly, if reliance on formal methods becomes the sine qua non of 'scientific' inquiry, then scholars who do not use them will eventually be marginalized within their respective fields."[14] Walt evaluates the contribution of rational choice theory to security studies and has three main conclusions: first,

> formal theory is most useful for enhancing the precision of a theory, and for verifying and refining its deductive logic. . . . [Second,] formalization has not led to powerful new explanations of important real-world phenomena. For the most part, recent formal work has tended to take arguments derived from other scholars and place them in mathematical form. . . . [Third,] recent formal work generally lacks rigorous empirical support.[15]

Walt argues that these three factors explain why formal work has had little to say about real-world security issues: to this extent it reflects the cult of irrelevance that pervades the social sciences. His response is to call for more methodological pluralism wherein all approaches are valued and esteemed; although in view of his previous comments about the irrelevance of most constructivism and all reflectivist work to the real world, I wonder if he means all approaches?[16]

The second group of traditional approaches is what Gideon Rose has called "neoclassical realism."[17] The thinkers Rose has in mind are writers such as Thomas Christensen, Randall Schweller, William Wohlforth, and

Fareed Zakaria, each of whom has written a major book in the area.[18] Rose sees neoclassical realism as distinct from three other schools of thought about foreign policy. The first of these are *innenpolitik theories*, which see foreign policy as the result of domestic factors such as political and economic ideology, socioeconomic structure, and national character. An example would be the democratic peace theory. The main weakness of these theories is that "they have difficulty accounting for why states with similar domestic systems often act differently . . . and why dissimilar states in similar situations often act alike."[19] The second are *offensive realism theories*, which see states trying to achieve security but in so doing end up in conflict with other states; domestic differences matter little because the pressures on security policy from the international environment are "strong and straightforward enough to make similarly situated states behave alike, regardless of their internal characteristics."[20] The third are *defensive realism theories*, which "assume that international anarchy is often more benign—that is, that security is often plentiful rather than scarce. . . . In the defensive realist world rational states pursuing security can often afford to be relaxed, bestirring themselves only to respond to external threats, which are rare."[21] In such situations, balancing usually makes the use of force unnecessary. Offensive and defensive realist theories suffer from the opposite problem to that which affects *innenolitik* theories, namely, that states in similar structural positions do not always act alike.

In contrast, neoclassical realism sees state policy as the result of systemic factors "as translated through intervening variables at the unit level."[22] Thus what matters are both the relative material power of states and the perceptions of this by political leaders and by key elements of their civil societies. Rose notes that neoclassical realists treat relative power as their chief independent variable but see states as less focused on security than on a desire to shape and control their external environments; this aim has to be mediated through internal political debate, and thus there may be a significant lag between changes in a country's relative power position and security policies that reflect these changes.[23]

The books by Christensen, Schweller, Wohlforth, and Zakaria each explain security policies by tracing the relationship between the changing relative power of the state and the internal perceptions and definitions of it. In my view, works such as these constitute a powerful reworking of realist security studies, one focused on the traditional concern of realism, namely, the military power of the state. In an important sense, they have reconstructed and reinvigorated realist accounts of security and together constitute a robust counter to approaches that seek to broaden and deepen the term. But the account remains focused on the state as actor and with the external military dimension of security paramount; the events of September 11, 2001, suggest that such an account is only of limited use. This is

because one of the key actors, Al-Qaida, was not a state and, more important, was not organized in the traditional way that states have been organized. It was not hierarchical but was organized in a cell-like fashion, and its
chains of command were very different to those of the modern state; it may
be difficult to prove, for example, that Osama bin Laden ordered the attacks
to take place in the places and at the times that they did. This makes it difficult for states to negotiate with such organizations, especially when they do
not share a similar set of goals. In an important sense, Al-Qaida is not a
self-interested, unitary, and "rational" (in the sense of Western rationality)
actor maximizing power. Accordingly, rational choice theory will be of
very limited utility in explaining its actions, since its identity constructs its
interests and rationality in a way that rational choice theory simply cannot

factor in. Neoclassical realism is also of very limited use in explaining its
actions since the group does not have the same internal/external structures
that characterize the contemporary state.

Having summarized the main features of the mainstream literature on
the concept of security, I now turn to more radical assessments of the status
of security studies. I will look at six main areas of developments in the nontraditional literature.

The Copenhagen School and Security

The work of Barry Buzan has been enormously important in the development of security studies, at the core of what Bill McSweeney has dubbed
the "Copenhagen school."[24] There are many scholars involved in this
school, but Buzan, along with Ole Wæver, has had the most influence on
the debate. As Ken Booth argued in 1991, Buzan's 1983 book, *People,
States, and Fear*,[25] was "the most comprehensive theoretical analysis of the
concept of security in international relations literature to date."[26] The key
move made by Buzan in this book was to broaden the security agenda so as
to involve five sectors rather than the traditional focus on only one: military
security. To this, Buzan added political, economic, societal, and ecological
security sectors. These new sectors needed to be discussed because of
changes in the policy environment facing states in the 1980s. Importantly,
Buzan also discussed the individual as the "irreducible base unit" for discussions about security. But for Buzan, individuals could not be the referent
object for the analysis of international security. That had to be the state for
three reasons: It was the state that had to cope with the substate-state-inter-
national security problematic; the state was the primary agent for the alleviation of insecurity; and the state was the dominant actor in the international
political system. In this sense, Buzan sought to widen the definition of
security to encompass five sectors and to focus discussions about security
on three levels (the substate, the state, and the international system). But in

all of this the state was the referent object, as it is the state that stands at the interface between security dynamics at the substate level and the security dynamics operating at the level of the international system. As such, despite widening the definition of security, Buzan presents what is a sophisticated neorealist account of security. He has been criticized by, among others, Richard Wyn Jones for his focus on the state and for his quest for scientific objectivity. As Wyn Jones notes, the book should really have been entitled *States and Fear*.[27] For Buzan, however, strategic studies had become a subset of security studies, dealing with issues of military technology and the use of force.[28] This widening fits well with the kinds of security issues thrown up by the events of September 11, in that the debate over how to respond has involved much wider notions than military security alone. Economic, societal, and political security issues have been major considerations in how the alliance decided on its goals and strategies, with the political need to maintain an alliance of paramount importance. In this light Buzan's notion of widening security seems to fit events.

However, other aspects of his work do not match the events after September 11; the most important of these is his reliance on the state as the referent object. Ken Booth and I both wrote critically about Buzan's focus on the state as the referent object for security studies, preferring instead a focus on the individual.[29] Booth argued that the state was not the primary referent for security for three reasons: "states are unreliable as primary referents because whereas some are in the business of security (internal and external) some are not"; "even those which are producers of security (internal and external) represent the means and not the ends"; and "states are too diverse in their character to serve as the basis for a comprehensive theory of security."[30] In place of the state, Booth wants to place human emancipation at the center of security studies: "The litmus test concerns the primary referent object: is it states, or is it people? Whose security comes first? I want to argue . . . that individual humans are the ultimate referent."[31] Martin Shaw criticized Booth for this focus on the individual, arguing instead that society is the "missing dimension" of security studies, with the concept of social relations needing to "be interposed between and around the terms 'state' and 'individual.'"[32] For Shaw, both state and individual need to be understood within a sociological context, and neither is seen as standing alone.

By the early 1990s, the massive changes in European security meant that it was difficult for Buzan to maintain his view that the state was the referent object for security. In a series of publications with Ole Wæver, he developed the notion of *societal security* as the most effective way of understanding the emerging security agenda in post–Cold War Europe.[33] This shift was a very important one. Whereas state security focuses on sovereignty as the core value, societal security focused instead on identity, as represented in the ability of a society to maintain its traditional patterns of language, culture, religion, and national identity and customs. For Buzan and Wæver, societal security should not replace a focus on state security but should be more at the center of analysis, since it was societal security issues that seemed far more relevant to the debates of the 1990s than were the old state security ones: there was "a duality of state security and societal security, the former having sovereignty as its ultimate criterion, and the latter being held together by concerns about identity."[34] Prominent among these were issues such as migration, which simply could not be fitted into the state security debate.

Crucial in this move toward societal security has been Ole Wæver's work on the idea of "securitization,"[35] and the events of September 11 illustrate the salience of this idea. For Wæver, security is best understood as a discursive act, as a speech act. By this he means that labeling something as a security issue imbues it with a sense of importance and urgency that legitimizes the use of special measures outside of the usual political process to deal with it. This is exactly what many critics of the U.S. response to the September 11 bombings fear; by securitizing the attack, rather than, for example, treating it as a criminal act, the administration of George W. Bush made the overthrow of Al-Qaida a military rather than a legal or political action. Similarly, the antiterrorist measures being introduced in many Western countries after September 11 threaten to erode significantly individual security in the name of the state. This is clear in the British reaction, where the government under Tony Blair suspended age-old laws concerning detention without trial as a means of defeating terrorism. The implication is that the usual political procedures do not apply in a state of war, and so responses to September 11 fall outside standard political practices; these implications arise directly from the securitization of the issue. Wæver is concerned that securitization results in a militarized and confrontational mind-set, which defines security questions in an us-versus-them manner. Instead, Wæver proposes desecuritizing issues, that is, removing them from the security agenda. Thus, for the Copenhagen School the center of analysis is "the practice of securitization."[36] In one Copenhagen School book, Barry Buzan, Ole Wæver, and Jaap de Wilde define the focus as follows: "securitization studies aims to gain an increasingly precise understanding of who securitizes, on what issues (threats), for whom (referent objects), why, with what results, and, not least, under what conditions (i.e., what explains when securitization is successful)."[37] A successful securitization attempt requires that the actor has the position of authority to make the securitizing claim, that the alleged threats facilitate securitization, and that the securitizing speech act follows the grammar of security. Buzan, Wæver, and de Wilde then relate this securitization approach to the five sectors outlined by Buzan back in 1983 and to a regional focus, rather than a state focus, on security.

The work of the Copenhagen School has sparked considerable debate. I want to look at three main critiques. The most extensive has come from Bill McSweeney,[38] who makes three main criticisms of their work. First, they conceive of society and identity in an objectivist, positivistic way: "Society is conceived as a social fact, with the same objectivity and ontological status as the state."[39] What this means is that the society and identity are seen as "objective realities, out there to be discovered and analyzed."[40] McSweeney thinks that such a focus is inappropriate since it means that society and identity are seen as social realities that have an independent existence rather than being created and re-created by changing social forces. Second, McSweeney argues that, following from this view of society, Buzan and Wæver therefore misunderstand the nature of identity. They see identity as something "real" that exists for any society, whereas McSweeney sees that identity as something to be negotiated not discovered:

> Who we are is not a matter of fact imposed on individuals who "belong" to the "society" of Wæver et al. Their idea of a collective identity as a social fact projects the image of a collective self to be discovered: we are who we are . . . [whereas] we are who we want to be, subject to the constraints of history.[41]

Third, McSweeney argues that they are wrong to see society as embodying the one value of identity as the only object of vulnerability relevant to security analysis. This results in identities being given for any society and thus not open to criticism—they just are: "We are stuck with every other community's account of its identity also, and have no intellectual means of passing judgment on these accounts. We may not like who they are, but if they think that way, so be it."[42] For McSweeney, disagreements about identity are normative, not objective.

McSweeney also notes that there is a discontinuity between the focus of Wæver and Buzan's work and Buzan's earlier work on security: in *People, States, and Fear*, Buzan, breaking with realist assumptions, had introduced the domestic environment by arguing for the need for strong states that would result in a mature anarchy of security communities (a move that introduced change at the international level). This would be a more secure international system. As McSweeney notes,

> The problem, then, is to understand how the identity thesis is compatible with Buzan's security theory. The concept of a strong state rested on the subordination of society to the state. Now, in Waever et al. the state is no longer the uniquely privileged actor. . . . If society is now an independent variable, no longer subordinate to the state, then it appears that the Copenhagen school has undermined Buzan's original thesis.[43]

Buzan and Wæver responded to this critique,[44] and McSweeney replied in turn.[45] The core of their disagreement concerns the objectivist nature of identity, with Buzan and Wæver arguing that their approach to identity was pragmatic, not objectivist. Nonetheless, they claimed that over time certain characteristics remain unchanged and thus these become socially sediment-ed and can be taken as a given. McSweeney fundamentally disagrees with this and claims that identity can only be understood as a process—it does not sediment and cannot be taken as a given. And whereas Buzan and Wæver do not see a contradiction between the work of Buzan on the state and the focus of the Copenhagen School on identity and societal security, McSweeney maintains that

> Buzan has pulled the rug from under his earlier thesis. . . . Identity figured in this schema as an element of the domestic sphere under the control of the state. Now identity figures as a potential rival to the state, generated outside its control, and standing with the state as an equal priority for security concern and policy.[46]

The second critique, by Johan Eriksson, focuses on the nature of secu-rity as a social construction.[47] Eriksson argues that since security is a social construct, then "there are no objective threats, only attempts to saddle issues with 'security' implications. Thus anyone who classifies an issue as a 'security problem' makes a political rather than an analytical decision."[48] Accordingly, Eriksson believes that the Copenhagen School should acknowledge its own responsibility for widening the agenda of security. He claims that there is a contradiction between them saying that they are observing that security is now being widened and also taking on the role of advocating that the security agenda should be widened. In this sense, he believes that they are acting as much as politicians (and securitizers!) as analysts. Eriksson believes that this inconsistency can only be solved in two ways: "either its own political responsibility for making the case for a widened agenda is admitted and seriously discussed, or the multisectoral agenda is abandoned altogether, in exchange for a more rigid securitization approach."[49] Ole Wæver's reply to this claim is that Eriksson is simply mistaken that there is a logical contradiction:

> The set-up with five sectors is an analytical net to trawl through existing security discourses to register what is going on. Whether we then find that there is lots of securitization in the environmental sector or not is a prod-uct not of the sectoral approach but of actors' practices . . . the logical error is Eriksson's of mixing up a typology with claims about the empiri-cal existence of the different types.[50]

Jef Huysmans[51] has also assessed this aspect of the Copenhagen

School. He argues that it is Eurocentric not so much in its focus of study but more in the fact that its underlying argument about the logic of security is a culturally specific one. As such the school "has difficulties in including social challenges to their understanding of the logic of security itself"[52]; by this he means that its notion of securitization is predicated on a logic of the need to securitize, and this may well be a peculiarly Western notion.

A third, and very significant, critique is that of Lene Hansen,[53] who points to the absence of gender-based insecurity in the work of the Copenhagen School, primarily because when they write about security it is generally about societal, not individual or group (e.g., gender or ethnic), security. Using the case study of honor killings in Pakistan, she argues that there are two "silences" in the Copenhagen School: the first is "security as silence," by which she means that the securitization approach assumes that it is possible to speak about the security issue. The honor-killings case shows that it is not possible for this issue to be securitized: if women speak up about the problem, then they might increase the threat to themselves. The second problem is that under the Copenhagen School's definition of securitization, this can only take place when a referent object is existentially threatened; yet gender-based security issues do not fit within any of their definitions of referent object. As Hansen summarizes the problem, "The focus on speech produces problems in situations where the possibilities of speaking security are constrained, and the conditions for becoming a referent object are such that gender security is almost excluded from qualifying."[54]

In my view, the work of the Copenhagen School is one of the most interesting developments in the contemporary study of security. Although it is true that there are tensions between the positions of the two main members, Buzan's neorealism and Wæver's poststructural realism (by which I mean his use of the tools of poststructuralism to examine the ontology of the realist world), it is nonetheless the case that some innovative work is going on here. The members are to be admired for working together and trying to see how they can develop accounts of security, albeit from different starting points. Specifically, I find the intersection between Wæver's work on securitization and Buzan's focus on system structure to be compatible, since each can agree that, in the contemporary international system, securitization is overwhelmingly carried out in a realist way. I do see some conflict between the joint foci of societal security and the state, but there is no doubt that the school, via its clear research program, has been carrying out work that is far more innovative than anything in the mainstream of the subject. Despite this, it remains focused on the state as referent unit, and this is a limitation on its ability to analyze important parts of the September 11 events.

Constructivist Security Studies

By *constructivist security studies* I refer to those writers who have brought
the assumptions of social constructivism into security studies. What this
involves is adopting the infamous statement of Alex Wendt—that "anarchy
is what states make of it"—to the security realm: thus security is not something that exists out there waiting for analysts or politicians to discover it.
Instead it is created by human intersubjective understandings, as the social
world is something that is made and remade by those in it. Thus, much of
the reaction to the September 11 attacks concerned exactly what constituted
our security and how *we* should react so as to make ourselves more secure
in the future. The considerable public debate in all alliance countries—
except the United States—well illustrates this main theme of constructivist
security studies that security is something we define not something out
there that we respond to.

There are several major constructivist security studies,[55] and I will
focus on two examples. The first is the edited collection of Emmanuel
Adler and Michael Barnett, *Security Communities*.[56] In this collection, the
editors combine Karl Deutsch's work on security communities with social
constructivism. They quickly move to distinguish their approach from poststructuralism and see social constructivism as "well-suited to consider how
social processes and an international community might transform security
politics."[57] The central theme is that security communities are best understood as path-dependent and socially constructed, with the trigger mechanisms for security communities having both material and normative bases.

The important insight that this volume develops is that state actors
might see security as achievable through community rather than through
power. Security, therefore, is something that can be *constructed*; insecurity
is not simply the given condition of the international system. Security is
what states make it. Thus they believe that "a constructivist approach,
which recognizes the importance of knowledge for transforming international structures and security politics, is best suited to taking seriously how
international community can shape security politics and create the conditions for a stable peace."[58]

The second major volume developing a constructivist account of international security is Peter Katzenstein's *The Culture of National Security*.[59]
Katzenstein presents the volume as one written by international relations
scholars "rummaging in the 'graveyard' of sociological studies."[60] The central theme of the book is that national

> security interests are defined by actors who respond to cultural factors.
> This does not mean that power, conventionally understood as material
> capabilities, is unimportant for an analysis of national security . . . but the
> meanings that states and other political actors attach to power and security
> help us explain their behavior.[61]

Despite the arguments for broadening security studies, the Katzenstein volume looks at the social determinants of "a traditional, narrow definition of security studies."[62] This is because the editor sees this as a hard test of the use of cultural explanations. This test, however, is to be undertaken according to the dominant epistemological and thus methodological rules; thus cultural explanations compete with those of liberalism and realism.

Note that for all the focus on identity, norms, and culture in this volume, the state is still the actor, and military security remains the form of security to be explained. All of this is to be undertaken using the traditional forms of analysis. I find this last point to be absolutely crucial, since it means that there is an enormous limitation on the form of investigation that can be carried out. Despite the fact that these two volumes deal with culture and identity, they do so in such a way as to produce a very restricted notion of these phenomena. Not surprisingly, in a concluding chapter to the Katzenstein volume, Paul Kowert and Jeffrey Legro argue that the focus on norms, culture, and identity essentially does no more than to "fill gaps where other perspectives fall short."[63]

In a major review of constructivist security studies, Michael Desch examines precisely this question.[64] His main claim is that while they might tell us something about state behavior,

> The crucial question, however, is whether these new theories merely supplement realist theories or actually threaten to supplant them. I argue that when cultural theories are assessed using evidence from the real world, there is no reason to think that they will relegate realist theories to the dustbin of social science history. The best case that can be made for these new cultural theories is that they are sometimes useful as a supplement to realist theories.[65]

For Desch, the main limitation with cultural/constructivist security studies is that it adds little to existing theories. The main potential lies in helping realist theory by explaining lags between structural change and state policy. Beyond this, he believes that cultural variables have little explanatory power. Thus, he concludes that "the empirical track record of strategic culture suggests caution about how much of strategic behavior is explained exclusively by cultural variables. Therefore we should not abandon realist theories in favor of the new culturalism in security studies."[66]

Social constructivist security studies tend to be open to the same criticisms as social constructivism generally, namely, that it is essentially a form of rationalism, that it focuses on states, and that it is essentially social scientific (the "explanation" as distinct from the "understanding" sense of the word).[67] It uses terms that are also found in poststructuralism, feminist theory, and critical theory (terms such as "identity" and "culture"), but it can only conceive of these as causal (and usually intervening) variables rather than constitutive ones. They are phenomena that apply to preexisting (anthropomorphized) actors rather than things that constitute those actors. The clearest indicator of this is the way in which social constructivist writers on security studies wish to distance themselves from poststructuralism and other Parisian social theories.[68] This means that constructivist security studies can only go so far in accounting for the events of September 11, since they see culture as causal not constitutive.

The clearest lesson from September 11 is that the identity of those who undertook the attacks, and of those in both Al-Qaida and in states that supported them, was not some causal factor working on preexisting identities, but an essential part of their identity. Hence, for example, many Muslims would not believe claims that bin Laden had planned and ordered the attacks, whatever the evidence that the West put forward. This was not because of the strength or weakness of the evidence per se but because of the role of their identity in filtering the evidence. Finally, it is also important to note that constructivist security studies did not invent the notion that culture and strategy interacted: writers such as Ken Booth, Jack Snyder, and Colin Gray had each written about strategic culture in the 1970s and 1980s, and there has been a significant literature from outside the United States looking at non-Western examples of strategic thinking.

Critical Security Studies

Critical security studies is the most sustained and coherent critique of traditional security studies. The dispute between these two perspectives is often fought out in debates over whether courses should be called security or strategic studies in Europe (in the United States the term "strategic studies" was never popular and instead courses focused on "national security policy"). It is important to note that there are considerable differences within this broad approach. They are united more by perceived defects in the orthodoxy than by any particular alternative vision. There are two main streams in the writing in this area: the first is based around one book, and the second involves a much more cohesive school of thought.

The first is that of Keith Krause and Michael Williams. It was they who popularized the distinction between broadening and deepening security in 1996.[69] Their 1997 coedited volume[70] is self-consciously concerned with developing a critical security studies (as distinct from the critical security studies of the Welsh School, discussed below). Krause and Williams want to be theoretically inclusive in the sense of involving many different perspectives, all of which are outside the mainstream but that together do not add up to one view, let alone a Frankfurt School critical view. They cite Robert Cox's distinction between problem-solving and critical theories. The former takes the existing social and political relations and institutions

as the given starting point for analysis and then sees how the problems arising from these can be solved or ameliorated; the latter enquires into how
these given relationships and institutions came into existence and how they
might be changed.

Specifically, they want to question the focus of traditional security
studies on the state and to deconstruct prevailing claims about security. The
editors admit that "the reconstructive agenda of critical security studies is
more difficult to discern at this point."[71] Krause and Williams are not convinced that there is a new grounding for this reconstructive project; hence
the volume has a wide variety of approaches and positions in its separate
chapters, from subaltern realist (Mohammed Ayoob), through fallen realist
(Ken Booth), to postmodernist (Rob Walker/Simon Dalby). These contributors are united on two counts: a shared dissatisfaction with orthodox security studies, and a disillusionment with the agenda of mainstream security
studies after the end of the Cold War. The volume has four main themes:
first, to examine substantive as well as metatheoretical issues; second, the
need to rethink the nature of the political in security studies; third, to
explore what it means to be critical in security studies; and fourth, to begin
to reconceptualize the political once the state has been problematized. All
of these aims are consistent with the events of September 11 in that they
support the kind of wider interpretation of security that is needed to be able
to account for the complexities of those events. Krause and Williams make
an important contribution to the volume in which they outline the main
themes of critical security studies. They stress the need to move from a
focus on the military dimension of state behavior under anarchy to a focus
on individuals, community, and identity.[72] This will require not only a shift
in what we study but also a change in the ways in which the discipline has
treated critical work by marginalizing it; and Krause has written persuasively about the practices by which the discipline has been disciplined.[73]
But ultimately Krause and Williams are most interested in promoting intellectual pluralism and encouraging a variety of approaches to studying security rather than promoting one particular critical approach.

The second variant within critical security studies has a more defined
and focused definition of what critical security studies means. This can be
termed the Welsh School[74] and is based on the pioneering work of Ken
Booth[75] and Richard Wyn Jones[76] at Aberystwyth. It was Booth who coined
the phrase "critical security studies" at the conference convened by Krause
and Williams in 1994 (which became their edited book discussed above).
The "critical" here is different to that used by Krause and Williams. For
Wyn Jones it is decidedly critical, since the intellectual inspirations are the
works of Gramsci and the Frankfurt School. For Booth, although these
thinkers became influential after he first expressed his ideas (most influen-
tially in his 1991 paper titled "Security and Emancipation"),[77] his influences

were Kenneth Boulding, Johan Galtung, and Richard Falk.[78] Booth's 1991 paper and a series of conference papers by Wyn Jones in the early 1990s were the formative work of this school of thought. Wyn Jones's most extensive statement is to be found in his book *Security, Strategy, and Critical Theory*.[79] Wyn Jones firmly locates critical security studies within the intellectual tradition of writers such as Max Horkheimer, Axel Honneth, and Jürgen Habermas, where the focus of a genuinely critical theory is on emancipation; so it should be with critical security studies, argues Wyn Jones.

Using critical theory's distinction between traditional and critical theory, Wyn Jones argues that traditional security studies suffers from the same weaknesses as does traditional theory; namely, it reifies the existing order, treats the observer-observed relationship as unproblematic, reports "neutrally" on the existing natural order, and works within the scientific paradigm of positivism. Wyn Jones wants critical security studies to be firmly located within critical theory, and this implies a commitment to emancipation, a commitment that he sees as immanent in many other approaches to studying security (he cites poststructuralism and Wæver's concept of securitization as examples) but that must, he claims, rest on a notion of what emancipation means: only critical theory can provide this foundational notion of emancipation.[80] Similarly, Wyn Jones points to the role of critical security studies as emancipatory practice and, drawing on the ideas of Gramsci about hegemony, organic intellectuals and the role of a "war of position."[81]

For Booth, as well as for Wyn Jones, there is not only an explicit dissatisfaction with the statism and scientism of the orthodoxy; there is also a very clear view of how to reconceptualize security studies: it is to be focused on human emancipation. Only a process of emancipation can make the prospect of security more likely. Booth sees emancipation as *not* being the following: it is not a universal timeless concept; it cannot be at the expense of others; and it is not synonymous with Westernization. Instead it has the following three roles: it is a philosophical anchorage; it is a strategic process; and it is a tactical goal.[82] For Booth, emancipation "offers a theory of progress for politics, it provides a politics of hope and it gives guidance to a politics of resistance. . . . Emancipation is the only permanent hope of becoming."[83] Emancipation is explicitly linked to the critical project. "The next stage of thinking about security in world affairs should be marked by moving it out of its almost exclusively realist framework into the critical philosophical camp."[84] Booth argues that emancipation "should logically be given precedence in our thinking about security over the mainstream themes of power and order."[85] He defines emancipation as

> the freeing of people (as individuals and groups) from the physical and
> human constraints which stop them carrying out what they would freely

choose to do. War and the threat of war is one of those constraints, together with poverty, poor education, political oppression and so on. Security and emancipation are two sides of the same coin. Emancipation, not power or order, produces true security. Emancipation, theoretically, is security.[86]

Emancipation seems to be particularly helpful in thinking about September 11 because it forces us to think through the reasons for those undertaking the attacks as well as the complex question of how to respond. The motivations of those who carried out the attacks calls into question many dominant notions of a Western view of emancipation in that they were acting to oppose the very modernization that lies at the heart of the emancipatory process. Al-Qaida does not simply oppose the United States because of its presence in the Middle East generally and its support for Israel specifically; it opposes the United States, and regimes such as Saudi Arabia in the Middle East, because it sees them as pursuing modernization, which it deems as diametrically opposed to authentic Islamic identity. Similarly, the debate over how to respond to the attacks forces to the surface an entire set of questions concerning emancipation, the most problematic of which is whether the West has a right or an obligation to liberate the population of Afghanistan from the Taliban. Just as to many in the West this looks like emancipation, so to many in Islamic countries it looks like the latest version of imperialism, which in turn poses the question "What constitutes human emancipation?"

Another major statement that fits with a broad definition of critical security studies (although it has strong linkages with social constructivism) has been Bill McSweeney's *Security, Identity, and Interests*.[87] McSweeney's work is not easy to categorize because he is basically introducing a sociological turn (or, as he puts it, a reflective sociological approach) in security studies. However, I see his work as an example of critical security studies because its underlying intellectual theme concerns the emancipation of individuals: his referent point is clearly the individual. McSweeney's main worry about traditional security studies is that it has produced a very limited range of responses to contemporary threats precisely because it defines security so narrowly. Rather than seeing security as something out there, with no room for human agency, McSweeney sees security policies as involving choices and thus human agency. He argues that

security only makes sense if individual human beings are seen as its primary referent, or subject. . . . The basic need for security . . . is that which expresses itself as such in everyday life and in all social action. It is the security of social relations. . . . It is from this elemental experience, by definition common to all individuals, that we derive the social order as the general condition of ontological security.[88]

In short, security is something we choose, and we cannot escape our role in preferring one model of security to another simply by claiming that it is necessary. Security policy therefore inherently has a moral dimension, and it requires human agency. It is not to be understood deterministically.

Critical security studies was critiqued by Johan Eriksson, in the same article as he critiqued the Copenhagen School. Eriksson is particularly critical of the focus of critical security studies on emancipation, which he sees as continuing the peace studies tradition and, as such, is seen by Eriksson as "straightforwardly political: the established realism is blamed for the hostility, instability and injustice that unfortunately are a part of world politics. . . . Like classical idealism, critical security studies open up for discussion how things could and should be rather than how they are."[89] Eriksson has two main reservations about critical security studies. First, it is mainly a critique: "it is more a method of asking questions than a theory of politics . . . implications for political practice are not clearly discernible."[90] The second problem is "its instinctive moralism. . . . Like its idealistic forerunners, critical security studies implicitly assumes that good ends must be met with good means."[91] Above all, he feels that the approach does not have a theory of politics and power, and thus it limits the range of political choices. I do not want to spend much time dealing with this critique, since I feel that Eriksson is simply wrong in his interpretation of the work he cites. Michael Williams, one of the authors cited by Eriksson in his attack, has replied to the article and has effectively answered Eriksson's claims: Williams's main point is that Eriksson has reinstated the old idealist-realist divide and in so doing missed the point that critical security studies criticizes realism for being *unrealistic*![92] Andreas Behnke has also criticized Eriksson's "truncated and partially misleading representation of CSS."[93] This misrepresentation means that "Eriksson's rather limited conception of CSS as merely an 'apolitical' method prevents him from appreciating one of the central potential contributions of CSS, namely the possibility of reconceptualizing security and formulating alternative political strategies."[94]

A more substantial critique of critical security studies has been made by Mohammed Ayoob, who focuses on the stress on emancipation. For Ayoob,

> The problem with such semantic jugglery is that by a sleight of hand it totally obfuscates the meanings of both the concepts of security and emancipation. Booth's definition refuses to acknowledge that a society or group can be emancipated without being secure and vice versa. . . . Such semantic acrobatics tend to impose a model of contemporary Western polities . . . that are far removed form Third World realities.[95]

He adds that "to posit emancipation as synonymous with security and the panacea for all the ills plaguing Third World states can be the height of naïveté."[96] The problem for Ayoob is that Booth is concerned with human emancipation, whereas Ayoob wants to focus on the security of the state; his is an avowedly realist perspective. Thus he feels that "an explicitly state-centric definition of security is likely to provide an analytical tool of tremendous value that should not be sacrificed at the altar of utopian thinking, even if Booth would prefer to call it 'utopian realism.'"[97] The main weakness of Ayoob's criticism is precisely his realism: for Ayoob the state is the least worst option for third world states. The problem with this is that for many societies and populations the state is the main threat to their security. Therefore, Ayoob's disagreement with Booth ends up as a dispute over what is the referent point of security: for Booth it is individual, for Ayoob the state. On this I explicitly side with Booth, but the more important point is to note that Ayoob's critique turns on this one issue, and therefore his criticisms of critical security studies have to be interpreted in the light of his seeing the state as the only referent object of security.

In summary, the Welsh School of critical security studies offers both a powerful critique of the orthodoxy as well as a clear alternative foundation for thinking about security. In one sense it is a part of the wider literature on critical security studies represented by the Krause and Williams book, but in another it is a more coherent and focused conception. Of course, that fact opens it up to criticism by those who do not accept the focus on human emancipation, as well as by those who disagree with Booth and Wyn Jones's conception of emancipation, and the events of September 11 provide a fascinating case study of this problem. Having said that, it is particularly interesting to note that Booth and Vale[98] have applied this framework to southern Africa and that Booth and Trood have run a project on strategic culture in the Asia Pacific.[99]

Critical security studies, defined more generally, consists of alternatives for security studies to that offered by the mainstream. It is explicit in its rejection of realism, but it does not add up to an alternative theory. The Krause and Williams book contains a mixture of positions posing an alternative to realism (though Ayoob is in the volume as well) and thus offers a much wider perspective on security studies. And while the advantage of this is a wide-ranging critique of the traditional literature, the price is that there is less likelihood of an agreement on how to reconceptualize security: the book remains a set of chapters, not a coordinated alternative position to the traditional agenda. The Welsh School of critical security studies offers a very different focus to that of either social constructivism or the Copenhagen School, with the former concentrating on the state, the latter on state/society. Critical security studies is absolutely clear that emancipation is the goal of studying security, and it is this explicit normative focus that attracts criticism from those who believe that security studies should be objective and merely report on the world from a neutral vantage point. Like poststructural critics of the orthodoxy, adherents of critical security studies deny the very possibility of such a vantage point, meaning that all viewpoints involve normative commitments. The problem then becomes one of how to mediate between varying conceptions of security and emancipation, with the events of September 11 illustrating the difficulty of believing in a variety of routes to, and forms of, human emancipation yet having to face the unavoidable normative choice of preferring one set of answers to another.

Feminist Security Studies

Feminist work on security is extensive, although much of it deals with security implicitly as a result of a thoroughgoing critique of the gendered assumptions of traditional international relations, whereas other approaches, notably the Welsh School of critical security studies, deal explicitly with the gendered aspects of security. Within feminist work the central claim is that international relations is axiomatically gendered in its consequences, and in the forms of identities and subjectivities it constitutes, and yet the discipline is gender-blind. Interestingly, one of the main objections to the rule of the Taliban before September 11 came from feminist groups that repeatedly pointed out the appalling treatment of women in Afghanistan; yet this was deemed irrelevant to international politics, being seen as a domestic political matter. The case of Afghanistan under the Taliban powerfully illustrates the argument of feminist international relations scholars who claim that women are ignored yet centrally implicated in international relations. Similarly, Afghanistan shows how the processes of world politics constitute specific forms of gendered identities for both men and women.

The key writers in feminist international relations are Cynthia Enloe, Jean Elshtain, Jan Pettman, Spike Peterson, and Ann Tickner. Tickner has argued that while security has always been considered a masculine issue, "women have seldom been recognized by the security literature; yet women have been writing about security since at least the beginning of the century."[100] As Tickner notes, there are security issues that more directly affect women than men: 80–90 percent of casualties of war are civilians, the majority of them being women and children; the rape of women is commonly used as a tool of war; more than 80 percent of the world's refugees are women and children; and domestic violence against women is higher in militarized societies.[101] If the definition of security is broadened from one centered on the military dimension to include economic and environmental dimensions, then women's insecurity is even further highlighted: "while women represent half the global population and one-third of the paid labour force and are responsible for two-thirds of all working hours, they receive only a tenth of world income and own less than one percent of world property."[102] Tickner's conclusion is that this evidence shows the fallacy of the view that the state is the guarantor of security for its citizens; crucially, the state is "not neutral with regard to security provision for all individuals."[103]

In her review of the literature on gender and international relations, Jill Steans[104] notes the overlap between feminist and other critics of traditional security studies. But what feminists add is a concern with "what is lost from our understanding of security when gender is omitted."[105] For Steans, gender alters our thinking about security not by merely adding new issues and different perspectives but more by forcing us to reconceptualize security: "Rethinking security, therefore, involves thinking about militarism and patriarchy, mal-development and environmental degradation. It involves thinking about the relationship between poverty, debt and population growth. It involves thinking about resources and how they are distributed."[106]

There are four main strands to feminist security studies. First, there is the work of writers such as Carol Cohn and Miriam Cooke and Angela Wollacott on the masculinized nature of the language used in strategic discourse.[107] Second is the work of writers such as Jean Elshtain and Nancy Hartsock, who critique the conventional portrayal of the distinction between men and women as one of the "just warrior" and the "beautiful soul"; they note that these myths re-create the role of women as noncombatants and men as warriors.[108] Third, there is the focus on where women fit into international security. Here the work of Cynthia Enloe has been massively influential. Enloe asks the question "Where are the women?" and finds that they are implicated in international relations in fundamental ways.

Only by showing where women fit into international relations can we understand how power really operates. Thus Enloe looks at the roles of women as prostitutes around military bases, at how masculinity gets constructed in the military, and at the politics of how women soldiers are treated.[109] Finally, there is the work on the practical relationship between education, peace research, and feminism. For example, Birgit Brock-Unte shows the linkages between militarism and sexism in society and argues that both are maintained by a similar worldview, namely, that men are inherently aggressive and women inherently nonviolent, as well as that women are inferior.[110]

The contribution of feminist writers to security studies is in my view both considerable and ultimately destabilizing for the subfield. This is because feminist work simply undermines the distinctions central to security studies as traditionally conceived. Not only does much of this work subvert the notion of the state as neutral actor; it also problematizes the identities of men and women by seeing masculinity both implicated in and constructed by the interrelated processes of militarism and patriarchy. Crucially, looking at security from the perspective of women alters the definition of what security is to such an extent that it is difficult to see how any form of traditional security studies can offer an analysis. Even without falling into the trap of seeing a women's standpoint, there is nonetheless the obvious implication that traditional security studies is gender-blind and not gender-neutral. It is like looking at the world through completely different-colored spectacles, and I do not think that traditional security studies can accommodate such a fundamental challenge. And of course, the more that gender is constructed (as distinct from assuming that there are pregiven and fixed female and male identities and natures) the more that practices (and thereby the study) of security become implicated in reinforcing these practices. Security studies therefore becomes part of the process of securitizing the state and supporting the gendered nature of international politics; this is far from the self-image of traditional strategic studies, which dealt with how to explain and manage a world of recurring patterns, motives, and interests. Seeing these as gendered and as constructed implicates the study of security with the practice of security, and the resulting power/ knowledge relationship is most certainly not one conducive to a naturalistic social science.

The events of September 11 indicate just how gendered security processes in contemporary world politics are. On the one hand, the specific forms of gendered identity represented by the Taliban and Al-Qaida became important aspects of the debate over whether and how to oppose them. The security interests of women in Afghanistan as a group were highlighted among the reasons for coalition intervention. On the other hand, the alleged attitude of the hijackers toward women (in one case decreeing that they should not be present at the funeral, yet also allegedly employing female prostitutes) shows how important were conceptions of gender roles in the hijackers' identity and behavior. Theirs was a very specific form of masculinity, one that rejected the (Western-defined) emancipation of women along with other aspects of modernization. Finally, note that the consequences of intervention had significant gendered effects both in terms of freedoms restored and in terms of the humanitarian consequences of the intervention. In short, gender was a central component of the events and could not be treated as a side issue or as something to add a few comments about.

Poststructuralist Security Studies

Poststructural work on security represents another significant challenge to traditional security studies: like Welsh School critical security studies and feminist work, the poststructural approach is a school of thought that undermines the traditional conception of both security and its referent object. Some would argue that poststructuralism is the most extreme alternative to the traditional literature since it disputes the epistemological, methodological, and ontological assumptions of traditional security studies (and of many of the variants discussed above) in the most basic way possible. It is for this reason that most social constructivists and critical security studies writers are at such pains to establish the difference between their work and that of poststructuralists. Put simply, poststructuralists deny the form of foundations for knowledge claims that dominate the security studies debate. As can be imagined, this has led to much hostility toward poststructuralism in the discipline, usually along the lines that the work cannot be assessed using social science methods of scholarship. There simply are not the testable hypotheses and propositions that dominate traditional analysis; nor is there the same appeal to the "truth" of a historical account or narrative. It is also important to point out that most of the alternative accounts discussed above would also have major disagreements with poststructuralism, since each of them (with the exception of some feminist work) holds on to the kind of epistemological foundationalism that poststructuralism denies. The dispute between, say, the Welsh School of critical security studies, or social constructivist security studies, and poststructural security studies is a profound one.

Much that has happened since September 11 supports many of the main claims of poststructuralism. Central to any understanding of the events has to be an appreciation of the role of identity, discourse, and narrative. The parties involved in the conflict were not simply actors with different value structures and preference functions but instead had fundamentally different identities, which led them to see the world in terms of very distinct narratives. The story Al-Qaida told of the world was not just a different version of the story told by the Bush administration; instead it was a diametrically opposed narrative about human history. Similarly, the role of the discourse of security has been to construct notions of us and them, of inside and outside in ways that have presented as natural what are contingent and culturally/historically specific definitions of the participants and issues.

It is difficult to summarize the main themes of poststructuralist work because the picture of the world involved is so fundamentally different to that of mainstream and, indeed, most alternative approaches. A good discussion can be found in articles by Jef Huysmans and Lene Hansen.[111] What I will do is to point to two illustrative examples of work in this area. The first is the work of Bradley Klein, specifically his book *Strategic Studies and World Order: The Global Politics of Deterrence*.[112] Klein's aim is to look at strategic studies as a discourse closely allied to the processes of state formation and maintenance. Klein shows convincingly how the literature of strategic studies, far from being a neutral evaluation of the ineluctable condition of international anarchy, is instead a specific political move aimed at the defense of the state. As he puts it, "What else is Strategic Studies about but the political-military defense of the state? . . . Strategic violence is less a function of the state than an instance of its own assertion . . . an ongoing process of defining state boundaries."[113] This view is informed by poststructural writings because they encourage "an attitude of skepticism whenever certain key organizing principles are invoked."[114] These principles, such as the states system— the West—are, for Klein, cultural constructs "made intelligible to social agents through the medium of language. Instead of presuming their existence and meaning, we ought to historicize and relativize them as sets of practices with distinct genealogical trajectories. The issue, in short, is not whether they are true or false but how they have acquired their meaning."[115] Thus, for Klein, strategic studies itself is part of the process of defending the state, which is for him the very first question that should be posed: How do states capable of organizing violence emerge in the first place? "Strategic Studies relies uncritically on what most needs explanation."[116]

David Campbell has written some of the best empirical work in post-structuralist security studies. In his 1992 book, *Writing Security,*[117] he looks at how the practices of U.S. foreign policy construct the identity of the United States. Instead of the usual survey of how external dangers threaten the United States, "this book offers a non-essentialist account of danger which highlights how the very domains of inside/outside, self/other, and domestic/foreign—these moral spaces made possible by the ethical borders of identity as much as the territorial boundaries of states—are constituted through the writing of a threat."[118] Using Michel Foucault's notion of writing a "history of the present," Campbell wants to trace how the rituals of U.S. power develop over time. For Campbell, "security . . . is first and foremost a performative discourse constitutive of political order."[119] The book traces the ways in which U.S. foreign policy has served to articulate danger and difference to construct a specific identity for the United States as an international actor. This identity is never fixed and never final; it is always in the process of becoming and "should the state project of security be successful in the terms in which it is articulated, the state would cease to exist. . . . Ironically, then, the inability of the state project of security to succeed is the guarantor of the state's continued success."[120] The bulk of the book consists of a series of discussions of how this identity of the United States has been performed. The result is a very different account of state security, one that argues precisely against the consensus of the mainstream that state security policy is directed at protecting the state; rather, Campbell shows most effectively how that policy constitutes the identity of the state, the very thing that is the starting assumption for traditional approaches.

In a later book, *National Deconstruction*,[121] Campbell offers an illuminating account of the Bosnian war using Emmanuel Levinas and Jacques Derrida to discuss the nature of responsibility to the Other. Campbell argues that Levinas's work makes it impossible for anyone to say that the Bosnian war was not their concern. This is because Levinas's conception of responsibility toward the Other is not an add-on to already existing identities and subjectivities. Rather, "subjects are constituted by their relationship with the Other."[122] By reconfiguring subjectivity in this way, that is, by making it an effect of the relationship with the Other, Levinas also reconfigures ethics. Thus, the war in Bosnia gives us a lack of choice; we cannot opt out of involvement, because ethics "has been transformed from something independent of subjectivity—that is, from a set of rules and regulations adopted by pregiven, autonomous agents—to something insinuated within and integral to that subjectivity."[123] Campbell argues that this form of thinking "can help identify and energize the political ethos through which the development of a political life adequate to the complexities of Bosnia might be possible."[124] Crucially, Campbell shows how a deconstructive approach *can* say something detailed about what to do in a case like Bosnia, and he argues powerfully that deconstructive thought allows politics to be politics rather than a "predetermined technology or an undemocratic program hostile to the ethos of the Enlightenment."[125] In contrast to the international community's response, based on realism, which furthered the violence in Bosnia, he believes that "a range of political options informed by deconstructive thought might *possibly* better address the conflict."[126] He gives two reasons for this claim: the first is that whereas others might see contradictions as obstacles to a just politics, deconstructive approaches see these as the contradictions "necessary for a politics, and as such they have to be contested and negotiated rather than transcended and escaped."[127] The second, and, he claims, the more important, reason is that all political proposals "have to be *preceded* by the qualification of a 'perhaps' and *followed* by an insistent and persistent questioning."[128] In other words, deconstructive thought is never satisfied with claims that a lasting solution to problems can be, or has been, reached.

Human Security

The concept of human security has risen to prominence in the debate following the 1994 United Nations Development Programme (UNDP).[129] Starting from the premise that the end of the Cold War gave an impetus to rethinking the concept of security, the UNDP proposed that the focus should shift from nuclear security to human security:

With the dark shadows of the cold war receding, one can now see that many conflicts are within nations rather than between nations. For most people, a feeling of insecurity arises more from worries about daily life than from the dread of a cataclysmic world event. Will they and their families have enough to eat? Will they lose their jobs? Will their streets and neighborhoods be safe from crime? Will they be tortured by a repressive state? Will they become a victim of violence because of their gender? Will their religion or ethnic origin target them for persecution? In the final analysis, human security is a child who did not die, a disease that did not spread, a job that was not cut, an ethnic tension that did not explode in violence, a dissident who was not silenced. Human security is not a concern with weapons—it is a concern with human life and dignity.[130]

Such a conception of security fits well with the debates since the attacks on September 11. Much of the discussion over why the hijackers acted as they did, and more saliently why they received so much support in non-Western countries, focused on the role of poverty and despair. The hijackers and their direct sponsors justified their actions in terms of antagonism to the United States and its role in the Middle East, and most of the hijackers did not come from economically disadvantaged backgrounds. Nonetheless, the considerable amount of support they received—a level that shocked U.S. public opinion—can be directly traced to problems that a human security perspective highlights.

The UNDP report notes four main features of the concept of human security: It is a universal concern, relevant to people everywhere because the threats are common to all; its components are interdependent since the threats to human security do not stay within national borders; it is easier to achieve through early rather than later intervention; and it is people-centerd, in that it is concerned with how people "live and breathe" in society.[131] Human security is a narrower concept than the concept of human development, which the UNDP says deals with widening the range of choices that people can make (although, of course, there is an obvious link between the two since failed or limited development can lead to violence).[132] The UNDP argues that although there have always been two main components of human security—freedom from fear and freedom from want—the concept of security has tended to be more concerned with the former rather than the latter, and accordingly the concept needs to shift from stressing territorial security to stressing people's security, from concentrating on achieving security through weapons to concentrating on achieving security through sustainable human development.[133]

The UNDP report outlines seven areas of human security: economic security, food security, health security, environmental security, personal security, community security, and political security.[134] It also identifies six main threats to human security: unchecked population growth, disparities in economic opportunities, migration pressures, environmental degradation, drug trafficking, and international terrorism.[135] Since the initial annual report in 1994, the UNDP has refined the concept of human security, with the 1997 report introducing the distinction between income poverty and human poverty: the former refers to an income of U.S.$1 a day and less, and the latter to factors such as life expectancy and illiteracy.[136] The concept has also been taken up by international bodies such as the World Bank and the International Monetary Fund, as well as by some governments. The most significant of these has been the use of the concept by the Canadian and Japanese governments. The Canadian usage of the concept differs in an important way from the UNDP usage: although the Canadian government pointed to the important role of the UNDP in refocusing attention on human rather than state security,

> the very breadth of the UNDP approach . . . made it unwieldy as a policy instrument [and] largely ignored the continuing human insecurity resulting from violent conflict. By the UNDP's own criteria, human insecurity is greatest during war. Of the 25 countries at the bottom of the 1998 Human Development Index, more than half are suffering the direct or indirect effects of violent conflict.[137]

The Canadian government is mainly concerned with measures to lessen the effects of conflict on people and thus has concentrated on measures such as the ban on landmines and the creation of the International Criminal Court to hold people responsible for war crimes. The Japanese government's concept of human security is much broader than the Canadian government's in that it is very closely related to the UNDP view: specifically noting the work of those who press for banning landmines and creating international criminal courts, the government nonetheless states that "in Japan's view, however, human security is a much broader concept . . . it is necessary to go beyond thinking of human security solely in terms of protecting human life in conflict situations."[138] Astri Suhrke, in a review of the multilateral meeting of foreign ministers held in May 1999, concludes that "'human security' requires conceptual clarification if it is to be taken seriously as a vision or an instrument of foreign policy."[139]

The Commission on Human Security, chaired by Sadako Ogata and Amartya Sen, submitted a report to the UN in May 2003 calling for a new security framework focused on people and aimed at ensuring their security. The executive summary of the report states that peoples' security around the world is interlinked—as today's global flows of goods, services, finance, people, and images highlight. Political liberalization and democratization open new opportunities but also new fault lines, such as political and economic instabilities and conflicts within states. More than 800,000 people a year lose their lives to violence. About 2.8 billion suffer from poverty, ill health, illiteracy, and other maladies. Conflict and deprivation are interconnected. Deprivation has many causal links to violence, although these have to be carefully examined. Conversely, wars kill people, destroy trust among them, increase poverty and crime, and slow down the economy. Addressing such insecurities effectively demands an integrated approach.[140]

Outside governments, the concept has been important in linking the study of conflict and security to economic development. The leading exponent of this link is Caroline Thomas, who, in a range of publications going back to her 1987 book, *In Search of Security*,[141] has pointed to the connection between economic underdevelopment and security. For Thomas, human security involves not only a shift from a focus on the state to the individual but also a shift from notions of the security of the individual to a focus on individual needs.[142] She builds on the argument of Canadian foreign minister Lloyd Axworthy, who has emphasized the importance of a "human needs" approach to human security. Following the logic of writers such as Johan Galtung (on structural violence) and John Burton (on human needs), he claims that: "At a minimum, human security requires that basic needs are met."[143] For Thomas, material sufficiency is at the core of human security, but it involves more than that: "human security describes a condition of existence in which basic human needs are met, and in which human dignity, including meaningful participation in the life of the community can be realised."[144] Thus, human security requires both that basic material needs are met (food, shelter, education, health care, etc.) and the achievement of human dignity that "incorporates personal autonomy, control over one's life and unhindered participation in the life of the community."[145]

As Amitav Acharya notes,

> We have three different conceptions of human security today: one focusing on the *human costs* of violent conflict, another stressing *human needs* in the path to sustainable development. A third conception, approximating the first more than the second, emphasizes the *rights* (meaning human rights) dimensions of human security without necessarily linking to the costs of violent conflict.[146]

As this implies, there is no agreement on the meaning of the concept of human security, and it is not clear exactly how it can be operationalized. In my view, the most promising development is that of a link between security and development, as represented by the work of Thomas as well as work by Fen Osler Hampson and Jorge Nef.[147] Such an approach offers a more comprehensive way of analyzing the events of September 11 than does the traditional perspective, since it directs our attention to the reasons why many individuals outside the developed world felt some degree of support for anyone who attacked the power base of world capitalism. In this sense it was a lack of human security that explained the lack of sympathy at the bombings in the United States; at last they were feeling what it was like to be insecure and powerless. More important, human security alerts us to one (though not all) of the possible causes for terrorism, and the debate over how to respond to the attacks necessarily brought into play issues concerning wider definitions of security than those of the mainstream. But this raises the tricky question of whether the term "security" is being stretched too far to retain any analytical utility, and this will be the focus of the conclusion below.

Conclusion

My main conclusion is that the concept of security is now genuinely contested; as part of this contestation, it requires that concepts, such as the state, community, emancipation, as well as the relationships, such as those between the individual and their society and between economics and politics, are also subject to contestation. In this way, there is now far more debate about the term than ever before. Emma Rothschild has classified these debates about extending security into four strands. The first involves the extension of security

> from the security of nations to the security of groups and individuals: it is extended downwards from nations to individuals. In the second, it is extended . . . upwards, from the nation to the biosphere. . . . In the third operation it is extended horizontally, or to the sorts of security that are in question . . . the concept of security is extended, therefore, from military to political, economic, social, environmental, or "human" security. . . . In a fourth operation, the political responsibility for ensuring security . . . is diffused in all directions from national states, including upwards to international institutions, downwards to regional or local government, and sideways to nongovernmental organizations, to public opinion and the press, and to the abstract forces of nature or of the market.[148]

The massive expansion in the extension of the concept since the end of the Cold War has caused some to question whether this undermines the utility of the concept. David Baldwin has argued that the term may now have little analytical usage since it is used so widely that it no longer has a core meaning.[149] In his review of the state of the field, Patrick Morgan argues that there is a danger that the coherence of security studies is being eroded.[150] Although he accepts that boundaries of disciplines are always being debated, he believes that this can be taken too far:

> On "security" I remain a traditionalist. Security has long been about the survival and physical safety of the actors and their people; by extension it

concerns the *deliberate* use of force by states. . . . Broadening security studies to cover other "harms"—economic, environmental and so forth— is unfortunate for it lumps together deliberate, organized physical harm (or threats thereof) with other threats and pains.[151]

The result is that "we have been inclined to try and make 'security' cover too many things, making security studies too amorphous."[152] By way of contrast, another contributor to the collection in which Morgan's work appeared, Edward Kolodziej, argues that in stark contrast to the treatment of security during the Cold War, any conception capable of dealing with the current world order needs to be linked to a much wider notion of governance than that which characterized the Cold War.[153] For Kolodziej, security refers to such a vast range of problems related to order and governance that there can be no single universal solution to the resulting security dilemmas and no treatment of security as isolated from its political and social underpinnings.

Simon Dalby has noted two worries about the extension of the concept:

> First is the concern from traditional realist analysts of national security that the agenda is expanded in a way that dilutes concern with military matters, the primary concern of the military to fight wars may be compromised by competing "threats" that might better be considered by other policy discourses. . . . The second argument . . . is ironically the opposite of the first one. It suggests that military approaches are inappropriate tools to tackle many of the new items on the political agenda. . . . The argument here is for a demilitarization or "de-securitization" of many aspects of social life.[154]

Mohammed Ayoob clearly accepts the first objection when he writes about the dangers of defining security so elastically as to remove the focus on the military dimension of state behavior.[155] R. B. J. Walker discusses both of these objections and concludes that neither is well-founded, since the former assumes that it is possible to pin security down to specific institutions and practices, and the latter assumes that these wider areas are not already infused with practices of state security.[156]

Similarly, Keith Krause and Michael Williams, in their discussion of the broadening-deepening distinction, asked the question of whether there were risks associated with broadening the definition of security; their answer was that

> it may be necessary to broaden the agenda of security studies (theoretically and methodologically) in order to narrow the agenda of *security*. A more profound understanding of the forces that create political loyalties, give rise to threats, and designate appropriate collective responses could open the way to . . . "desecuritization"—the progressive removal of issues

from the security agenda as they are dealt with via institutions and practices that do not implicate force, violence, or the "security dilemma."[157]

In my view, the events of September 11 support those who wish to widen and deepen the concept of security, although it is important to note that there are also some contrary implications of the events. On the one hand, the events brought military security back to center stage, and the ensuing U.S.-led war on terrorism was very much state-led and state-based. The coalition was a collation of states, with regional and international institutions having little role. Thus NATO and the UN were relatively uninvolved in the war, with the United States dealing directly, and bilaterally, with alliance partners. The events also reinforced the role of the state as guarantor of personal security and led to states increasingly becoming national security states, with greater roles for intelligence and for state intrusion into what had previously been seen as areas of personal freedom and autonomy. On the other hand, both the causes and the form of the conflict cannot be explained by either the traditional conception of security or by approaches with its methodological assumptions. The conflict involved one party that was not a state and whose structure and working practices were far removed from those of the nation-state. The form of the attacks did not use traditional tools of war but instead used civilian airliners. The hijackers did not bargain to save their lives but instead deliberately engaged in suicide missions.

The roots of their determination lay in a deep antipathy toward modernization and the ideology of liberalism as much as it was opposed to specific U.S. policies in the Middle East. Above all, the way the U.S.-led coalition had to fight the war, and the ways in which populations in large parts of the world reacted, indicate that the traditional notion of security is unable to explain the events. The alternative conceptions discussed above offer much deeper and more powerful insights into the events than does the traditional realist conception of state-to-state military security. But this does not mean that traditional security studies has nothing to say about the events—only that it is a specific reading of them, reflecting underlying notions of security, community, and emancipation.

The concept of security is therefore a battleground in and of itself. There are those who wish to broaden and deepen it (indeed, broadening the term may well be the necessary consequence of deepening it); and there is now a reinvigorated neoclassical realist school focusing on the traditional meaning of the term: the military security of nation-states. To those working within the traditional area of the subject, broadening and deepening only threaten to undermine the utility of the concept and render it useless for analysis. If the concept of security refers to *any* threat, then it becomes meaningless. Broadening and deepening also carry the risk of undermining the important practices of state security, it is claimed, by undermining the core activity of state security. But I do not share these worries: perhaps the important questions to ask are "Who would want to keep the concept narrow and why?" and "Who might want to keep some issues off the security agenda and why?"

My primary aim in this chapter has been to outline the main components of the nontraditional debates about the concept of security. But mine is not a view from nowhere. I have no doubt that the concept of security needs to be challenged and contested and that the traditional definition—especially when linked to a naturalistic philosophy of enquiry that presented the world of international security as if it were external to and independent of our analysis of it—helped create that very natural, common-sensical world of international politics. This does not mean that merely contesting the meaning of the concept is sufficient to reconstruct security in world politics, but it is an undertaking that is necessary if such a reconstruction is to take place. For far too long security was not considered to be a contestable concept; for even longer it was never contested. Now the situation is one where not only the concept of security can and must be contested—but so can the intimately related concepts of community and emancipation.

Notes

I would like to thank Paul Williams for his research assistance on this paper.

1. Gallie, "Essentially Contested Concepts."
2. Lukes, *Power.*
3. Buzan, *People, States, and Fear*; and *People, States, and Fear: An Agenda.*
4. Buzan, *People, States, and Fear: An Agenda*, p. 7.
5. Little, "Ideology and Change," p. 35.
6. McSweeney, *Security, Identity, and Interests,* p. 83.
7. Ibid., p. 84.
8. Ibid.
9. Booth, "Security and Self."
10. Some sections of the following survey are based on an earlier paper on this topic, Smith, "The Increasing Insecurity of Security Studies."
11. Ibid.
12. Ibid.
13. Walt, "Rigor or Rigor Mortis?"
14. Ibid., p. 7.
15. Ibid.
16. Walt, "International Relations."
17. Rose, "Neoclassical Realism and Theories of Foreign Policy."
18. Christensen, *Useful Adversaries*; Schweller, *Deadly Imbalances;* Wohlforth, *The Elusive Balance;* Zakaria, *From Wealth to Power.*
19. Rose, "Neoclassical Realism and Theories of Foreign Policy," p. 148.
20. Ibid., p. 149.
21. Rose, "Neoclassical Realism and Theories of Foreign Policy," p. 149.

22. Ibid., p. 146.
23. Ibid., p. 152.
24. McSweeney, "Identity and Security."
25. Buzan, *People, States, and Fear*; *People, States, and Fear: An Agenda.*
26. Booth, "Security and Emancipation," p. 317.
27. Wyn Jones, "'Travel Without Maps,'" p. 210.
28. Buzan, *An Introduction to Strategic Studies.*
29. Booth, "Security and Emancipation"; Smith, "Mature Anarchy, Strong States, and Security."
30. Booth, "Security and Emancipation," p. 320.
31. Ibid., p. 319.
32. Shaw, "There Is No Such Thing as Society," p. 160.
33. Buzan, et al., *The European Security Order Recast*; Wæver, et al., *Identity, Migration, and the New Security Agenda in Europe*; Buzan, Wæver, and de Wilde, *Security*; Wæver, Lemaitre, and Tromer, *European Polyphony.*
34. Wæver, et al., *Identity, Migration and the New Security Agenda in Europe*, p. 25.
35. See Wæver, " Securitization and Desecuritization."
36. Buzan, Wæver, and de Wilde, *Security*, p. 32.
37. Ibid.
38. McSweeney, "Identity and Security."
39. Ibid.
40. Ibid., p. 83.
41. Ibid., p. 90.
42. Ibid., p. 87.
43. Ibid., p. 93.
44. Buzan and Wæver, "Slippery? Contradictory? Sociologically Untenable?"
45. McSweeney, "Durkheim and the Copenhagen School."
46. Ibid., p. 140.
47. Eriksson, "Observers or Advocates?"
48. Ibid., p. 315.
49. Ibid., p. 317.
50. Wæver, "Securitizing Sectors?" p. 335.
51. Huysmans, "Revisiting Copenhagen."
52. Ibid., p. 500.
53. Hansen, "The Little Mermaid's Silent Security Dilemma."
54. Ibid., pp. 299–300.
55. See also Johnston, *Cultural Realism*; Legro, *Cooperation Under Fire*; Kier, *Imagining War*; Price, *The Chemical Weapons Taboo.*
56. Adler and Barnett, *Security Communities.*
57. Ibid., p. 12.
58. Adler and Barnett, *Security Communities*, p. 59.
59. Katzenstein, *The Culture of National Security.*
60. Ibid., p. 1.
61. Ibid., p. 2.
62. Ibid., p. 10.
63. Kowert and Legro, "Norms, Identity, and Their Limits," p. 496.
64. Desch, "Culture Clash."
65. Ibid., pp. 141–142.
66. Ibid., p. 170.
67. Hollis and Smith, *Explaining and Understanding International Relations.*

The authors argue that one or the other accounts is possible, but not a combination: an explanatory account based on scientific principles or an understanding account based on hermeneutic principles.

68. See Jepperson, Wendt, and Katzenstein, "Norms, Identity, and Culture in National Security," p. 34.

69. Krause and Williams, "Broadening the Agenda of Security Studies."

70. Krause and Williams, *Critical Security Studies.*

71. Williams and Krause, "Preface: Towards Critical Security Studies," p. xiii.

72. Krause and Williams, "From Strategy to Security."

73. Krause, "Critical Theory and Security Studies."

74. This term was first used in 1993 by Booth and Wyn Jones.

75. Booth, "Security and Emancipation"; Booth, "Security in Anarchy"; Booth (ed.), *New Thinking About Strategy and International Security;* Booth, "Human Wrongs and International Relations"; Booth, "Dare Not to Know"; Booth, "Security and Self"; Booth, "Three Tyrannies"; Booth and Vale, "Security in Southern Africa"; Booth (ed.), *Statecraft and Security;* Bilgin, Booth, and Wyn Jones, "Security Studies."

76. Wyn Jones, "'Travel Without Maps'"; "'Message in a Bottle'?"; "The Nuclear Revolution"; *Strategy, Security, Critical Theory.*

77. Booth, "Security and Emancipation."

78. Personal communication, December 2000.

79. Wyn Jones, *Strategy, Security, Critical Theory.*

80. Ibid., pp. 117–123.

81. Ibid., pp. 153–163.

82. Booth, "Three Tyrannies," pp. 41–45.

83. Ibid., p. 46.

84. Booth, "Security and Emancipation," p. 321.

85. Ibid., p. 319.

86. Ibid., p. 319.

87. McSweeney, *Security, Identity, and Interests.*

88. Ibid., p. 208.

89. Eriksson, "Observers or Advocates?" p. 318.

90. Ibid., p. 320.

91. Ibid., p. 321.

92. Williams, "The Practices of Security."

93. Behnke, "The Message or the Messenger?" p. 89.

94. Ibid., pp. 89–90.

95. Ayoob, "Defining Security," pp. 126–127.

96. Ibid., p. 127.

97. Ibid., p. 128.

98. Booth and Vale, "Security in Southern Africa."

99. Booth and Trood (eds.), *Strategic Culture in the Asia-Pacific.*

100. Tickner, "Re-Visioning Security," p. 190. See also Tickner, *Gender in International Relations* and *Gendering World Politics.*

101. Tickner, "Re-Visioning Security," p. 191.

102. Ibid.

103. Ibid., p. 193.

104. Steans, *Gender and International Relations.*

105. Ibid., p. 109.

106. Ibid., p. 129.

107. Cohn, "Sex, Death, and the Rational World of Defense Intellectuals"; Cooke and Woollacott (eds.), *Gendering War Talk.*

108. Elshtain, *Women and War;* Hartsock, "The Barracks Community in Western Political Thought."

109. Enloe, *Bananas, Beaches, and Bases*; *The Morning After*; *Maneuvers.*

110. Brock-Unte, *Educating for Peace.*

111. Huysmans, "Security! What Do You Mean?"; Hansen, "A Case for Seduction."

112. Klein, *Strategic Studies and World Order.*

113. Ibid., p. 7.

114. Ibid., p. 10.

115. Ibid., p. 10.

116. Klein, *Strategic Studies and World Order*, p. 37.

117. Campbell, *Writing Security.*

118. Ibid., p. vii.

119. Ibid., p. 253.

120. Ibid., p. 12.

121. Campbell, *National Deconstruction.*

122. Ibid., p. 174.

123. Ibid., p. 176.

124. Ibid., p. 219.

125. Ibid., p. 243.

126. Ibid., p. 240.

127. Ibid., p. 241.

128. Ibid., p. 242.

129. United Nations Development Programme (UNDP), *Human Development Report 1994* (citations that follow are from a reprint of sections of the report "Redefining Security," in *Current History* [May 1995]: 229–236).

130. Ibid., p. 229.

131. Ibid., p. 229.

132. Ibid., p. 230.

133. Ibid., p. 230.

134. Ibid., pp. 230–234.

135. Ibid., pp. 234–236.

136. UNDP, *Human Development Report 1997.*

137. Department of Foreign Affairs and International Trade, Government of Canada, *Human Security*; quote from sec. 2.

138. Takasu, "Statement by Director General Yukio Takasu."

139. Suhrke, "Human Security and the Interests of States."

140. Commission on Human Security, *Human Security Now.*

141. Thomas, *In Search of Security.*

142. Thomas, *Global Governance, Development, and Human Security;* see also Thomas and Wilkin (eds.), *Globalization, Human Security, and the African Experience.*

143. Axworthy, "Canada and Human Security," p. 184.

144. Thomas, *Global Governance, Development, and Human Security*, p. 6.

145. Ibid., p. 6.

146. Acharya and Acharya, "Human Security in the Asia Pacific."

147. Hampson, *Madness in the Multitude*; Nef, *Human Security and Mutual Vulnerability.*

148. Rothschild, "What Is Security?" p. 55.

149. Baldwin, "The Concept of Security."

150. Morgan, "Liberalist and Realist Security Studies at 2000," p. 40.

151. Ibid., p. 40.

152. Ibid., p. 64.

153. Kolodziej, "Security Studies for the Next Millennium."

154. Dalby, *Geopolitical Change and Contemporary Security Studies,* pp. 12–13.

155. Ayoob, "Defining Security," pp. 137–142.

156. Walker, "The Subject of Security," p. 76.

157. Krause and Williams, "Broadening the Agenda of Security Studies," p. 249.

3

Military Force(s) and In/security

Graeme Cheeseman

Within the realist lexicon, military force represents the central component of state power. Military force is said to enable states and their leaders to protect and promote their particular interests, to defend national sovereignty and identity, to influence and, where necessary, compel others into their way of thinking, to deter war, and to shape the very rules that govern the maintenance of international order.[1] While it is recognized that a state's power also derives from factors other than military ones—economic and industrial capacity, technological know-how, volume of trade, and so on—military forces and capability have continued to be seen to play a crucial role in the quest for national and international security. This was especially the case during the Cold War, in which the precedence given to military power was evidenced by increasing worldwide military expenditures, an expanding global trade in arms and associated technologies, and the growing militarization of states, regions, and the world as a whole.

The quest for power and security during the Cold War was not without its problems and contradictions. The arming of the superpowers' various client states and supporters fostered political repression, armed rebellion, and conflict across areas of the globe that resulted in considerable loss of life and incalculable suffering among civilian populations. The diversion of more and more money and resources into nonproductive military uses threatened the social and economic well-being of peoples and states everywhere, but especially in the developing world.[2] The accumulation of nuclear and other weapons of mass destruction, the growing sophistication and destructive potential of conventional armaments, and the increasing integration of nuclear and nonnuclear arsenals threatened not only the security of the two belligerents but also the global environment as a whole.[3]

These problems highlighted the so-called defense and security dilemmas that are integral to the realist and neorealist approaches to strategic studies and international relations.[4] These approaches hold that in order to

63

be secure in an anarchical world states must seek to maximize their military power with respect to competitors and potential adversaries. But the unbridled pursuit of military power can serve to lessen the state's security by causing other states to follow suit, thereby precipitating an arms competition in which the security of all parties (and their peoples) steadily deteriorates. When nuclear weapons are involved, the consequences of the security dilemma are vastly multiplied; as Anatole Rapoport has aptly described, the "game of strategy" becomes transformed into "a plan of genocidal orgies."[5] These negative outcomes led scholars and practitioners alike to begin to look at ways of removing the security dilemma or at least ameliorating its effects and fostered a range of alternative ideas and prescriptions, some of which came eventually to be accepted by the strategic studies mainstream.[6] The first part of this chapter discusses two of these responses—nonoffensive defense (NOD) and confidence- and security-building measures (CSBMs)—which, while not exactly new concepts,[7] gained considerable currency during the Cold War.

Although NOD and CSBMs represented important examples of alternative security thinking at the time, we need to recognize that they addressed only problems and dilemmas associated with the (usually military) security of states and paid little attention to other, especially nonstate, actors, referents, and sources of insecurity. They remained located, in other words, within the conceptual confines of neorealism and, as such, were subject to the various contestations surrounding that basic approach to international relations. These contestations have, if anything, sharpened following the end of the Cold War, as the process of globalization has continued apace and its problems and pitfalls have become more evident, and in the wake of such events as the terrorist attacks of September 11, 2001, and the subsequent war on terrorism conducted by U.S.-led military forces in Afghanistan and Iraq. These developments have served to confirm and to question further the relevance and importance of traditional realist (or militarized) approaches to security. Some suggest that the world we live in has now changed in complex and unexpected ways and that the case for revisiting the principal means of seeking to make sense of what is occurring around us has strengthened immeasurably. As Richard Wyn Jones has argued, "What has previously passed muster as timeless wisdom" now needs changing. To progress, we have to draw up "new maps for understanding the post–Cold War world."[8] Others, including many within the national security establishments of the United States and its key allies, see the acquisition and use of military power and associated militarized discourses as being as important as ever in the pursuit of national security interests both at home and abroad.

The remainder of this chapter looks at some of the potential implications for, debates over, and trends in the role of military force and forces in a post–Cold War, post–September 11, and increasingly globalized world. The analysis is more interrogative (and necessarily speculative) than prescriptive or analytical, raising questions and issues for consideration and debate rather than dissecting particular events or providing decisionmakers with specific advice or policy proposals. This is because, like the disciplines of security studies and international relations more generally, the issue of the future deployment of force(s) is both highly complex and contested, with dilemmas, divergences, contradictions, and contestations abounding.

Responding to Cold War Security Dilemmas: NOD and CSBMs

The problems associated with extended nuclear deterrence fostered, from the early 1980s, a growing interest in the concept of nonoffensive defense particularly within West Germany and the Scandinavian countries. This initial work was largely carried out by peace researchers and disenchanted military specialists and was supported by reformist political parties such as West Germany's Social Democratic Party (SPD).[9] In view of the location and nature of the research, it tended, not surprisingly, to reflect European Cold War needs and experiences.

Also known as "nonprovocative defense," "preservative defense," and "defensive deterrence," NOD is a strategy for providing for the credible defense of one's own territory while rejecting any means of invading or attacking the homeland of a potential adversary. This can be achieved in a number of ways, including by relinquishing all components of a "critical" range or mobility in favor of a stationary network of defenses, eschewing clearly offensive military capabilities—such as strategic strike assets—from the overall force structure, and "linking" mobile units to stationary networks in order effectively to immobilize the posture as a whole.[10] These kinds of constraints can be applied voluntarily or, preferably, be implemented as part of a series of formal cooperative security arrangements between two or more countries. In this last regard, NOD was compatible with the notion of common security that had been advanced by the Independent Commission on Disarmament and Security Issues (the Palme Commission) and others concerned with finding ways of managing the nuclear competition between the superpowers.[11]

As Bjørn Møller has described, the purposes of adopting an NOD posture are generally to: prevent war occurring by improving crisis stability and reducing incentives for preemptive attack; limit damage should war nevertheless take place; facilitate arms control and disarmament; and "promote detente, mutual confidence, and rapprochement between states with a view to minimizing the international system's political propensity for war."[12] NOD strategies are also said to provide the basis for establishing a stable balance of power at lower levels of arms and to remove the incentive for arms-racing. Faced by purely defensive forces, rational opponents who have no aggressive intentions of their own need make no military response to their opponent's defensive restructuring and so do not enter into the action-reaction cycle of the security dilemma.

NOD also recognizes that there may be situations where a state may be confronted by an irrational or an aggressive adversary. The concept therefore seeks to provide a sufficiently credible self-defense posture to deter or be able to defeat such an adversary. This generally means making defensive forces hard to attack and difficult to defeat and the defender's own territory expensive to invade or occupy. In satisfying these objectives, NOD strategies seek to exploit defensive technologies and the advantages of local terrain, and they give emphasis to such notions as defense-in-depth, sustainability and endurance in defense, decentralized and dispersed deployments, delay and denial tactics, and self-reliance.

NOD strategies and postures are not without their problems and disadvantages. The principles of defensive defense can be difficult to apply in the case of those states, such as Australia, whose internal geographical dimensions exceed those between the country and neighboring states, or states such as Indonesia whose territory encompasses extensive waterways, or very small states like Israel that lack strategic depth. An NOD posture would be vulnerable to any enemy who would attack or threaten to attack the defender with missiles or other offensive weapons launched from its own territory. It would allow aggressors to concentrate forces and launch initial and follow-up attacks with impunity. It would limit the defender's strategic options, reduce its capacity to defend remote interests, and ensure that military conflict, should it occur, would take place on or near the defender's own territory. Since an NOD posture would limit a nation's capacity to deploy forces beyond its shores, it might call into question—or at least serve to complicate—existing alliance or security arrangements and constrain its ability to conduct peacekeeping and other international humanitarian operations. It might be more expensive to implement than more traditional postures and, in some cases, could lead to the militarization of society and, as witnessed in the former Yugoslavia, provide the means by which internal groups may seek to challenge or secede from the state.[13] These kinds of concerns are important and should not be ignored when considering whether and how NOD concepts could be applied to a particular situation. But neither should they be used to dismiss the concept out of hand since many of the disadvantages only apply if conflict actually breaks out, a situation NOD is designed to prevent occurring.

Bjørn Møller also notes that NOD strategies and systems of defense are not suitable for implementing certain military and political-military roles that have been seen to be important in the past and may continue to be so in the future. These include the tasks of war-winning and territorial expansion, coercive diplomacy, foreign intervention, and the demonstration of national prestige (or *gloire*). While acknowledging that this is generally true, Møller suggests that the removal of these options from states' armories may not be such a bad thing. He further argues that in the nuclear era war-winning strategies may no longer represent a rational or even feasible means of pursuing political objectives—a point I will return to. Moreover, while an NOD posture may serve to constrain a state's capacity to conduct coercive diplomacy, it provides a more than adequate means of withstanding such pressure from someone else and, in the event of conflict, makes it clear to the world who is the aggressor.[14]

Perhaps because of these problems and concerns, the consideration of NOD during the period of the Cold War remained largely restricted to academics and peace researchers, although the concept was taken up by certain opposition parties in Europe, and it informed the 1990 Conventional Forces in Europe (CFE) Treaty that reduced NATO's and the Warsaw Pact's capacities to launch a surprise attack or engage in large-scale offensive action.[15] To the extent that they recognized and sought to accommodate the security dilemma, governments and official advisers on both sides of the East-West divide preferred to emphasize so-called confidence-building measures (CBMs), which were later called confidence- and security-building measures.

As in the case of NOD, the contemporary discourse on CBM/CSBMs gained considerable impetus during the Cold War. Initially this thinking focused on minimizing the risk of unwanted military conflict between the two superpowers and their allies in Europe and beyond. Thus, in the early 1970s, the United States and the Soviet Union signed a number of agreements aimed at preventing nuclear accidents and collisions and other incidents at sea. From the mid-1970s, the Conference for Security and Cooperation in Europe (CSCE) negotiated a range of CBMs that aimed at promoting greater military openness and included advance notification of military exercises and troop movements, as well as a range of verification procedures such as on-site inspections and the exchange of military observers.[16] These kinds of operational initiatives attracted growing interest among the academic and policy communities largely because they appeared to avoid some of the difficulties associated with more traditional, structural disarmament, and arms control proposals (including NOD). As Ariel Levite and Emily Landau subsequently described:

> Their integral nature allows adversaries to accept confidence building measures even when the political basis for fundamental restructuring of the relationship between them is still missing. Their evolutionary nature,

and focus on intentions, in turn, mean that their adoption neither diminishes either side's security margins, nor, at least initially, does it require large and painful practical (as distinguished from psychological) adjustments on either side.[17]

Later thinking on the subject moved, at least conceptually, beyond the earlier concern with possible means of limiting military activities to embrace the process of confidence-building itself. This expanded approach emphasizes greater transparency, consultation and dialogue, and cooperation at all levels and seeks, in the words of James Macintosh, the "transformation of senior decision-maker beliefs about the nature of threat posed by other, formerly antagonistic states, primarily entailing a shift from a basic assumption of hostile intentions to an assumption of nonhostile intentions."[18]

Immediately after the end of the Cold War, interest in CSBMs dramatically increased with scholars and policymakers alike advocating their use in a range of different circumstances and institutional contexts.[19] An important practical example of a post–Cold War CSBM is the United Nations *Register* of conventional arms, which came into operation in 1993 and provides public details of major weapons transfers between states. The idea of an arms register has been around for some time. It was included in the Covenant of the League of Nations and informs the Stockholm International Peace Research Institute's extensive database on weapons production and arms transfers that provides the basis for the summaries published annually in its *SIPRI Yearbook*.[20] Proposals for an arms register were also regularly advanced within the United Nations, but with little effect until the end of the Cold War and subsequent revelations over arms transfers to Iraq and its neighbors in the lead-up to the 1991 Gulf War.[21] These led to UN General Assembly resolution 46/36L, which tasked the UN Secretary-General with maintaining a register of transfers of battle tanks, armored combat vehicles, large-caliber artillery systems, combat aircraft, attack helicopters, warships, and missiles or missile systems. Member states were also asked to inform the Secretary-General of their national arms imports and export policies, as well as to provide background information regarding their military holdings, national production capabilities, and related policies.

Contemporary research on NOD also continued. Although it has tended to be European-centered, there have been proposals for NOD-type postures for both individual countries and groups of countries in other parts of the world. The latter, usually advanced as part of broader systems of common or cooperative security, have included the western Mediterranean, southern Asia, and parts of the Asia Pacific.[22] The proposed Conference on Security and Cooperation in the [Western] Mediterranean (CSCM), for example, seeks to include the northern countries of Spain, Italy, France, and Portugal and the southern states of Morocco, Algeria, Tunisia, and Libya in a CSCE-type arrangement. In addition to various nonmilitary issues and concerns, the CSCM's proposed agenda would include disarmament and arms control measures, the "reorientation of national defence postures towards defence," and "confidence-building measures and the development of mechanisms for regional conflict resolution."[23] Some researchers have sought to extend the principles of NOD beyond its traditional emphasis on land operations to include the air and maritime domains,[24] while others have compared the basic tenets of NOD with those of maneuver and other emerging land warfare doctrines.[25]

Yet there is a feeling, too, that the relevance of the concept of NOD (and by extension CSBMs) may be actually declining as we move further into the 2000s. In considering whether NOD has a future in the post–Cold War world, Barry Buzan concludes, for example, that "the ending of the Cold War has largely undermined the relevance of the original formulations of NOD for the situation in Europe, though not the relevance of the ideas in and of themselves. The challenge now facing the advocates of NOD," Buzan continues, "is to rework the specific proposals for military and political policies and structures to suit the rather different conditions in the places in which NOD now has some chance of being implemented."[26]

In Buzan's view, however, these places are likely to be quite limited. He considers that NOD is unlikely to figure much in future Western European military calculations that, to the extent they even appear on the emerging security agenda, seem to be focused on structuring for possible out-of-area operations by NATO forces. There may be a greater potential role for NOD in Eastern Europe and parts of Asia and the third world, although even here there are problems. According to Buzan, "NOD is easier during periods of detente than when tensions and threat perceptions are high"—which is the case in many of the trouble spots that remain after the end of the Cold War—and "where there is a high level of integration between government and society," which is not the case in an increasing proportion of the developing world.[27] Buzan proceeds with the important observation that the post–Cold War world is "not going to be just a more congenial version of the old one." In his view, we are entering a "completely different" era some of whose characteristics are clear—the end of geopolitical bipolarity and ideological rivalry for example—but whose probable ending point remains both uncertain and sharply contested. "Wherever it may be going," Buzan concludes, "this emerging new world (dis)order would seem to pose a crisis of relevance for NOD."[28]

Although not disagreeing with this conclusion and its implications, I would argue that Buzan's analysis may be unduly restricted by his tendency to focus on the evolving distribution of political and economic power among states. If we extend our purview beyond states and state-based inter-

ests and include the major social, technological, and other systemic
changes that are taking place around us, and that prefigured the end of the
Cold War, a more complex picture emerges that has important implications
both for NOD and the future role of military force(s) more generally. As we
will see, continuing developments in weapons and other technologies are
raising questions about the capacity of defensive forces to prevail in combat. They are encouraging the growing interest, being shown by policy analysts and practitioners alike, in military intervention to protect or extend
Western/developed world political or economic interests, to provide
humanitarian assistance or infrastructure support to failed or failing states,
or to deal with actors who choose to operate beyond international norms.
Most important of all, systemic changes may be leading to a relative
decline in the importance of the state in international affairs and, in so
doing, altering the place and continuing relevance of existing state-based
military structures, doctrines, and understandings.

Military Force and Armed Forces in a
Post–Cold War and Rapidly Globalizing World

The military forces we are generally familiar with are inextricably linked
with the states and societies they serve. Military forces are often the agent
of the state's birth. Military experiences and traditions play a central role in
the construction of national identity. Military service—particularly service
in combat in the defense of the state or its interests—is often posited as the
most important and noble responsibility of the state's citizens.[29] During
peacetime and especially in the face of adversity or change, national military forces or values are often seen as appropriate vehicles or models for
maintaining internal order, cohesion, and legitimacy. Indeed, in a rapidly
globalizing world, state-based militaries and militarized cultures provide
one of the few remaining means of demonstrating national independence,
pride, and assertiveness.

  Today most of the traditions, practices, and assumptions that underpin
and inform state-based militaries and their uses are being questioned or
challenged. As described in more detail below, the Westphalian world order
that gave birth to the modern state and its armed forces is said to be ending,
and we are entering a fundamentally new era in international politics. The
role of the state in these new times, and those of its key agents, are being
challenged and circumscribed by forces and actors operating beyond their
control. The twin dynamics of globalization and fragmentation are, for
example, serving to blur previously clear distinctions between peace and
war, between the state's domestic and external environments, and between
society and the military. Traditional notions of citizenship and belonging
are also changing, affecting in complex ways notions of duty, service, and

identity. These various pressures and changes are seeing, in turn, changes occurring in the roles, doctrines, and capabilities of the armed forces of many states. They are fostering the emergence, or countenance, of new forms of military organizations, structures, and cultures. And they are accompanying significant and continuing changes in the broader political, strategic, and security contexts within which armed forces—both old and new—must now operate.

From Defense to Security: The Changing Roles of Military Forces

Contrary to realist expectations, military forces today are being employed less and less in the defense of the state and more and more on broader regional and international security tasks. The post–Cold War era has witnessed a significant number of UN-sponsored or -sanctioned military interventions, including the establishment of the safe havens and no-fly zones in northern and southern Iraq, the U.S. and UN operations in Somalia, NATO incursions in the Balkans and Afghanistan, and the deployment of Australian-led coalition forces in Cambodia, East Timor, and the Solomon Islands. Most of these interventions have been triggered by human rights violations and suffering of such magnitude (and public exposure) that they have been seen by the UN to constitute potential threats to international peace and security and, as such, warrant collective action under Chapter VII of the UN Charter. Together they may represent a new, if qualified, norm in international relations: a right to intervene militarily in the internal affairs of states or, more specifically, a "right to secure the delivery of humanitarian assistance by force."[30] Even if this is not the case, calls for the United Nations and other multilateral institutions to intervene in various civil emergencies and intrastate disputes seem likely to continue and grow. The meaning of peacekeeping is also likely to continue to expand beyond earlier, Cold War understandings to embrace so-called second-generation or wider peacekeeping activities that include the option of peace enforcement.[31]

In a post–Cold War and rapidly globalizing world, the answer to the perennial question "Security from what?" is also being expanded beyond other states and their military forces to include such new sources of insecurity and conflict as: disputes over the control of, and access to, resources; various nonmilitary threats to societal harmony and well-being posed by such things as traditional and cyberterrorism, drugs, transboundary crime, epidemics, and disease; population migration caused by poverty and overcrowding, political oppression, and instability; and growing environmental degradation. Armed forces in many places are now expected to be able to help deal with these "threats without enemies"[32] and to contribute to the pursuit not only of military security but economic security, energy security, food security, societal security, and environmental security as well.[33]

The growing employment of national military forces on peace operations and other nontraditional security tasks is requiring them to expand the existing repertoire of functions, capabilities, and skills. Post–Cold War peace operations, for example, have required the intervening forces to, among other things, provide humanitarian assistance of various kinds, manage the movement of refugees and displaced persons, help conduct elections, provide safe havens and protection for humanitarian workers, establish cantonment areas or demilitarized zones between warring parties, disarm military or paramilitary forces, clear mines and other leftovers from war, negotiate local cease-fires or the safe passage of aid, provide civil administration, help restore civil society, and contribute to the reconstruction and development of local economies.[34] Military establishments are, to varying degrees, beginning to recast their policies and doctrines to accommodate these broader roles and responsibilities. The armed forces of both Great Britain and Australia, for example, are now described as forces for good. Both are being required to defend security interests that extend well beyond their territorial boundaries. And both are expected to help deal with such nontraditional military threats as illegal immigration, terrorism, and cyberattack.[35]

While acknowledging that their military forces will be involved more and more in so-called operations other than war, however, defense planners in most countries also remain reluctant to restructure their military forces for such operations. As Ian Malcolm describes in the case of Canada, they tend to see peacekeeping as an "accepted activity rather than a core concern"[36] and argue that national forces should continue to be structured and prepared primarily for defending the state against armed attack or threat of attack by another state. They further insist that forces structured for the defense of the state are generally sufficient for carrying out likely nontraditional security roles. This determination of many defense decisionmakers to continue to see military force(s) in traditional terms is arguably being reinforced by continuing technological change and the so-called revolution in military affairs (RMA), which are serving to increase the reach, lethality, and destructive efficiency of conventional weapons and are "making it increasingly possible to apply decisive force with a minimum of both friendly and enemy losses."[37] According to the proponents of RMA, those nations that possess such capabilities will be able to dominate the conventional battlefields of the future, engage in so-called third-wave or cyberwars against their adversaries and, as we witnessed most recently in Afghanistan and Iraq, and earlier in the former Yugoslavia, use military power (and especially airpower) to compel individual rogue states or other organizations to cease hostilities and desist from pursuing certain foreign or domestic policies or practices.[38]

But changes in the roles and responsibilities of today's military forces may be only a small part of the overall story. The same basic forces that are leading militaries in the industrial world to adjust their roles and structures are serving also to alter the contexts in which conventional military forces operate and are understood. We are, in short, in the midst of a much more important and far-reaching process of change, one that threatens to revolutionize not only how militaries will act in the future but also their purpose and basic raison d'être.

The Changing Nature of Armed Forces:
From Modern Toward Postmodern Militaries

The growing incidence of peace operations and other nontraditional security missions mirrors an underlying shift in the type and general nature of military organizations. Military forces are becoming, at one level, increasingly transnationalized, with national forces becoming more cosmopolitan-minded and being deployed increasingly (albeit reluctantly in some cases) under the control of such international and regional organizations as the United Nations, NATO, and the Commonwealth of Independent States.[39] We are also seeing the emergence of a growing array of private military services and mercenary organizations, some of which are "organised around a charismatic leader" or "attached to political movements or organized criminal networks or both."[40] Although they may not have cruise missiles and the other high-technology weapons that are owned by national and transnational forces, these "post-Fordist" militaries can easily access the range of small arms that have flooded world markets since the end of the Cold War.[41] According to Charles Moskos and colleagues, armed forces in the United States and other Western industrialized nations are also gradually evolving into postmodern variants that differ from their modern predecessors in quite significant ways. Whereas the modern military organization is "war-oriented in mission, masculine in makeup and ethos, and sharply differentiated in structure and culture from civilian society," the postmodern military is "more multipurpose in mission, increasingly androgynous in makeup and ethos, and [has] greater permeability with civilian society."[42]

These trends are part a much wider process in which the sovereignty of the state and its longstanding relationships with the military and society are being challenged. In a rapidly globalizing world, the economic, physical, cultural, and psychological underpinnings of state sovereignty are being eroded or circumscribed by the unimpeded flow of goods and capital, ideas and information, lifestyle cultures and values, criminal activities, drugs, and pollution.[43] Governments are having to contend with increasingly powerful transnational economic and political actors as well as global social movements of various kinds. They are also being confronted by a growing array of what Anthony Giddens calls "manufactured risks"—nuclear oblivion, global environmental pressures of various kinds, AIDS and other pandemics, and so on—which are a product of human activity and against which individual states are relatively powerless.[44] As a result, the image and role of the state as posited by classical realist and neorealist thinking are becoming increasingly problematic.[45] In some places, the sovereign or territorial state is being reduced to what some describe as the residual state and others as the enabling state, one that is more and more the agent of global capitalism and less and less the representative of domestic civil society.[46] In other areas we are witnessing the appearance of so-called phantom states, or failed or failing states—states that exist on paper, that may have a government and be represented at the UN, but have ceased to provide the services that are paid for and expected by peoples within their borders.[47]

These pressures are producing, in turn, a crisis of governance in which people everywhere are beginning to question traditional sources of authority and to look to other institutions and ideals for meaning and leadership. Citizens in the postmodern era are assuming multiple identities or have multiple (and sometimes conflicting) loyalties that are often locally and globally as well as nationally based.[48] Military organizations are not immune from these processes. As James Rosenau describes, today's servicemen and women are likely to identify themselves not only with a particular service or country but also with specific religious, ethnic, or secular groupings that exist within the state—and that also often have global connections—as well as broader social movements concerned with such global issues as gender, human rights, and environmentalism. This disaggregation of interests within the military itself is likely to have important operational and other policy consequences, ranging from the need to adhere to a range of global norms and obligations through balancing the expectations of the state with those of self or family, to dealing with soldiers who refuse to fire on fellow or like-minded citizens.[49] The crisis of governance also raises questions about who does and should military forces now serve: governments or their citizens, local or global economic interests, and states, the society of states or some wider cosmopolis.

The Changing Nature of Armed Conflict: From Inter-State to New Wars

The primary declared purpose of modern militaries is to be able to fight and win wars against other states. Yet there is a growing view that major inter-state wars may be becoming a thing of the past, particularly in the case of industrialized countries. This view, which admittedly is not shared by everyone, coincides with the appearance of weapons of mass destruction, which have changed forever rational war calculations, at least among nuclear players.[50] It is said to be heightened by the end of the Cold War—the phenomenon of globalization that is facilitating growing levels of interaction among states and the gradual spread of globalized cultures and associated norms, and, more contentiously, the continuing spread of democracy.[51]

The decline in the prospect of war between industrialized nations does not mean, of course, that armed conflict will disappear completely. As evidenced in the upsurge of violence in Africa and the Balkans, the post–Cold War political landscape continues to witness a range of armed disputes and conflicts that are variously called "new wars," "uncivil wars," or "wars of the third kind."[52] As Mary Kaldor has described, these conflicts differ from classical interstate conflicts in a number of important ways. They are taking place largely within society rather than between bordered states and in relatively remote regions on the periphery of the developed world. They often arise in the wake of the disintegration of existing states or the destruction or marginalization of local economies. They are more often directed at civilians than opposing military forces. They are marked by both a decline in earlier patron-client state relations and the emergence of a range of new external connections and actors, including various diaspora communities, transnational commercial networks (both legal and illegal), foreign mercenaries, and nongovernment organizations (NGOs). And they tend to be more about the politics of identity than traditional concerns over realpolitik.[53]

Many argue that the ascendancy of high-tech Western military forces and capabilities, so evident in the Gulf War, has also led to a change of tactics by those developing states and other organizations that are in conflict with first world or first tier countries—spawning the prospect of *asymmetric warfare*. Writing well before September 2001, Alvin and Heidi Toffler argued that the adversaries of the developed world will be able to access the increasingly sophisticated weapons and techniques being developed for conventional armed conflict in order to blackmail, threaten, or destroy their competitors and ideological opponents. Their aims will be helped by the fact that, in addition to affecting conventional warfare, the continuing revolution in information and associated technologies is also creating enormously sophisticated, postindustrial or third wave economies that will become more vulnerable not only to terrorists and suicide bombers but also to various "ideological, religious, or cultural warriors who roam the planet, and computer 'crackers' [who] can turn up in countries like Colombia or Iran, placing their talents at the service of criminals or fanatics."[54]

These kinds of developments raise important questions about the future role and functions of armed force(s). As Martin van Creveld argues, traditional Clausewitzian strategies and structures may be of little use for either understanding or responding to many of the situations governments and their leaders will face in the future,[55] a point underscored by both the U.S. occupation of Iraq and the ongoing conflict between the Palestinians and

Israel. As we have seen, military forces will increasingly be called on to conduct a growing range of nonmilitary tasks and functions and to contribute to postconflict peacebuilding as well as fighting and winning wars. Indeed, some scholars, such as Carl Builder of the RAND Corporation, argue that the size of active forces required for conventional war-fighting roles will almost certainly decrease, whereas missions and associated forces "involving the rapid projection of infrastructure (transport, communications, surveillance, rescue, medical, humanitarian assistance, civil emergency, and security) are likely to increase disproportionately."[56] Others see an expanding need for special forces or special operations units to deal with low-intensity conflicts and to conduct such missions as clandestine raids for intelligence gathering, sabotage, hostage rescue, assassination, and "antiterrorist or antinarco operations."[57] Some, like Robert Kaplan, even suggest that defenders of the state will begin, in many places, to look more and more like existing police and civilian security services than the armed forces we know today.[58]

The Changing International Political Context: Toward a Post-Westphalian World?

States and their military forces are the products of the Westphalian age. Yet in the view of many commentators that age has ended and we are entering a new era in international politics. Just what the post-Westphalian world will end up looking like remains a matter of considerable contention.[59] Some see the world returning to the kind of situation that existed before the Treaty of Westphalia—a world of chaos and anarchy as portrayed on the screen by the Mad Max movies and we find in reality in places like Rwanda and West Africa.[60] Some see a continuation of existing state-centric structures based around realist, rationalist, or liberal internationalist systems of world order in which states remain the key actors.[61] Some suggest that future fault lines will occur between civilizations or so-called zones of peace and zones of turmoil.[62] Others argue that existing state-based systems are being complemented or replaced by a complex, increasingly interconnected global political economy and associated civil society, a world that has porous or no borders, and is increasingly dominated by a range of nonstate entities, transactions, structures, and norms.

These contending world visions have different implications for the meaning of security—in particular who or what is being secured and against what—as well as the future roles of military force and armed forces. Traditional balance-of-power prognoses, whether stressing unipolar, bipolar, or multipolar structures, represent a continuation of existing priorities and mindsets. These would continue to privilege the state as the key actor in international affairs and the use or threatened use of military force in the pursuit of national or global interests. Military conflict would still be posited as the most important issue affecting national and international security, armed forces would continue to be structured and trained primarily for traditional war-fighting roles, and national strategic postures would continue to emphasize sovereignty defense, power-balancing, coalition warfare, and the management of alliances.[63] The conduct of warfare and the organization of military forces within this realist world will continue to evolve to accommodate technological change and emerging social pressures and expectations, but not radically or evenly across the globe. State-based forces will be required to take part in UN-sanctioned peacekeeping, humanitarian assistance, and other nonmilitary operations, but these will be as ad hoc coalitions of the willing and able. Such operations, moreover, will not determine, except at the margins, the military structures or basic doctrines of their component forces. This future vision of international politics may be of comfort to those who fear or wish to control change, but it will also invoke unchecked security dilemmas, continuing militarization and conflict, arms-racing, and the prospect of wars between major powers or across major fault lines.

Those who see the twenty-first century dominated by geoeconomics rather than geopolitics suggest that the place of both the state and military power in international affairs will become much less relevant, although they will continue to have a role.[64] Increasing economic interdependence, the rising power of transnational corporations, and the triumph of liberal capitalism raise questions about the importance of sovereignty and territoriality in security calculations. They also hold out the prospect of slowly expanding zones of peace or democratic economic (or security) communities within which there would be no expectation of major war and no need for either state-based sovereignty defense forces or the maintenance of internal military balances of power. Military forces will still be required for a degree of internal reassurance, to protect those in the zones of peace against threats emerging from the surrounding zones of turmoil, and, occasionally, to intervene in these latter areas to safeguard peoples and resources or help protect or resurrect failed or failing states or communities. Given that the zones of peace will be inhabited by highly advanced, third wave economies that are able to capitalize on the ongoing RMA, it is unlikely that they will be challenged militarily by the large, but technologically inferior, conventional armies located in the more advanced parts of the zones of turmoil. Rather, for first tier countries, the key security issues are likely to be nonmilitary rather than military ones—such as population movements, pandemics, and transboundary environmental pressures—although the various terrorist and other asymmetric threats described above will not be able fully to be discounted.

Proponents of a globalized world see the expansion and eventual overlap of the zones of peace, the replacement of nation-states by regional or global communities, the expansion of international regimes and associated norms, and increased global governance through either a system of world government or some form of transgovernmentalism.[65] Such a system of geogovernance could be inequitable, unjust, unrepresentative, and, for many, profoundly insecure, marked by structural inequalities and conflict "between the forces of globalization and the territorially-based forces of local survival seeking to preserve and to redefine community."[66] Or it could be both enlightened and humane; in Richard Falk's words, a

> community for the whole of humanity which overcomes the most prob-
> lematic aspects of the present world scene . . . [and where] difference and
> uniformities across space and through time are subsumed beneath an over-
> all commitment to world order values in the provisional shape of peace,
> economic well-being, social and political justice, and environmental sus-
> tainability.[67]

However structured, systems of global governance are likely to be much less warlike. The key security issues and associated dilemmas will be largely nonmilitary in nature and either transnational or local in focus. Traditional alliances will be replaced by common security arrangements. Society will become progressively demilitarized. To the extent they exist at all, military forces will be largely collectively organized and will tend to be employed in security rather than traditional defense roles. These roles might include, in an unjust and inequitable world, enforcement of the global economic order and protection of its key interests. In a world motivated more by human and environmental security concerns, they could include the management and protection of planetary resources, the policing of UN or other global norms and conventions, and the provision and maintenance of infrastructural and other forms of support to areas or regions of need.[68] Some collective traditional military actions or interventions will still occur, although within a system of humane governance it would be generally viewed "as a failure of 'security' not as its embodiment."[69]

It is difficult to tell at this stage that one or a combination of these visions of the future is the most appropriate or will prevail. Depending on when and where we look, some models seem to be more valid than others. Certain parts of Africa, for example, seem closely to fit the new medievalism thesis, while the expanding European Union is a clear exemplar of the economic security community postulated in both the liberal internationalist and zones of peace/zones of turmoil models. Given that the process of globalization cannot be reversed, it would seem reasonable to suggest that we are slowly moving toward some form of system of global order or geogovernance. How quickly and how uniformly we complete this transition and what kind of system of geogovernance we end up with, however, remain uncertain and will depend, in large measure, on the actions and decisions we take now.[70]

Conclusion: Responding to the New Security Agenda

I have suggested that we are currently confronted by a world in transition, one characterized by rapid change, new sources of unease and insecurity, and contradictory trends and prospects in both military and international affairs. How have first world militaries, in particular, and their security advisers responded to these changing circumstances and their associated agendas, issues, and concerns? The answer, like the question itself, is mixed. It is clear that most defense policymakers and security advisers are conscious that we have entered new and uncertain times. This is reflected in the spate of national strategic reviews and the fact that, since the end of the Cold War, academic and the professional journals of the United States and other armed forces have been full of articles on the revolution in military affairs, the future of warfare, and the nature of what has been termed the "military after next." Major studies have been initiated to try to forecast alternative strategic futures and their implications for militaries. And numerous conferences and workshops have been run on such topics as new-era security, information warfare, and, since September 11, global terrorism and its connections to Islamic fundamentalism.[71] As we have seen, existing military missions and operational doctrines are beginning to be extended beyond traditional war-fighting concepts and techniques to encompass such things as peacemaking, conflict resolution, and operations other than war. In the wake of the terrorist attacks in New York, Bali, and Madrid, governments everywhere, but especially those in the West, are seeking to upgrade their human intelligence and antiterrorist forces and capabilities.

Although much has occurred, there remains much to be done. As evidenced by their general response to September 11 and subsequent acts of international terrorism, Western security planners tend to see unconventional threats and new sources of insecurity in largely conventional terms, focusing on symptoms rather than causes. They continue still, in other words, to posit nonmilitary sources of insecurity as dangers to be defended against rather than problems to be solved and, as such, often ignore or downplay their social, political, and historical roots. As Mary Kaldor argues, they appear not adequately to recognize the increasing predominance and special character of the new wars that are now dominating the global strategic landscape, seeing them as of secondary importance to traditional interstate conflicts and, when they are engaged, responding to them in largely traditional or Clausewitzian terms.[72] Key decisionmakers in many countries continue also to resist suggestions that it is time to broaden our traditional and largely militarized understanding of security to include various nonmilitary sources of insecurity, or to have individuals or the globe as a whole replace, or join, the state as the key referents in future security calculations. This is usually on the grounds that any such redefinition would serve to divert attention from more serious threats to national security and overly complicate defense and security planning. Yet as we have seen, the world is becoming more complex, not less so, requiring policymakers to develop more sophisticated and nuanced ways of examining and responding to the global security problematique.

In spite of the impressive amount of theoretical and empirical evidence brought against it, then, the realist-neorealist perspective continues to be the one most favored by national security planners across the globe and their mainstream advisers in academe. Indeed, since the inception of the war on terrorism under the administration of George W. Bush, the space and incentives for alternative or critical thinking about security have been progressively closed down and its proponents ignored, marginalized, and stigmatized. This return to tradition is occurring at a time, ironically, when new ideas and new and critical approaches to security are most desperately needed. Why is this happening?

It is possible that the realist inclinations of Western security planners and policymakers are the most appropriate for the troubled times we are now in, although the clear and emerging policy failures in Israel, Afghanistan, Iraq, and parts of the former Soviet Union might suggest otherwise. It is possible, too, that the sheer shock of September 11 generated within the policymaking fraternity (and the broader communities to which they belong) a kind of strategic reflex whereby reason gave way to more instinctual responses. Faced with uncertain and troubling times, strategic planners, like drunkards and religious zealots, have turned to what they are most comfortable with. Or, to paraphrase the Australian historian Henry Reynolds, admittedly in another but not entirely unconnected context, when the chips are down, history and culture will always triumph over geography.[73]

The fact that security policymakers everywhere seem naturally predisposed toward realist understandings and solutions points to a number of other important (and related) factors and determinants. The first is the crucial role of the U.S. strategic studies mainstream and its military history wing, which have continued to dominate ways of viewing and responding to world affairs, acting as intellectual gatekeepers, and patrolling the boundaries of their disciplines repelling intruders and heretics. Another is the ascendancy within Western democracies everywhere of neoconservative political forces and actors who have long been wedded, emotionally as well as intellectually, to realist political and strategic axioms and are prepared, ruthlessly, to invoke national military myths, exploit popular fears and prejudices, and spend as much of their national treasures as is necessary to advance their own particular personal or party political interests. Within such a closed environment, traditional discourses of security, international relations, technological progress, and cultural relativism serve as useful and effective means of constituting reality in ways that can serve to advance or protect the interests not of peoples or humanity but those of the power holders themselves.[74]

A third and important factor is our own culpability in this process. We need to realize and accept that the siren calls of our politicians, teachers, and expert policy advisers connect as much to our emotional as our intellectual selves. As Martin Shaw has argued in *Post-Military Society*, while the move toward a more harmonious, cooperative, and peaceful world depends, at one level, on the progressive weakening of the power of established military (and militarized) institutions and thinking in favor of alternative structures and perspectives, these structural changes need also to be accomplished by a shift in societal values and beliefs. As Shaw puts it,

> Beyond specific political tasks, culture will remain the last refuge of militarism. A fully postmilitary citizenship will be achieved only when the ideas, values, and concepts of military culture, which permeate society at the deepest levels, have been genuinely domesticated.[75]

Any move beyond the strictures of realism will ultimately depend on us coming to terms with our own understandings and prejudices, how these have and continue to be shaped by our particular histories and experiences, and how they can be open to exploitation and manipulation. Such knowledge can provide us with a better and more informed understanding of who and what we are and, in the process, make us not only more resilient and discerning but also more open to humanity's common experiences, heritages, and destiny. These underlying processes of personal and community consciousness and empowerment are, for this writer at least, the essence of critical security thinking.

Whither NOD and CSBMs and the other elements of the original alternative security agenda in all of this? Clearly they can and should play a role for some time yet, both in the prevention and management of military conflict and in strengthening the kinds of cultures of cooperation that must underpin any move toward a more peaceful and harmonious society of states and beyond. The concepts themselves and their potential application will need, of course, to be adjusted to take account of the effects of the continuing revolution in military affairs and the other technological developments that are increasing the range and potential lethality of conventional and unconventional military forces and are clearly shifting the perceived balance of military advantage from defense to attack. This latter trend is likely to at least complicate—and could even undermine completely—

future efforts to devise purely defensive military force structures and so reinforce the preference of policymakers, described earlier, for CSBMs rather than more fundamental ways of dealing with existing and emerging defense and security dilemmas. This is unfortunate since, while such measures are important, they do little to halt or reverse the underlying structural, political, and cultural forces that give rise to continuing national and international militarization and its consequences. For all its faults and limitations, NOD and arms control and disarmament proposals more generally tend to require their proponents to view the issues at hand in a more critical and historically nuanced way than CSBMs, which deal simply with the here and now.

In other words, while the two concepts may be less applicable in a rapidly globalizing world, the thinking behind them remains relevant, perhaps even more so as the certainties associated with the period of the Cold War diminish further. So is their underlying purpose, which is to provide a better appreciation of the nature of security dilemmas and ways to deal with them. As we have seen, as the security agenda is expanding, so are the various security dilemmas associated with it. The possession of strong military forces provides little protection against suicide bombers, cyberterrorists, and other third wave warriors. They are largely ineffective against such manufactured risks or threats without enemies as AIDS and other epidemics, transnational crime, drugs, and environmental degradation. The untrammeled application of militarized thinking (and military force) to solve continuing social and political problems, moreover, can set off all kinds of reactions and conflict spirals that will serve to undermine security and well-being not only in the places directly affected but also in other parts of the world. This new and more complex security environment requires a much more democratic, empathetic, and cooperative approach to problem-solving, one that embraces the basic principles of NOD and CSBMs but extends their application well beyond states to include individuals and other forms of community. The end of the Cold War gave some hope that we might be moving in this direction, although the response to the September 11 attacks, the subsequent U.S.-led war against terrorism in Afghanistan and Iraq, the continuing imbroglio between Israelis and Palestinians, and decisions by the Bush administration not to ratify the Kyoto Accord, to revoke the 1972 Anti-Ballistic Missile Treaty, and to pursue its policy of preemptive intervention show we have still some way to go.

Notes

1. See Art, "To What Ends Military Power?"; Art and Waltz (eds.), *The Use of Force*; and Rothgeb, *Defining Power*.

2. Sivard, *World Military and Social Expenditures*.

3. There is a huge and varied literature on the nuclear and conventional arms races and their potential consequences. Some examples include Schell, *The Fate of the Earth*; Independent Commission on Disarmament, *Common Security*; and *SIPRI Yearbook* (Oxford: Oxford University Press/Stockholm International Peace Research Institute, various years).

4. Discussions of the security dilemma are contained in Jervis, "Cooperation Under the Security Dilemma"; Buzan, *People, States, and Fear*; and Butfoy, *Common Security and Strategic Reform*.

5. Rapoport, "Critique of Strategic Thinking," in Rosembaum (ed.), *Readings in the International Political System*, p. 224, cited in Møller, *Common Security and Nonoffensive Defense*, p. 21.

6. McInnes, "Alternative Defence," in McInnes (ed.), *Security and Strategy in the New Europe*; and Booth, "Strategy," in Groom and Light (eds.), *Contemporary International Relations*, at p. 114.

7. See Wiseman, *Common Security and Non-Provocative Defence*.

8. Wyn Jones, "'Travel Without Maps,'" p. 197.

9. For a discussion of the German debate on NOD, see Møller, *Resolving the Security Dilemma in Europe*.

10. See Ter Borg and Smit (eds.), *Non-Provocative Defence as a Principle of Arms Reduction*; Boserup and Neild (eds.), *The Foundations of Defensive Defence*; and Møller, *Dictionary of Alternative Defense*, esp. pp. 242–243 and references therein. To help overcome the intrinsic difficulty of distinguishing offensive from defensive weapons, NOD proponents suggest that national defense postures as a whole be examined rather than each and every weapons system.

11. Independent Commission on Disarmament and Security Issues, *Common Security*. See also Wiseman, *Common Security and Non-Provocative Defence*, and Møller, *Common Security and Nonoffensive Defense*.

12. Møller, *Common Security and Nonoffensive Defense*, p. 2. See also Møller and Wiberg (eds.), *Non-Offensive Defence for the Twenty-First Century*, pp. 1–4.

13. Gates, *Non-Offensive Defense*; Cheeseman, "The Application of the Principles of Non-Offensive Defence Beyond Europe"; and Butfoy, "Critical Reflections on Non-Offensive Defence." For a recent discussion of some of these kinds of criticisms, see Møller, "Small States, Non-Offensive Defence, and Collective Security."

14. Møller, *Common Security and Nonoffensive Defense*, pp. 199–207.

15. Dean, "Using Arms Control to Promote NOD in Europe," in Møller and Wiberg (eds.), *Non-Offensive Defence for the Twenty-First Century*.

16. Alford, "Confidence-Building Measures in Europe"; Møller, *Dictionary of Alternative Defense*, pp. 57–59; and Desjardins, *Rethinking Confidence-Building Measures*.

17. Levite and Landau, "Confidence and Security Building Measures in the Middle East."

18. Macintosh, "Confidence- and Security-Building Measures," p. 9. See also Macintosh, "Confidence Building and the Arms Control Process"; and Desjardins, *Rethinking Confidence-Building Measures*, pp. 18–19.

19. See Pederson and Weeks, "A Survey of Confidence and Security Building Measures," in Cossa (ed.), *Asia Pacific Confidence and Security Building Measures*; Ball, "Building Confidence and Security in the Asia-Pacific Region," in Klintworth (ed.), *Asia-Pacific Security*; Chalmers, *Confidence-Building in South-East Asia*; and Ganguly and Greenwood (eds.), *Mending Fences*.

20. Laurance, Wezeman, and Wulf, *Arms Watch*, pp. 5–6.

21. Chalmers, Greene, Laurance, and Wulf (eds.), *Developing the UN Register of Conventional Arms*, pp. 3–4. According to the authors, "as information about arms exports to Iraq and its neighbours during the 1980s became disseminated, proposals to increase transparency of the international arms trade gained high-level political support in the EC, G7 and P5 states amongst many others." The permanent five members of the UN Security Council also began meeting to consider the establishment of multilateral constraints on the export of destabilizing weapons systems to the Middle East and beyond.

22. Singh and Vekaric (eds.), *Non-Provocative Defence*; United Nations Institute for Disarmament Research, *Nonoffensive Defense*; Cheeseman, *The Search for Self-Reliance*, pp. 201–214; and Møller, "A Common Security and NOD Regime for the Asia-Pacific?" An excellent (and exhaustive) source of contemporary research on NOD and associated concepts is the International Research newsletter *NOD and Conversion* (previously entitled *NOD. Non-Offensive Defence*), edited by Bjørn Møller and published monthly by the Copenhagen Peace Research Institute.

23. Armengol, "NOD and the Western Mediterranean," in Møller and Wiberg (eds.), *Non-Offensive Defence for the Twenty-First Century*. In most of these cases, various practical difficulties led their proponents to give priority to confidence-building measures at least in the short term. In the case of the western Mediterranean, for example, Armengol notes that the adoption of fully developed NOD structures is hampered by, among other things, imbalances in existing force projection capabilities, the inclusion of rapid intervention or nuclear forces in some national military postures, the presence of a "multitude of bases and auxiliary installations belonging to non-Mediterranean powers, and the northern state's membership of, and connections to, NATO and the WEU."

24. Hagena, "NOD in the Air," in Møller and Wiberg (eds.), *Non-Offensive Defence for the Twenty-First Century*; Booth, "NOD at Sea," in Møller and Wiberg (eds.), *Non-Offensive Defence for the Twenty-First Century*.

25. Gongora, Fortmann, and Lefebvre, "Modern Land Warfare Doctrines and Non-Offensive Defense."

26. Buzan, "Does NOD Have a Future in the Post–Cold War World?" in Møller and Wiberg (eds.), *Non-Offensive Defence for the Twenty-First Century*, p. 24.

27. Buzan, "Does NOD Have a Future in the Post–Cold War World?" pp. 19 and 22.

28. Ibid., pp. 14–15. See also Buzan, "The Present as a Historic Turning Point"; and Møller, "Small States, Non-Offensive Defence, and Collective Security," pp. 128–129.

29. See Porter, *War and the Rise of the State*, and Holsti, *The State, War, and the State of War*. For an excellent discussion of the gendered nature of national military and social identities, see Enloe, *Does Khaki Become You?*

30. Knudsen, "Humanitarian Intervention Revisited." Not everyone agrees with this view of course. Wheeler and Morris argue, for example, that the cases of Iraq, Rwanda, and Somalia provide "no more than the most tentative support for the descriptive claim that the concept of humanitarian intervention is now seen by the international community as legitimate." They also assert that the idea of humanitarian intervention may not be as attractive to non-Western governments such as China and Indonesia or to NGOs and the publics in these countries. See Wheeler and Morris, "Humanitarian Intervention and State Practice at the End of the Cold War," in Fawn and Larkins (eds.), *International Society After the Cold War*, p. 160.

31. There is a huge literature on the emergence, characteristics, and implications of this new form of peacekeeping. Some examples include Daniel and Hayes (eds.), *Beyond Traditional Peacekeeping*; Ratner, *The New UN Peacekeeping*; and Mackinlay (ed.), *A Guide to Peace Support Operations.*

32. Smith and Kettle (eds.), *Threats Without Enemies,* and Prins (ed.), *Threats Without Enemies.*

33. Discussions of these are contained in Barnett, *The Meaning of Environmental Security*; Buzan, Wæver, and de Wilde, *Security*; Krause and Williams (eds.), *Critical Security Studies*; Lipshutz (ed.), *On Security*; and Terriff, Croft, James, and Morgan, *Security Studies Today.*

34. See Findlay, "The New Peacekeepers and the New Peacekeeping," in Findlay (ed.), *Challenges for the New.*

35. Wing, *Refocusing Concepts of Security.*

36. Malcolm, *Does the Blue Helmet Fit? The Canadian Forces and Peacekeeping.*

37. Lambeth, "Technology Trends in Air Warfare," in Stephens (ed.), *New Era Security*, p. 135. A useful treatment of the Revolution in Military Affairs is contained in Metz and Kievet, *The Revolution in Military Affairs and Conflict Short of War.*

38. Toffler and Toffler, *Wars and Anti-Wars*; Pape, *Bombing to Win*; and Gates, "Air Power and the Theory and Practice of Coercion."

39. A discussion of cosmopolitan and cosmopolitan-minded military forces is contained in Elliott and Cheeseman (eds.), *Forces for Good? Cosmopolitan Militaries in the 21st Century.*

40. Kaldor, "Introduction," in Kaldor and Vashee (eds.), *Restructuring the Global Military Sector*, p. 13. See also Brooks, "Messiahs or Mercenaries?" and Mandel, *Armies Without States.*

41. See Klare, "An Avalanche of Guns," in Kaldor and Vashee (eds.), *Restructuring the Global Military Sector.*

42. Moskos, Williams, and Segal, "Armed Forces After the Cold War," in Moskos, Williams, and Segal (eds.), *The Postmodern Military*, at pp. 1–2.

43. An excellent overview of the process of globalization and its various causes, characteristics, and contestations is provided in Scholte, *Globalization.*

44. Giddens, *Runaway World.* Useful overviews of the environmental problems currently confronting the world and their potential security implications are contained in Elliott, "Environmental Conflict," and Duedney and Mathews (eds.), *Contested Grounds.*

45. The degree to which state sovereignty is being undermined by the twin forces of globalization and fragmentation is subject to considerable debate. Some contending positions on the issue are contained in Camilleri and Falk, *The End of Sovereignty?*; Devetak and Higgott, "Justice Unbound"; Mann, "Has Globalization Ended the Rise and Rise of the Nation-State?"; and Weiss, "Globalization and the Myth of the Powerless State."

46. See, for example, Gray, *False Dawn,* and Botsman and Latham (eds.), *The Enabling State.*

47. See Holsti, "The Coming Chaos?" in Paul and Hall (eds.), *International Order and the Future of World Politics.*

48. See Linklater, "What Is a Good International Citizen?" in Keal (ed.), *Ethics and Foreign Policy;* and van Steenbergen (ed.), *The Condition of Citizenship.*

49. Rosenau, "Armed Force and Armed Forces in a Turbulent World," in Burk (ed.), *The Military in New Times*; and James N. Rosenau, *Along the Domestic-Foreign Frontier.*

50. See Mueller, *Retreat from Doomsday.*

51. These latter developments are thought to lessen the prospect of interstate wars by increasing the number of stakeholders in international disputes as well as the potential costs of military conflict, reducing the importance of territorial conquest in the calculation of national power, increasing the incentives for institutional cooperation, and enhancing the view among state elites that war is no longer a rational way of achieving national political objectives. For contending views on the end of interstate war, see Russett, *Controlling the Sword*; Thompson, "The Future of Transitional Warfare," in Burk (ed.), *The Military in New Times*; and Weart, *Never at War.*

52. See, for example, Callahan, *Unwinnable Wars*; Freedman, "The Changing Forms of Military Conflict"; and Snow, *Uncivil Wars.*

53. Kaldor, *New and Old Wars.*

54. Toffler and Toffler, *Wars and Anti-Wars*, p. 161.

55. van Creveld, *The Transformation of War.*

56. Builder, *The Icarus Syndrome*, p. 255. See also Snow, *National Security*, 3d ed.

57. Toffler and Toffler, *Wars and Anti-Wars*, pp. 91–92.

58. Kaplan, "The Coming Anarchy."

59. See Fry and O'Hagan (eds.), *Contending Images of World Politics*; Harkavy, "Images of the Coming International System"; Walker, *One World, Many Worlds*; and Walt, "International Relations."

60. Kaplan, "The Coming Anarchy."

61. Fawn and Larkins (eds.), *International Society After the Cold War.*

62. Huntington, *The Clash of Civilizations and the Remaking of World Order*; Singer and Wildavsky, *The Real World Order.*

63. An exemplar of this view is Dibb, *Towards a New Balance of Power in Asia.*

64. Drucker, "The Global Economy and the Nation-State."

65. Slaughter, "The Real New World Order."

66. Harkavy, "Images of the Coming International System," p. 585. For a discussion of such a world order, see Chomsky, *World Orders, Old and New.*

67. Falk, *On Humane Governance*, p. 243.

68. Gurtov, *Global Politics in the Human Interest*, 2d ed.

69. Falk, *On Humane Governance*, p. 70.

70. As Ken Booth argues, any such consideration of the future must include an appropriate "ethicscape" for the twenty-first century—the kinds of values and principles that should determine how we might organize our lives and experiences. Booth's own preferred ethicscape emphasizes cosmopolitan over communitarian values, especially those concerning human rights and emancipation. It follows the tradition of those who conceive of humanity as a whole and seeks to build on the "variety of historical and contemporary theories" that already promote the ideals of world community, human needs, and environmental sustainability (a position this writer broadly shares). Booth, "Human Wrongs and International Relations." See also Booth, "Security and Emancipation," and Booth, "Conclusion," in Booth (ed.), *Statecraft and Security*. In this last work, Booth makes the powerful point that "the main question . . . is not 'What will the twenty-first century be *like*?' but 'Who will the twenty-first century be *for*?'" (p. 346, emphasis in the original).

71. Examples include Bracken, "The Military After Next"; Biddle, "Victory Misunderstood"; Metz, *Strategic Horizons*; and Thomas (ed.), *The Revolution in Military Affairs*.

72. Kaldor (ed.), *Global Insecurity*.

73. Reynolds, "Catching Up with Our Geography."

74. Klein, "How the West Was Won," and *Strategic Studies and World Order*. See also Campbell, *Writing Security,* and Dalby, "Contesting an Essential Concept," in Krause and Williams (eds.), *Critical Security Studies*.

75. Shaw, *Post-Military Society*, p. 188.

4

Militarized Masculinities and the Politics of Peacekeeping

Sandra Whitworth

The image of a Canadian soldier wearing his blue beret, standing watch at some lonely outpost in a strife-torn foreign land, is part of the modern Canadian mosaic, and a proud tradition.

—*General Paul Manson*[1]

Arone lapsed in and out of consciousness during the beating. When he was conscious, he was heard to scream "Canada! Canada!" on several occasions.

—*Account of the murder of Shidane Arone by Canadian soldiers, March 16, 1993*[2]

The image of Canada as peacekeeper,[3] so aptly described above by former chief of the defense staff General Paul Manson, has long served as one of the "core myths"[4] of Canada's "imagined community."[5] That myth locates Canada as an altruistic and benign middle power, acting with a kind of moral purity not normally exhibited by contemporary states. Thus when two Canadian soldiers beat to death a Somali teenager, Shidane Abukar Arone, in March 1993—using their fists, their boots, a baton, a metal rod, and cigarettes—the myth was reasserted at the very moment it began to disintegrate. Arone's only words in English that night were to repeat "Canada . . . Canada" throughout his ordeal. The myth had been sold so well, even a sixteen-year-old Somali shepherd, murdered by those who were supposed to be its exemplars, apparently believed in it.

Arone's tragic death, and the shooting two weeks earlier of two Somali men by Canadian soldiers, sparked a series of courts-martial and eventually prompted the Canadian government to launch a commission of inquiry to investigate the activities of its forces in Somalia. Intended as much to resuscitate the image of Canada's military and Canada's reputation internationally, many of those investigations focused on problems of a few bad apples or otherwise lamented a decline of traditional military values. More

89

rarely were the events of Somalia associated with the problems of militarized masculinity and the use of soldiers—people trained to destroy other human beings by force—in peace operations.[6] However, the dramatic expansion of peacekeeping missions in the post–Cold War period demands such an analysis. The events in Somalia not only revealed some of the contradictions of one of Canada's core myths but also underscored the pervasiveness, and effects of, militarized masculinity within issues of international security.

Masculinities and Peacekeeping

Since the end of the Cold War, it has become commonplace to note that there has been a proliferation of peacekeeping missions: the United Nations launched fifteen between 1956 and 1989 and a further twenty-two peacekeeping missions between 1989 and 1995 alone.[7] The proliferation of missions has led also to a proliferation of peacekeeping personnel deployed around the world: in 1991 the UN deployed some 11,000 blue helmets, and by 1994 the number of peacekeepers in the field numbered well over 75,000.[8] Those missions also have become much more complex, departing from the traditional interposition of neutral forces between belligerent groups to include, for example, military and police functions, the monitoring of human rights, the conduct of elections, the delivery of humanitarian aid, the repatriation of refugees, the creation and conduct of state administrative structures, and so on.[9]

Peacekeeping, and peace operations generally, became the way in which the UN asserted its visibility internationally, and many cited peacekeeping as "perhaps the major instrument of diplomacy available to the United Nations for insuring peace and international security."[10] That instrument, however, continues to depend primarily on the use of soldiers to serve as the personnel for peace operations. Nobody knows better than militaries themselves what is involved in the creation of a soldier. As Major R. W. J. Wenek wrote in 1984: "The defining role of any military force is the management of violence by violence, so that individual aggressiveness is, or should be, a fundamental characteristic of occupational fitness in combat units."[11] These are the kinds of qualities feminist scholars point to when they note the way in which most militaries promote a particular kind of masculinity, one premised on violence and aggression, institutional unity and hierarchy, "aggressive heterosexism and homophobia," as well as misogyny and racism.[12]

My argument in this chapter is that peacekeeping may have resolved what was a crisis of legitimation for some post–Cold War militaries, but it did so in a way that is not fully or properly militaristic. Restrictions on firing weapons only in self-defense and a sometimes multilateral chain of command disrupt prevailing notions of military purpose and structure. Within traditional military culture, peacekeeping and peace operations are often ridiculed and demeaned: much as they have become increasingly important within the post–Cold War era, there is not the same prestige associated with a blue beret fight for the mostly young men trained to do battle who we deploy on these missions. The resolution of the military's legitimation crisis becomes to some extent a crisis of masculinity. The tensions that emerge, and their sometimes horrifying consequences, are made clear by examining the Canadian case.

Canada and Peacekeeping

As has been suggested, peacekeeping is an extremely popular activity within Canada. This is in contrast to the far more ambivalent position found in the United States, where peacekeeping does not appear to receive the same widespread public support as in Canada and where peace operations generally are treated with considerable caution and sometimes outright hostility (a caution that will be heightened by the experience in Iraq following the 2003 war). It is difficult to imagine the Canadian state falling into arrears to the UN for peacekeeping contributions, a consistent problem with the United States; and it is equally unthinkable that a Canadian soldier would be lauded by some political elites for refusing to serve under UN command as occurred in the United States with the 1995 case of Specialist Michael New.[13] Peacekeeping in Canada, by contrast, was critiqued favorably in reviews of both foreign and defense policy as central, primary to our foreign and security policies. As the 1994 Report of the Special Joint Committee on Canada's Defence Policy statement noted:

> In virtually every one of these [successful peacekeeping] cases, Canada has played a constructive and often leading role. Canadians are rightly proud of what their country—their military—has done in this regard. Indeed, the demand for our services, and arguably the need, is growing. Since 1988, the United Nations has undertaken more peacekeeping missions than in the previous thirty-five years, and Canada has been a key participant in almost every one of them.[14]

Likewise, as Janice Stein reported to the special joint committee reviewing Canada's foreign policy in 1994, "The overwhelming sense [is] that this is an area of comparative advantage for Canadians."[15]

Canadian government documents reveal an assumption not only that Canadians are experienced and committed peacekeepers but also that peacekeeping is a clear extension of Canadian values on the international stage. As the 1995 government statement, *Canada in the World,* noted:

Canadians are confident in their values and in the contribution these values make to the international community. . . . Our principles and values—
our culture—are rooted in a commitment to tolerance; to democracy, equi-
ty and human rights; to the peaceful resolution of differences; to the
opportunities and challenges of the marketplace; to social justice; to sustainable development; and to easing poverty.[16]

Or as Stéphane Dion, president of the Privy Council and minister of
intergovernmental affairs, enthusiastically commented: "Canada is a good
global citizen, projecting beyond our borders our values of generosity, tolerance and an unswerving commitment to peace and democracy."[17]

Such widespread government support does not mean that there are not
disagreements within the Canadian government about peacekeeping. The
Department of National Defence's enthusiasm for peacekeeping is tem-
pered somewhat by the disadvantages associated with the popularity of an
activity that does not require nearly as much capital expenditure as the
geostrategic defense of Canada and its allies. As the Defence White Paper
stated repeatedly, there is more to defense than peacekeeping; as Major
General (ret.) Glen Younghusband pointed out to the special joint committee reviewing Canada's defense policy in 1994, "To believe that Canada
will never require a greater military capability than peacekeeping is wishful
thinking, and a defence policy based on wishful thinking would be dangerous indeed."[18]

But in general, the advantages of peacekeeping are widely accepted,
and government support for peacekeeping is reflected also within the general population. In the 1995 foreign policy review conducted by the
Canadian government, women's groups that appeared before the joint
committee provided a number of important criticisms of peacekeeping, but
most of the groups were supportive and viewed it as an element of defense
that should be expanded.[19] Peace groups often note the importance of
shifting the emphasis of the Canadian military from combat to peacekeeping.[20] In 1992, even the Citizens' Inquiry into Peace and Security (an alternative foreign and defense review organized by the Canadian Peace
Alliance and funded by a number of largely peace, native, and labor
NGOs) found that support for peacekeeping activities was "virtually unan-
imous."[21]

The image of Canada as peacekeeper has also served a variety of
important political goals of the Canadian government. As Joseph T. Jockel
notes, "Canada's reputation as a good international 'citizen,' a reputation
acquired partially through extensive peacekeeping, may have strengthened
its position in the UN across a wide range of issues on the world agenda."[22]
It certainly played a role in Canada's successful bid for a Security Council
seat in 1998; Jockel notes that in the post–Cold War period

> Canada was the peacekeeping country *par excellence*, having contributed
> to virtually all UN peacekeeping operations . . . [its] peacekeeping experi-
> ence, coupled with its well-recognized commitment to the UN, appeared
> to have left it especially suited to play if not a leading role, then at least a
> significant one in the building of the new world order.[23]

Indeed, as numerous commentators have noted, it has been Canada's involvement in peacekeeping and its "history of altruism, compassion, fairness, and of doing things irrespective of our own national interest" that gives it influence internationally far out of proportion to its military or economic power."[24] As Carol Off writes: "Canada is one of only a handful of nations that include peacekeeping as a permanent part of their national defence, and no other country gives peacekeeping such a defining role in its international politics. It's in our genetic code as a nation."[25]

The Canadian soldier as peacekeeper is not a warrior but a protector. These are assumptions that fit very well with the more generalized notions of moral purity that pervade Canadian foreign policy[26] and the much-touted view of Canada as a middle-power that has informed most government statements and mainstream analyses of Canadian foreign policy since World War II. As the seasoned veterans[27] of peacekeeping, Canadian soldiers are expected to know how to act when deployed abroad. It is that reputation that makes the experience of Canadian soldiers in Somalia so revealing of the practices associated with militarized masculinity.

The Reputation Tarnished:
Canadian Peacekeepers in Somalia

The very favorable image associated with Canadian peacekeeping was shaken to its core when reports emerged from Belet Huen, Somalia, of the shooting of two Somali men and then the subsequent torture and murder of Arone by members of the elite Canadian Airborne Regiment.[28] The two men, one of whom died, were shot in the back, and while an initial investigation concluded that the soldiers had acted properly, a Canadian military doctor later reported that the dead man had been shot once in the back and then "someone had finished him off with a . . . lethal shot to the head."[29] The doctor reported, moreover, that he had been pressured to destroy his medical records concerning the alleged murder.[30] Canada's peacekeeping image was rocked even further when, at court-martial proceedings, it was revealed that Arone's torturers had photographed his ordeal. The photographs, described as trophy photos, depicted two soldiers, Master Corporal Clayton Matchee and Private Elvin Kyle Brown, striking various poses with the bloodied Arone, one of which showed Matchee holding a loaded pistol to Arone's head and another in which Matchee forced Arone's mouth open with the riot baton.

The first reaction by mainstream observers of peacekeeping in Canada to the Arone murder was to dismiss it as the act of a few bad apples,[31] most likely the result of years of underfunding, which had led to the deployment of a unit not ready for duty.[32] The bad-apple theory was undermined when, some months after the inquiry was called into the events in Somalia, a number of videos were released to the Canadian media. The first was a video from the Somalia mission taken by Canadian soldiers on duty there as a personal record, portions of which portrayed Airborne soldiers describing it as "Operation Snatch Niggers," with others lamenting that "they had not shot enough niggers yet." The second video depicted hazing (or initiation) rituals that included, among other things, images of Airborne soldiers vomiting or eating vomit, being smeared with feces, and the single black soldier in the regiment being forced to walk around on all fours with the phrase "I love the KKK" written on his back.[33] The problem, it would appear from the videos, was far more pervasive than could be accounted by blaming only a few bad apples.

The courts-martial eventually found one of the men involved in Arone's murder, Elvin Kyle Brown, guilty of torture and manslaughter; it sentenced him to five years in prison and dismissed him in disgrace. Clayton Matchee tried to commit suicide after his arrest in Somalia, suffered brain damage, and was found unfit to stand trial at his subsequent court-martial. Other soldiers who had heard but not stopped the beating and murder were found guilty of lesser charges, and after the release of the hazing videos the Airborne Regiment itself was disbanded.

The government inquiry that had been called to investigate the events in Somalia was halted before it could actually examine Arone's murder. The inquiry had exceeded the set time limit for its investigation, and the Canadian government refused any further extensions. This was the first time in Canadian history that a commission of inquiry of this magnitude was brought to a halt before its completion. But the commissioners did hear extensive evidence on predeployment issues as well as the shooting on March 4, 1993. Its five-volume report, *Dishonoured Legacy*, while critical of the military in a number of important respects, picked up on the theme that had already been emphasized by military apologists. The problem was not one of the military itself but rather one of a military gone wrong. As military historian David Bercuson noted, the Canadian military had become stifled by budget cuts, was overbureaucratized, and was staffed by career-minded cover-your-ass officers who have replaced the disciplined and honorable leaders of the past.[34] The problem, in short, was a failure of traditional military values.

Feminist and Critical Questions

Feminists and critical theorists might ask instead whether the problem was actually one of military values. Theorists of both militarism and of masculinity have long argued the intimate connection between military organizations and hegemonic representations of masculinity.[35] As David Morgan writes:

> Of all the sites where masculinities are constructed, reproduced, and deployed, those associated with war and the military are some of the most direct. Despite far-reaching political, social, and technological changes, the warrior still seems to be a key symbol of masculinity. In statues, heroic paintings, comic books, and popular films the gendered connotations are inescapable. The stance, the facial expressions, and the weapons clearly connote aggression, courage, a capacity for violence, and, sometimes, a willingness for sacrifice. The uniform absorbs individualities into a generalized and timeless masculinity while also connoting a control of emotion and a subordination to a larger rationality.[36]

And this is as true of Canada's ostensibly benign and altruistic peacekeepers as it is of soldiers elsewhere. Indeed, what has been particularly revealing in the Canadian case has been the dangerous behavior that erupts when soldiers trained "to engage in wanton destruction and to slip the bonds of civilized behaviour"[37] are limited and constrained to mere peacekeeping duty. From this perspective, what Somalia demonstrated was not a departure from traditional military values but rather their brutal conclusion.

Most feminist analyses of militaries and militarism focus on the ways in which the qualities demanded by militaries—the requisite lust for violence (when needed) and a corresponding willingness to subordinate oneself to hierarchy and authority (when needed)[38]—are not natural but must be self-consciously cultivated. Few new male recruits arrive as ready-made soldiers, and as Barbara Ehrenreich notes, "the difference between an ordinary man or boy and a reliable killer, as any drill sergeant could attest, is profound. A transformation is required."[39]

Historically, that transformation has been accomplished in different ways, but by the seventeenth century in Europe, as Ehrenreich describes it, the process had become highly organized:

> New recruits and even seasoned veterans were endlessly drilled, hour after hour, until each man began to feel himself part of a single, giant fighting machine. The drill was only partially inspired by the technology of firearms. It's easy enough to teach a man to shoot a gun: the problem is to make him willing to get into situations where guns are being shot and to remain there long enough to do some shooting of his own. . . . In the fanatical routines of boot camp, a man leaves behind his former identity and is reborn as a creature of the military—an automaton and also, ideally, a willing killer of other men.[40]

The contemporary practices of boot camp are remarkably similar across most modern state militaries. They entail a tightly choreographed process aimed at breaking down the individuality of the recruits and replacing it with a commitment to, and dependence upon, the total institution of which they are now a part.[41] By the end, recruits should conform to the official attitudes of military conduct, be able to follow orders instantly and without question, and commit themselves to the larger group (whether that is corecruits, barrack, regiment, battalion, military, or state) over any personal or individual commitments they previously held.[42]

The new soldier faces the humiliation strategies that are common to most national militaries. The tactics used to humiliate and degrade the recruit will vary depending on the military. In some, physically brutalizing new recruits remains an acceptable strategy, whether by officers or more senior recruits. In other militaries where physical punishment in principle is prohibited, drill sergeants often have at their official disposal only the threat of violence and verbal assaults. Here the new recruit is not only reminded constantly of his or her incompetence but faces a variety of gendered and raced insults crafted to play upon her or his specific feminine or masculine anxieties, including "whore," "faggot," "sissies," "cunt," "ladies," "abortion," "pussies," "nigger," "Indian," and sometimes simply "you woman."[43] Even in militaries that ostensibly outlaw physical violence toward new recruits, unofficial initiation rituals and general hazing are still common and regularly conducted in the presence of superior officers.[44]

Ominously, and in an observation that might have served as a prediction of the murders in Somalia some ten years later, Major R. W. J. Wenek wrote in 1984 that:

> Aggressiveness must be selected for in military organizations and must be reinforced during military training, but it may be extremely difficult to make fine distinctions between those individuals who can be counted on to act in an appropriately aggressive way and those likely at some time to display inappropriate aggression. *To some extent, the risk of erring on the side of excess may be a necessary one in an organization whose existence is premised on the instrumental value of aggression and violence.*[45]

The recipe for creating soldiers thus involves not only selecting for and reinforcing aggressive behavior; it usually entails also an explosive mix of misogyny, racism, and homophobia. A deeper analysis of the murders in Somalia and Canada's Somalia inquiry reveals all of these ingredients to have been present in Canada's beloved, benign, and altruistic armed forces.

Rereading the Somalia Crisis

Soldiers in the Canadian Airborne Regiment were excited to be going to Somalia, especially as it became clear that it might become a mission authorized under Chapter VII of the UN Charter. As the only soldier charged in Arone's murder said after his release from prison (and apparently with no intended irony): "The fact is, peacekeeping is boring and we were much happier to be going to Somalia in a chapter 7 role. Personally, I was delighted."[46] Airborne had been chosen to go while Somalia was still designated a blue beret mission, but the mission was changed to a Chapter VII mission in early December 1992, just before Airborne deployed. As one soldier commented, "I think the men were glad when the mission changed from peacekeeping to peace making . . . this was more real. We're training for war all our lives, and the guys all want to know what it is like. That's why they join the army, to soldier."[47]

Apparently so excited by the prospect of real soldiering, a number of Airborne soldiers allegedly torched an officer's car, and others went into a provincial park and fired off their weapons in a small shooting spree. Asked at the inquiry whether this might have signaled discipline problems within the Airborne, Major-General (ret.) Lewis Mackenzie's response was revealing: while it didn't excuse what the soldiers did, he said, these incidents could be explained by the fact that there had been few Chapter VII missions in UN history to that point and the soldiers were all psyched up. Somalia had become a non–blue beret fight, and while some of this is macho stuff, there was more prestige for Airborne soldiers being deployed on a Chapter VII mission than a Chapter VI mission.

But after their training, preparation, and anticipation of real soldiering, Airborne discovered that the war had moved on from Belet Huen. The country was hot, dusty, dry, and full of scorpions—which provided a certain amount of danger during otherwise boring daily routines, but little in the way of exciting military action. Life in Somalia was unpleasant, but Belet Huen was not a war zone. One soldier remarked, "When we got there, there was no war. The war had gone by. Probably for some guys that was a disappointment."[48] As Donna Winslow notes, "Once the Canadians concluded that they were 'wasting their time' in Somalia, came the brutal conclusion that one could die 'for nothing.'"[49] And when Canadian soldiers came to that conclusion, their own violence began.

The Canadians, indeed, had already decided that Somalis—in particular Somali men—could not be trusted. They were black, they were the enemy, they had no respect for their women, they were liars and thieves, they were not grateful for Canadian efforts, and they were even, in the opinion of many Airborne soldiers, homosexuals. Marked in this way, the violence perpetrated upon them seems almost inevitable. As Sherene Razack argues, it "is a short step from cultural difference to naturalized violence,"[50] and this was certainly in evidence in Somalia.

While the release of the two videotapes (the first from Somalia and the second from the Airborne Regiment's 1 Commando Unit hazing rituals) gave perhaps the most obvious indications of racism within Airborne—and apparently shocked many Canadians—officials at the Department of National Defence might not have been surprised at all. It was learned within the first week of the Somalia inquiry's hearings that the department had been investigating the presence of racist skinhead organizations and neo-Nazi activities within the Canadian Forces and had identified the entire Canadian Forces Base (CFB) at Petawawa (home of the Airborne Regiment) as "one of the several areas where right-wing activities are centred."[51] Senior military officials, in other words, had allowed members of Airborne who were either known members of racist skinhead organizations or who were under investigation for suspected skinhead and neo-Nazi activity to be deployed to Somalia.[52]

Whether or not the racism exhibited by Airborne soldiers was organized, much of the evidence from testimonies, photographs, diaries, and letters home from Canadian soldiers reveals the ways in which racism pervaded Airborne. From posing in front of the Confederate flag (the rebel flag often used by white supremacist groups in the United States), through tattooing themselves with swastikas, to calling Somalis any number of racist pejoratives ("smufty," "smoofties," "moolie," "flip-flop," "nig nog," "nigger," and "gimmes"),[53] Canadian soldiers demonstrated repeatedly that they viewed the Somali people as both other and inferior.

Many of the Canadians assumed that the desperate poverty they witnessed in Somalia was the result of a backward culture that fostered laziness. As paratrooper Robert Prouse reported in his diary from the mission, fellow soldiers said that Somalia should be used "as a nuclear dump, it's worthless" and others asked: "F_____ tar monkeys, why should we help them? If they haven't improved in the last thousand years, they won't improve now. They're so backwards, why bother?"[54] As Prouse commented, "The majority of our people hate the Somalis and the country."[55] Many also considered Somalis a people with little respect for human life who had different standards and different expectations about death and violence.[56] Kyle Brown reported that in Somalia "[violence is a] part of their culture, and a language they understand."[57] If nothing else, one soldier complained, it was hard to distinguish between the good guys and the bad guys: "They're all Black, who's who? They all look alike."[58]

Somalis were different not only in terms of their skin color, their poverty, and their values; for Airborne they were also different from Canadians in terms of their attitudes toward women. In interviews with sociologist Donna Winslow, soldiers reported how angered they were by the way Somali men treated women and children. As one soldier reported, "It's frustrating to see. Women do everything over there. They get the water, cook, do everything. . . . But the men, they sit around, don't do anything all day long. They visit their friends and that's about it."[59]

Somali men seemed different not only in terms of how they treated women but also in terms of how they interacted with one another. Many of the Canadian soldiers quickly concluded that "Everybody's gay here!"[60] Somali men wore sarongs, they held hands with one another as expressions of friendship, and they urinated by squatting. As one soldier described it: "Real men wear pants and stand to urinate and they certainly don't hold hands."[61] Soldiers reported to Winslow that the hand-holding was evidence that "there was quite a lot of homosexuality" in Somalia.

The reviled and hated ethnic other all looked the same, treated their women badly, and were a bunch of homosexuals. But the last straw was that they also did not act nearly grateful enough to the soldiers who had gone to Somalia as a result of Operation Deliverance. Razack writes that "the Canadian military understood its role as 'putting that region of Somalia back on the path to a normal lifestyle.' Or, in the more direct language of the troops, their task was to 'look after' Somalis who, as it turns out, were neither properly grateful nor deserving, a source of considerable aggravation for the troops."[62] The reality on the ground for Canadian soldiers included having rocks thrown at them, being called insulting names, and confronting people, many of whom did not seem to appreciate the work that the Canadians were doing for them.[63]

As the soldiers became increasingly frustrated with the apparent lack of gratitude, the rock-throwing, the begging, and the petty thefts, their own responses became correspondingly more violent. Soldiers started throwing rocks back at the Somalis, sometimes in order to disperse children begging for food and water.[64] One photograph depicted a Canadian chaplain standing guard over a number of bound and blindfolded Somali children with a sign that read "I am a thief" hanging around their necks. As one soldier reported to Winslow, "Basically everybody beat up on the Somalis. Everybody did."[65]

Warrior Princes?

The racism and violence witnessed in Somalia were largely attributed to the frustration, stress, and the profound culture shock Airborne members experienced upon arrival in Somalia.[66] Arone's murder was linked also to the particular antimalaria drug used by Canadian soldiers in Somalia.[67] Each of these types of explanation depoliticizes the events in Somalia, excuses and explains away the racism and violence in a way intended not to disrupt prevailing myths about both Canadian soldiers and Canada itself. Canada's so-called Somalia crisis was a crisis only insofar as it laid bare the fundamental contradiction of relying on soldiers in so-called peace operations. And it was Somalis, in particular Somali men who were marked as different, who bore the brunt of those contradictions.

If we examine the ways in which race, gender, and sexuality are privileged sites in the creation of a soldier, we might be less surprised that these were the lines around which Canadian soldiers reacted and understood both their difference and expressed their violence. Race and racism often figure in military hazing and initiation rituals, as noted above. Race was apparently a factor in Brown and Matchee's hazing, especially upon entering Airborne. Matchee is full Cree and Brown part Cree, and reports indicate that in Matchee's case in particular his "Cree heritage became a focus" of his hazing upon arriving at Canadian Forces Base Petawawa to join Airborne. Matchee, in turn, became one of Brown's "most feared hazers" when he arrived at Petawawa.[68] Alfred McCoy has argued that soldiers subjected to brutal hazing as cadets repeat that behavior later in their careers.[69] Thus as Matchee beat Arone he told fellow soldiers that "the white man fears the Indian and so will the black man," and when asked the next day about the murder, he boasted, "Indians: two, White man: nothing."[70]

Brown himself claims to have experienced his Airborne hazing as "a lot of fun." It was a ritual that did not involve the feces and vomit-filled celebration of 1 Commando but was rather a "Zulu Warrior" ritual in which new recruits tried to drink a bottle of beer before a strip of burning toilet paper stuck in the cheeks of the soldier's buttocks burned to the end. Brown commented that "no one was seriously hurt—a lot of soldier's bravado— but we all felt closer-knit and united after it."[71]

It is precisely that sense of unity that initiation or hazing rituals are intended to promote. As Alfred McCoy describes it, the hazing is often brutal and normally aims at "breaking down a cadet's civilian identity . . . creating what one study called a 'remarkable unity.'"[72] If Kyle Brown felt a greater comradeship with his compatriots after having his buttocks singed, so too—more surprisingly—did Corporal Christopher Robin. Robin was the only black soldier in the Airborne Regiment's 1 Commando Unit who was depicted in the hazing video being forced to walk around on all fours and to bark like a dog with "I love the KKK" written on his back. He was also shown on all fours while another soldier pretended to sodomize him and he was tied to a tree as fellow soldiers poured white powder on him. When Robin was asked at the inquiry whether the acts depicted in the video were racist, he said that they were. When asked if he had ever experienced racism in Airborne, he said that he had not; rather, these incidents showed "what you can take under adverse conditions." He said also that no matter what people now thought, he was very proud of the regiment of which he was a part and said further that "I would do everything I could to protect" its good name.[73]

Along with race, gender is a locus of organizing a soldier's sense of self, and some indication of the Canadian military's attitudes toward women was conveyed in one of the first documents tabled at the inquiry. The Hewson Report was a 1985 inquiry investigating whether there was a higher rate of criminal behavior within the Canadian Forces than within Canadian society more generally.[74] It was introduced at the inquiry because Major General Hewson reported that while there was no higher general incidence of crime within the forces, there were two exceptions to this observation: First, there did appear to be a higher frequency of sexual offenses within Canadian Forces than within the larger Canadian population; and second, there was a higher incidence of violent crime within the Canadian Airborne Regiment.[75] It was the latter observation that mattered most at the inquiry, but it was Hewson's explanations for both of these exceptions that unintentionally revealed some of the Canadian military's assumptions about women.

Hewson explained the higher incidence of violent crime within Airborne in straightforwardly gendered terms: local "girls," he said, tended to be attracted to the "young single soldier with his new 'sporty' car, regular and higher pay and job security." The local male population was described as "robust and tough," and there simply were not enough girls to go around; "disputes over girls," in other words, were almost unavoidable.[76] But not particularly worth investigating further. As it would be summarized later by David Bercuson, the earlier troubles in the Airborne resulted from the social climate in Petawawa: "There were too few ways for single soldiers to blow off steam; there was too much drinking; there were too few available women."[77] In this way, the strutting between males over "girls" was depicted as natural.

While the Hewson Report addressed directly, and in an openly gendered way, the question of crime within Airborne, it was more circumspect—but equally revealing—in its analysis of the higher incidence of sexual offenses within the Canadian Forces. Hewson never stated *how much* higher the level of sexual offenses were but indicated that an appendix outlining crime case synopses "does not, statistically, reveal any significant or alarming trends."[78] This was far from the case. Hewson's crime case synopsis, in fact, indicates that the incidence of sexual crimes was dramatic. If one includes within the category of sexual assaults all assaults in which the victim was a woman, more than half of the 141 crimes listed were either sexual assaults or physical assaults against women: seventy-six out of 141 cases, or 54 percent.[79] This is hardly a figure that could be described as insignificant. What the Hewson Report indicated to the Canadian military—but what was never followed up either after the report was issued or at the Somalia inquiry more than ten years later[80]—was something that feminists have long argued, namely, that the level of violence against women is disproportionately high within militaries, and this is true also of the Canadian military.[81]

That level of violence toward women is quite at odds with the self-representations of Canadian soldiers as warrior princes, providers of humani-

tarian services, and helpers to the women and children of Somalia. It was
but one of the ways that Somali men were designated as inferior, and yet
from Hewson's studies, the Canadian military's attitudes toward women
may have been little different than that of the denigrated Somali other.
Certainly the evidence of violence toward women within the Canadian
Forces suggests that this is true, as does the Hewson Report's cavalier attitude toward "disputes over girls." But even more dramatically, early questioning at the inquiry by the Canadian Jewish Congress alleged also that
members of Airborne held a celebratory dinner to honor Marc Lepine,[82] the
man who massacred fourteen women at the Université de Montréal in 1989,
shouting at them as he did so, "You're all a bunch of feminists!" Airborne
soldiers claimed they did not like the way Somali men treated their women
and insisted that this was a cultural difference between Somalis and
Canadian soldiers; yet at the same time participated in celebrations of a
man who had massacred fourteen women in Canada.

Conclusion

Canadians had never before seen their soldiers accused of atrocities against
civilians. They did not have any public experiences that corresponded to
Vietnam, to attacks like that at My Lai, or to the kind of cultural reflection
as was witnessed in the post-Vietnam United States, through novels, docu-
mentaries, and Hollywood movies. Why would they? Canada's imagined
community had long distinguished itself through different representations
of the military: Americans fought wars, Canadians made peace.[83] The
extent to which the notion of a soldier as benign, altruistic, and morally
superior is, quite simply, a contradiction had never before been confronted
in Canada. That this contradiction might also exist at the level of Canada as
a nation was unthinkable. As Razack writes: "Canadian naïveté and passivi-
ty as a nation constitute a narrative of innocence that blocks accountability
for the violence in Somalia, just as it blocks accountability for racist violence within Canada. A nation so gentle could not possibly have participated in the acts of violence reported by the press."[84]

An analysis of Canada's reputation as a country committed to the
ideals of peacekeeping, and the way in which many features of that reputation were seriously challenged by the murders of Somali citizens by
Canadian soldiers, leads us to question the constitution and effects of militarized masculinity. Militaries depend on attracting young people, but especially young men, to the idea of becoming real men through the initiation
rituals associated with soldiering. As Judith Stiehm has written: "all militaries have . . . regularly been rooted in the psychological coercion of
young men through appeals to their (uncertain) manliness."[85] What militaries do is replace that uncertainty with a certainty that is, at least in part,

constituted through norms of masculinity that privilege violence, racism, aggression, and hatred toward women. And its effects were dramatically depicted in Somalia. What this means for students of critical security studies is that a change of mission does not by itself transform the years of training and socialization that have gone into the creation of a soldier. What this suggests, quite dramatically, is that the skills of war are often quite at odds with those required for peace operations. Indeed, it is often the non-military contributions that Canadian peacekeepers make for which they are best remembered. In Somalia, these included reopening a local school and hospital. In other settings it has included building parks for children and serving as mediators in difficult situations. This means that we need to acknowledge that soldiers *don't* always make the best peacekeepers—sometimes it is carpenters, mediators, and doctors who best perform that function and who best contribute to a people's sense of a meaningful security. It means also that when we *do* send soldiers on peace operations, they need to be soldiers who have been trained and encouraged to understand that properly masculine behavior need not be dependent on misogyny, racism, or violence.[86] Keeping the peace positively demands it.

Notes

1. Manson, "Peacekeeping in a Changing World," in *Canadian Speeches* 2, no. 8, December 1988, pp. 35–41.

2. From the General Court Martial Transcripts of Private Brocklebank, 1994, vol. 3, entry 19, in Government of Canada, *Information Legacy.*

3. The author is grateful for financial support received from the Social Science and Humanities Research Council of Canada. This is drawn from a chapter in my book, *Men, Militarism, and UN Peacekeeping.*

4. Francis, *National Dreams*, p. 10.

5. Anderson, *Imagined Communities*, p. 6.

6. An important exception here was one study produced for the Commission of Inquiry into the Deployment of Canadian Forces to Somalia by Donna Winslow. Though she does not discuss problems of militarized masculinity, she does address the problems of sending soldiers trained for combat on peacekeeping missions. See Winslow, *The Canadian Airborne Regiment in Somalia.* I make the same argument in Whitworth, "The Ugly Unasked Questions About Somalia," *Globe and Mail*, 14 February 1997, p. A27.

7. Sens, *Somalia and the Changing Nature of Peacekeeping,* A Study Prepared for the Commission of Inquiry into the Deployment of Canadian Forces to Somalia, p. 22.

8. Coulon, *Soldiers of Diplomacy*, p. ix.

9. Heininger, *Peacekeeping in Transition*, p. 5; see also Coulon, *Soldiers of Diplomacy*, p. 26.

10. Rubinstein, "Cultural Aspects of Peacekeeping."

11. Wenek, *The Assessment of Psychological Fitness*, p. 13; cf. Commission of Inquiry into the Deployment of Canadian Forces to Somalia, *Document Book No. 1, Hewson Report*, p. 46.

12. As soon as one makes any claims about what militarized masculinity *is*, it is important to note that militarized masculinity, like all masculinities, is not one unitary set of qualities or characteristics that remain constant across time and place. See, for example, Morgan, "Theater of War," pp. 165–182.

13. See Sokolsky, "Great Ideals and Uneasy Compromises"; "U.S. Soldier Discharged for Refusing to Serve UN," *Ottawa Citizen*, January 25, 1996, p. A8.

14. Government of Canada, *Security in a Changing World*, p. 12. See also Government of Canada, *Security in a Changing World, 1994*, p. 12.

15. Government of Canada, *Canada's Foreign Policy*, p. 16.

16. Government of Canada, *Canada in the World, Government Statement*, p. 8.

17. Dion, "Canada Is Going to Make It After All!" cited from Cox and Sjolander, "Damage Control," in Pal (ed.), *How Ottawa Spends, 1998–1999*, pp. 217–242

18. Government of Canada, *Security in a Changing World, 1994*, p. 14.

19. See Whitworth, "Women, and Gender, in the Foreign Policy Review Process," in Cameron and Molot, *Canada Among Nations 1995*, pp. 83–98.

20. See, for example, Project Ploughshares, *Report to Donors*.

21. *Transformation Moment*, The Report of the Citizens' Inquiry into Peace and Security, p. 23.

22. Jockel, *Canada and International Peacekeeping*, p. 15.

23. Ibid., p. 1.

24. Cited from Cooper, *Canadian Foreign Policy*, p. 20.

25. Off, *The Lion, the Fox, and the Eagle*, p. 2.

26. A similar argument is made about Dutch national identity in Dudink, "The Unheroic Men of a Moral Nation," in Cockburn and Zarkov (eds.), *The Postwar Moment*, pp. 146–151.

27. This term is used to describe Canada's role in peacekeeping in Morrison and Plain, "Canada."

28. Some of this material is drawn from Whitworth, "Gender, Race and the Politics of Peacekeeping," in Moxon-Browne, (ed.), *A Future for Peacekeeping?* pp. 176–191.

29. Testimony of Major Barry Armstrong, Commission of Inquiry into the Deployment of Canadian Forces to Somalia, 12 March 1997.

30. Pugliese, "Somalia: What Went So Wrong?" *Ottawa Citizen*, October 1, 1995, p. A6.

31. I raise this in my "The Ugly Unasked Questions About Somalia." It is discussed also in Government of Canada, *Dishonoured Legacy*, ES-1 and passim and in Desbarats, *Somalia Cover-Up*, p. 3 and passim.

32. Jockel, *Canada and International Peacekeeping*, p. 33.

33. Dornan, "Scenes from a Scandal," *Globe and Mail, 21* January 1995, p. D1.

34. Bercuson, *Significan Incident*, p. vi and passim.

35. R. W. Connell has developed the notion of "hegemonic masculinity" by which he means the way in which some forms of masculinity, at different periods of time, become "culturally exalted." See his *Masculinities*, pp. 77–78.

36. Morgan, "Theater of War," p. 165.

37. Bercuson, *Significant Incident*, p. 29.

38. Charlotte Hooper notes the way in which soldiering also involves many traditional "feminine" traits such as "total obedience and submission to authority, the attention to dress detail, and the endless repetition of mundane tasks that enlisted men as opposed to officers are expected to perform." But these activities are not

emphasized in representations of soldiering, illustrating the way in which, for Hooper, "it is not the actions themselves but the gendered interpretations placed on them that are crucial in determining which activities count as masculine and valued and which count as feminine and devalued." Hooper, *Manly States*, pp. 47–48.

39. Ehrenreich, *Blood Rites*, p. 10. See also Ehrenreich, "Fukuyama's Follies," p. 118.

40. Ehrenreich, *Blood Rites*, pp. 11–12.

41. For an excellent summary of the goals and procedures of basic training, see Harrison and Laliberté, *No Life Like It*, chapter 1. See also Davis, *The Sharp End*, chapter 2; Goldstein, *War and Gender*, chapter 5; Arkin and Dobrofsky, "Military Socialization and Masculinity," pp. 151–168; McCoy, "'Same Banana,'" pp. 689–726; Gill, "Creating Citizens, Making Men," pp. 527–550.

42. Arkin and Dobrofsky, "Military Socialization and Masculinity," p. 158.

43. Gill, "Creating Citizens, Making Men," p. 534; Davis, *The Sharp End*, p. 14; Appy, *Working-Class War*, p. 101. Linda Bird Francke notes that the same techniques are sometimes also applied to women: at Fort Jackson in the United States, a 1991 strategy was to shout at female recruits: "You wuss, you baby, you goddamn female." Reverse psychology, by contrast, doesn't seen to work: a female instructor who yelled "You boy!" at a straggler discovered, in the context of basic training, that it sounded more like a compliment than an insult. Francke, *Ground Zero*, pp. 155–156.

44. Landay, "Hazing Rituals in Military Are Common—and Abusive." Donna Winslow notes that a 1908 U.S. Secretary of War Board of Inquiry into hazing at West Point Military Academy indicated that the practice of hazing—a continued period of abuse of an initial entry period into the military—had been going on since the 1860s. See Winslow, "Rites of Passage and Group Bonding in the Canadian Airborne."

45. Wenek, *The Assessment of Psychological Fitness*, p. 13; cf. Commission of Inquiry, *Document Book No. 1, Hewson Report*, p. 46.

46. *Document Book No. 1, Hewson Report*, p. 70.

47. Winslow, *The Canadian Airborne Regiment in Somalia*, p. 198.

48. Ibid., p. 231.

49. Ibid., p. 231.

50. Razack, "The Violence of Canadian Peacekeepers," p. 146.

51. Pugliese, "Military Brass Let Racist Skinheads Go to Somalia."

52. Commission of Inquiry into the Deployment of Canadian Forces to Somalia, *Document Book No. 8, Racism.*

53. The latter was intended to refer to the constant begging by Somalis—and Winslow reports that the Canadians also purchased a "commemorative T-shirt with an outstretched Somali hand and the word 'gimme' on it." Winslow, *The Canadian Airborne Regiment in Somalia*, p. 252. See also Government of Canada, *Information Legacy*, Hearing Transcripts, Tuesday, October 10, 1995, vol. 3, p. 584, vol. 4, p. 595; Monday, January 15, 1996, vol. 32, p. 6086.

54. Prouse, "The Dark Side That Emerged in Somalia Is Inside All Canadians," pp. A4–A6.

55. Ibid.

56. Winslow, *The Canadian Airborne Regiment in Somalia*, p. 235.

57. Worthington and Brown, *Scapegoat*, p. 123.

58. Winslow, *The Canadian Airborne Regiment in Somalia*, p. 249.

59. Ibid., pp. 233–234.

60. Ibid., p. 232.

61. Ibid.

62. Razack, "The Violence of Canadian Peacekeepers," p. 137.

63. Winslow, *The Canadian Airborne Regiment in Somalia*, pp. 236–238, and Razack, "The Violence of Canadian Peacekeepers," p. 138.

64. Winslow, *The Canadian Airborne Regiment in Somalia*, pp. 253, 256.

65. Ibid., p. 255.

66. Much of Winslow's analysis focuses on these.

67. See, for example, Worthington and Brown, *Scapegoat*, pp. 220–228.

68. Cheney, "Canada . . . Canada."

69. McCoy, "Ram Boys."

70. Testimony by Corporal B. J. MacDonald, Volume 3, and Testimony by Private D. J. Brockelbank, Volume 4, both in Government of Canada, *Information Legacy*. The final statement refers to the fact that it was a native soldier who shot and killed Arun Ahmesh in the March 4 incident.

71. Worthington and Brown, *Scapegoat*, p. 56.

72. McCoy, "Same Banana," p. 695.

73. Corporal Christopher Robin, Testimony to the Commission of Inquiry into the Deployment of Canadian Forces to Somalia, 12 October 1995, Ottawa, Canada.

74. Pugliese, "Almost 20% of '85 Airborne Unit Had Police Record, Report Found"; Wenek, *The Assessment of Psychological Fitness*, p. 13; cf. Commission of Inquiry, *Document Book No. 1, Hewson Report*, p. 15.

75. Commission of Inquiry, *Document Book No. 1, Hewson Report*, p. 17.

76. Ibid., p. 19.

77. Bercuson, *Significant Incident*, p. 209.

78. Commission of Inquiry, *Document Book No. 1, Hewson Report*, pp. 20–21.

79. Ibid., annex G.

80. Hewson recommended that the higher level of sexual offenses be studied further, though he did not seem to think that this recommendation merited inclusion within his "Main Summary of Recommendations."

81. Much, though not all, of this violence is directed at the women (and children) within military families. A 1994 U.S. study indicated that the rate of domestic violence within U.S. army families was twice that of comparable civilian families. See Harrison and Laliberté, *No Life Like It*, p. 189.

82. "Soldier Confirms Airborne Held Massacre Party"; "Army Commander Probes Report of Lepine Dinner."

83. Government of Canada, *Dishonoured Legacy*, Volume 1, p. 198, quoted from Razack, "The Violence of Canadian Peacekeepers in Somalia," p. 156, fn 5.

84. Razack, "The Violence of Canadian Peacekeepers in Somalia," p. 135.

85. Stiehm, *Arms and the Enlisted Woman*, p. 226.

86. I have borrowed this formulation from Enloe, *Maneuvers*, 2000, p. xiii.

Part 2

COMMUNITY

PART 2 FOCUSES ON A concept that is even more contentious than security: "community" is surely one of the most problematized ideas in the study of politics and society. Nevertheless, "Where do *we* end and *they* start?" remains a fundamental question for all students of security, and community remains an indispensable way of expressing what it means to be a politically-relevant *we*.

Despite familiar warnings from sociologists and others about the problems of defining community,[1] there remains no better idea for thinking about organizing societies in the human interest. And for a species that is programmed for "sociality,"[2] security—like other important values—can only be furthered within complex relationships (such as community). Rather than rejecting the notion of community because of its difficulties and ambiguities, we should recognize that in working through its potentialities and problems we are in fact helping to constitute a different type of world politics. The task is therefore more than merely semantic; it is part of constructing a more progressive politics. The latter includes the development of ideas of political community with the potential to further multidimensional and inclusive emancipatory politics.

With such considerations in mind, I define an emancipatory community (the only sort Frankfurt School critical theory wants to embrace) as follows: *A community is a free association of individuals, recognizing their solidarity in relation to common conceptions of what it is to live an ethical life; it binds people together, providing a distinctive network of identity and ideas, support and society. Communities in general are social organizations whose separateness expresses human variety, but an emancipatory community will recognize that people have multiple identities, that a person's identity cannot be defined by one attribution, and that people must be allowed to live simultaneously in a variety of communities. Emancipatory communities, in recognizing the right of individuals to express themselves through multiple identifiers of difference, will, above all, celebrate human equality.*

Ethical universalism or cosmopolitanism is the idea that people should be treated as equals and that moral differences should not rest on contingent factors such as nationality, gender, race, and so on. From this viewpoint, a continuing and expanding development of networks of emancipatory communities, horizontally and vertically, is the desirable growth pattern for global governance. Out of the imagining of common humanity might come the construction of an actually existing global political community of communities.[3] Such an outcome has the potential to meet human needs for

109

identity while tying down and civilizing the divisive and power-seeking dynamics of both the sovereign states system and globalization.

In opening Part 2, Andrew Linklater (Chapter 5) suggests that the plight of refugees—a tragically familiar feature of world politics these days—shows in a direct way that security is inextricably linked with membership in a political community. It is in a settled political community, he argues, where members respect one another and have some say in shaping a valued form of life, including one in which we can look for the promotion of human security. He believes that this relationship between security and community needs to be set against a long history dominated by realist attitudes and practices in which security was conceived in terms of strategic action to advance the interests of the state. Linklater's thesis, in contrast, derives from the Kantian proposition that everything hinges on how political community is constructed. Whereas realists have favored the politics of outwitting, containing, and overpowering adversaries, Linklater favors approaches deriving from the ideas of one of the leading figures in the Frankfurt School, Jürgen Habermas. Politics here becomes a search for agreement and understanding—communicative action—and beyond that communicative or discourse ethics.

Whereas realists might dismiss such approaches as relevant only to narrow concerns, or as being utopian, Linklater argues that the prospects for reforming world politics and its constituent sovereign parts are greater than realists would allow. This does not mean that communicative action and ethics will banish strategic action entirely—only that it might be progressively marginalized to play a lesser role. He is careful to point out that critical theory does not assume that the condition of permanent peace is ever likely to be achieved, while any progress in that direction will require the support of states, especially the great powers. More generally, progress toward the ideal of a security community requires the emergence of more dialogic forms of life; it is the latter that is the key to the Kantian ideal of a cosmopolitan condition of general political security.

Political communities seeking to promote emancipation, justice, and fairness require a political economy that allows their members to engage in appropriate communicative action. In this and other ways, security, community, and economics are inseparable. None of us in the comfortable parts of the world, for example, should ever forget that poverty is a bigger daily killer than war, and any approach that purports to study security in global perspective must reflect this in its central concerns. While never neglecting the military dimension of security, students of CSS must seek above all to try to overcome the traditional prioritizing of the victims of politics (wars/tyranny) over the victims of economics (poverty/oppression). As a result, they must engage more fully in their work with those economic theories and practices that contribute to creating and replicating conditions of insecurity.

Roger Tooze (Chapter 6) undertakes such an engagement, with a central theme being the parallels between orthodox economics and orthodox security studies. Both, he argues, are in need of critical thinking because of the way they take the politics out of what they seek to analyze. Both project an image of neutrality and technicality when they are themselves politicized; what is more, this politicization serves interests that are not friendly to human security generally. This means that movement toward real security, community, and emancipation will be intimately bound up with our ability to retheorize international political economy (IPE); such a critical IPE will not be dependent upon concepts defined and constrained by what Tooze believes has been the hegemony of economism and a mute acceptance of the separation of economics and politics. Orthodox IPE does not help, for it puts up barriers against alternative conceptions of politics and power. Central to Tooze's view is the claim that most of the practitioners of orthodox IPE have accepted a predefined notion of what constitutes economics; this hegemony of legitimate knowledge is absolutely politically defined, he argues, though it is not understood to be. It imports a particular theorization of economics, one that is analyzed as a purely rational activity and to whose problems technical solutions are possible. As Tooze puts it, the claim that economics is nonpolitical is itself a political claim. Orthodox IPE, therefore, acts as an authoritative allocator of value that is neither neutral, natural, nor outside the realm of power. His chapter ends with a discussion of the need for a differently constructed notion of economics. This, for Tooze, is the core problem facing the development of a critical IPE alongside a critical security studies. Without such a development, he does not foresee the construction of the sort of community that will deliver human security and emancipation.

All questions of community are questions of identity. The boundaries of duties, the nationality printed on one's passport, the collection of taxes, the definition of citizenship, and the group for whom one might ultimately be willing to die (or to kill)—these and many other issues are all at some level questions of identity. Identity is everywhere and is everywhere political, and so it can become one of those explanations—like power or human nature—that ostensibly answer all questions and therefore none. What is interesting and important are the concrete issues relating to the who, how, and why of identity. *Who* gets to ascribe identity? *How* do identities relate to interests? And *why* have certain identities come to be important? It would have been possible to have chosen any among many empirical cases to illustrate the work done by identity in the domestic and foreign policies of states. The specific illustration chosen is an analysis of Australia and

Asia by Jan Jindy Pettman (Chapter 7). While avoiding the overt violence that characterizes the identity politics of some situations (such as Northern Ireland; see Chapter 10), the relationship between Australia and Asia illustrates some of the roles identity can play in a complex regional setting. The designation of the politically relevant *we* in this context has been a prize struggled over by states and nations, ethnic groups, and cultural traditions, the forces of history, and the dynamics of contemporary world politics.

Pettman's chapter develops three main themes in relation to her exploration of the development of Australian national identity in the context of its European history and Asian geography. First, there is the claim that mainstream security studies and state practice are shaped by ideas of elite security and privilege and that it is the task of critical approaches to challenge the orthodoxies that ensue. Second, it is argued that community and other referents are neither inevitable nor fixed but are sites of political contestation and the outcomes of power struggles. And third, realist-speak is said to have silenced—while deploying—racialized and other understandings of identity. Pettman argues that immigration into Australia has become reracialized and foreign policy remilitarized, not least in the context of the U.S.-led war on terror. Readers will immediately recognize parallels between this situation and others across the world.

Part 2 begins with Linklater emphasizing the relationship between security and political community; it ends with Pettman emphasizing the complexities of developing political community when state practices are dominated by ideas of elite security and privilege, with the interests of the rest being marginalized. It is in this familiar top-down world that the need for emancipatory politics for those whose lives are determined by elite oppression are all the greater. This theme links directly with the concerns of Part 3, on emancipation.

Notes

1. The standard reference is Williams, *Keywords.*

2. See Carrithers, *Why Humans Have Cultures*, pp. 12–13.

3. Andrew Linklater has done the most relevant work on political community in international relations. See in particular, his *Transformation of Political Community.*

5

Political Community and Human Security

Andrew Linklater

Refugees repeatedly express the wish to make a new life for themselves in another state that is free from the devastation and violence from which they have fled, and admission into another society is often the simplest solution to their immediate problem of insecurity. In this way, they can avoid the acts of violence that may have existed in their original societies, and they can escape the squalor and agonies of the refugee camps. The right to reside in another place can meet their most urgent needs, but it may not end all their insecurities. Racial threats, acts of violence and discrimination, and poor opportunities for advancement are some of the hardships that refugees often encounter in their new land. Entry into another society can bring an end to direct and immediate threats to their security, but the mere right of residence may simply mean that one form of tyranny is exchanged for another. Refugees need more than the right to inhabit another society without fear of eviction: they have to be granted all the legal, political, and social rights that citizens enjoy. Without these endowments, they cannot be at home in their new society.[1]

The plight of refugees is a simple reminder that security is inextricably linked with membership of a political community in which all members respect one another and in which all of them have some say in shaping a form of life that they regard as their own. Some may wish to go further by suggesting that the predicament of the refugee is a fine illustration of the timeless wisdom of political realism. From this vantage point, the viable state remains the chief guarantor of security. What is more, the stateless person usually wants to belong to a secure state more than anything else, since this is the prerequisite for living a decent life, and peoples without states invariably strive to establish their own sovereign communities rather than celebrate their avant-garde status as harbingers and heralds of the forthcoming neomedieval or post-Westphalian international order. For realists, there is a short step from acknowledging these truths to recognizing that states, which are the main containers and providers of security, are surrounded by other states and, increasingly, by the architects of transnational crime and private violence that threaten their citizens. If they are to survive in this contest, states must monitor the strength of neighboring or threatening powers and make sure that the requisite counterweights are in place as quickly as possible. They must prepare for war, realizing that a neighbor's capacity to destroy or inflict damage may soon be succeeded by the intention to cause violent harm, and they must take part in an ongoing war against drugs, terrorism, and crime. To secure the community in the face of internal and external challenges and threats, the state must have long-term investments in the politics of strategic action: in outwitting or outmaneuvering, in weakening or eliminating, actual or potential adversaries.[2]

Deep controversies now surround the contention that the merits of political realism can be illustrated by recalling the plight and predicament of the world's refugees. Proponents of critical security studies have challenged the realist's belief that the state is the main container of security and that strategic action is the rational response to the security dilemma.[3] They have provided radically new answers to the question of whose security is being advanced (but also endangered) by strategic action. They have identified other subjects or referents of security, and they have explored means of providing security that break with the pessimism of political realism, including the contention that anarchy in itself compels states to participate in geopolitical competition and prepare for war.[4]

In the course of making these claims, the critics stress the ambiguities of the state since it is often a source of, as well as a threat to, human security.[5] The brief discussion of refugees above suggests they are right to do so. The critics recognize the connection between security and community while casting doubt on the contention that even viable sovereign states are adequate forms of political community; they also treat the proposition that security is best provided by strategic orientations toward outsiders with deep suspicion. From this vantage point, there is no doubt that security is inextricably linked with community and emancipation.[6] From the perspective of the realist critics, however, these developments should be resisted. Critical security theorists stretch the notion of security too far; they confuse it with concepts, such as emancipation, with which it has no obvious or even helpful links; and they operate at a level of generality that empties the discussion of security of useful policy relevance.[7]

The following sections explore the relationship between security and community and consider the extent to which the concept of emancipation either hinders or advances efforts to develop a critical security agenda. Some comments on the intricate connections between human security and political community begin the discussion, and particular attention is paid to the respects in which improved forms of political community are required to overcome the moral deficits of modern sovereign states. Quite how far such an approach is too remote from the concerns of policymakers to make any sensible contribution to security studies is an issue that cannot be escaped, as was emphasized in an academic controversy in Britain in the 1990s.[8] The response to this question is that political realism, which was long thought to have a special relationship with, and sympathy for, the problems facing policymakers, has tended to prioritize strategic over communicative action in world affairs. This formulation acknowledges that realism has not entirely neglected the importance of communicative action, although it has been inclined to maintain that its labors are confined to a narrow domain and are always in danger of being consumed by the sphere of strategic interaction. Whether this is correct is one issue that has been central to critical approaches.

Almost all critical approaches argue that the prospects for reforming world politics and its constituent sovereign parts are much greater than realists allow. This is not to envisage a future world order in which communicative action banishes strategic action entirely. Doubtless the two realms will continue to coexist in a state of tension, and progress toward a world in which strategic action plays a lesser role in world politics will continue to come up against the unyielding barriers of distrust between many communities. The point, however, is not to regard a world order that revolves around strategic action as somehow embodying permanent truths about international politics or the human condition, but rather to regard such a world as the defacement and disfigurement of the human potential to enlarge the social realm that can be governed by dialogue and trust.[9] When characterizing the current debate between critical security analysts and their opponents, it is useful to recall Immanuel Kant's efforts to preserve the strengths of realism in his ethical vision of a universal kingdom of ends and in his related comments about how this ideal can influence the world of policy and practice. Kant's belief that orientations toward communicative action are the prerequisites for radical global reform is central to debates surrounding critical theories of world politics in general and the more specific domain of security studies.

Security and Community

The need to consider security and community together is a central theme in Niccolò Machiavelli's writings in which at least one definition of security smacks of patriarchy and possessive individualism: a man would only feel secure, Machiavelli argued, when he could regard his possessions without anxiety, live without fear for the honor of his wives and children, and conduct his everyday business without being afraid for himself.[10] A simpler and more straightforward approach would be to regard security as involving the "absence of threats."[11] But however one chooses to define security, there can be no doubt that it has to be underpinned by the appropriate form of political community. Hermits can be secure only in communities that are happy to leave them alone. Moving from the meaning of security to how it might be realized, Machiavelli argued that human beings could be secure in monarchical regimes, but they would be more secure under democratic governments in which they are involved in decisions about their collective life. This stress on dialogue and deliberation identifies the crucial link between political community and human security.

Though not entirely absent from political realism, the elements of dialogue and deliberation have usually been subordinate to the dictates of strategic action for exponents of this perspective. As noted earlier, and as stated in considerable detail elsewhere, realism assumes that the state is the safe haven that protects citizens from the intrusions of anarchy and disorder.[12] Cold War realists presumed that some states were more secure than others and that Western democracy was clearly superior to Soviet totalitarianism, but what has usually been emphasized in interpretations of realism is its more general claim that states provide security for their citizens and render each other insecure in the process by unstintingly preparing for war. Whether this assessment is entirely fair to realism, others must decide.[13] Perhaps it applies more readily to neorealism, although it is immediately important to add that structural realists are well aware that sovereign states are simultaneously a pillar of, and danger to, human security. In an important passage, Barry Buzan notes that "the security of individuals is locked into an unbreakable paradox in which it is partly dependent on, and partly threatened by the state" and continues: "Individuals can be threatened by their own state in a variety of ways, and they can also be threatened through their state as a result of its interactions with other states in the international system."[14] Working through the implications of these remarks has been a central preoccupation of critical security studies.[15]

Leaving aside important respects in which states provide security, one might consider three respects in which states are a source of insecurity.[16] First, they are a source of insecurity where migrants, gypsies, minority nations, and indigenous peoples, among others, do not enjoy the protection of the rule of the law or are barred from enjoying the political and other rights that full members of the community already enjoy. Second, they are a source of insecurity for their own citizens where they have recourse to reckless or aggressive foreign policy behavior, where they miscalculate in their dealings with other states or cause them to miscalculate in ways that lead the parties into war. Third, as this last point indicates, and as realists have long argued, states are also a source of insecurity to one another, often accidentally rather than intentionally as they cope with security dilemmas.

Conventional strategic studies focused on the second and third of these phenomena, regarding the first as the business of political science rather than international relations and assuming that states will have to deal with international threats and dangers long after they have removed any threats they may pose to their own citizens. (Critics of conventional approaches dispute the value of this division of labor, and rightly for reasons to be considered later.) Traditional studies of national security have been concerned with the respects in which reckless foreign policy can endanger the state and its citizens, and they developed studies of crisis management in this context.[17] But above all else, realists are associated with the belief that the security dilemma is inescapable in the context of anarchy, that states are condemned to engage in balance-of-power politics, and that the tragic consequence of their defensive efforts to provide for their security is a general condition of insecurity that is the breeding ground for war.

Realist approaches to national security have a special interest in how states can mitigate the worst effects of international anarchy. Exercises in self-help that include efforts to outmaneuver, contain, or eradicate adversaries are available to states, as are more cooperative ventures to preserve the balance of military power or to accommodate conflicting interests. Strategic action is often taken to be the essence of realist praxis, although a more balanced interpretation highlights its stress "on the need for military preparedness supplemented by negotiation."[18] Illustrations of this latter theme abound, ranging from Hans Morgenthau's emphasis on the necessity for diplomatic efforts to accommodate equally legitimate strategic interests to Henry Kissinger's stress on the need for adversaries to negotiate mutually acceptable levels of security and insecurity.[19] Realism possesses its own hermeneutic commitment exemplified by its hostility to ideological approaches to foreign policy that demonize the other instead of appreciating that states would probably behave in much the same way as their adversaries if strategic positions were reversed.[20] Classical realists stress the importance of empathy as well as control and emphasize the value of communicative as well as strategic action even in relations between adversaries.

Realists are nevertheless deeply suspicious of optimistic claims that cooperation can extend very far, or last particularly long, in the context of anarchy. Neorealists such as Kenneth Waltz go farther by arguing that strategic action is the norm in world politics, and communicative action is the precarious exception to this more persistent trend. In consequence, high levels of cooperation in Western Europe were thought to depend ultimately on strategic equilibrium between the superpowers.[21] The collapse of bipolarity did not release potentials for greater communicative action from the constraints of superpower rivalry but unleashed new and more violent forms of strategic action spearheaded by aggressively nationalistic movements in various parts of the former socialist bloc. The logic of anarchy was not halted by efforts to widen the European security community or to lay the foundations for a bold new experiment in transnational democracy. Strategic orientations reasserted themselves as societal security dilemmas replaced the more familiar dilemmas that bedevil nation-states.[22]

Critical analysts and their realist or neorealist opponents disagree about how far security communities can develop or endure in world politics. Realists do not rule out the possibility that robust security communities can develop. Morgenthau clearly thought that the main challenge in world politics was to develop such arrangements, as did E. H. Carr, whose relationship with political realism is undoubtedly complex.[23] Waltz concedes that there is something to be said for the concept of the liberal zone of peace, although he is quick to add that the more significant point to remember in the unipolar era is that unbridled or unchecked power brings its own dangers.[24] Security communities will in any event last only as long as they enjoy the support of the dominant powers, and they can always be destroyed by hostile forces.

For their part, critical theorists do not underestimate the obstacles to global political reform; nor do they subscribe to any notion of inevitable and irreversible progress. They argue there is nothing in international anarchy that makes competition and conflict permanent features of world politics. The qualities of anarchy, especially as neorealism characterizes that condition, are at heart the attributes of the dominant powers. This is why critical theory can start with the Kantian proposition that everything hinges on how political community is constructed, particularly in the most powerful regions. From this vantage point, it is a profound mistake to ignore the respects in which states threaten their own citizens so that the study of international relations is free to develop its specific focus on the ways in which states interact with and threaten each other. The important point is that societies that are quick to resort to strategic action in their internal relations are improbable advocates of communicative action in world politics, unless foreign policy pragmatism suggests that commitments to dialogue will produce national advantages; conversely, societies that have standing commitments to communicative action domestically already have the potential to bring similar orientations to bear on relations with outsiders. Consequently, critical theory does not begin with how independent political communities conduct their external relations but with the deeper question of how they are constituted in the first place.

Transforming Political Community

Conventional security studies is concerned with how states interact with one another, not with the ways in which they treat their national citizens. The billiard-ball model started with the assumption that the inside of the state is of little import unless, of course, despotic rule creates hardships for other states (e.g., by forcing them to bear the burden of coping with the rapid influx of significant numbers of refugees). In such cases, however, the domestic realm is captured only in the lens of conventional security studies because of its consequences for international order and stability. The rejection of reductionist, inside-out analysis—which is central to neo-realism—is part of a larger challenge to liberal and socialist accounts of the possibility of internally generated processes of global change. The most important statement of the competing position is to be found in the writings of Kant and in restatements of liberal political theory that argue that the transformation of political communities is the key to developing lasting international security arrangements.

Kant has been portrayed as a second-image analyst of war whose belief that popular checks on executive power would bring an end to war neglected the desperate logic of international anarchy.[25] His position was more complex. Kant did have enormous faith in the pacifying tendencies of republican regimes in which executive and legislative power were clearly separated, but this idea was linked with the belief that their progressive role was anchored in a commitment to the politics of publicity and consent and in their moral belief that all human beings, and not only fellow-citizens, deserve recognition as ends in and of themselves. Michael Doyle's claim that liberal states are ill disposed to coerce other liberal states that are equally committed to organizing their societies consensually captures part of the central point. The deeper truth is that such societies must be uneasy about using coercive power at all whether they deal with liberal or illiberal states.[26] They can never comfortably purchase their own security by imposing insecurity and heteronomy on others, and they cannot happily punish unrepresented peoples for the sins and misdemeanors of despotic regimes.[27] Put differently, good liberals must be deeply uncomfortable with an international system in which strategic action thwarts the possibility of generalized commitments to communicative action.

Inside-out analysis works in liberal international political theory by arguing that the way in which states treat national citizens is not simply a domestic matter that can be ignored in accounts of external affairs. If strategic action prevails in domestic politics, then the commitment to communicative action is unlikely to shape that state's foreign policy, other than—as noted earlier—for pragmatic and self-interested reasons. But if communicative action is central to the domestic political order, then the prospects for transcending purely strategic concerns in foreign policy will be significantly enlarged.[28] These are the considerations that underpin Kantian and more contemporary liberal analyses of the relationship between the transformation of political community and the advancement of human security.

The liberal approach to security and community therefore generates an emancipatory politics that is designed to enlarge the realm of human inter- action that is governed by publicity, dialogue, and consent, but whether its concept of emancipation goes far enough is the crucial question. Socialists in the nineteenth century regarded classical liberalism as flawed because it privileged negative liberty and property rights over the values of communi- ty, solidarity, and equality. Defenders of the rights of minority nations and indigenous peoples have suggested that the liberal-individualistic claim that all citizens should have exactly the same rights ignores the need for group-specific rights that ensure due respect for cultural differences within society.[29] Feminists have also protested against the ways in which the seemingly benign liberal account of the equal rights of all citizens allows patriarchy to go untouched.[30] For such reasons, critical theorists have argued that the emancipatory project must transcend liberal horizons.

The issue of how far liberalism has been, and can be, modified to meet these criticisms is too complex a task to undertake here. Suffice it to note that the vision of social arrangements that are governed by publicity, dia- logue, and consent requires an emancipatory politics with the following three ambitions: first, the development of social arrangements that do not rest on morally irrelevant or problematical differences between individuals (including differences of ethnicity, class, religion, gender, and race and the distinction between citizens and aliens)[31]; second, the transformation of societies so that they are more respectful of the cultural differences between human beings; and third, the reduction of material inequalities that mean the underprivileged are barred from effective participation in public affairs notwithstanding the juridical truth that they possess the same legal and political rights and entitlements as the more privileged members of society. These are the ingredients of an emancipatory politics that is geared toward developing forms of political community that promote not only national but also human security. The task is twofold: to promote political frameworks in which communicative action will be free to develop; and to secure the material and other conditions that will ensure that larger num- bers of the human race (and particularly the weakest and most vulnerable members) can determine their fate within dialogic arrangements.

Earlier, it was suggested that dialogue and deliberation form the link between community and security: the previous discussion indicates how the idea of emancipation strenghens this link, but considerable unease sur- rounds the concept of emancipation within critical approaches to interna- tional relations, as well as within the wider branches of social theory from which they so freely draw. In some quarters, emancipation immediately conjures up images of revolutionary political movements that are all too willing to force others to be free. In his comments, Jürgen Habermas expresses a preference for using the concept of understanding rather than emancipation, as well as for using the latter term to refer to changes within the self rather than the broad movement of society and history.[32] An alternative approach, which is endorsed here, is Karl-Otto Apel's claim that emancipation refers to advances in "nonrepressive deliberation."[33] This formulation has the double merit of staying clear of untenable historical metanarratives while supporting moves toward domination-free communication that run through much contemporary critical theory.[34] Whether this way of conceptualizing emancipation meets all the objections to notions of emancipation raised within critical debates will long be disputed; but what is clear is that some realists think that the flirtation with notions of critique and emancipation has had a corrupting influence on security studies.

Two themes stand out in realist responses to the critical turn in security studies and to the wider domain of critical international theory. The first is that efforts to link security with emancipation are dangerously naive because they invite every ethnic group in the third world to exercise the right of self-determination with potentially destructive consequences for domestic stability.[35] However relevant it may be to Western Europe, the linkage between security and emancipation courts disaster when applied to the majority of third world states, where civil order is often precarious.[36] The second contention—which features in an attempt to set out the ethical dimensions of classical realism—is that notions of critique and emancipation are notoriously vague and devoid of any direct relevance to substantial issues of international affairs.[37] This objection runs parallel to the objection that much critical theory, and especially postmodernism, prefers theoretical obscurantism and self-indulgence to the more urgent political task of tackling critical issues of policy and practice that burden decisionmakers.[38]

Regarding the first of these criticisms, emancipation understood as the progress of nonrepressive deliberation does not invite every ethnic group to exercise the right of national self-determination without any regard for the other members of society. Support for emancipation does not give groups or individuals the green light to defend their interests or express their identities in ways that may prove harmful to their neighbors; it urges these groups or individuals to remake, but not to shed their identities, in the light of the dialogic imperative, and to engage those who stand to be harmed by their actions as moral equals in open dialogue.[39] This is why dialogue and emancipation are essential to any improved account of human security: they take issue with essentialist accounts of political community that suppose that identities and interests provide their own justification and are free from the obligation of answerability to those who are adversely affected by the actions that follow from them.[40] These sentiments are common to the different tendencies within current critical theory, and, as previously noted, they form part of the ethical content of classical political realism.

Regarding the second criticism, which is that critical perspectives invariably lack serious policy relevance, it is useful to begin by noting that many of the ethical concerns of classical realism are reaffirmed and taken further in contemporary critical theory. George F. Kennan's argument is that the state should "concede the same legitimacy to the security needs of others that it claims for its own"[41] and urges empathetic orientations toward others that critical-theoretical accounts of dialogue are equally at pains to defend. Parallels exist between the realist case for "avoiding . . . the alienation of others by the arbitrary imposition of one's own particular values,"[42] and one central claim of the discourse theory of morality, which is that subjects must resort to dialogue since none can claim any special access to ethical and political truths.[43] There are parallels between the claim that realism has a special interest in promoting "mutual understandings," particularly in the context of "divergent value systems,"[44] and a range of critical approaches that take respect for the difference of the other as their ethical starting point.[45] There are similarities, too, between the realist argument that consent should govern the affairs of states wherever practicable and the normative aspirations of critical theory—although, at least since Michel Foucault, critical theorists have been keen to stress that consensual arrangements may well rest on, and be intertwined with, subtle exclusionary practices and intricate matrices of power.[46]

If these parallels do exist, then it is mysterious to learn that realism has a special relationship with the world of everyday practice while critical theory remains disturbingly aloof and disengaged from the challenges of current politics. The mystery deepens when it is suggested, from within a subaltern realist perspective, that security studies should move beyond the classical focus upon relations between states to deal with the domestic insecurities of multiethnic third world states.[47] All the moral considerations that classical realism commends to adversaries (empathy, efforts to reach an understanding, and to proceed by mutual consent) are as relevant to efforts to improve the relations between mutually suspicious ethnic or national groups involved in a bitter struggle to control the state's monopoly powers as they are to attempts to reduce tensions between states. The resources of communicative as opposed to strategic action are at least as relevant to the world of societal security and insecurity as they are to relations between viable nation-states.[48] If classical realism is especially attuned to the substantial issues of world politics, then critical theorists have every right to claim at least the same status. Empathy, understanding, dialogue, and consent are—and to an even greater extent than is the case with realism—the basic tools of their trade.

It has been suggested that critical security studies fails to recognize that the security of the state is key to order and stability in the multiethnic societies of the third world.[49] On this analysis, many of those societies are still in the early stages of state formation, when the territorial concentration

of state power is urgently needed to prevent civil unrest and societal breakdown. Eroding the state's monopoly powers by devolving some responsibilities to substate authorities while others are conferred upon transnational
organizations may be appropriate in the more secure and prosperous
regions of Western Europe, but such practices inevitably court disaster
where state-building is in its infancy. Critical security studies therefore
stands accused of ethnocentrism and irrelevance to the plight of many
states in the third world.[50]

It is important to examine this belief that realism has a special relationship with the substantial issues of world politics, as well as to show that
critical approaches have a greater claim to be relevant to the immediate
questions of security. Statism, as defended in subaltern realism, masquer-
ades as a strategy that can provide security for all, but the reality is that the
monopolization and concentration of state power often comprise the principal threats to various subaltern groups including ethnic minorities. Their
security is more likely to be enhanced by devolving power to democratically elected representatives and by ensuring that existing political elites are
answerable to global agencies with responsibility for the international protection of human rights than by preserving and consolidating territorial
concentrations of power. Suggesting instead that third world societies
should seek to replicate the state-building project that characterized
European history for three and a half centuries is the more obvious case of
ethnocentrism. Subaltern realism highlights the plight of the weaker states
of the third world but has had remarkably little to say about subaltern people and territories such as Tibet, or East Timor prior to its detachment from
Indonesia.[51] For those who live in those regions, the problem of security is
intimately connected with the project of transforming political community
so that territorial concentrations of power are checked by the devolution of
political responsibilities and the international protection of human rights.[52]
Efforts to build confederal political arrangements rather than to persevere
with unitary sovereign states may be the most effective ways of attempting
to solve, or at least dampen, ethnic rivalries.[53] Critical theory, which contests the modern fusion of sovereignty, territoriality, citizenship, and
nationalism with all its destructive consequences, need not defer to subaltern realism in the sphere of policy relevance.[54]

A Kantian Approach to Human Security

Critical theory links the discussion of security with the wider analysis of
community and emancipation in the belief that advances in communicative
action can often play a vital role in solving or reducing human conflicts. To
some extent, the supposition that critical theory has an overriding interest
in identifying the sources of structural change, in providing normative

visions of alternative world orders, and in offering ways of assessing the merits of current forms of political practice has obscured its problem-solving dimension.[55] This has encouraged the skeptics in their belief that critical theory may be strong on vision but has nothing profound to say about the strategies of transition that would lead to a new world order or about the stubborn issues of world affairs that confront policymakers.[56]

There is no political theory, realism included, that offers an instruction manual for dealing with the most intractable forms of ethnic or ethnoreligious communal conflict. There are no conflict resolution kits that explain how intersocietal estrangement can be replaced by confidence and trust, or that show how deeply ingrained habits of resorting to strategic action can be cured by advances in communicative action and discourse ethics.[57] Revising political structures and constitutional arrangements may ease social tensions even in the most intractable cases, but lasting solutions invariably require profound cultural changes and parallel modifications in individual psychologies that can only take place over many generations.[58] Efforts to solve ethnic conflict are a permanent reminder of the truth of Max Weber's observation that politics is the slow boring of hard boards. Progress from essentially strategic to communicative responses to such conflict is the normative goal of critical theory, which also finds muted expression in classical political realism. However, what may be described as the Kantian project in international relations surpasses realism by combining problem-solving and critical concerns in an analysis that begins with the prospects for radical breakthroughs in communicative action across world society as a whole. Notions of empathy and understanding exist in realism, but they often illustrate a limited problem-solving orientation that leaves the basic structure of world politics untouched.

Analyses of Kant's writings stress his vision of a future world order in which the citizens of sovereign states regard themselves as colegislators within a universal kingdom of ends, and they note how this vision informed his critique of the barbaric freedom of the modern territorial state. Kant was much more than a normative theorist, however. He recognized that violence would long remain an essential feature of world politics and that force might never be eradicated entirely from the world of states. His writings recognized that there was a role for strategic action while this condition prevailed, and they did not rule out violence where adversaries preferred coercion to communication. But at the heart of Kant's project is the fundamental question of how the realm of strategic action can be pushed back gradually over time by stronger commitments to communicative action.

His answer blended realism with more utopian concerns.[59] Kant advocated several transitional strategies that were divided into two main groups: those that were immediately binding on political subjects (such as ensuring the ethical conduct of war), and those that could only be realized gradually, conceivably over centuries, as estrangement and suspicion yielded to mutual respect and trust (such as abolishing standing armies). Kant's inventory is obviously dated, but his act of dividing strategies of transition into two main groups has more contemporary illustrations. Approaches that distinguish between immediately binding duties to promote confidence-building measures and the longer-term goal of negotiated demilitarization rest on the same dichotomy.[60] The key point behind this distinction is that common interests may permit limited experiments in transparency and reciprocity from which more radical commitments to publicity, dialogue, and consent may develop in time.[61] Problem-solving responses to conditions of insecurity should be informed then by the longer-term ethical aspirations of critical theory; these are also the means by which the more demanding normative aspirations of critical theory can be embedded in political institutions and practice.

The Kantian project transcended the stark opposition between problem-solving and critical theories by withholding support from short-term measures that hindered or failed to encourage respect for a universal kingdom of ends.[62] Responses to immediate security problems and longer-term ethical goals were locked in a dialectical relationship. The approach was far from silent on specific courses of action, but it avoided an essentially instrumental approach to political life that assumes that human affairs can be guided by some instruction manual or recipe book.[63] Like realism, Kantian critical theory was at odds with rationalism in politics in the Oakeshottian sense of applying abstract moral and political principles without regard for the nuances of social contexts. It was less concerned with recommending specific courses of action than with highlighting the cognitive changes that they should bring about. As noted, it agreed with the classical realists that deep and lasting solutions to conflict required greater empathy and understanding, but it parted company with realism by assuming that the opportunities for enlarging the sphere that is governed by consent as well as empathy and understanding are far greater than most realists have supposed.[64] The belief that realism is gripped by an unwarranted pessimism has meant that critical theory in the Kantian mode has been especially interested in the much-neglected areas of culture, communication, and possible extensions of the moral boundaries of existing forms of life.

Uppermost in Kant's normative international theory was the possibility of transforming the conceptual framework that human beings apply to conflicts of interest and identity. Kant stressed the importance of developing conceptual systems that gave expression to the human capacity for living in accordance with moral universals. Critical theory in the Kantian mode insists that these universals do not require the dissemination of any specific form of life or particular conception of the good. Nor do they require that separate individuals scrutinize their actions to ascertain whether or not the maxims that underlie them can be universalized in principle. What is required is a willingness to engage those who may be harmed by one's actions in an open dialogue in which all human differences are treated with respect and in which no prior assumptions are made about where the dialogue will lead or about how, ideally, it should end.[65] This is what separates communicative action that is concerned with reaching mutual understanding from communicative or discourse ethics concerned that agreements are as free from all known forms of power and coercion as is possible. Actors who acquire these psychological qualities enter what Habermas calls the "domain of postconventional morality."[66] Such actors do not abandon their particularity—which is impossible in any case—but they recognize that demeaning representations of others are always possible in the context of plurality and diversity and that the resultant challenge is to reach agreements in which each actor has attempted to take the place of all others and to understand radically different political positions.[67] Postconventional ethics requires a reflective orientation toward the forms of unjust exclusion that subjects have created in the process of pursuing interests and protecting valued differences. Additionally, it involves the desire to engage the unjustly excluded in an open dialogue in which the latter can protest against the systematic neglect of their legitimate concerns. Forms of political community with these attachments to communicative as opposed to strategic action are the true foundations of human security.

Conclusion

In the 1950s, Karl Deutsch coined the phrase the "security community" to describe those regions in which a sense of "we-feeling" had softened the edges of national differences and in which the desire for peaceful change had abolished the use of force.[68] His analysis neatly captured the basic truth that security ultimately requires a shift from strategic to communicative orientations toward others. Elements of this approach exist within classical political realism, although they have not been developed very far because of a pessimistic analysis of world politics that assumes that communicative action might ease tensions between adversaries but cannot solve the intractable security problems in world politics. Critical theory takes these themes more seriously in the belief there are no systemic or ontological barriers to breakthroughs in communicative action and discourse ethics across world society as a whole. To put this differently, realism regards empathy and understanding as important ways of mitigating the worst effects of international anarchy, but it is disinclined to believe that they could ever provide the foundations of an alternative world order; critical theory maintains that empathy and understanding can provide the bridge to a world order that revolves around the principles of publicity, dialogue, and consent (without assuming that the condition of permanent peace is ever likely to be achieved and recognizing that progress toward this end requires the support of states, especially the great powers).

From the critical perspective, security requires the development of forms of political community in which the constraints on actors are, as far as possible, the constraints they willingly impose on themselves.[69] It requires the establishment of political structures that guarantee effective participation in dialogic arrangements (either directly or indirectly through democratically elected representatives). It involves the willingness to extend these arrangements across both domestic and international politics. An ideal security community will take the form of an unlimited speech or communication community in which the right to participate in dialogue is possessed by one and all. Progress toward this ideal cannot take place without the prior transformation of political community. The emergence of more dialogic forms of life is the key to advancing the Kantian ideal of a "cosmopolitan condition of general political security."[70]

Notes

1. The main themes of this paragraph are drawn from Michael Walzer's account of the distribution of membership in Walzer, *Spheres of Justice*, chap. 2.

2. Habermas, *Justification and Application*, p. 78 describes strategic action as action that is governed by the subject's concern with personal success whereas communicative action involves the search for agreement and understanding. For further discussion see Johnson, "Habermas." We shall return to this distinction later.

3. Wheeler and Booth, "The Security Dilemma" in Baylis and Rengger (eds.), *Dilemmas of World Politics*.

4. For an astute discussion of these themes, see Mutimer, "Beyond Strategy."

5. Buzan, *People, States, and Fear*, p. 364.

6. Booth, "Security in Anarchy" and "Security and Self."

7. Ayoob, "Defining Security."

8. Wallace, "Truth and Power"; Booth, "A Reply to Wallace"; and Smith, "Power and Truth."

9. The question of trust has been strangely ignored in the study of international relations. See Rengger, "The Ethics of Trust in World Politics."

10. Pettit, *Republicanism*, p. 28.

11. Booth, "Security in Anarchy," p. 319.

12. Krause and Williams (eds.), *Critical Security Studies*, p. ix.

13. See Murray, *Reconstructing Realism*.

14. Buzan, *People, States, and Fear*, p. 364.

15. Mutimer, "Beyond Strategy."

16. The argument that is developed here does not deny that states may be the containers of security for their citizens but shifts the emphasis onto how their moral deficits can be reduced and advances in human security achieved.

17. But some approaches were also quick to stress the "rationality of irra-

tionality" especially but not only in the context of nuclear deterrence. For a critical discussion, see Midgley, *The Natural Law Tradition and the Theory of International Relations*, chap. 12, pt. 1.

18. Mutimer, "Beyond Strategy," p. 73.

19. Morgenthau, *Politics Among Nations*, chap. 32; and Kissinger, *The White House Years*.

20. For a detailed discussion of philosophical hermeneutics and international politics, see Shapcott, *Justice, Community, and Dialogue in International Relations*.

21. Waltz, *Theory of International Politics*, p. 71.

22. See Wæver et al., *Identity, Migration*.

23. Booth, "Security in Anarchy"; and Linklater, "The Transformation of Political Community."

24. Waltz, "America as a Model for the World?" pp. 667–670.

25. Waltz, "Kant, Liberalism, and War."

26. Michael Doyle argues that liberal states tend not to go to war with one another, but are less inhibited when dealing with regimes that lack any commitment to the politics of consent. See Doyle, "Liberalism and World Politics," *American Political Science Review* 80: 1151–1168. MacMillan, "A Kantian Protest" and *On Liberal Peace*, develops the bolder argument that liberal states must proceed in a consensual fashion in all their external relations if they are to remain true to their deepest moral convictions.

27. MacMillan, "A Kantian Protest" and *On Liberal Peace*, argues that liberal states may well behave in this way, but in so doing they allow their liberal sentiments to be overpowered by nonliberal convictions in government or society.

28. The skeptic may want greater precision about the extent to which domestic political change makes a measurable difference to foreign policy behavior. This is not a question that can be answered here. A larger study of these themes would also need to make further progress on the conceptual front. A society that combines investments in communicative action with an ethnic conception of citizenship is unlikely to behave in the same way as a society in which communicative action is linked with a civic conception of citizenship. (I am grateful to Don MacIver from Staffordshire University for highlighting this point.) The link between the inside and the outside, between domestic structures and communicative action in foreign affairs, will presumably be stronger if citizenship is thought to embody universal or cosmopolitan commitments. The belief that there may be good reasons for treating insiders and outsiders differently but not for subjecting them to different forms of politics (to the politics of communicative action in the case of citizens, to the politics of strategic action in the case of aliens) is crucial here.

29. Kymlicka, *Liberalism, Community, and Culture*.

30. Steans, *Gender and International Relations*, chap. 1.

31. Abolishing forms of politics that rest upon morally irrelevant distinctions between insiders and outsiders (citizens and aliens) is a crucial extension of this process. This is not to argue that national loyalties are incompatible with a cosmopolitan community, or to suggest that duties to humanity must always override duties to other citizens and to the state. But it is to suggest that the differences between insiders and outsiders are not so profound as to justify confining the politics of communicative action to the domestic sphere. Put another way, the similarities between insiders and outsiders are such as to require efforts to enlarge the speech community or to promote an unlimited or universal communication community. See Lyotard, "The Other's Rights," in Shute and Hurley (eds.), *On Human*

Rights; Apel, *Towards a Transformation of Philosophy*; and Habermas, *Justification and Application*. Moral agents must become troubled by the fact that "the idea of an ideally extended communication community is paradoxical in that every known community is limited and distinguishes members from nonmembers through rules of inclusion" (Habermas, *Justification and Application*, p. 54). Concern about the harm that may be caused to outsiders requires measures to solve this paradox by creating a more inclusive speech community. For further discussion, see Linklater, *Transformation of Political Community*, chap. 6.

32. Habermas, *The Past as Future*, p. 104.

33. Apel, "The Conflicts of Our Time," pp. 98–99.

34. See Linklater, *Transformation of Political Community*, chap. 3. The notion of domination-free communication can be found in Rorty, *Contingency, Irony, and Solidarity*, p. 68.

35. Ayoob, "Defining Security," p. 127.

36. Ibid. Ayoob takes issue with Booth's claim that "emancipation is the freeing of people (as individuals and groups) from the physical and human constraints which stop them carrying out what they would freely choose to do" (quoted by Ayoob, "Defining Security," p. 126). With this definition in mind, Ayoob argues that endorsing the right of self-determination for ethnic groups ("which can be considered a major manifestation of emancipation") will "increase disorder in the Third World because of the multiethnic character of almost all Third World countries" (Ayoob, "Defining Security," p. 128). An alternative way of reflecting on these matters is suggested in the next paragraph of this chapter.

37. Murray, *Reconstructing Realism*, pp. 202–203.

38. Wallace, "Truth and Power." For responses to this argument, see Booth, "A Reply to Wallace," and Smith, "Power and Truth."

39. Habermas, *Justification and Application*, p. 58, argues that ideal argumentation "leaves the identity of the participants . . . untouched. The moral point of view calls for the extension and reversibility of interpretive structures so that alternative viewpoints and interest structures and differences in individual self-understandings and worldviews are not effaced but are given full play in discourse." Parallels with Gadamer's notion of the fusion of horizons are considered in Habermas, *Justification and Application*, pp. 104–105. For further comments on harm and discourse, see Linklater, "Citizenship, Humanity and Cosmopolitan Harm Conventions," *International Political Science Review* 22: 261–278.

40. This is why it still makes sense to think in terms of the "emancipatory potential of moral universalism." See Habermas, *Justification and Application*, p. 125 and also p. 24.

41. Quoted by Murray, *Reconstructing Realism*, p. 123.

42. Ibid., p. 8.

43. On the importance of moral fallibilism for classical realism, see ibid., pp. 119–120. See Habermas, *Justification and Application*, p. 164, for a statement of the fallibilist theme in the discourse theory of morality.

44. Murray, *Reconstructing Realism*, p. 8.

45. Campbell, "The Deterritorialisation of Responsibility," *Alternatives* 19: 455–484.

46. Murray, *Reconstructing Realism*, p. 132, highlights the importance of consent for Butterfield, who many would regard as a member of the English School. For further discussion, see Dunne, *Inventing International Society*.

47. Ayoob, "Defining Security," pp. 121–124.

48. Works that bear on these themes include Vayrynen, "Phenomenology and Conflict Analysis"; Jones, *Cosmopolitan Mediation?*; and Murithi, *Moral Development*.

49. Ayoob, "Defining Security."

50. Ibid.

51. This is to endorse the claim that the allegations that critical theory fails to address the real world problems of the policymaking community wrongly privilege the interests of state managers over the interests of groups in civil society. See Booth, "A Reply to Wallace," p. 375; and Smith, "Power and Truth," p. 510.

52. For the background to this claim, see Linklater, "Citizenship and Sovereignty in the Post-Westphalian State," *European Journal of International Relations* 2: 77–103. For a discussion of its relevance outside the European context, see Booth and Vale, "Critical Security Studies and Regional Insecurity," in Krause and Williams (eds.), *Critical Security Studies*, pp. 349–352. For an account of its relevance for the remaking of Europe, see Wæver et al., *Identity, Migration, and the New Security Agenda in Europe.*

53. Communitarians such as Michael Walzer are right to argue that confederalism, and even secession itself with the appropriate safeguards for minorities, are often the best means of promoting the security of subaltern ethnic or national groups. See Walzer, "Notes on The New Tribalism," in Brown (ed.), *Political Restructuring in Europe.*

54. Carr, *Nationalism and After,* remains one of the best accounts of these destructive consequences.

55. On this distinction, see Cox, "Social Forces, States and World Orders: Beyond International Relations Theory."

56. On the contention that critical theory has very little to say about strategies of transition, see Murray, *Reconstructing Realism*, p. 185.

57. Whereas communicative action refers to efforts to reach an agreement or understanding, discourse or communicative ethics refers to the specific moral principles that subjects bring to this project. Discourse ethics is "a reflective form of communicative action" since it urges everyone to "act with an orientation to mutual understanding and allow everyone the communicative freedom to take positions on validity claims." See Habermas, *Justification and Application*, pp. 1 and 66. Another way of highlighting the differences between communicative action and communicative or discourse ethics is suggested by the claim that "we cannot rationally *convince* anyone, not even ourselves, of something if we do not accept as our common point of departure that all voices that are at all relevant should be heard, that the best arguments available given the current state of our knowledge should be expressed, and that only the unforced force of the better argument should determine the 'yes' and 'no' responses of participants" (Habermas, *Justification and Application*, p. 145, italics in original). Communicative action that is concerned with reaching an understanding or agreement may not involve this effort to purify relations of the effects of power inequalities. For further discussion of the differences between communicative action and discourse or discourse ethics, see Johnson, "Habermas."

58. See Murithi, *Moral Development,* chap. 7, on the importance of generational change.

59. See Giddens, *The Nation-State and Violence, Volume 2: A Contemporary Critique of Historical Materialism,* chap. 11; and Booth, "Security and Emancipation."

60. An intriguing example is Kenny, *The Logic of Deterrence.*

61. These are crucial themes in neoliberal studies of cooperation under anarchy and in English School accounts of international societies. The transition from a system to a society of states, as members of the English School argue, involves the increased importance of communicative as opposed to strategic action.

62. It is worth noting Kant's somewhat consequentialist argument that action should be judged by the extent to which it hampers or promotes the development of a universal kingdom of ends. See Linklater, *Men and Citizens in the Theory of International Relations*, p. 117. For an illustration of this approach in connection with responses to the terrorist attacks on September 11, 2001, see Linklater, "Unnecessary Suffering," in Booth and Dunne (eds.), *Worlds in Collision*.

63. This is echoed in the more recent contention that participants themselves must choose their path to liberation. See Habermas, *Justification and Application*, pp. 175–176. It is worth adding that early peace research was inclined to regard conflict as the medical profession regards disease. See Lawler, *A Question of Values*, pp. 56–60.

64. Habermas (*Justification and Application*, p. 174) argues that "empathy," which is "the ability to project oneself across cultural distances into alien and at first sight incomprehensible conditions of life . . . is an emotional prerequisite for ideal role taking, which requires everyone to take the perspective of all others." Universal communication, as Habermas understands it, requires this ability to understand the position taken by all others (see also Habermas, *Justification and Application*, p. 154).

65. This approach is indebted to Seyla Benhabib's distinction between ethics that deal with the specific, and ethics that deal with the generalized other—and with the related distinction between substitutionalist and interactive universalism. See Benhabib and Cornell, (eds.), *Feminism as Critique,* chap. 4. See also her account of postconventional contextualism in Benhabib, *Situating the Self*. Linklater, *Transformation of Political Community*, chaps. 2–3, discusses these issues in more detail.

66. Habermas, *Justification and Application*, chap. 3.

67. Ibid., p. 154.

68. Deutsch, *Political Community at the International Level*.

69. The theme is Rousseau's.

70. On the cosmopolitan condition of general political security, see Kant, "Idea for a Universal History with a Cosmopolitan Purpose," in Reiss (ed.), *Kant's Political Writings*, p. 49.

6

The Missing Link: Security, Critical International Political Economy, and Community

Roger Tooze

This chapter, like all academic writing on security, approaches the concept through a particular set of values, a range of philosophical assumptions, and certain analytical practices linked to a particular academic discipline—in this case the disciplinary knowledge and precepts of a critical international political economy (IPE). The chapter does *not* set out to provide an alternative, emancipatory view of the global political economy: rather, it offers a way of thinking *critically* about the current theorization of international political economy. By the way it is argued, the chapter suggests a method for moving toward security, community, and emancipation. The argument[1] that is advanced below has three equally important, interlinked strands:

1. Given the success of advanced or financial capitalism in becoming *the* world economic system, any and all critical attempts to understand and theorize security must be constructed to recognize and integrate the study of international political economy. This is not the case today, when the economic elements of security are theorized as functional. That is, they are regarded as purely economic aspects of a predefined *political* concept of security; as a result, they are then either tacked onto existing analyses or are merely considered separately under the rubric of economic security.

2. The goal of achieving security, via the theories and practices of critical security studies (CSS), is hindered, and quite possibly even denied, by the current theorization of orthodox and even much heterodox IPE; this is illustrated by the way that the issue of economic security has been articulated and theorized in the mainstream, state-based IPE literature. It is not that *national* economic security, however defined, does not matter. It clearly does. The problem is that the *sole* focus on national economic security, theorized only through mainstream positivist methodology and with the economic being defined in the way it is by orthodox IPE, is too narrow, claims

too much, and is increasingly partial and inappropriate. The failure of IPE theory in this regard demands the construction of a critical IPE.

3. The achievement of security, as defined by CSS, ultimately demands the integration in theory and in practice of security, community, *and* international political economy. This in turn demands a genuine and critical IPE, which among other requirements entails the theoretical reembedding of economy into society and polity. By this I mean a practice of IPE that is democratic, historical, and reflexive. This should allow us to understand the processes by which the separation of politics and economics is achieved, reproduced, and utilized.[2]

In terms of disciplinary knowledge within orthodox international relations (IR) and IPE these arguments challenge both the existing theorizations of politics, economics, and international political economy, as well as the various ways in which politics and economics are separated and then related to each other by and within these theories. All this has profound implications for the way we think about security and community—and hence emancipation.

The Dominance of Neoliberal Discourse

If my arguments in this chapter are to be successful they have to confront the power of the predominant, embedded, and common-sensical discourse of neoliberal economics, which either consciously or unconsciously form the starting point for most people in the rich states of the Organization for Economic Cooperation and Development (OECD). The existence and power of this discourse are not fortuitous, inevitable, or natural. They are constitutive of and a consequence of the hegemony of the United States beginning around 1900. And despite the domination of public and policy discussion by a specific and partial conception of security since September 11, 2001, in response to the threat of international terrorism, the fundamental significance of the theory and institutionalized practice of neoliberalism remains; indeed, it comprises the core set of assumptions and values upon which U.S. hegemony is predicated and hence upon which the world political economy is constructed. Among other fundamental claims, this discourse sets out a specific and special relationship between politics and economics in which the rationality of economics should generally triumph over the irrationality of politics.[3]

Today in the OECD states and beyond, neoliberalism has come to prefigure much of the language and predefine the core concepts that are used to describe economic activity. For example, when we talk about the market, the range of assumptions that is embedded in this concept already construct it as benevolent, desirable, and, of course, nonpolitical. In much the same way as CSS contests a fundamental statism, a critical IPE *has* to contest a fundamental economism (as well as statism!) in which the only legitimate language to speak about the world economy has come to be that of economics (note *not* the world political economy). The terms used here, "economics" and "political economy," and "world economy" and "world political economy," are fundamentally important as they denote very different ontologies. By "ontology" here I mean the notion used by Robert Cox that "we cannot define a problem in global politics without presupposing a certain basic structure consisting of the significant kinds of entities involved and the form of significant relationships among them."[4] "Economics," as used to refer to both the discipline and the daily activity, accepts and reproduces the separation of economic activity from other forms of human activity; it makes a claim to the distinctiveness of economic life in that it can be separated out from society and polity and understood on its own terms. But the use of the term "political economy" reclaims the integration of politics and economics and denies the meaningful separation of the two. Hence, when we talk about the "world economy" we are constructing a very different ontology than that constructed by the term "world political economy." Much of the disciplinary knowledge, and certainly many of the universal claims of economics have become legitimized as common sense and, as such, are beyond everyday questioning.[5]

Mainstream IPE includes a wide variety of approaches and methodologies that, within mainstream epistemologies, make it superficially difficult to make general observations about the field as a whole; and within mainstream thought the resulting perspectivism serves as an effective barrier to its practitioners, questioning the key political process of how we know what we know. However, IPE as a whole field of knowledge is constructed socially as a practice of orthodoxy, with particular heterodox versions outside of this orthodoxy, but both orthodox and heterodox versions are contained within an unarticulated *doxa* (or body of beliefs) that sets the unspoken and unacknowledged limits of such discourse.[6] Pierre Bourdieu's notion of *doxa* is useful here, as it identifies and denotes what he calls the "universe of the undiscussed" and "that which is beyond question" and taken for granted.[7] In the sense that *doxa* "delimits the *universe of possible discourse*," the investigation and identification of doxic relationships is a fundamental aspect of any critical theory. Here it is particularly important in understanding the way in which, in matters of political economy, neoliberal ideas are often presented by those whose interests are being served by these ideas as *doxa*, that is, as constituting a "self-evident and natural order which goes without saying and therefore goes unquestioned."[8] Such a social construction of disciplinary IPE knowledge practices allows a clear, critical, and analytical focus on the power of its orthodox representations and their claims to legitimacy. The rewriting of IPE that is implied by the

points above is a major task and would take much more than this short
chapter, but I will endeavor to bring out the core arguments, as well as their
problems and limitations. It is worth noting that the similar contest now
taking place within security studies over the discourse of security and its
articulation in mainstream international relations is unfortunately still taking place *in parallel* to critical IPE rather than *as part of it*, thus continuing
to support the separation of the "economic" from the "political."[9]

International Political Economy:
Its Role in Security, Community, and Emancipation

One of the central themes of Part 2 is that security *must* be closely related
to some notion of community. One of the core arguments of this chapter is
that the underpinning of security by community constitutes the sine qua
non of genuine emancipation, of genuine human security. Given this reality,
the necessity to assert and then interpret the ontological interconnections,
albeit in the form of complex and often obtuse relationships and structures,
between security, community, and international political economy is clear.
If the study of international political economy is *really* about political economy—the unity of politics and economics, as I would argue—then such
political economy must be intimately and necessarily embedded in social
practice and institutions, with the institution of community being historically central, in whatever form community has been historically and culturally
experienced and conceptualized.

However, because of the historical centrality of the three notions of
security, economy, and community in the evolution of modern state forms,
it is important briefly to consider these (particularly the security-economy
nexus) in their historical context; this will avoid making the mistake of taking for granted the current formulation of their meaning and referents.

The history of the modern state is the history of the institutionalization
and capture of the actual condition and discourse of security. Indeed, it is
possible to argue that in its centrality to the development of the state, security is one of the key constitutive elements of modernity[10] and, as such, is
intimately bound up with conceptions of human progress. However, it is
likely that this link might now be corrupted. In this historical process,
notions of state security, particularly in and after Jeremy Bentham, were
inseparable from the idea of *economy*. In the words of Anthony Burke,
"This involved a series of shifts, firstly from economy as a principle for the
government of the family to one for the general organisation of society, and
then of sovereignty from a rule over territory to the government of a 'complex of men and things' which would incorporate territory into a set of economic relations."[11] Hence political economy comes from the actuality and
perception of the closer relations between territory, wealth, and population

locked together in the problem of what Michel Foucault has called "governmentality."[12]

The key point for this chapter is that security and political economy, historically, are two inseparable elements in the construction and continuing reproduction of the state and modernity. Only later came the process of the explicit, formal, and state-constructed internationalizing of political economy and the separation of economics from politics on the basis of the political imposition and then elevation of the capitalist market to become the core necessary social formation, as so well analyzed by Karl Polanyi.[13] Once political economy became established, and defined directly as being constituted by the interests of the state through the doctrine of mercantilism (in which power was identical to wealth), any political challenge to the state from those who gained power and wealth from incipient capitalist industrialization and the creation of surplus capital would eventually necessarily require the separation of the realm of economy from that of political economy. This partly accounts for the liberal doctrine of the separation of politics and economics, a separation reemphasized and doctrinally embedded in both the theory and practice of contemporary neoliberalism.[14] The separation became professionalized at the end of the nineteenth century with the creation of the modern discipline of economics, which in its mainstream form then became an essential part of the social mechanisms for reproducing liberal political economy.

Community, Emancipation, and Political Economy

There has been an effective forgetting of the common historical and structural roots of security and political economy, with the invisibility of their necessary fusion created by contemporary categories. Further, as we shall also see later, there has also been the almost unquestioning acceptance of an economics-defined ontology of political economy by those members of the discipline of international relations who have considered themselves as "security" specialists. It is not therefore surprising that security has been understood in the way it has.

More problematic is the notion of community under capitalism. I do not want here to rehearse all the problems of defining community or even what or who should define community. What *is* central here is the question of the very possibility of real community under advanced forms of market capitalism. The same processes that led to the creation of what Karl Polanyi called an "economic sphere," separated out from society and polity, also constructed community in a particular configuration and in a specific relationship to capitalism. For historical materialists, as critical theorists, this relationship is one of opposition. Partha Chatterjee has no doubt on this:

> If there is one great moment that turns the provincial thought of Europe to
> universal philosophy, the parochial history of Europe to universal history,
> it is the movement of capital—capital that is global in its territorial reach
> and universal in its conceptual domain. . . . For this narrative to take
> shape, *the destruction of community is fundamental.*[15]

And later in the same piece he adds:

> Community is not easily appropriated within the narrative of capital. . . . It
> is not so much the state–civil society opposition but rather the capital-
> community opposition that seems to be the great unsurpassed contradic-
> tion in Western social philosophy. . . . The modern state, embedded as it is
> within the universal narrative of capital, cannot recognize within its juris-
> diction any form of community except the single, determinate, demo-
> graphically enumerable form of the nation.[16]

For Chatterjee the very success of capitalism and now neoliberal globalization means the denial of community. But at the same time, community
becomes a means of responding to and fighting the social and personal consequences of advanced capitalism. This is not a view that is easily marginalized by the orthodoxy, as would normally be the case, because it is held
by a growing number of nonhistorical materialists as well. Many of the
responses to globalization from those concerned with broader aspects of
society emphasize the destruction—and rebuilding—of community as *necessary first steps* in the political process of reclaiming security.[17] Clearly, if
in the process of rethinking security we accept the necessity to reintegrate
economics and politics as a basis for this rethink, we also need to consider
our whole understanding of community.

Here, then, the relationships between international political economy
(as advanced capitalism), security, community, and emancipation are
brought together and intensified under the conditions of globalization,
although analysis reveals the globalization process to be far more complex
and subtle (particularly in terms of the international/national) than previously thought.[18] Yet it would be too easy simply to assert, following
Chatterjee's analysis above, that we should change the system of global
finance capital or mediate its effects, although mediation by and through
the organs of civil society is more possible than fundamental change in the
near future.

As I suggest throughout this chapter, the *possibilities* of security, community, and emancipation must at first be recognized—identified and theorized—before change can take place. Bourdieu suggests that what he calls
the "theory effect" is "the properly political effect that consists in making
tangible (*theorein*) a 'reality' that cannot entirely exist insofar as it remains
unknown and unrecognized."[19] Inasmuch as the relationships between
political economy, security, community, and emancipation are obscured and

hidden by orthodox disciplines, the first stages of emancipation are necessarily making tangible this reality. But this process is all too often confined to those of us privileged to be members of the academy, without concern for the theory's effect (or lack of it) in our work. In this regard, Bourdieu argues that we as academics "can escape the alternative of populism and conservatism, two forms of essentialism which tend to consecrate the status quo, only by *working to universalize the conditions of access to universality.*"[20] This, I suggest, provides the basis for theorizing the emancipation of everyday life.

The Relevance of the World Political Economy

Acknowledging the importance of *the* international political economy for the current and future life chances of the majority of the world's population implies that the theory and the practice of the study of international political economy have become a necessary part of the unity of security, community, emancipation, and economy—where *economy* is political economy at every level of society. Hence IPE is a necessary part of the constitution of critical security studies.[21] Those who still harbor any doubt about the central relevance of IPE to security, community, and emancipation need only briefly reflect on two pivotal developments.

First, we should consider the stormy events of the world political economy since July 1997. At that moment, a breakdown of the financial system in Thailand precipitated a massive economic crisis in the Far East, impacted on the world political economy in concrete terms, and resulted in changed policies and attitudes toward future developments. These developments within the global financial structure had a real and severe impact upon hundreds of millions of people's lives through mass unemployment, political instability, and the vast increase in the number of suicides in the main affected economies. What price security for these human beings?

Second, there are the continuing reverberations of the events of September 2001. These not only produced major changes in the interstate political system and the conduct of domestic politics in many states but also revealed (and legitimized) for many the reality and extent of U.S. hegemonic power. (As a condition for its existence and reproduction, U.S. hegemonic power at a structural level necessarily integrates politics and economics—and belief systems—while publicly maintaining the separation of politics and economics within the doctrine of neoliberalism.) Almost all the consequent analyses of global terrorism implicitly or explicitly make a substantive link between the military, political, economic, and ideological bases of terrorism. Furthermore, almost all recognize the direct and indirect relationship between politics and economics in that they call for the longer-term alleviation of the economic conditions and structures that are identified as contributing to global terrorism.[22] Yet if anything, the global political economy has become even more neoliberal since September 2001. The citizens of the OECD countries (and others) are warned by their national politicians that security cannot now be total—although, of course, it never has been. However, the political and economic costs and responses to global terror are now beginning to threaten the very basis of our own civil society, perhaps as much as the original acts of global terror themselves. What price security here?

We are living at a time of underlying but largely unrecognized economic and financial crisis. In these first years of the twenty-first century, the world's financial, investment, and trading structures are creaking. Former U.S. president Bill Clinton has described this time as offering the biggest challenge facing the world economy for over fifty years. It is a time of high drama and much talk of systemic risk and threats to security, a time when the world economy is affected by uncertainty, risk, and the impediments to economic activity imposed in the search for security, for which the world's governments are desperately seeking solutions.[23] Suddenly, past orthodoxies, embedded and institutionalized at every level of government and economy, are no longer automatically seen by academics and policymakers alike as the common sense they have been portrayed as. The values and policies that have driven the operation, institutions, and governance of the world political economy are now part of the problem rather than part of the solution. Although it often seems easy to put the blame for problems on the intransigence or self-interest of the United States or the European Union, this is to mistake the symptoms for the structural imperatives of the embedded logic of neoliberalism. That being the case, the crisis that CSS has identified in common-sense IR with respect to security converges dramatically with the crisis that a critical IPE reveals in orthodox IPE.

The continuing concern over financial structures and the failure of the post-2001 Doha Round of the World Trade Organization are fundamental in the sense that these structures and their associated modes of behavior are a necessary and integral part of the system of advanced financial capitalism. Yet from the gaze of a critical IPE this concern is just one element of a larger problem that very few of the analysts and commentators on the world economy acknowledge or, indeed, can even recognize given their assumptions, concepts, and values. Other manifestations of this larger problem include the massive and increasing disparities of wealth and poverty that have accompanied the overall growth of the world product—both within and between national political economies.[24] By the early 1990s, for example, the top 1 percent of earners in the United States received more income than the combined total of the bottom 40 percent, and the 400 richest individuals listed by the U.S. *Forbes* magazine had a net worth equal to the gross domestic product (GDP) of India, Bangladesh, Nepal, and Sri

Lanka—which together had a combined population of more than 1 billion.[25] There has been increasing world unemployment and underemployment, with all the implications of these conditions; the total is now more than 1 billion people, one-third of all possible employees. There is a growing search for meaningful alternatives and complementary forms of community in the face of the manifest problems and limitations of the state, as shown both by the efforts of regional organizations and subnational social movements. And not least, we can see the hardening of the global scientific consensus on the conclusion that human beings, through our economic activities, have destroyed one-third of *our* natural habitat since 1970 and are also destroying the ozone layer at rates previously thought impossible.

Together, these elements making up the contemporary global situation indicate a far broader and a far deeper problem than the myriad economists and business analysts who regularly pontificate in and on our media are able and willing to recognize and discuss. Despite this, these are the people to whom we—as concerned and aware citizens—invariably turn to for knowledge. Our societies have seemingly given them legitimacy to be the only bona fide interpreters of these matters (apart from politicians, who properly claim democratic legitimacy, but most of whom have simply accepted the values and assumptions of a neoliberal economism). Moreover, as this chapter illustrates, we do not seem to be getting much help from those academic disciplines that we might have expected to have had the expertise and critical distance to provide analyses and understanding, namely, international political economy, international relations, and economics.

To the extent that these disciplinary practices of knowledge in their mainstream or orthodox manifestations have accepted particular values and assumptions, they have weakened their own ability to offer anything other than system-supporting analyses. This is particularly the case when the prevailing structures of neoliberal capitalism are under threat or are under conditions of longer-term change. Practitioners of orthodox disciplines (particularly, but not solely, economics) are content to offer us their solutions, derived from universal and nomological categories, on the implicit basis of problem-solving theory,[26] rather than acknowledge the limitations and inappropriateness of such knowledge for the conditions in which we now find ourselves.[27]

Robert Cox has developed an important and original critical perspective on political economy.[28] He makes and uses the fundamental distinction between two types of theory defined by their purpose: critical theory and problem-solving theory. For Cox problem-solving theory takes the existing institutions and structures as given and attempts to resolve problems within this existing framework, whereas critical theory stands apart from and questions the historical and structural context of problems and attempts to make clear the broader and more long-term forces at work in political economy.[29] Cox's two categories are helpful in distinguishing between theories, in setting up different ontologies, and in posing some of the essential questions for a critical IPE. In particular, whose interests are being served by theory and whose purpose is this theory for?

What is clearly at stake within the gyrations of the world political economy is our security as individuals and groups. What happens in and to the world political economy today has an impact on most of the world's population, and that impact can be life-threatening or merely lifestyle-threatening, direct or indirect, immediate or long-term, concrete or ideational, and/or any combination of these. The threat often appears to be in the conditions of high instability, high risk, and the demonstrated propensity for rapid, directionless change (with the possibility of systemic crisis and meltdown). Yet, it would be wrong to focus only on the crisis, because it is not only in crisis that our security may be challenged. The very operation of the system of global financial capitalism creates significant insecurity for many through the spread of uncertainty but principally through the growth of inequality and poverty.

In 1998, Paul Volcker, the former chairman of the U.S. Federal Reserve Board—in effect, the world's most powerful financial institution—wrote that "the problems we see with such force today are systemic—they arise from *the ordinary workings of global financial capitalism.*"[30] The crisis of the war on terror and the overwhelming mass of debate, discussion, and political noise following developments associated with it, have all worked to obscure this fact. But it is a core feature of capitalism. Barry Buzan argued that "competitive capitalism is . . . founded on a considerable degree of permanent insecurity for all the units within it (individuals, firms, states), making the idea of economic security within capitalism seem a contradiction in terms."[31] He concluded: "Without a substantial level of insecurity the system does not work."[32] This is an important and often forgotten conclusion which highlights a key structural feature of security within a capitalist system. However, because of the inherent limitations of his approach, Buzan was unable to resolve the more intractable problems of the political economy of security; these stem from his misunderstanding of history, his ontological categories, and his understanding of reality.

The impact of normal systemic crisis amplifies the ordinary workings of the world political economy, and the results clearly impact on the security of individuals, families, companies, organizations, and states and governments. But as we said earlier, those ordinary workings in and of themselves increasingly constitute insecurity.[33] In this way, the activities of global corporations, rather than constituting the economic security that they and neoliberal commentators claim, can be and are seen by many as a threat. In David Korten's view, "The protection of people and communities from predatory global corporations and finance is arguably the central security issue of our time."[34]

The human consequences of the structural insecurity of the current world political economy are unfortunately all too easy to illustrate: the closing of factories in Scotland and the North-East of England through the global restructuring of the silicon chip industry; the major disruptions in and the coming closures of automobile and steel factories in the new "old industrial areas" of the United States, which throw whole families and towns out of work; the enormous and unprecedented mass migrations in China from country to city in search of jobs; the daily insecurity of child labor in India, where whole families become dependent upon their children because their parents' labor is too expensive in the global marketplace; the corruption of Colombia by a drug cartel whose legitimacy derives from the fact that the world demand for cocaine provides a better living for the people than the subsistence agriculture under which they previously existed; and the millions directly affected by the problems of the Indonesian economy, many of whom are now living off the contents of municipal rubbish dumps. Each of these illustrations is a powerful indictment of the abstract and formal analysis offered to us daily; it reflects the total failure of the mainstream view (what became labeled the Washington Consensus) on how the world political economy *actually* works and how it *should* work.

Indeed, for many in the world, through their understanding of what constituted common sense, the key element of security has come to be understood and constituted as economic security—security of sustenance and shelter, security of employment and income, security of energy supplies, security of savings, security of the economy, and security of the global economic system. This does not mean that other aspects of social existence[35] are not constituted as relevant to security, but it does reflect what I understand as the economization of both material and ideational life, which together construct the basis and framework for common sense.[36] By this, I mean the way in which the values and language of economy have come to dominate and construct *all* our social, political, and personal lives and spaces; as a result, market values become the sole criteria for social and personal behavior. And notwithstanding all the debates on the nature and extent of globalization,[37] the focus on economic security also reflects the widely held perception that there *is* a global economy and that it is largely uncontrollable by any of the actors who claim to be able to exert control, including the government of the United States. It is the apparently increasingly arbitrary, random, sudden, and unpredictable nature of the workings of the global economy that have heightened the sense that these matters concern our security.

At the heart of the problem of making sense of these developments is the limitation on our understandings imposed by the theories and concepts we use. This in turn inhibits our understanding of the links between economy, security, and community. The concepts and language we use to describe and interpret what is going on in the world political economy are not neutral—in their origin, use, or purpose. Nor are they merely instruments through which we can discover an autonomous preexisting reality of political economy.[38] Economic theory, concepts, and language are constitutive of reality; this is only too well demonstrated through the problems faced by the poor and the dispossessed in the world political economy.[39] In this epistemology, the distinction between theory and practice held by orthodox neopositivist international political economists such as Stephen Krasner[40] is dissolved. Here, theory and practice are mutually constitutive. No less a successful capitalist than George Soros has clearly identified the centrality of this mutuality when he writes, in an article entitled "The Capitalist Threat," that markets must be understood "reflexively" because "buyers and sellers in financial markets seek to discount a future that depends on their own decisions."[41]

The change in our understanding that is brought about by such a recognition of a constitutive theory of IPE is as dramatic as it is fundamental. It is dramatic because it should make us reflect on our own daily lives as a place where the struggles of world political economy are carried on—not at some distant and abstract level of globalization. Consider, for example, that over the period of the most recent crisis in global finance, whose public beginnings were in July 1997, the knowledge most used to comment on the situation, and to make public analyses of it, in most of the media has been through what I call a socialized form of economics—notably economists employed by banks and investment houses. Think of this when you next watch TV news and see who is brought forward by Fox News, BBC, CNN, or whatever broadcasting system. It will normally be an individual working for a bank or financial organization such as NatWest or Morgan Grenfell. The knowledge that is put before viewers and listeners constructs economics as an autonomous, self-contained, objective, rational, and nonpolitical realm of activity and, as such, takes "one part of the human experience—the interaction between buyers and sellers—and makes it the narrow and fragile base for a rickety and unstable Theory of Everything."[42]

The 1997 global economic crisis was portrayed as a major threat to economic stability and hence to our security. It was explained as a failure of Asian governments to supervise and regulate their banking sectors, or the failure of Japanese policymakers to reflate the Japanese economy, or a failure in the architecture of governance of the world financial system. The crisis was portrayed as the result of contingent factors and not a product of the political, social, and economic forces of the very system so lauded by mainstream analysts. The analyses of the latter are characteristically offered as neutral, objective, disinterested, factually based comment by technical experts, in line both with the social status of economics and the presumed scientific status of the knowledge so promulgated. However, the nature of the analysis offered, based on assumptions and concepts of rationality and of the market, have been widely discredited by other—and I believe—more reflective economists[43] and also attacked by political economists.[44] Even so, the authority given to these experts serves not only to insulate the system of global financial capitalism from its critics but also to maintain the legitimacy, validity, and social and political hegemony of the theories, concepts, and knowledge used in these expert analyses. The most significant import of these economic theories and concepts for our understanding of security and political economy is that they define and then describe a world of rational economic man in which economics is both separated from polity and society and made the dominant, privileged, and defining sphere of human life.

Security, Community, and the Practice of IPE

A central feature of contemporary U.S.-structured economic and technological globalization has been the longer-term deterritorialization of significant economic and financial activity. One of the main consequences of this tendency is the dislocation and destabilizing of the experience and idea of community.[45] The phenomenon of deterritorialization is an important element of the structure of a world political economy characterized by instantaneous real-time communication, what Manuel Castells has called "the logic of informationalization and globalization."[46] This has occurred as part of, and over the same historical period as, the growth of new structures of political economy. The consequence is that we now have an internationalized and globalized political economy characterized by uneven levels of integration into these structures. The operation and sometime severe instability of this world political economy has come to present a pressing problem of security. In these new structures our lives as human beings (wherever we live in relation to the world political economy) are subject to all kinds of possibilities and pressures that fundamentally disrupt existing communities already likely to have been fractured by capitalism itself.[47] They have yet to offer the possibility of new forms of community, yet they call into question current understandings of our values and identities, the ways we relate to each other, our relationships to place, space, and territory,[48] our means of economic survival and of generating wealth, our personal and collective happiness, our assumptions concerning how we achieve personal and collective security, and how we achieve directed change in our lives. The questions raised by such outcomes demand a more philosophically sensitive and reflexive knowledge of the world than is currently offered by conventional economic and political concepts: they require, as a necessary but not sufficient element, a deep understanding and analysis of power in the world economy.

The Failure of Orthodox IPE

One would hope that the disciplinary knowledge of IPE could provide the required analysis. My sense is that it cannot yet do this. The reason for this is the failure of critical thinking: mainstream IPE is still locked into an ontology and epistemology that reproduces a very specific and partial interpretation of international political economy, based around the state and the shared commitment to a method of positivism.[49] Mainstream IPE grounds its analysis in a world in which the state is the fundamental unit and legitimate knowledge is gained through the objective testing of propositions against an external and knowable reality. My negative conclusion is all the more disappointing given that the origins of modern IR-based international political economy lie in the very dissatisfaction felt with the limitations of a traditional military security-focused study of international relations, coupled with the inability and unwillingness of economics and international economics to handle questions of power.[50]

IPE as a distinct field of knowledge has been an academic growth industry since the early 1970s, particularly in the United States. Its growth has reflected events in the world political economy and the perceived needs of policymakers (again mainly in the United States). It is now a substantial field of knowledge, with all of the professional structures necessary to that success.[51] As it has been primarily located within the larger field of international studies, the core theoretical frameworks of a U.S.-dominated IR, with its particular philosophical and political values and assumptions, have been transposed into IPE itself. Moreover, under the hegemony of economics in the social sciences in general, the exponents of IPE have increasingly also transposed the assumptions and methodologies of economics, including rational choice theory, and a fixation with formal, quantifiable, modeling, and microsystems explanations. All these elements constitute a deep commitment to positivist epistemology. As defined above, positivist epistemology entails a claim that the only legitimate knowledge of IPE is gained through the objective testing of propositions against an external and knowable reality. The influence of this double and mutually supportive hegemony[52] has produced a distinct form of IPE, in which a contest between the competing perspectives of liberalism, nationalism, realism, and Marxism has veiled a basic orthodoxy constructed around an epistemological commitment to positivism, a theoretical commitment to methodological individualism, an ontological commitment to the state, and a domination by the agenda and interests of the United States.[53]

The commitment to positivism is a serious limitation on the ability of orthodox IPE to construct a knowledge sufficient to suggest adequate understandings of security and community under today's conditions and therefore appropriate to the complex, multilayered world we live in (as exemplified by some of the problems we have already identified). By denying the social construction and reproduction of reality (and the social reproduction of itself), orthodox IPE cannot take into account the intersubjective basis and realities of power in the world political economy. Moreover, in the context of the argument here, it places a fundamental epistemological barrier to the integration of political economy and (critical approaches to) security. A detailed epistemological critique of orthodox IPE has been articulated elsewhere[54]; the following analysis will focus on the principal ontological questions and the core problem of the theorization of politics and economics.

In terms of the basic structure of assumed entities and their relationships, IPE was initially constructed as "the politics of international economic relations."[55] In other words, the focus was to be the politics of interstate economic relations, with the unit of analysis being the territorial economy of the state, the politics being intergovernmental, and the realm of economics being given the generative role in the construction of the issues and concerns of governments. In this ontology, IPE draws upon classical political realism for its statism and liberal economic theory for its understanding of economics. And although it is an attempt to bridge the gap between international relations and international economics, it also shares with IR a marked tendency to equate politics (i.e., the realm of the state), with force and economics (linked to civil society), with rule by consent.

In this equation the politics of interstate economic relations was already demonstrating the power of the yet-to-be-articulated neoliberal ideology and neorealist IR theory.[56] Even after the politics of international economics became international political economy (around the same time that mainstream IR moved to embrace neorealism) the academic mainstream of IPE continued to conceive the state as the ontological core entity. Statism remains the core ontological commitment for orthodox IPE. At the same time, there is a willingness to recognize that other entities are possibly significant and other forms of politics may occur, but all are subservient to state structures, processes, and purposes. Within IPE statism is more than putting the state at the center of analysis (state-centrism), as it involves the commitment to the state as the only legitimate framework for political economy.[57] With regard to the argument of this chapter, the nature and limitations of this statism are best understood in relation to the way in which the joining together of economics and IR in the concept and issue of economic security has been theorized by orthodox IPE.

Economic Security

The consideration of the economic in the theory and practice of security, and security in the theory and practice of political economy, has taken place on the basis of prevailing discourses in economics, political science, political economy, and international political economy. As we have seen, these discourses not only embody deep commitments to specific (orthodox) methodology, epistemology, and ontology; they also construct both economics and politics, and the relationship between them, in very particular ways. This seems to have led to the possibility of a twin track for investigations into security by political economy and into economics by security. One track starts with politics (the traditional concerns of security) but with economic added on as a new domain of threat to states. The other track starts with a (repoliticized) economics, leading to a whole literature on economic security, vulnerability, and systemic risk (with particular reference to the global financial system). But the way that the economic is then related to the political (and vice versa) seems to depend upon prior ideological commitments as to the nature of the relationship between economics and politics, normally expressed in paradigmatic terms of perspectives or contesting approaches. For instance, a liberal interpretation of economic security is conditioned by the prior assumption of the link between economic prosperity and war based on the assumed beneficial rationality of markets.

In this sense, economic security as a concept and as an issue has been clearly constructed as an extension of statist, positivist IPE, which brings together the twin tracks by grafting the agenda of economics onto the classic concerns of state security via neorealism. Of course, the tradition of mercantilist thinking, or economic nationalism, as Robert Gilpin prefers to describe it, clearly locks economic security into physical security—but on, and only on, a state basis. In this tradition, power and wealth, and hence national security, are inseparable and complementary, particularly in what are regarded as strategic industries, that is, those industries whose healthy development is considered necessary for the maintenance of national military-political security.[58] Notwithstanding the mercantilist imperative for both states and theorists, the post-1945 international economic structure emerged as a U.S. hegemony that was articulated and developed on the public basis of a liberal trade and investment order with a constituting, rationalizing, and legitimating ideology of liberal political economy. Hence, for twenty years after IR and economics were theoretically linked in mainstream academic practice, it was only to the extent that a strong, broad-based modern economy was regarded as necessary to maintain security.

However, the early intimations of the failure of U.S. policy to keep apart the Bretton Woods institutional twin-track system set up after World War II—separating international politics (as politics) and international economics (as technical management)—manifested themselves in the problems of the dollar and U.S. payments in the late 1960s. The unwillingness of the United States to tolerate a massive outflow of dollars forced a reconnection at the policy level of politics and economics, and this led to an upswing of interest in the international politics of economic conflict. The possibility of trade wars was mooted.[59] But the real spur to the study of what became labeled "economic security" came with action by the Organization of Petroleum Exporting Countries (OPEC) in 1973 and the resultant oil-supply threats and related price shocks for the international economic system.[60] The changing structure of the international political economy at that time, with the move to floating exchange rates and the rediscovery by the West (and the South) of economic vulnerability, brought forth a large number of studies on the issue and problems of economic security.[61]

The studies of economic security stemming from the crises of the 1970s defined their focus principally in terms of the interests of the state. Equally significant, their definition of economics prioritized issues of trade and trade relations and tended to ignore other potentially significant elements. This meant that deep structures of international political economy—finance, production, and knowledge[62]—and the changing international division of labor (and its implications) were not seen as part of this conception of economic security. In effect, IPE and IR (including that branch conceiving itself as security studies) meekly adopted the agenda of U.S. policy economists. After all, from the perspective of this approach, what matters when all states have adopted the goal of long-term economic growth are threats to the economic security of the state, and the territorial economy of the state, in terms of the ability of the state to deliver on its claimed economic goals. Such is particularly the case when this ability is made vulnerable by an apparent change in trade relationships or is made more sensitive to the problems of deepening economic interdependence.

In his attempt to provide an overview of the changing system that explicitly linked security and economics, Richard Rosecrance tried to reflect this new reality by explicitly linking the goal of economic growth to patterns of state behavior, with states choosing between trading or territorial expansion as means of enhancing their power and security.[63] However, most international political economists have maintained the narrower focus on economic security. They theorize the conditions of interdependence in more structural ways and take account of specific domestic factors and industries.[64] But the problem for a critical political economy is that the international political economy of economic security remains steadfastly statist.[65] Current manifestations of concern about economic security focus on high-technology industries (microchips, computers, civil aircraft manufacturing, etc.), the exemplars of twenty-first-century national strategic manufacturing and knowledge-based systems engineering.[66] The state focus remains despite the questions posed by those who have tried to analyze the underlying nonnational structure of contemporary economic forces.[67]

To restate the basis of the argument: it is not that *national* economic security, however defined, does not matter; it clearly does, but it is that a *sole* focus on national economic security, theorized only through positivist methodology and where the economic is defined in the way it is by orthodox IPE, is *too narrow, claims too much, and is increasingly partial and inappropriate.* An exemplar of this weakness is the otherwise excellent analysis of economic security and the problem of cooperation in post–Cold War Europe by Jonathan Sperling and Emile Kirchner.[68] This is an important article, both for security studies and IPE, as it argues for a redefinition of security in that "the European security system has two mutually constitutive elements, the political-military and the economic."[69] This achieves (in my view) the necessary elevation of economic matters above the secondary level afforded by most analyses of security *and* makes the link between security and political economy equally important; this link is all too often ignored by mainstream IPE outside the specific focus on economic security. The article offers a powerful argument showing the mutually constitutive structures and processes that together may bring about comprehensive security in Europe. Yet despite discussing societal security in a spatial political economy that is more integrated than within many states, and despite the extensive discussion of European institutions, this argument still relies on a statist ontology. This limits its epistemological and political constructivism to the activities of states and state-based institutions. Here, in effect, politics is defined as what is done by governments, agents of states, or those involved in formal political structures and roles. But are agents of European states the only institutions relevant to comprehensive security? Do the large corporations and banks (e.g., Shell, Volkswagen, Credit Suisse) or mass social movements (e.g. antiglobalization, antinuclear, environmentalist) have no relevant power in Europe? Does the European economy exist in isolation of the world market economy? One would think so from this analysis. In holding this position, Sperling and Kirchner maintain a particular conceptualization of both politics and economics but inadvertently contradict their own assertions through the assumed definitions and predefined relationships that they (and all orthodox IPE) import into their political economy from the discipline of economics.

Quite simply, the approach of Sperling and Kirchner shares with orthodox IPE the characteristic of importing into political economy a particular theorization of economics that has major consequences for our ability to understand political economy. Economics is analyzed as a purely rational activity to which a technical solution is possible, that is, economics is accepted as defined by and for economists. The analysis of the guns-versus-butter issue by Sperling and Kirchner, for example, employs a resolutely rationalistic and economistic argument, which seems to specify the problem in order to make it amenable to rational analysis. I would argue that the move to butter—social welfare—is the product of much more complex forces than they identify.[70] Moreover, note the argument that "until transition (to stability) is completed and consolidated, issues of political economy must be treated as elements of the new security order *rather than as simple issues of welfare maximization.*"[71] Does the achievement of stability really mean that issues of political economy are magically depoliticized and/or stripped of their power content, to make them amenable to technical rational economic resolution? Can, for example, the support for agriculture, which directly affects the price of food, be defined as a simple issue of welfare maximization when it is clearly and necessarily a concern of the democratic polity? It can, but only if one understands how simple issues of welfare maximization are treated in economics and if we accept the argument of Sperling and Kirchner.

The move to link security, politics, and economics is desirable and important. Most of the practitioners of orthodox IPE, however, have accepted a predefined notion of what constitutes economics and what the social role of economics is and should be. This notion is, it must be stressed, *absolutely politically defined*, in the sense *that it acts as an authoritative allocator of value*, and it *reflects and influences who gets what, when, where, and how*, and is therefore clearly *not neutral, not natural, and not outside of the realm of power*. This might be a common-sense definition or view of economics, but common sense is constructed.[72] Essentially, the view of economics imported from the economics profession—both the corporate and academic worlds—is largely neoliberal. This means that economics is separated from politics and is regarded as a rational, self-serving activity with economic issues amenable to technical resolution, whereas politics is regarded as both residual and irrational, in the sense that the intervention of politics prevents the efficient operation of the market. However, Enrico Augelli and Craig Murphy[73] in their discussion of Gramsci's notion of civil society provide the basis to suggest that such a conception of economics reinforces the distinction between two worlds of power constructed by different social processes: the world of force (realist states in a condition of anarchy), and the world of consensus (transnational social relations and economic cooperation). Such a position makes the articulation of an international political economy of security highly problematic because the conceptions of economics and politics used are contentious and contradictory, and the contention cannot be resolved by merely reframing the problem as one of "competing perspectives" (paradigmatism) in which either politics determines economics or economics determines politics. Nor can it be resolved by the otherwise reasonable assertion about the "mutually constitutive" meaning and practices of both spheres.

Politics, Economics, and Security

The third and final strand of the argument of this chapter is that the achievement of security, as defined by CSS, will ultimately demand the integration of political economy into the theory and practice of security, community, and emancipation. As suggested earlier, in the practice of disciplinary knowledge within IPE this proposed integration challenges: first, the existing theorizations of politics, economics, and international political economy; and second, the various ways in which politics and economics are first separated and then related to each other by and within these theories.

The foundations of this strand of the argument are laid in the critique of conventional security studies mounted by CSS itself; it is also evident in the critique of orthodox IPE that has begun but has yet to be fully articulated.[74] The core elements of this critique are that a primarily U.S.-centered, statist IPE privileges a particular, fundamentalist, and ahistorical conceptualization of the structure of the world political economy and that the explication of this structure offered by the mainstream is not sufficient to produce any real understanding of the political economy it purports to address. This orthodox IPE is both made possible by and uses instrumentally an empiricist epistemology that in buttressing its limited understanding fails to take account of any form of the intersubjective construction and understanding of world political economy. This means that it can never capture or understand the power of institutionalized ideas, such as the view of the world political economy put forward and supported by the World Bank. Because people behave as if the World Bank view is real and right, it has enormous power. Moreover—and crucially—the orthodox combination of ontology and epistemology is not fortuitous or accidental; as Robert Cox points out, "positivism is less well adapted to inquiry into complex and comprehensive change."[75] As such, positivism is perfectly suited to supporting and explicating an ontology that argues for the fundamental continuity of an IPE based solely on states.[76] If (as in the case in IPE) ontology provides for a fixed and historically continuous framework, then a problem-solving theory based in positivism is perfectly adequate, but for most purposes a critical approach would find such problem-solving theory inappropriate and inadequate. Finally, the practice of orthodox IPE reproduces by way of discourse both a specific conception of politics *and* a specific imported conception of economics. Each of these conceptions resists the integration of politics and economics that is necessary if a real understanding of security is to be achieved.

The statist nature of orthodox IPE is one of the major constraints in working toward an international political economy in which security is an integral factor. This is not only because statist IPE seems to preclude the kind of security that CSS envisages, and often works directly against emancipation, but also because statist orthodox IPE contains and reproduces an ahistorical universalized conception of politics in which politics is forever embedded in and contained by the state and its territorial trap.[77] Hence the ontological underpinnings of statist IPE privileges a particular universe of structure and process and, within this universe, a very specific politically and historically defined conception of politics. This conception is one in which there is an identity between state and politics that is reflected in the meaning of the political concepts we use, such as authority—the meaning of which is embedded firmly in a practice of state politics.[78] Unless and until we can redefine our understanding of the nature of politics to be more than simply state-based and referenced, we are stuck with language and concepts, including notions of authority and security, that constantly help to reproduce the situation that we are hoping to change. As Susan Strange has forcefully argued, politics is "no longer confined to the state, to the functioning of government by states."[79] She asks: "Why should we imagine that states are the only institutions which exercise authority over others in setting not only rules but norms and customary procedures?"[80]

Turning to the problem of the conceptualization of economics, we find even greater resistance to an integrated political economy than in traditional political analysis and hence great resistance to an integrated theory and practice of security. This is because a specific notion of economics has become hegemonic, especially since the 1970s. Among critical theorists, Richard Ashley has done most to identify the problematics of knowledge and the consequences of economism for real political agency.[81] For Ashley the move from classical political realism to IR's neorealism was the formal manifestation of a powerful and relentless economism, expressed under and through the same conditions that in orthodox IPE gave rise to the concern with economic security. In Ashley's words:

> The "given" order, including the separation of political and economic spheres, was no longer self-evident. In matters of resource vulnerability and petroleum embargoes, monetary crises and worldwide recession, economic processes and relations no longer seemed independent of political interventions. . . . Suddenly, the ever-so-commonsensical realist depiction of international politics in terms of an autonomous power-political logic lost its magic.[82]

The resulting theorization was the statism of neorealism, embedded within which is a logic of economy and technical rationality.

Ashley's work helps us to understand the deep relationship between

politics and economics laid down within and prefigured by a statist, orthodox IPE framed by neorealism. This is an important critical uncovering of
hidden theoretical assumptions. Yet as important as Ashley's insights are,
perhaps they do not go far enough. My sense is that the fundamental basis
of this economism *is already laid down*, not in the theories of IR and IPE
but in the construction of a hegemony of legitimate knowledge driven by
the emergence of economics as a sphere of human activity and the market
as its institutionalized form within the overall development of capitalism.

The emergence of a realm of human economic activity that required
and requires a special knowledge of economics in order for it to be made
sense of within society is the province of capitalism.[83] The rise and consolidation of capitalism is one, moreover, with which the fields of IR and security studies had and have a very ambivalent and troublesome relationship,
particularly given the primacy of politics that is embedded in both fields.
To assert the primacy of politics, as we saw in the discussion of politics and
economics in the last section, presupposes not only the ontological separation of the interstate political system and "a highly integrated, incompletely
regulated, rapidly growing . . . world economy"[84] but also the prior separation of politics and economics as distinct spheres of activity. This separation is a necessary and integral part of the process of the construction of
self-regulating markets in the dynamics of capitalist growth.[85] As Karl
Polanyi has pointed out,

> A self-regulating market demands nothing less than the institutional sepa-
> ration of society into an economic and political sphere. Such a dichotomy
> is, in effect, merely the restatement, from the point of view of society as a
> whole, of the existence of a self-regulating market. It might be argued that
> the separateness of the two spheres obtains in every type of society at all
> times. Such an inference would be based on a fallacy.[86]

Polanyi then shows how the existence of a separate economic system is
a specific and historically distinct creation of nineteenth-century English
capitalism and indeed is a political creation, "the outcome of a conscious
and often violent intervention on the part of governments which imposed
the market organization on society *for noneconomic ends*."[87] The construction of the market and its corollary, the separation of economics from politics, is thus political.

If the construction of an economics separate from politics and society
is itself a political act and remains a political act in that economic structures and processes serve particular interests, it is highly problematic when,
as Polanyi calls it, the economic sphere comes to be in turn constructed and
justified as neutral, as nonpolitical, and as natural, above politics. The historical processes by and through which the construction of such a depoliticized political economy has occurred are complex. They link directly to the

professionalization of knowledge,[88] to the political triumph of a specific and partial view of human rationality at the beginning of the twentieth century,[89] and to the ability of those with wealth to wield the power to reproduce and enhance those structures that guaranteed and enhanced that wealth. Suffice to say that the thirty-year hegemony of neoliberalism in the world political economy has constructed the economic sphere in such a way as to claim that a neoliberal economic way of organizing society within its scale of values is natural, inevitable, neutral, and rational, with no indication of the inherently and structurally political nature of economics itself. In other words, the claim that economics is nonpolitical is a political claim.

Conclusion

The maintenance of claims to political neutrality or to having a value outside of, above, or beyond politics is a core problem for the development of an integrated theory of the international political economy of security. Today the hegemony of a socialized economics is still intact. Although initially challenged by responses to the crisis of 1997, and by the meltdown of world stock markets, it was reestablished under the smokescreen of the war on terror. But even these responses in the main used the same understandings of politics and economics that have been constructed to ensure the hegemony of economism. This is clearly demonstrated in the practices of mainstream IPE, particularly in its focus on economic security. Movement toward a real security based in human emancipation is intimately bound up with our ability to retheorize an international political economy not dependent upon concepts defined by the hegemony of economism and not derived from our mute acceptance of the universality of the separation of economics and politics.

The struggle to break away from this dominant understanding is, of course, a political struggle. Within this, academic analysis can form the basis of a new understanding, through what Bourdieu calls "the power of theory,"[90] but it cannot create this understanding. Within the political economy of our everyday life we as human beings and as citizens are all presented with the evidence of the unity of security, polity, and economy. Have we as academics so forgotten the objective conditions that make possible our scholarly activities that the majority of us (in the field of IPE, at least) do not even inquire into the possibilities of a theoretical understanding of our *own* political economy? For the adherents of conventional social science, the answer is simply yes.

Although the argument of this chapter has been that joining politics and economics is necessary for the real achievement of security and that this can *only* be done through a *critical* articulation of the field of international political economy, what underpins this possibility, and equally underpins the whole project of critical security studies, is the understanding provided by a reflexive theory of the political economy of knowledge.

Notes

1. This chapter draws heavily on the arguments developed over many years working in IPE, particularly with Craig Murphy. I would like to thank him and many other colleagues for their interest and contributions. I would also like to thank Ken Booth for his encouragement and support over this chapter.

2. Tooze and Murphy, "Epistemology of Poverty."

3. Gilpin, *Political Economy*.

4. See Cox, "Post-Hegemonic Conceptualization," p. 132.

5. Augelli and Murphy, *America's Quest*; Murphy and Tooze, *New International Political Economy*.

6. Murphy and Tooze, *New International Political Economy*; Bourdieu, *Outline*; Bourdieu, *Acts of Resistance*; Bourdieu, *Practical Reason*.

7. Bourdieu, *Outline*, pp. 168–169.

8. Ibid., p. 166.

9. Booth, "Security and Emancipation"; Bilgin, Booth, and Wyn Jones, "Security Studies"; Krause and Williams (eds.), *Critical Security Studies*.

10. This is the core argument made by Burke in "Security and Antipodean Echoes." I am grateful to him for his thoughts on this and other philosophical points.

11. Burke, "Security and Antipodean Echoes," p. 7.

12. Foucault, "Governmentality," in Burchell, et al. (eds.), *The Foucault Effect*.

13. Polanyi, *Great Transformation*.

14. Ibid.

15. Chatterjee, "Response to Taylor," pp. 129–131, emphasis added.

16. Ibid.

17. Elliot and Atkinson, *Age of Insecurity*; Mander and Goldsmith (eds.), *The Case Against the Global Economy*.

18. Sassen, "Globalization of Denationalization."

19. Bourdieu, *Acts of Resistance*, p. 11; Bourdieu, *Practical Reason*, p. 11.

20. Bourdieu, *Acts of Resistance*, p. 137; Bourdieu, *Practical Reason*, p. 137, emphasis in original.

21. Booth, "Security and Emancipation."

22. Johnson, *Blowback*.

23. Stiglitz, *Globalization and Its Discontents*.

24. This has been well documented by various World Bank Reports on an international basis, but see also the eye-opening figures in Korten, *When Corporations Rule the World*.

25. Elliot and Atkinson, *Age of Insecurity*, p. 223.

26. Cox, "Social Forces."

27. For some helpful remarks on this problem, see Robert Cox's comments on the problems of theory in "an era of structural change" in Cox, "Post-Hegemonic Conceptualization," pp. 132–146.

28. Cox, *Approaches to World Order*.

29. Cox, "Social Forces"; Cox, *Approaches to World Order*.

30. Volcker, "Can We Bounce Back?" *Financial Times*, October 7, 1998, p. 18, emphasis added.

31. Buzan, *People, States, and Fear*.

32. Ibid., pp. 235–236.

33. Elliott and Atkinson, *Age of Insecurity*.

34. Korten, "Your Mortal Enemy."

35. Latham, "Thinking About Security After the Cold War."

36. See also Ashley, "Three Modes"; Gill, *American Hegemony and the Trilateral Commission*; Gill (ed.), *Gramsci, Historical Materialism and International Relations*.

37. Hirst and Thompson, *Globalization in Question*; Mittelman (ed.), *Globalization*.

38. Tooze, "International Political Economy"; Tooze, "Unwritten Preface."

39. Cox, "Social Forces"; Tooze, "Unwritten Preface"; Tooze and Murphy, "Epistemology of Poverty"; Burch and Denemark, *Constituting*; Bilgin, Booth, and Wyn Jones, "Security Studies"; Ruggie, *Constructing the World Polity*.

40. Krasner, *National Interest*; Krasner, "Accomplishments."

41. Soros, "The Capitalist Threat."

42. Elliott and Atkinson, *Age of Insecurity*, p. 122.

43. Albelda, et al. (eds.), *Alternatives to Economic Orthodoxy*; Ormerod, *The Death of Economics*; Heilbroner and Milberg, *Crisis of Vision in Modern Economic Thought*; Lawson, *Economics and Reality*.

44. See, for example, Strange, "Beyond Economics."

45. Strange, "Towards a Theory of Transnational Empire," in Czempiel and Rosenau (eds.), *Global Changes and Theoretical Challenges*; Agnew and Corbridge, *Mastering Space*; Corbridge, Martin, and Thrift, *Money, Power and Space*.

46. Castells, *End of Millennium*, p. 1.

47. Chatterjee, "Response to Taylor."

48. Gallagher, *The Power of Place*.

49. Murphy and Tooze, *New International Political Economy*; Strange, "Beyond Economics"; Higgott, "International Political Economy," in Groom and Light (eds.), *Contemporary International Relations*.

50. Strange, "International Economics and International Relations."

51. Perkin, *Third Revolution*.

52. Tooze, "Unwritten Preface."

53. Murphy and Tooze, *New International Political Economy*.

54. Ibid.; Tooze and Murphy, "Epistemology of Poverty"; Burch and Denemark, *Constituting*.

55. Spero, *The Politics of International Economic Relations*.

56. Augelli and Murphy, *America's Quest*; Ashley, "Poverty of Neorealism."

57. Krasner, *National Interest*; Krasner, "Abiding Discord"; Krasner, "Accomplishments"; Strange, "Wake Up"; Strange, *The Retreat of the State*.

58. Viner, *The Long View and the Short*; Knorr, *Power and Wealth*; Gilpin, *Political Economy*.

59. For example, Malmgren, "Coming Trade Wars."

60. Among many others, see Cooper, "Security and the Energy Crisis"; Nye, "Collective Economic Security."

61. For example, Knorr and Trager (eds.), *Economic Issues and National Security*; Alting von Geusau and Pelkmans (eds.), *National Economic Security*.

62. Strange, "Beyond Economics."

63. Rosecrance, *The Rise of the Trading State*.

64. Moran, "The Globalization of America's Defense Industries"; Kapstein, *The Political Economy of National Security*.

65. Crawford, *Economic Vulnerability in International Relations*. In an otherwise exemplary discussion by Crawford, there is no questioning of the assumed identity of state interests with citizen interests, or of the possibility that the economic vulnerability of individuals or collectivities may be increased by the same state policy that brings "security" at the state level.

66. Tyson, *Who's Bashing Whom? Trade Conflicts in High Technology Industries*; Ostry and Nelson, *Techno-Nationalism and Techno-Globalism*.

67. Reich, *The Work of Nations*.

68. Sperling and Kirchner, "Economic Security."

69. Ibid., p. 222.

70. Elliott and Atkinson, *Age of Insecurity*.

71. Ibid., p. 222, emphasis added.

72. Augelli and Murphy, *America's Quest*.

73. Ibid.

74. See, for example, the two very different but equally critical articles: Crystal, "The Politics of Capital Flight" and Hills, "Dependency Theory and Its Relevance Today.

75. Cox, "Post-Hegemonic Conceptualization."

76. See, for example, Krasner, "Abiding Discord."

77. Agnew and Corbridge, *Masterning Space*, pp. 78–100.

78. Strange, *The Retreat of the State*; Strange, "Beyond Economics."

79. Strange, "Beyond Economics," p. 19.

80. Strange, *The Retreat of the State*; p. 32.

81. Amongst others, Ashley, "Three Modes"; Ashley, "Poverty of Neorealism"; and see Youngs, "From Realism." I am grateful to Gillian Youngs for sharing with me her interpretations of Richard Ashley's work.

82. Ashley, "Three Modes," p. 468, as quoted in Youngs, "From Realism," p. 92.

83. Heilbroner, *Twenty-First Century Capitalism*.

84. Strange, "Wake Up," p. 212.

85. Wood, "The Separation of the Economic and the Political in Capitalism."

86. Polanyi, *Great Transformation*, p. 71.

87. Ibid., p. 250, emphasis added.

88. Perkin, *Third Revolution*.

89. Augelli and Murphy, *America's Quest*.

90. Bourdieu, *Acts of Resistance*; Bourdieu, *Practical Reason*.

7

Questions of Identity: Australia and Asia

Jan Jindy Pettman

Security, and danger, have as much to do with who we are (seen to be) as where we live, or which state recognizes us as a citizen. To explore this proposition, this chapter locates itself at several intersections or disjunctions: first, between Australia and Asia; second, between Asia and the West; then between national security and identity and different political communities within states. These dis/connections are further complicated by the tension between statist and interstate constructions of security and identity, as well as globalizing processes propelling liberal marketization. An exploration of these problematics enables us to ask whose understandings of security are obscured or silenced by dominant representations of state and region and whose evidence we might seek out to inform this interrogation of the relations between community, identity, and security.

The Problem

Conventional security studies invests in the idea of state security, which often translates as elite security. State elites seek to legitimize their own power and interests by claiming to be representative of, or defenders of, the community. They mobilize particular understandings of the people, the nation, of culture, of national identity; and seek to suppress other imaginings of community. Attempts to broaden notions of security, or to reconfigure its referent, for example as people, individuals, or humankind, are crucial political moves. They unsettle the state-security assumption and make a space in which it is possible to see the state itself, in particular the militarized agents charged with its protection, as the primary threat to many people's security. Any such critique of statist security needs to ask who is included within a state's community and who is excluded; to interrogate the ways in which community is imagined in relation to others. Identity is constructed through difference, along boundaries of inclusion and exclusion.

These boundaries can become the limit of the moral community, beyond which violence and other deadly practices are ignored or sanctioned.

Recent writings on collective political identities such as nation, ethnicity, and race insist that these are imagined communities and that they are discursively constructed through histories and stories about who we are and who is not us. These writings draw attention to the constitutive effects of mapping, naming, and imagining our community, the nation, our world, the region, and to the processes whereby identity is constructed through difference: insiders and outsiders, Us and Them. Identity-making is thus boundary-making, determining, through contests located within specific relations of power, both where the boundary lies and what criteria are used to identify people within and outside that boundary. Thus identity and difference—boundaries of belonging—are not natural, inevitable, or fixed, though it is part of the politics of identity to make them appear so. Identities are the product of struggle. Political identities like nation, race, or ethnicity are practices of power and sites of contestation and resistance.

The realist-speak of conventional international relations (IR) and security studies (SS) homogenizes states, by disguising or disregarding differences within them, as well as by assuming that the category of states is composed of (more or less successful, or powerful) things of the same order. Issues to do with identity and culture have been neglected,[1] despite the enormous political work that goes into the construction and deployment of international identities like the West, the third world, and Asia. Such identities guide state practices and have real material effects. On closer examination, it becomes evident that they are racialized and bear the traces of the vast, and violent, processes of colonization and decolonization. It seems all the more strange, then, that IR/SS have maintained silences around colonization, anticolonialism, and postcoloniality. They routinely deploy but rarely interrogate racialized international identities. Yet an awareness of the constructions of international difference is intrinsic to any understanding of national identity, security, and danger.

Australia and Asia

In the 1980s and early 1990s especially, Australian foreign policymakers and opinion leaders directed considerable energy and imaginative geopolitical work into redefining Australia's relations with Asia.[2] Engagement with Asia was viewed as essential for Australia's security and well-being—though the 1997 economic crash and consequent uncertainty regarding the Asian miracle has unsettled this claim.

Australia was originally conceived as a distant prison and British Empire lookout. Settler interests were consolidated through the rapidly increasing population from the gold rushes of the 1850s and through nativist (meaning European Australian-born) and nationalist movements of the late nineteenth century. This led to federation in 1901. As a settler state, Australian national identity was problematic and ambiguous, set against both Britain, as mother country, and against indigenous people, whose prior claim to occupation and belonging had to be erased, and forgotten, to make space for the new Australian nation.[3] This nation was cast as European, indeed British, and (so) as white. While relations with Britain were ambivalent—there were both monarchist and republican tendencies at work—most Australians accepted their belonging within an imperial frame. Australia actively participated in many empire wars, notably in World War I, whose disastrous Gallipoli campaign is still celebrated as "the birth of the nation."[4]

The cultural and racialized associations of the new nation were, then, with places and people far away. This set up the recurring history-versus-geography tension frequently observed in academic and popular commentaries on Australian nationalism. It also meant that Australian national identity was constructed, from the beginning, against Asia.[5] The first act of the new Australian parliament was what became known as the White Australia Policy, consolidating earlier and separate colonial legislation directed especially against Chinese immigrants. This policy instituted a racially and culturally exclusivist immigration policy to keep the nation white, preferably British. The racialization of the nation meant that immigration was always seen as intimately related to national identity and security. (This connection is evident in Western European states as migrant laborers often from former colonies are used to fuel reactive nationalisms and closure against strangers.) So, too, European colonization of most parts of Asia, and imperial domination of those who escaped "geographic captivity,"[6] were understood to enhance Australia's security by providing a buffer between Australia and the racialized, culturalized Other, namely, the endlessly substitutable and recurringly threatening Asia.[7] Japan's military successes in the early years of World War II, especially the fall of Singapore and consequent collapse of British power in the region, were registered as a profound security shock.

This trauma has been replayed since through frequent national remembrances and anniversaries, for example, in the recalling of the brutal treatment of Australians by Japanese military on the Thai-Burma railway. Such rememberings can become complicit with racialized understandings of difference equated with savagery and violence and of Australia's Asian neighbors as embodiments of this difference.

Australian policymakers opted briefly for liberal internationalism in the immediate postwar period, but the advent of the Cold War and of a conservative Australian government in 1949 saw a return to traditional, statist, and power-political understandings of national security. Britain's retreat from the region and decolonization in Asia coincided with the rising specter of communism. The search for another great and powerful friend to stand between Us and Them quickly bound Australian defense and foreign policy to the U.S. military alliance, which in turn consolidated Australian national identity as white and Western. It also prompted forward defense—to fight them there, before they could get here. Australia was the first ally to join the United States in the Korean War and introduced selective conscription to support the United States in the Vietnam War. That debacle and the subsequent 1969 Guam doctrine confirmed what many feared—that the United States might not necessarily continue to act as regional security guarantor for Australia. Thus Australian governments were faced with the necessity to deal directly with Asia.

At the same time, progressive social movements and new identity contests arose at home. These different politics ushered in moves to deracialize immigration and citizenship policy. The social democratic Labour government under Gough Whitlam, elected in 1972, recognized limited indigenous rights and claims and declared Australia a multicultural society—though there was little agreement about what that might mean. The subsequent Conservative government under Malcolm Fraser from 1975 softened but did not reject these moves. All the major political parties stressed the need for a more inclusive national identity, in part to prove to Asia that we had indeed changed, as well as to gain some distance from the racist discrimination and exclusions that had humiliated and angered many Asian state leaders.[8] Increasing immigration from Asian states, including significant numbers of Vietnamese refugees, was offered as evidence of closer relations with Asia. The irony of so many Asian Australians coming to Australia to escape precisely those governments or cultures that Australian leaders sought to impress appears to have been overlooked.

Recasting Australia's national identity was seen as a precondition for acceptance into the region's fora and collaboration;[9] being accepted was felt necessary to further both military security and trade interests. So in the 1990s, Labour prime minister Paul Keating pursued his (Irish background) republicanism as a means of demonstrating to the region that Australia had indeed grown up and left home and was no longer tied to the maternal—imperial—apron strings.[10] But the strangeness of the attempt to become accepted by Asia led to some peculiar identity contortions. So in 1991 Labour foreign minister Gareth Evans informed a Tokyo audience of Australia's aim to move from being odd man out in Asia to odd man in.[11]

Cultivating links with Asia became doubly urgent as globalization proceeded apace. In the late 1980s through the 1990s, the Australian government adopted neoliberal policies that aimed to increase its international competitiveness. The consequent opening up of the economy, the deregulation of banking and financing, and the reduction of protective tariffs made

Australia increasingly vulnerable to the whims and fancies of global capital. In the meantime, the celebrated Asian miracle joined the longer-established Japanese exceptionalism on the global stage. East Asian states (South Korea, Taiwan, Hong Kong, and Singapore by association) were identified as global growth centers. Then some Southeast Asian states—Thailand, Malaysia, and Indonesia—also experienced rapid growth and were given International Monetary Fund (IMF) and other global capital agents' approval.[12] Australia could not afford to be excluded from these centers of growth and trade.

Australian views of Asia were subsequently forced to change. Having been long seen by many as inferior, as disorderly and threatening to security, Asian states appeared quite suddenly to be thriving in a global political economy that was providing many Australians with severe and painful challenges. One commentator represented these changing relations as moving Australia from the role of "elder brother" to "little brother struggling to catch up." According to Gabriel Lafitte,

> If the classic orientalist imagery of Asia was decidedly feminine in its confessions of receptiveness, passivity, mystery, treachery and unpredictability, the new image is decidedly masculinist. The new Asian tigers are rising fast, unshackled by maternal environmental or labor laws, thrusting into new markets. The secret of their success is that their leaders . . . work as a phalanx, united in brotherhood against the world.[13]

Such representational shifts modernize but do not supersede Orientalism. The use of gendered language signals changing power relations and prevailing assumptions about connections between dominance and having what it takes to succeed in international politics. Gendered discourse marks challenges and changes in Asian-West relations, for different masculinities also mark hierarchies among different men.[14] These gendered constructions feed resentments and anxieties that suggest that even more than military security and economic well-being are at stake. Loss of national status in regional and global politics could also threaten national demasculinization in international, and racialized, identity politics.

Recasting national identity always involves rethinking national security, too. Official declarations on security through the 1990s stressed its new agenda. These declarations sought to ensure a place for Australia in the new global configuration of wealth-making and consumption. They also sought to guard against environmental degradation and refugee or other perceived threats to Australian borders and lifestyles. These have often been add-ons or cautions attached to primary interests, along with the need to redefine identity and security to include economic interests. During this period, the locus of foreign policy and security policy pronouncement shifted from the Department of Defence toward the Department of Foreign Affairs and

Trade, from a classic military-security focus to a market-driven focus.[15] Australia had to be remade, in new nationalist strength and energy and intelligence, equipped to stand alone and unprotected by either foreign ally or national protectionism (even while maintaining controls against the movement of people, as against movement of capital), to compete against and forge collaborative ventures with the rest of the world—especially the growth centers in Asia.

But many Australians, especially those associated with defense interests, continued to think in terms of military threats and invasion, possibly reflecting the shadow memories of an Australia already forcibly seized from its indigenous inhabitants.[16] So too the new agenda revealed more continuity than break with more conventional attachments to security. The dominant application of direct realism in Australian official discourses suggests a self-evident "world out there."[17] David Sullivan notes continuities in official and much academic discourse on Australia's defense and security policies, finding in the 1994 *Defending Australia* White Paper, for example, "an extremely narrow definition of security."[18] He suggests that the addition of new agenda issues represented "at best a tactical shift." States, nations, and peoples are articulated as pregiven identities, and the discourse is constructed in terms of order, stability, and economic miracles, though possible dangers and threats can be associated with the region as well. There are token inclusions in such discourses, but there is no critical questioning of either the notion of security or the politics of identity that lie behind such conventional security narratives. According to Sullivan,

> When the Australian security community's discursive representations of post–Cold War Asia-Pacific security are analyzed, orthodox security studies and politics . . . are seen to encode powerful political representations that discipline subjects, normalize state violence, and champion "order," "stability" and "cooperation." . . . Regional security literature, in particular, functions to marginalize and delegitimizes non-state, non-military, non-elite issue. Identity, gender, representation—these are three overlapping sites of critical investigation excluded from academic and policy agendas set in place by Australia's professionalized security community.[19]

Nevertheless, changes in the relations between Australia and its regional neighbors, even when each side is understood as an unproblematic or fixed entity, can cause anxiety. Attempts to engage with Asia, and so relocate Australia in the imaginative geography of Asia,[20] challenge particular constructions of national identity. Many Australians' resistance to this relocation lies, in part at least, in the discomfort and insecurity that accompany such dramatic changes, in particular the perceived reversal in power relations between Australia and Asia during the celebrated Asian miracle. This resistance reflects deeply embedded notions of security as zero-sum relations, tied to power in terms of dominance. These notions generated fear that Australia's dependence on booming Asian economies is constructing it as an appendage to Asia or as "a bit on the side."[21]

The feelings of insecurity generated by Australia's engagement with Asia come from deep within the perceived disjunction between, or presumed incompatibility of, what it is to be Australian and to be Asian. These identities reflect still powerful racialized and culturalized understandings of difference and of the incommensurate and threatening nature of national difference. These understandings feed into conventional notions of security and of the obligation of the state to defend its people against outsiders. These notions prevail despite the fact that Asia is already in Australia, in the bodies of many Australian residents and citizens of Asian background.[22]

The ongoing constitutive power of identities constructed through binaries is clearly demonstrated in the emergence in 1996 of the tellingly titled One Nation Party, Australia's own belated version of new-right, protectionist, and racist parties better known in Britain, France, and Germany.[23] The party's appeal was partly explained as a familiar reaction to the pain and confusion of economic restructuring and the consequent undermining of state provision and support. Not coincidently, One Nation sought to restore protective tariff barriers, restore national control over banking and finance, and to regulate and severely restrict foreign investment. It also sought to end immigration, with occasional qualifications.[24]

By the 2001 election, One Nation was waning, undermined by the Conservative Howard government's abandonment of a model of inclusive and engaged Australia, in preference for home defense against refugees, migrants, and indigenous claims and military adventures abroad. A remilitarization of Australia's foreign policy through the East Timor crisis propelled national security to center stage once more. Australia led an international peace enforcement operation following the deadly violence and militia revenge that met East Timor's August 1999 vote for independence. The rhetoric was not however of a collaborative peace initiative but rather a celebration of militarism and of recovered masculinity.[25] At one stage, Prime Minister John Howard suggested a role for Australia in Asia as deputy sheriff to the United States. Then September 11, 2001, witnessed a further reversion, as the Australian government immediately committed military support to the United States without undertaking consultation with Asian neighbors, including the world's largest Muslim nation, Indonesia.

Shortly before September 11, the Australian government, facing an election, adopted the twin priorities of productive (read neoliberal) economy and national (read military) security. It ruthlessly exploited perceived threats to security as border transgressions and the danger of difference.[26] It moved the navy to prevent the landing of refugee boats on Australian soil. Ironically, those boats carried mostly Iraqi and Afghani asylum-seekers, fleeing the very governments that were identified as our enemy, too. Popular support for these moves underlined the extent to which immigration to Australia has been reracialized. Being anti-immigration was again coded as anti-Asian—and now as anti-Muslim, too. However, racism is denied, deflected into assertions of cultural difference and understandings of that difference as threatening our culture and identity. Once again, colonial and racialized constructions of difference are replayed through defensive reimaginings of who we are, of who can belong, and who threatens us.

Colonizing and Racializing

Opponents of a more multicultural or Asian-engaged Australia are able to tap into deep and abiding constructions of identity and difference that are still saturated with the power and imagination of Europe's colonial encounter with Asia.[27] Through this encounter, Asia was constructed as a bounded object, a cohesive identity. (While Asia is an older construction, Southeast Asia is a more recent military and strategic identity, growing out of World War II.) A separate and singular Asia, or Southeast Asia, is a fabrication.

Edward Said's *Orientalism* revealed ways in which the Orient was constructed through difference, and in which difference was utilized in colonial rule. Subsequent studies have interrogated the close links between imperial power, colonizing knowledge, and disciplining practices. Identities, like theories, are always constructed for someone and in someone's interest.[28] There are now complex and productive debates around the discursive construction of the Orient and its material effects, as well as of the complicity or subversion on the part of those orientalized.

In a familiar colonial ploy, the inferior races/peoples were both feminized (against the masculinism of the dominant colonial power) and infantilized (as children, or adolescents, in need of the strong hand of a responsible father).[29] In the process, colonizing women, and colonized women, were subsumed within their nation or race. When they did become visible, it was as symbols of their nation, markers of boundaries, and signifiers of difference.

Defending the boundaries of colonial power and privilege necessitated policing those boundaries against sexual transgressions or, more especially, from the claims to citizenship or colonial right by children of mixed liaisons. Colonial power made use of certain patriarchal ideas about women and sexuality to construct and police the boundaries.[30] Colonizing women were distinguished from colonized women according to a good woman–bad woman dichotomy, though colonized women could also be constructed as the innocent victim of colonized men, which appeared to justify colonial intervention to save them. Colonizing men had access to colonized women as part of the spoils of power, as long as those relations did not threaten the purity of the race. So, too, the honor of colonizing women had to be enforced to maintain their function as reproducer of the race. In the process, racialized boundaries were sexualized, infused with the erotics of power, replayed now through sex tourism, which reproduces colonialist and racist fantasies of pleasure and conquest.[31]

Anticolonial nationalist movements in Asia organized against colonial power and set out to build a nation to claim the state. Nationalism infuses political identities with meaning and passion. National humiliations and exclusions become the stuff of identity, demanding recompense or recovery.[32] Colonial occupation was articulated as such a humiliation, represented often as heterosexual rape: the nation was represented as a violated woman, whose national men must come to her rescue, to recover both her honor and their own masculinity. Women were deployed symbolically, both to mark difference and facilitate calls on national men to avenge women's/nation's honor. In the process, difference was asserted against the West and located in culture and family, those sites and relations that were less public and less conspicuously foreign-dominated. In the words of Gayatri Gopinath, "Women's bodies, then, become crucial to nationalist discourse in that they serve not only as the site of biological reproduction of national collectivities, but as the very embodiment of this nostalgically evoked communal past and tradition."[33]

In anticolonial and early independence times, nationalist movements constructed a nation that would both include and supersede more particular identities of language, religion, region, and caste. Once the state was won, its coercive and educative capacities were focused on consolidation and on nationalization of the populace. While taking very different forms in different states, state elites defined the nation and identified as its custodians. These definitions were gendered, and women and gender roles, asserted by states and in antistate movements, signaled different political projects. Within these contested politics, state elites were engaged in a double move against the continued domination of the West and against those within the state who contested the state's nation.

Reorientalizing, or East Versus West

Neglecting to consider experiences of colonization and imperialism can obscure both the legacy and force of anticolonial nationalism in Asian states and the deep desire to escape from the "abject status" of colonization.[34] It also facilitates the reproduction of older readings of difference and encourages complicity with new Orientalisms that replicate the boundary between Asia and the West, Them and Us. That Asians, too, participate in these reconstructions of Asia does not make these constructions politically innocent. It is useful to think of Orientalism as a language that can be used by those from outside and from within the Orient.[35]

Taking seriously the ongoing effects of colonization and decolonization on international identities and national identities can reveal that all of us are implicated in these politics. "Both 'we' and 'they' have been mutually reconstructed over four centuries of imperialist interaction."[36] The world is postcolonial now, and all of our national identities are contested within this frame. This does not mean that colonization has passed. While formal political occupation is now relatively rare, the region includes conspicuous examples of ongoing colonization, including of East Timor by Indonesia until 1999. In addition, many indigenous people see themselves as entrapped, still, within colonial relations. This is clearly evident in Australia, where ongoing conflicts over land rights and indigenous status reveal the unresolved and everyday legacy of colonialism.[37] As well, colonial histories are deeply implicated in a number of current ethnonationalist conflicts, for example, in Sri Lanka. There is nowhere, or more precisely no understanding of anywhere, that is not transformed by the experience of colonization and by resistance to it. Asia and the West have been engaged in a complex politics of mutual identity construction for many generations, though always located within asymmetrical power relations.

The prosperity and economic ascendancy that led to a growing cultural self-confidence among East and Southeast Asian elites through the 1980s and 1990s marked "a transformation, but not a cancellation, of the parameters of the discourse of the West versus the rest."[38] This transformation from a powerless, colonized Asia to an empowered Asia was often seen as threatening by outsiders. Particular Asian state identities were reconfigured in part through disassociation with the West, reproducing Asian difference through Asian values, or the Asian way. This neo-Orientalism has been played out through complex identity dynamics, as Asian elites and their friends, and bemused Western commentators, searched for the key to Asian success—finding it, often, in cultural values or distinctive relations between state and people and between state and market. These Asian values were posited as communitarian rather than individualist, building on family virtue and individual duty. So, for example, the Singapore government's statement "Shared Value"[39] expressed its fears that foreign (U.S./Western) values were threatening Singaporean community values. While distinguishing between different ethnic communities, the statement was especially concerned with distinguishing Asian values as community-oriented, laying the groundwork for articulating a kind of community corporatism that both legitimized authoritarian rule in the name of culture, stability, and order and supported state developmental strategies.[40]

The dramatic changes in East and Southeast Asia, and the cultural assertions of difference they generated, raised questions concerning the nature of Asian capitalism, that is, whether Asian authoritarian and interventionist states represented an adaptation of Western or global capitalism or a distinctively Asian form of capitalist development. Some claimed that "Asian countries have discovered divergent trajectories of modernisation."[41] A study of Southeast Asian modernity identified market corporatism in Malaysia, market socialism in Vietnam, and high-tech developmentalism in Singapore, linking "market fundamentalism" to the emergent middle classes and regime consolidation. Aihwa Ong interrogated narratives of Chinese nationalism and capitalism and notes that "visions of Chinese modernities depend on self-orientalising strategies that critique Western values like individualism and human rights," and saw these narratives as intersecting with counterhegemonic voices raised against U.S. domination of the Asia Pacific.[42] Lily Ling labeled the mix of rapid economic growth, Confucist-identified culture, and authoritarian rule as "Asian corporatism."[43] Arif Dirlik cautioned against culturalist explanations of Chinese capitalism. He argued that "Chinese culture conceived homogeneously provides an ideological alibi to new developments within [global] capitalism, as well as a means to check the disruptive effects of capitalist development in Chinese societies."[44] These studies, while coming to rather different conclusions concerning the relation between culture and political economy, demonstrate how important it is to analyze globalization and social change "as a process of *situated* transformation."[45]

Too often, though, Asian difference remains essentialized, resting on "a sharp distinction between East and West and on a generally fixed conceptualization of culture/race, which overlooks the hybrid character of the history of the region."[46] The rising wealth and power in the region created considerable alarm in the West, at times exhibiting a kind of colonial/race memory, prompting some to prophesy intensifying civilizational conflicts.[47] In turn, Asian assertion of exceptionalism or difference has been articulated as an explicit critique of the West. This critique is counterhegemonic in that it claims both competence (and therefore independence) and suggests reasons for then-perceived comparative Western decline. It was largely directed against the United States, especially by those whose states have most felt the effects of U.S. hegemony: Japan through postwar occupation and reconstruction; South Korea in its client status after the civil war; and those states that had until recently hosted, or still host, a strong U.S. military presence.

Asian difference has also been mobilized against U.S. surrogates or poorer relations. Thus former prime ministers Lee Kuan Yew of Singapore and Mahathir Mohamad of Malaysia both strongly resisted Australian attempts to join Asia.[48] They attempted to block this particular ambition/pretension by explicit declarations of Asian values that necessarily exclude Australia. Mahathir in particular has sought to bolster his anticolonial credentials by attacking Australia as representative of the West and calling up by way of contrast the values and identities that other elites in the region are presumed to share.

Some states are more vocal defenders of Asian values than others. In Southeast Asia, the Philippines occupies an ambiguous position in these discourses. It has much more visible critics within, including feminists who analyze former military base prostitution, sex tourism, and international labor migration within a critical international political economy perspective that also challenges state militarism and political violence. The Singaporean and Malaysian governments especially use Asian values to deflect international criticism of authoritarian and militarized states' human rights records. This "culturalist alibi" claims an Asian priority to social and economic rights over supposedly Western civil and political rights. However, most of these governments show reckless disregard for social or economic rights—workers' rights, for example, or social security. They mean, rather, a priority to economic development, or growth, over human rights. These same governments cheerfully and sometimes aggressively espouse Western notions of development and the market,[49] even while claiming a different way. Crediting Asian values with responsibility for economic growth and dynamism is deployed by some to legitimize, even necessitate, authoritarian rule.

The high value given to family in Asian values implicates women and gender relations in familiar ways, as cultural markers and symbols of difference. Thus Asia appears a region where "men are men and women are women"[50] in defiance of the family breakdown and consequent moral and social ills that supposedly bedevil the hapless West. Accordingly, refiguring gender relations in Asian states becomes a way of recovering Asian masculinities in the face of previously hegemonic Western (including military) masculinity, as well as of marking changes and challenges within Asian-Western relations. At the same time, these gender constructions naturalize the Asian woman and disguise actual Asian women's often violent incorporation into their states' economic miracles, as labor made cheap, as global assembly workers, as labor migrants, and as sex workers.[51] As well, such constructions deny a space for Asian feminisms, associating feminist critique with Western contamination and antinationalist persuasion.

Australian leaders and commentators have often been complicit in reorientalizing politics, including through attention to cultural sensitivities supposedly on the part of states but actually on the part of their elites. So successive Australian governments had sought good-neighbor relations with long-ruling President Suharto of Indonesia until his fall in 1998, choosing to value stability and growth over human rights. Australia became the only state to effectively recognize Indonesia's devastating takeover of

East Timor.[52] Good-neighborliness and cooperative security became covers for cultivating relations with current leaders. Statism and Asianism combined to discipline and contain Australian governments' political imagination where both security and region were concerned.

In part attempting to compensate for past racist slights, Australian governments have attempted to purchase closer relations and security by turning their backs on the blood and pain of those who pay for reasons of state.[53] In the process, they condone elitist and authoritarian behavior of state elites and military violence against their people. This complicity manifests in the continuing effect of the statist security trap, where states and governments are so closely associated that the people slip from view. Dissidents, democrats, union organizers, women's movement activists, students, and many others are abandoned. So, too, a national security value is set on stability, which strong governments are seen to provide, even if the cost is paid in human rights. However, the delivery of both wealth and order throughout the region is now under serious threat as a result of the Asian crisis.

Elites Versus the People?

Identity can be seen as a strategy that individuals, groups, and state elites deploy to mobilize support, access resources, or enhance their own security. A critical security approach problematizes state and oppositional exclusivist identities. When Asia is called up, for praise or blame, we must ask which Asia? whose Asia? and whose security is it that the state/these states should be held responsible for? We must also ask who is Australia? and what might that mean for different kinds of associations with different Asias?

State elite formulations of culture and nation become part of the politics of legitimation within the state. State elites must define the community and the nation in such a way as to validate their own claims as its protector and defender. They must also suppress or defuse alternative constructions of identity that might threaten their own hold on power. In this process, Asian values are deployed for domestic, as well as international, consumption.

State consolidation, and state transformation in the face of globalization processes, have aggravated disparities within and between states. The Asian miracle disguised or silenced those who have paid for economic success,[54] including workers who have experienced exploitation and been prohibited from unionism; labor migrants who lack citizenship rights and face discrimination and superexploitation; women who have provided cheapened labor for local factories and export processing zones; women who serve as sex workers to contain the sexual aggression of U.S. military men

based on other states' soil; those displaced by large-scale commercializa-
tion of agriculture or forest clearing; and refugees fleeing across borders
escaping repression and discrimination.

The costs of growth were dramatically demonstrated by two related
catastrophes in Southeast Asia in 1997. Forest fires in Indonesia created a
deep and poisonous pall that drifted into neighboring states; this was a
health and economic hazard and source of much alarm. The currency crash
that began in Thailand in July 1997 with the devaluation of the baht spread
rapidly and caused severe currency convulsions throughout Southeast Asia.
Among the most damaged economies was that of Indonesia, where the
growth of three decades was wiped out in a few months, reducing more
than half of the population to poverty. This crash came close after the
IMF's rescue of South Korea and during continued expressions of doubt
over the capacity of Japan to recover its economic energies. It destroyed the
international financial market's faith in the Asian miracle and significantly
reduced Asian state governments' bargaining power. It also revealed the
enormous coercive power of the IMF,[55] whose interventions some critics
saw as fueling the fires and whose prescriptions spread severe hardship and
impoverishment to many millions of people. For some, including Mahathir,
these interventions amounted to an attempt to reassert Western hegemony, a
payback for upstart states.

It is remarkable how quickly the Asian miracle was called into doubt.
But this doubt did not undermine the essentialized and racialized construction of Asian difference; it merely altered judgment upon it. What formerly
had explained success now explained failure. The economic meltdown led
to suggestions that perhaps they did not have what it takes to do international wealth and politics after all. Asian values were quickly translated by
some commentators into negative manifestations of crony capitalism, corruption, and an almost feudal misunderstanding of the requirements of
global capital. The Australian government moved quickly to distance itself
from Asia, arguing to domestic and international financial audiences that
Australia was not part of Asia after all, that we may be close by but we are
economically and socially different and should not be identified with
"them."[56]

So, too, Asian ways of governance and production came under attack.
The highly prized stability of Southeast Asian states dissipated in the face
of straitened economic circumstances. The bloody May 1998 riots in
Indonesia following the withdrawal of fuel and food subsidies saw Asia yet
again associated with disorder, irrational behavior, and mob violence
(although reports also showed students, housewives, and other protesters
with whom some Australians could readily identify). As the troubles spread
in Indonesia, reports began to surface of attacks on the property and persons of ethnic Chinese, though many of those of Chinese descent were

Indonesians, long resident over many generations. In some areas, the attacks witnessed systematic sexual violence against ethnic Chinese women, including by military or regime-supported men.[57] These attacks demonstrated yet again the dangers of dominant and/or popular constructions of nation that exclude others, as well as the subsequent vulnerability of such others to scapegoating, or to communal violence, in times of crisis. Symptomatic of this process of othering was the stereotyping of Indonesians of Chinese background as overseas Chinese, as merely sojourning, with their hearts still in their homeland, making wealth at the locals' expense.[58]

The antidemocratic practices authorized through Asian values discourses have severely weakened progressive political movements and alliances. Linkages and identities that seem less overtly political can thrive. Reactive nationalisms and political religious movements mobilizing against the state might be met with states' adoption, for example, of some demands of political Islam in an attempt to co-opt and defuse Islamicist appeals.[59] These strategies offer more communal control over women in return for regime security. At the same time, states move against dissenters, including democratic mobilizations, and generate a spiral of violence. The targets of violence, whether state-sponsored or communally based, are most likely those who are defined as other and whose otherness is seen as a threat to national or identity security.

Into this fraught identity/security environment came September 11 and the war on terror. Prime Minister Howard, coincidentally in Washington at the time of the attacks, immediately declared that Australia should stand shoulder to shoulder with the Americans, because September 11 represented an attack on the way of life both held dear in common. He continued to reiterate that his government had rebalanced Australian foreign policy more toward the United States and Europe, so (re)placing Australia clearly within an imagined white, Western community. He committed Australian troops to Afghanistan and, even more controversially, to Iraq in 2003. In addition to confirming Australia's identity reversion, these moves made a militarized response and the U.S. alliance the center points of Australian foreign policy. They reintroduced the older notion of forward defense and appeared to many critics to be bypassing the region.

National security was declared paramount; threats were mostly associated with difference, especially Islam, even if usually labeled radical or militant Islam. There were frequent reminders that Australia's close neighbor, Indonesia, was the most populous Muslim state in the world. This uncomfortable closeness was brought even closer to home with the Bali bombing in October 2002, in which a number of Australians died along with others, including Indonesian nationals. This tragedy closed the circle of Australian foreign policy, for it brought the war on terror and our global realignment back into the region. Our neighborhood was now seen as a link in the chain of terror, as some formerly Asian were reinscribed as Muslim, and civilizational rhetoric mobilized religion along with race to mark the borderlines.

There were many critics of both the militarist/masculinist turn of Australian foreign policy and the (related) heightened border protection that turned those fleeing the enemy states into threats and enemies themselves.[60] In the immediate aftermath of the Bali bombing, for example, Keating declared: "We must find our security in Asia, not from Asia."[61] Heading into a new election year in 2004, Howard continued to emphasize national security in terms of strength and alliance. The new Labour leader, Mark Latham, also asserted strength, but with a more pluralistic and region-sensitive approach. He announced the opposition's three pillars: "Our membership of the United Nations: our alliance with the United States; and comprehensive engagement with Asia. But Labour's three pillars rest on a rock. And the rock is an independent, self-reliant Australia strong, proud and independent."[62]

Conclusion:
In/security and the Boundaries of Community

Who you are (seen to be) can cost you your life. Identities are often imposed from the outside; and those in power can impose their own determinations of who belongs to the political and moral community and who does not. Exclusion or discrimination can generate reactive identifications and mobilizations that challenge the boundaries or the consequences of such boundaries. Alternatively, they can lead those seen as outsiders to attempt strategies of assimilation or disguise, though in the case of race, ethnicity, or other ascribed markings there is no guarantee of safety in these strategies.

A robust politics of identity can work toward more inclusive and emancipatory accounts of security, asking questions and seeking to learn from ordinary people's experiences of identity and security. This is a powerful corrective to more visible elite, statist, and militarized constructions of the identity-security nexus. These interrogations must involve both respect for and critique of difference. We can never assume that identity is aligned in any simple or obvious way with political positions. We must caution, too, against geographic or state essentialism, which reproduces singular, bounded, and culturalized identities ("Australia," "Japan," "Indonesia," "Asia"), and against identity politics that reproduce ethnicity, culture, or religion as prepolitical or fixed. Collective political identities are multiple, contingent, contested; they are racialized and gendered. We each perform our identities in our own ways, but we do so within imagined possibilities and actual power relations not of our choosing.

Notes

1. Exceptions include Doty, "Immigration and National Identity"; Krause and Renwick (eds.), *Identities in International Relations*; Darby (ed.), *On the Edge of International Relations*; Pettman, "Nationalism and After," *International Studies Quarterly*; Ling, *Postcolonial International Relations*; and numerous articles within *Millennium* and *Alternatives*.

2. Evans, *Australia's Regional Security*; Cheeseman and Bruce (eds.), *Discourses of Danger and Dread*; McGillivray and Smith (eds.), *Australia and Asia*; Cotton and Ravenhill (eds.), *Seeking Asian Engagement*.

3. Pettman, "Gender, Ethnicity, Race, and Class in Australia."

4. Lake, "Mission Impossible."

5. Milner, "The Rhetoric of Asia."

6. Chow, *Writing Diaspora*.

7. Hamilton, "Fear and Desire."

8. Smith, "Australia's Political Relationship with Asia."

9. Though the boundaries of the region have never been agreed on. The region is frequently used as a codeword for Southeast Asia, often including East Asia, but rarely including South Asia. Pacific Island states are usually forgotten, but occasionally referred to as the neighborhood or our backyard, for example in response to French nuclear testing in the Pacific.

10. Curthoys, "Feminism, Citizenship, and National Identity."

11. Evans, "The Asia-Pacific and Global Change."

12. *The East Asian Miracle: Economic Growth and Public Policy.*

13. Lafitte, "ReOrientations." Note that this decidedly feminine aspect contrasted strongly with the brutal masculinist image associated with the Burma railway. Orientalist imagery, like racist imagery more broadly, is often contradictory and shifting.

14. Pettman, "A Feminist Perspective on 'Australia in Asia.'"

15. See Crane, "Imagining the Economic Nation."

16. Pettman, "Border Crossings/Shifting Identities."

17. "Introduction," Cheeseman and Bruce, *Discourses of Danger.*

18. Sullivan, "Sipping a Thin Gruel."

19. Ibid., p. 107.

20. Halperin, "Review: A Bit on the Side."

21. Berry, *A Bit on the Side.*

22. Ang and Stratton, "Asianing Australia."

23. Curthoys and Johnson, "Articulating the Future and the Past." In the 1998 federal elections, One Nation won only one seat, but did attract over 8 percent of the overall vote.

24. *Canberra Times*, July 2, 1998.

25. Pettman, "Gender in Australian Foreign Policy."

26. See "Opinion," *The Australian,* November 7. 2001, p. 15.

27. Intra-Asian colonization is put to one side here; though it is clear that "race," civilization, and cultural hierarchies inform colonizing practices of the Chinese, Japanese, etc., too.

28. Cox, "Social Forces, States, and World Orders."

29. McClintock, *Imperial Leather*; Doty, "Immigration and National Identity"; and Doty, *Imperial Encounters*.

30. Pettman, *Worlding Women*; Stoler, *Race and the Education of Desire*.

31. Note here Berry's uncomfortable question: "Is this what they mean by 'Australia in Asia'?" *A Bit on the Side*, p. 21.

32. Pettman, "Nationalism and After."

33. Gopinath, "Nostalgia, Desire, and Diaspora."

34. Ang and Stratton, "Asianing Australia."

35. When we speak against Orientalism and nativism, we understand them as *languages* that can be used by natives and nonnatives alike. A critique of Orientalism in East Asian pedagogy neither implies that only "natives" of East Asian cultures are entitled to speaking about those cultures truthfully nor that "natives" themselves are automatically innocent of Orientalism as a mode of discourse." Chow, *Writing Diaspora*, p. 7.

36. Ling, *Hegemony and the Internationalizing State*.

37. Rowse, *After Mabo*.

38. Ang and Stratton, "Asianizing Australia"; Berger, "Yellow Mythologies"; Sopiee, "The Development of an East Asian Consciousness."

40. Ghai, "The Politics of Human Rights in Asia, the United Nations."

41. Kahn, "Malaysian Modem or Anti–Anti Asian Values."

42. Ong, "A Momentary Glow of Fraternity"; see also Ong and Nonini (eds.), *Underground Empires*.

43. Ling, *Hegemony*.

44. Dirlik, "Critical Reflections on 'Chinese Capitalism' as Paradigm."

45. Van den Berge, "Culture as Ideology in the Conquest of Modernity: Japan's Regional Regulation Strategies" (emphasis added).

46. Berger, "Yellow Mythologies."

47. Huntington, *The Clash of Civilizations*.

48. Wong, "Touchy Neighbours"; Viviani, "Australia and Southeast Asia."

49. Ghai, "The Politics of Human Rights," p. 20.

50. Moon, "East Versus West."

51. See Hyan Yi Kang, "Si(gh)ting Asian/American Women," for a careful exploration of "metaphors, plots and images" by which "Asian women" are represented, in ways that hide the politics and power that goes into constructing and exploiting many Asian women as cheap labor, and national resources in competition for global capitalism.

52. Goldsworthy, "An Overview." Note that following the fall of Suharto, the Australian prime minister quickly changed track to suggest that Indonesia might like now to solve the East Timor problem, which he identified as "an irritant." *Canberra Times*, May 26, 1998.

53. Burke, *In Fear of Security: Australia's Asian Anxiety*. Note that several Australian governments were reluctant to antagonize Indonesia by protesting ongoing and systematic violence against East Timorese, and even as horrific postreferendum militia destruction was beamed into world living rooms, would not intervene until given an Indonesian invitation to do so.

54. Pettman, "Women on the Move"; McGibbon, *Engaging with the Asia-Pacific*.

55. Bello, "East Asia."

56. See, for example, *The Australian* headline "Australia Escapes Asian Crisis," November 10, 1998.

57. *China Post,* July 15, 1998.

58. Reid, "The Ides of May for Two Sino–Southeast Asian Minorities." Competing constructions of the Chinese diaspora in Southeast Asia and elsewhere are a fascinating example of the international politics of identity; and more recently of the emergence of transnational business communities; though of course only some Southeast Asians of Chinese descent are party to these particular linkages. See Ong and Nonini, *Underground Empires.*

59. Moghadam, *Identity Politics and Women.*

60. Burke, *In Fear of Security*; Pettman, "Feminist International Relations After 9/11."

61. *Canberra Times,* November 4, 2002.

62. *Sydney Morning Herald,* January 30, 2004. The gendered language that legitimized militarism continued when, for example, the Labour left sought at the National Conference to end mandatory detention of refugees, and was defeated, a move described as Labour's refusal to soften its refugee and asylum-seeker policy.

Part 3

EMANCIPATION

EMANCIPATION IS AT THE CONTROVERSIAL heart of critical security studies. It is a much disputed concept, attracting criticism from Western political realists, neorealists, subaltern realists, postmodernists, poststructuralists, some postcolonial theorists, opponents of human rights, political tyrants, and others. While their warnings should be heeded, most of their criticisms are misconceived.[1]

It is important to keep in mind that emancipatory politics need not be dominated by what are often loosely called "Western" ideas. Nor should ideas of universal significance be dismissed just because they are identifiable as having origins within the multifaceted Western world. A more benign world politics needs to reject both ethnocentrism and ethnoguilt. All ideas come from somewhere, and it is foolish and naive to dismiss something simply because of its geographical or cultural origins. At some place, at some time, in the distant evolution of human society, life-enhancing concepts such as love and hospitality were invented. These are now universal ideas, though obviously with local (indeed individual) manifestations in practice. Who in their right minds would want to abolish love or hospitality because they were first invented by alien ethical communities? If we are to take these universal ideas seriously, should we not—*at least in principle*—be prepared to consider the validity of other values such as tolerance, nonviolence, democracy, and human rights? Vulgar relativistic thinking is calculated to replicate only a dismal and impoverished world. What matters is whether ideas are true or false, with the grain of humanity or against it, emancipatory or oppressive: what matters is not where ideas come but how well they travel.

Humans need emancipatory politics as guides for judgment and action. Without belief in ideals, traditional power elites and their oppressive common sense will perpetuate human wrongs, and humanity will never be what it might become.[2] From this, I define emancipation, in the broadest of terms, as follows: *Emancipation is the theory and practice of inventing humanity, with a view to freeing people, as individuals and collectivities, from contingent and structural oppressions. It is a discourse of human self-creation and the politics of trying to bring it about. Security and community are guiding principles, and at this stage of history the growth of a universal human rights culture is central to emancipatory politics. The concept of emancipation shapes strategies and tactics of resistance, offers a theory of progress for society, and gives a politics of hope for common humanity.*[3]

Several roles are envisaged for the concept of emancipation:

1. As a philosophical anchorage. By this I mean that emancipation can serve as a basis or test for saying whether something is true; in other words, whether particular claims to knowledge should be taken seriously. An anchorage is not a neutral foundation but rather a historically contingent yet powerful position from which people can begin to discuss what to do next in their political projects.

2. As a strategic process. Emancipation should not be considered in terms of any timeless endpoint but as a dynamic process with changing targets. It is strategic in the sense that it is concerned with bringing about practical results, but it is a process in the sense that it is a project that can never be completed. Its practicality lies in its being based in immanent critique.

3. As a guide for tactical goal setting. As a result of engaging in immanent critique emancipatory ideas can develop that in turn can be translated into tactical action. Praxis is the coming together of one's theoretical commitment to critique and political orientation to emancipation in projects of reconstruction.

The relationship between emancipation and security is more difficult to explain in theory than in practice, but it is the latter that is more important; the real test of emancipatory politics always takes place in concrete historical circumstances to the extent individuals and groups are freed from oppression.[4] One way of explaining the relationship is in terms of security as a means and emancipation as an end, though holding on as far as possible to the Gandhian conceptualization of a nondualistic ends-means relationship. While means are something to utilize instrumentally, our ideals should inform the manner in which means are employed, as well as defining the end condition. In this sense, ends/means should be regarded as being almost synonymous, in that "the same moral demands apply to both."[5] Such an outlook is identical to the Kantian injunction to consistency in one's actions. Machiavellian behavior always carries the risk of undermining itself: if a leader lies on some issue (and is discovered), it will not be long before the electorate will cease to believe him or her on any issue.[6] The imperative for consistency may be thought less important in international relations than domestic politics, in the sense that raw power can sometimes overcome the demands of justice or democracy. But consistency is an imperative for those who would construct a more benign world order. If one's ideal is a law-governed world, one should behave lawfully in trying to achieve it, even if one sometimes has to bear a heavy cost. If one's ideal is a democratic world, one should respect the weight of opinion of others, even if that sometimes means losing an argument. What one believes is right in the end one seeks must also be right in the means one chooses to pursue it.

What does this mean for the relationship between security and emancipation? First, one should eschew the powerful tradition of believing that the ends justify the means. To do otherwise is to risk corrupting the good ends one seeks by violent or iniquitous means. Second, the corollary of this is that one should as far as possible seek to pursue actions that create a virtuous circle of security and emancipation. This occurs when the pursuit of security (reducing the threats that impose life-determining conditions of insecurity on individuals and groups) promotes emancipation (freeing people from oppression and so giving them some opportunity to explore being more fully human), while the pursuit of emancipation (reducing structural oppression) promotes security (opening up space in which people can feel safer). The ideals in the goals of emancipation must be reflected in the emancipatory politics chosen to achieve those goals. There is no other way, if emancipation is to be true to itself.

Enough has been said in this book already to show the need in world politics for emancipatory politics on the part of those many people whose lives are deformed by structural and other forms of oppression. Emancipation was described above as the political discourse of human self-creation. Part 3 offers various perspectives on that claim.

In his broad-ranging sweep of the theoretical horizon of conceptualizations of emancipation, Hayward Alker (Chapter 8) brings together (among many others) the unlikely bedfellows of Franklin D. Roosevelt and Jacques Derrida. He quotes from the former's "Four Freedoms" and the latter's embrace of the "great classical discourse of emancipation" to illustrate the validity of what he calls "several relatively promising ways" in which more broadly based emancipatory themes might be developed within critical approaches to security. He outlines what he thinks are the key features of the CSS project, particularly the relationship he sees between critical theory, security, and emancipation. His main point is that while different approaches exist within the overall critical project, there is nevertheless a widespread emancipatory concern with freedom from exploitation and repression, together with ideas about greater human self-realization and community-building at different levels.

Challenges exist to traditional Western Enlightenment ideas about emancipation from non-Western, postcolonial, feminist, and postmodern perspectives, but there are also linkages. The chapter suggests that the urgency of a "globalizing search" for intersubjective agreements has grown since the September 11 attacks on the United States; nevertheless, the author does not shy away from the difficulty of achieving them. Brute relativism is rejected, and it is argued that different groups might agree on culturally sensitive concepts of emancipation and seek to further them in a posthegemonic way. Alker is encouraged by evidence offered by both non-Western and postmodern writers of the seriousness and salience of the

emancipation theme. His own view is that even in the era of the global war
on terror, and against a background of globalizing emancipatory discourses (which have to be looked upon with a "certain skepticism"), pragmatic
convergences are possible on concrete issues to augment emancipatory
concerns.

Alker's chapter supports the view that emancipation is not the dividing
concept it has often been thought to be among critical scholars; instead, he
argues that it is embraced by a variety of critical approaches. This theme is
also developed in Chapter 9, by Richard Wyn Jones, on "concrete utopias."
To date, emancipation has seemed to be a major issue dividing two of the
main schools of thought within CSS, namely the Frankfurt School tradition
of social theory and postmodern and poststructuralist approaches to international relations. Whereas emancipation has been central to thinking
about security "in the light" of the Frankfurt tradition of critical theory, it
is seen as one of the many negative ideas associated with the metanarratives of modernity in the opinion of those drawn to the *rive gauche* tradition of postmodernism and poststructuralism. Wyn Jones challenges this
view, arguing that the gap between Frankfurt School critical theory and
poststructuralist conceptualizations of emancipation can be exaggerated;
his contention is that, whatever the rhetoric of poststructuralist critics, a
concept of emancipation is a necessary element in any form of analysis
that attempts to problematize, and take on, the status quo. In support, he
offers a textual analysis of a range of poststructuralist writing and shows
that the critical edge of the poststructuralist approach to international relations depends—whether its exponents recognize it or not—on the possibility of progressive alternatives to the status quo. Having shown the pervasiveness of an emancipatory spirit (indeed logic) even among some of
those who would deny it, the chapter proceeds to its main theme, a discussion of the different and sometimes contradictory ways in which the
Frankfurt tradition has conceptualized humanity's capacity for emancipatory transformation.

Wyn Jones argues that the Frankfurt School is an "invaluable
resource," but that does not mean that what it has to offer is not without
problems, including differences of opinion among its exponents and contradictions within itself. He shows this by tracing the theme of emancipation
in the work of such key Frankfurt School figures as Horkheimer, Adorno,
Habermas, and others. Newer conceptualizations developed by contemporary theorists are identified, such as deliberative and cosmopolitan democracy (David Held) and political community (Andrew Linklater). The chapter ends by reaffirming the centrality of a concern with emancipation for
any form of CSS and of the particular importance of the archive of the
Frankfurt School in revealing its possibilities and pitfalls. Michel Foucault,
the obligatory authority in all poststructuralist writing in international rela-

tions, is remembered as having said that he would have "saved useful time" and "avoided certain errors" had he encountered the work of the Frankfurt School earlier than he actually did.

One of the most familiar lines of attack on the idea of emancipation by political realists is that critical perspectives represent only a theoretical ideal. And when not actually making things worse by privileging the hopes of the oppressed over the "necessities of state," emancipation is said to be much too abstract a concept to help real politics in real situations. In the final contribution, Joseph Ruane and Jennifer Todd (Chapter 10) argue that emancipation can be much more than political rhetoric or academic theory. For them it can be the most practical of politics, and they show this in relation to one of the toughest cases facing students of security, communal conflict. This, it hardly needs emphasizing, is one of the most pervasive causes of insecurity in the world today.

Chapter 10 examines the prolonged conflict in Northern Ireland and the role of emancipation in the peace process. While acknowledging the strictures of those who criticize the concept of emancipation (alongside the values and principles of the Enlightenment more generally), Ruane and Todd attempt to show the concept's continuing political value in concrete historical situations. Though critics might see emancipation as "idealistic and nebulous" and "irrelevant to practical affairs," the chapter argues that now, as in the past, the emancipatory aim of dismantling the conditions that give rise to conflict, and in the process changing aims, identities, and aspirations, remains urgent and practical. For most of the period since the current Troubles began in Northern Ireland in the late 1960s, it is argued that a realist approach was adopted in the search for a settlement. As a result, the situation was understood as inherently conflictual, and so the only solution was seen to lie in some form of deal based on the compromising of interests. In the 1990s, however, the authors note that greater openness was shown to emancipatory ideas (while not eschewing realist strategies). The centerpiece of this policy was the Belfast Agreement (April 1998), which offered an institutional framework for managing conflict in the short and medium terms while seeking to transform the conditions of conflict. The latter was to be achieved by identifying the social and cultural bases of existing conflictual interests and identities, as well as by changing the conditions under which those engaged in the conflict could act upon and change them. It was this move—transforming conditions and changing interests and identities—that for Ruane and Todd comprises the emancipatory dimension of the peace process.

The conflict in Northern Ireland is far from over, but if the peace process is to work, the authors argue that the "tensions and contradictions" in the Belfast Agreement, and the system of relationships that generate the communal conflict, can be addressed only by strengthening the emancipatory elements of the process. Going beyond the realist project, which seeks order through brokering political compromise, the authors offer concrete illustrations of what an emancipatory process entails in this concrete struggle, namely, a "clear and attainable set of policy priorities and goals" to address the conflict at source, building on what has been achieved. Rather than being utopian in the negative (unworldly) sense, Ruane and Todd argue that in the real politics of Northern Ireland emancipatory processes are practical, necessary, and urgent. These arguments are of direct relevance to many other conflicts that scar world affairs and the lives of so many individuals, families, and communities. These conflicts include some of the most violent and apparently intractable in the world today, such as the struggles between the Israeli state and the Palestinians, the bloody wars in central and west Africa, and the potentially catastrophic clash between nuclear-armed rivals over Kashmir.

The illustrative chapters at the end of each main section of this volume—revealing important dimensions of militarized masculinity (by Whitworth), identity issues (by Pettman), and communal conflict (by Ruane and Todd)—point to the obvious fact that the empirical agenda for students of CSS is overflowing. Insecurity seems always to be in season. But hope should not be lost. Rivalries can be overcome. The traditional enemies in Western Europe came together to form the European Union. The Cold War ended without nuclear catastrophe. Argentina and Brazil stepped back from becoming nuclear-armed neighbors. South Africa moved beyond institutionalized racism without the long-predicted bloodbath. What is more, moral progress is possible, evident in international standard-setting (such as the delegitimization of racism or the creation of a human rights culture), even though the record of compliance often leaves much to be desired. Standard-setting offers some promise of a better future, though everybody must accept the difficulty of turning humanizing ideas into political realities. This will be the case in the future, as it was in the past, but perhaps even more so given the growing complexities of world politics. In the decades ahead, old and new challenges abound for students of security, but even in dark times hope is rational. History is not only a miserable record of human wrongs; it is also a resource for, and reminder of, truly amazing humane possibilities.

Notes

1. For an elaboration, see Booth, "Three Tyrannies," pp. 36–64.
2. This is a theme of the work of Philip Allott. See, for example, *Eunomia*; "Globalization from Above," in Booth, Dunne, and Cox (eds.), *How Might We Live? Global Ethics in the New Century*; and *The Health of Nations: Society and Law Beyond the State*.
3. Booth, "Three Tyrannies," p. 46.

4. My first explicit discussion of emancipation in the context of security was Booth, "A New Security Concept for Europe," pp. 1–7 in Eavis (ed.), *European Security: The New Agenda*. See, for fuller developments, Booth, "Security and Emancipation," and "Three Tyrannies." Unless otherwise stated, the argument in this section is based on these sources.

5. Richards, *The Philosophy of Gandhi,* p. 31.

6. For an overview of the Kantian approach to world politics, see Williams and Booth, "Kant," in Clark and Newmann (eds.), *Classical Theories of International Relations.*

8

Emancipation in the Critical Security Studies Project

Hayward Alker

> Freedom of speech
> Freedom of worship
> Freedom from want
> Freedom from fear
> —*Franklin D. Roosevelt, 1941[1]*

> I refuse to renounce the great classical discourse of emancipation. I believe that there is an enormous amount to do today for emancipation, in all domains and all the areas of the world and society.
> —*Jacques Derrida, 1996[2]*

After a brief restatement of what Ken Booth has called the critical security studies project,[3] I wish here to explore several relatively promising ways in which its emancipatory theme can be developed. The first is historical contexting: I shall suggest that an important ancestor of that project was expressed in and through Roosevelt's World War II leadership and his call for the realization of the "Four Freedoms" in that war. Just as emancipation has historically been associated with controversial Marxist claims concerning the emancipatory potential of working-class and anti-imperialist revolutions, the above historical insight similarly roots more recent, comprehensive concerns with individual human security in a more recent version of a Western hegemonic project. Hence further critical, but open-minded, scholarly discussion is required, especially in an era where a loose coalition of Muslim extremists is at war with the West.

Besides historically informed reanalyses of security-emancipation linkages, the basic concepts themselves need rethinking. Operationally, I suggest that Ole Wæver's promising securitization approach to identifying concrete threats to existential security might be cautiously linked, via its nonfoundationalist use of communicative rationality, to emancipatory concerns in intracultural, cross-cultural, and transcultural ways. If emancipation points toward deeply held dispositions toward freedom, emancipation, and redemption, at individual and group levels, I shall then argue, with Fred Dallmayr and Jacques Derrida as allies, that these are genuinely universal concerns, although differently shaped in different contexts. With an attentive ear to premodern, modern, and postmodern security analysts, I shall next suggest epistemologically and ontologically sensitive ways in which the reshapings of collective memories and imagined futures can be emancipatory. Rather than confront contemporary ethnic and political-religious conflicts directly, I shall raise the related issue of politically motivated, distorting, and self-serving retellings of the past from a little greater historical distance. Focusing on ways in which the role of violence in intergroup and intracommunity relationships can be transformed, I shall critically examine examples from retellings of Japanese and U.S. history; hopefully, this review will be informed by the earlier discussion of Allied World War II aims. In conclusion, I suggest that culturally sensitive concepts of emancipation can be linked to concretely researchable, equally sensitive conceptions of existential security in a posthegemonic fashion.

The Critical Security Studies Project

Critical security studies has its roots in internationally relevant critical theory, conventional and alternative strategic or security studies, security studies initiated within or oriented toward the third world during the Cold War period, peace research, the English School of international relations, and postpositivist approaches to international politics and security. Their crystallization into a relatively coherent and visible project, evident in diverse approaches to international security issues, is nonetheless a post–Cold War phenomenon.[4] Important milestones in this regard are a 1991 article by Ken Booth[5] and the publication of Keith Krause and Michael C. Williams's book on the subject, principally the results of a York University conference in the mid-1990s.

How are critical theory, security, and emancipation related to each other? What project or projects lie within this nexus? In the past, revolutionary change has been justified in emancipatory terms; perhaps in the future it will be again, as when the U.S.-led international order declines. For contemporary international relations scholars, however, talking about a critical theory immediately brings to mind the way in which Frankfurt School theorists, Gramscian political economists, and others of a critical or reflective historiographic cast have linked emancipatory, or repression-reducing, projects to their theorizing of sociopolitical change.[6] Just as Robert Cox criticizes alternative problem-solving theories as "serving particular national, sectional, or class interests, which are comfortable within the given order," Booth's perspective arises out of a personal effort to dissociate himself from the "Luttwak simplifier"—"strategy as enthnocentrism writ large"[7]; in this fundamental respect, then, the emancipatory focus of his work is clearly linked to the broader concerns of critical social and political theory.

Similarly, Booth is concerned generally with human well-being, in its many individual and social manifestations and broadly reconceptualizes insecurity, war, and emancipation in these terms. If security is characterized conventionally as "the absence of threats,"[8] the list of relevant threats is not defined in state-centric terms. Aside from the occasional problem of "Napoleonic neighbors," for the most part "economic collapse, political oppression, scarcity, overpopulation, ethnic rivalry, the destruction of nature, terrorism, crime and disease" provide more serious threats to "the well-being of individuals and the interests of nations." More radically, "to countless millions of people in the world it is their own state, and not 'The Enemy' that is the primary security threat."[9] Continuing, he identifies war prevention as part of a larger project of human emancipation:

> Emancipation is the freeing of people (as individuals and groups) from those physical and human constraints which stop them carrying out what they would freely choose to do. War and the threat of war is one of those constraints, together with poverty, poor education, political oppression and so on. Security and emancipation are two sides of the same coin. Emancipation [which he conceives of as a process], not power or order, produces true security.

Following Hedley Bull and the World Society School, Booth advocates considering the individual human's security as more fundamental than states' security, because individuals are the "ultimate units of the great society of all mankind." And with cites to critical international theorists like Held and Hoffman, plus Caroline Thomas's work on third world and North/South security, he suggests that an egalitarian concept of liberty, reciprocity of rights, and the breaking down of barriers between domestic and foreign policy are all integral to, or derivable from, security thought of as a process of human emancipation.[10] Through different lenses, these goals could be defined as liberal, enlightened, modern, cosmopolitan, social-democratic, or globally humanistic.

More cautiously, and more heterogeneously, Krause and Williams accept a nonethnocentric, Coxian concern to go beyond problem-solving theory to address, both historically and philosophically, the changing and sometimes contingent subject-objects of conventional security studies and its frameworks of situation analysis and (sometimes coercive) response recommendation.[11] But they do not want their conception of critical security studies to be fully identified with any particular critical orthodoxy (Gramscian, Frankfurt School, or otherwise) or an associated emancipatory project.

Although they do not want to foster an indiscriminant, incoherence-generating approach to security studies,[12] like Booth they clearly are uncomfortable with the conventional focus on state-centric uses of force offered by Stephen Walt and other contemporary neorealists. While presenting Mohammed Ayoob's developmental view advocating security through the realist path of increasing state strength, they nicely problematize neorealist perspectives by summarizing the neorealists' ahistorical worldview of sovereign states in an anarchic world with the subtitle: "States Are the Subjects; Anarchy Is the Condition; Contractarianism Is the Solution."[13]

Krause and Williams are evidently aware of the problematical nature of an exclusive focus on states and their "Others" in a way that ontologically and epistemologically excludes the life needs and concerns of their citizens.[14] Thus they are well aware of, and sensitive to, feminist critiques of the domination relations within the private spheres generated by supposedly voluntaristic public economic and political contractual relations,[15] as well as sustainability-motivated ecological reconceptualizations of sovereignty and security concerns.[16] Critical security studies in their senses, then, represents several projects overlapping with, but not necessarily identical with, Booth's conception.

Although critical security studies authors, with the exception of Booth, are not as clearly focused on the emancipatory potential of "utopian realism,"[17] can one discern some commonalities across all or most of these writers, especially concerning emancipatory concerns such as freedom from exploitation, repression, or unjustifiable intervention? Evidently, they, too, are sympathetic with the concern of critical international theorists[18] to reconnect security theorizing with ameliorative, if not emancipatory, ethical-political theories pointed toward greater human self-realization, autonomy, community, security, and well-being on a transnational, perhaps even a global, scale. Within limits, they support historical, constructivist accounts of security arrangements.[19] At least implicitly, therefore, many of their contributors make a link from community-building to security enhancement—and thus freedom from threats or fear—through the relevant international community-building or state-building activities.[20]

A Return to the Roots of
the Critical Security Studies Project

Is the critical security studies project a Western invention? Does it therefore embody suspect, discredited, or at least sharply contested Enlightenment, liberal, or social democratic ideals? Does its comprehensive, universalistic character reflect to some extent hegemonic aspirations that we should be critically skeptical about, either in terms of the value concerns and loyalties embodied in that project or from the perspectives of nonsupporters? I have returned with renewed admiration, but a more critical historical eye, to the Franklin Delano Roosevelt Memorial in Washington, D.C. On reflection, that visit gives significant support for a cautionary, nondismissive attitude toward such questions.

Located across from the Thomas Jefferson Memorial, the FDR Memorial is also not far from the moving Vietnam Memorial; for those sensitive to the unequal treatment of blacks in the United States, these neighbors provide mute testimonies to some of the broader societal contradictions associated with Jefferson's and Roosevelt's noble American ideals. The Roosevelt Memorial's stirring inscriptions, imposing stone courtyards, and waterworks—linked to each of his four terms in office as president—should, and will, appeal to many Americans besides myself, as well as to foreign visitors. Figure 8.1 lists the last ten of the memorial's twenty-one inscriptions, associated with his last two terms, including the war years.

Walking through the memorial, contemplating the engraved inscriptions, or reading their source texts available in the adjoining bookstore, one relives in memorial awe selected highlights of Roosevelt's presidential life. Because it physically comes last in the narrative trajectory I followed, Inscription 19, concerning the Four Freedoms, deserves special attention. In the context of the other internationally oriented inscriptions, and on the basis of a reading of the 1941 Annual Message to Congress (now called the State of the Union speech) and two associated texts made available at the memorial bookstore as sources of FDR's words on this subject,[21] I was struck by the commonalities of FDR's hegemonic vision of Allied/U.S. war aims and the themes in the previously cited literature on the critical security studies project. In the security studies literature of my acquaintance, only Randall Forsberg's writings resurrect as many of these themes, but in a more defensively oriented fashion.[22]

With the hindsight of six decades of world history, let me recall some of these originating, common themes. Clearly grounded in FDR's New Deal effort of active, planned, socioeconomic, governmental responses to Depression crises, and his memorialized 1933 Inaugural claim that "the only thing we have to fear is fear itself" (Inscription 5), the Four Freedoms did not actually appear in the partly decontexted forms that the memorial presents. Such language evolves from Roosevelt's earlier public remarks, appearing most succinctly in a letter of acceptance to what appears to be an interdenominational churchmen group.[23] As evidence for a global hegemonic perspective, the "everywhere ['or anywhere'] in the world" rhetoric of the first (State of the Union) presentation is particularly striking. It is repeated four times, as each freedom is introduced:

Figure 8.1   The FDR Memorial's Last Ten Inscriptions

12. We must scrupulously guard the civil rights and civil liberties of all our citizens, whatever their background. We must remember that any oppression, any injustice, any hatred, is a wedge designed to attack our civilization. (1/9/40)

13. We must be the great arsenal of Democracy. (1/29/40)

14. We have faith that future generations will know that here, in the middle of the twentieth century, there came a time when men of good will found a way to unite, and produce, and fight to destroy the forces of ignorance, and intolerance, and slavery, and war. (2/12/43)

15. They (who) seek to establish systems of government based on the regimentation of all human beings by a handful of individual rulers . . . call this a new order. It is not new and it is not order. (3/15/41)

16. I have seen war. I have seen war on land and sea. I have seen blood running from the wounded . . . I have seen the dead in the mud. I have seen

cities destroyed . . . I have seen children starving. I have seen the agony of mothers and wives. I hate war. (8/14/36)

17. More than an end to war, we want an end to the beginnings of all wars. (4/13/45)

18. Unless the peace that follows recognizes that the whole world is one neighborhood and does justice to the whole human race, the germs of another world war will remain as a constant threat to mankind. (2/12/43)

19. Freedom of speech
    Freedom of worship
    Freedom from want
    Freedom from fear (1/6/41)

20. The structure of world peace cannot be the work of one man, or one party, or one nation . . . it must be a peace which rests on the cooperative effort of the whole world. (3/1/45)

21. The only limits to our realization of tomorrow will be our doubts of today. Let us move forward with strong and active faith. (prepared for 4/13/45)

Source: National Parks Service, "Franklin Delano Roosevelt Memorial: Guide to Inscriptions and Sculpture" (Washington, D.C.: U.S. Government Printing Office, 1997).

In the future days, which we seek to make secure, we look forward to a world founded upon four essential human freedoms.

The first is freedom of speech and expression—everywhere in the world.

The second is freedom of every person to worship God in his own way—everywhere in the world.

The third is freedom from want—which, translated into world terms, means economic understandings which will secure to every nation a healthy peacetime life for its inhabitants—everywhere in the world.

The fourth is freedom from fear—which, translated into world terms, means a world-wide reduction of armaments to such a point and in such a thorough fashion that no nation will be in a position to commit an act of physical aggression against any neighbor—anywhere in the world.

That is no vision of a distant millennium. It is a definite basis for a kind of world attainable in our own time and generation.[24]

In addition to a subsequent claim that "freedom means the supremacy of human rights everywhere,"[25] calls for the building of armaments to help our prewar allies, the treatment of our increasing military involvement as an act of defense, the mention of Napoleonic incursions in the United States, a commitment to realism and increased efficiency in weapons production, the rejection of tyrannical, imposed world orders, and the need to work in concert with others, there is a clear, processual commitment to a broad kind of security for ordinary people (and nations, not states): "We believe that the men and women of such nations, no matter what size, can, through the process of peace, serve themselves and serve the world by protecting the common man's security."[26] That the fourth freedom is associated with disarmament in our lifetime is also emphasized. Many of these themes are reechoed in Inscriptions 12–18, 20, and 21, as well as in the critical security studies literature reviewed above.

If security and emancipation are seen to go together in Rooseveltean projects, our skeptical reflections suggest that they need not always do so, for the same people. Recall that before and during the Roosevelt era a freer future was linked in controversial Marxist claims to the emancipatory potential of peasant working-class and anti-imperialist revolutions. The vast majority of international scholars today would agree that a historically balanced, multiperspective appraisal of such claims is needed and can be approximated in the making of such appraisals. Is it too much to hope that someday, if not now, Rooseveltean projects linking comprehensive security concerns and individual emancipation will receive similar critical, but open-minded, balanced, multiperspective scholarly discussions including scholars from Western and non-Western countries? And should we not try to approximate such ideals in our own contemporary policy-oriented research and discussion?

Rethinking the Links Between Security and Emancipation

How might the emancipatory project (or projects) of critical security studies be better defined, their tendencies be empirically studied, and their impressive-sounding ideals be criticized and improved upon in practice? The broadening of security concerns to include individual men's and women's experiences of threat, as well as other well-being aspirations, makes many students ask: Shouldn't a workable scholarly conception of common security or human security be made more specific, practically helpful, yet still criticizable in scholarly or policy-oriented ways?

An awareness of the pre–Cold War Western roots of many key ideas in critical security studies makes others object that a genuinely cross-cultural, autonomy-respecting, critical approach to security concerns has yet to be established. Those hoping to achieve a scientific, international/global scholarly approach to international/world security issues in today's subnational/international/global world need to know how this goal might at least be approximated in an eventually posthegemonic, difference-respecting, culturally specific yet cross-cultural or transcultural fashion. Or with less universalistic aspirations, they might suggest that a more productive focus would be on how projects claiming to enhance both security and emancipation could be operationally defined as relevant to the lives or existence of particular individuals, peoples, practices, organizations, or countries in various parts of the world. And should not such projects be subjected as well to careful but serious criticism from a variety of Western normative, conceptual, and empirical perspectives, including postmodern ones, on the meanings of freedom?

The remainder of this chapter suggests preliminary answers to these seemingly divergent questions. Of course, outside stirring speeches, good things are less likely always to go together. Taken together, the answers given here will nonetheless argue for the possibility and actuality of defensible linkings of emancipation to concretely researchable, yet cross-cultural, variants of existential security.

To progress toward this goal, I want first to recast slightly the individual-level focus emphasized by Booth, Hedley Bull, and others above. If, as argued, individuals or families are the ultimate units of world society, I think it appropriate for specialists in international security studies to focus instrumentally on the contributions that larger entities—minority groups, regimes, communities, sectoral practices or institutions, technologies, societies, economic-ecological arrangements, states or international/transnational organizations—provide for meeting their security concerns. When these larger entities represent collective agencies, they, too, can have security needs or objectives worth studying, but not in isolation from the impact of these pursuits on their constituent members and on outsiders.

Recognizing Security Threats
Constituted by Securitization Processes

If we are to explore links between emancipation and security, we must know somehow which threats to which groups, practices, or institutions—and ultimately their constituent individuals or families—deserve to be labeled "security issues." As a way of giving coherence and focus to the security-emancipation relationship, I suggest using the antiessentialist "securitization" approach to defining security issues offered by Barry Buzan, Ole Wæver, and Jaap de Wilde.[27] As a kind of emergency breaking of the rules, securitization should be seen as extreme or abnormal politicization (more of it is not thus better). It is concerned with an "existential (life- or existence-challenging) threat [that] has to be argued" successfully to a relevant public as an intersubjectively agreed upon threat/survival issue requiring rule-breaking (and possibly force-employing) practices for a certain more or less extended period of time.[28]

Due principally to Ole Wæver, the securitization approach to situation-specific characterizations of security issues/threats may be described as an antiessentialist or poststructural attempt to (re)join Hobbes to the English School of international relations (Martin Wight, Hedley Bull, etc.), rather than leave him to the misinterpretations of Hobbesian anarchy typically associated with neorealist readings thereof; international relations usually do not occur within a nasty, brutish, and short, precontract, domestic, anarchic wilderness but within an international/world society of mutually recognized states reluctantly, unevenly, but increasingly recognizing individuals or households as their and its ultimate units. In that world, "security is about survival [concerning] an issue posing an existential threat to a designated referent object (traditionally, but not necessarily, the state, incorporating government, territory, and society)."

In recent centuries in world history, the religiously/aristocratically/ethnically structured character of certain regimes and the genocidal devastation of certain ethnic populations have surely justified describing their defense in such existential security terms as well. The extent to which identity-specific values or symbols are severely threatened enough within particular communities or societies to require securitization responses must be further researched. Retrospective policy justifications or critiques require both cultural-specific discursive analyses, in which all major viewpoints on an issue are given careful attention, and the careful checking of such views through historical/scientific research. Accepting the *relevance* of such analyses does not imply support for genocidal politics! At a time when ethnic conflicts are abundant, I also do not want to suggest that every secession is truly emancipatory, and I am very skeptical that any form of ethnic cleansing can adequately be justified in emancipatory terms.

It is key to Wæver's conception that the securitizing speech act, which has traditionally legitimated the use of force, has also invoked the right of a "state to mobilize, or take special powers, to handle existential threats." As Buzan, Wæver, and de Wilde carefully illustrate, such invocations can be regarding political, economic, cultural, societal, or environmental sectors of a domestic or international society; just as clearly, the mere invocation of the words "security" or "defense" or "survival" does not, by itself, make something a security/securitized issue or threat.

Previous case studies of security-enhancing successes, or breakdowns, need to be reanalyzed in these terms in order to derive more perceptive and practically useful ways to prevent debilitating and/or unsuccessful securitization dynamics. And the approach needs to be extended critically to include the much richer existing literature on strategies for crossing thresholds of violent collective behavior in ways that effectively allow for relatively prompt returns. And when reliably generalizable ways of characterizing emancipation are available, we can develop and better defend empirical generalizations linking or delinking emancipation, securitization, and human well-being.

The securitization approach is constructively and practically oriented toward the multileveled analysis of the variety of security-needing social entities I have just proposed.[29] It certainly does not discredit the evaluative study of their impacts on ordinary human lives!

It responds constructively, discursively, to the transnationalizing of concerns and the broadening of possibilities for reconceptualizing threats clearly present in, and encouraged by, critical security studies.[30] Moreover, I find this discursive, intersubjectively oriented, community-linked, yet coherent approach suggestive of how to proceed in further decentering the statist bias of conventional security/strategic studies, without denying the relevance of states' contributions to vital topics like nuclear arms control, Napoleonic neighbors, and civil wars. Refocusing critical security studies to point toward existential threats to important groups, nations, practices, organizations, or technologies within particular transnational or international societies or places gives concrete meanings to freedom from fear. Whether or not securitization helps achieve that goal—at what price for discursive communal-will formation—must be answered empirically, historically, discursively. The corresponding search within relevant societies and communities for remedial, preferably nonsecuritized or desecuritizing, emancipatory, or redemptive practices is based on the pacifist belief that peace is best waged by peaceful means rather than the alternative maxim: to secure peace, prepare for war.[31]

Within critical security studies, security and community are closely related concepts[32]; importantly, this linkage depends on the equally close relationship between self-realization, autonomy, self-determination, and freedom for the collectivities involved. Processes or threats that serve to demobilize or sidestep discursive community responses to them undermine the collective, rational, and deliberative capacities of communities autonomously and freely to meet such threats.

For our purposes, it is important to recognize that there are a variety of things societies, groups, and individuals can do to prevent doleful securitizations of their lives. For example, consider the mobilization of existence-enhancing (inter)communal problem-solving practices or, in a noncrisis mode, the writing and diffusing of balanced precedential histories. Easier to describe than actually to write, these histories would more clearly attribute responsibilities for past failures and be suggestive of how existentially threatening violence can be avoided. Such peacebuilding activities are not normally on the agendas of conventional security/strategic specialists trained in exemplary studies of extended deterrence or the less-than-peaceful proclivities of mature or immature democratic states!

Using the securitization approach, recognizing the internal relations of community-supporting and desecuritizing practices, can the emancipatory thrust of critical security studies be further articulated? In my earlier work[33] on emancipatory empirical peace research, I used a mixture of Jürgen Habermas and Roy Bhaskar to describe the emancipatory knowledge interest as "an attitude which is formed in the experience of suffering from something man-made, which can be abolished and should be abolished"; and I focused on the "uncoupling [of] the present from the causality of the past," replacing "depotentialising (disempowering, oppressive)" psychological, social, and ecological structures by "potentialising (empowering, enhancing) ones." I suggested that practically achievable emancipation was a "special qualitative kind of becoming free" that "consists in the self-directed transformation from an unwanted and unneeded to a wanted and needed source of determination."[34]

Rather than continue to broaden the discussion of freedom/liberty typically offered in Western social and political theory,[35] I would like to comment further on the tendency observed by Andrew Linklater in later Habermasian writings to be "rather careful these days about using the expression 'emancipation' beyond the realm of biographical experiences" because "neither social collectivities nor society as a whole can be regarded as a subject writ large."[36] It turns out that by recognizing that the Enlightenment and modernity no longer come along with "a promise of happiness," Habermas is only secure in talking about a "history of political emancipation." He defined the latter in terms of a political and constitutional point of view, of principles that were "achieved only over the course of centuries of struggles, and of the collective experience of social recognition that at the end were finally assimilated into our political culture."[37]

Could it be that Habermas—the late modern, communicatively rational, critical Kantian democrat—had rediscovered Erich Fromm's or Harold Lasswell's devastating, Freud-inspired indictments of ideologically charged, irrational projections of domestic views onto the world scene? Less plausibly, one might even ask if Habermas, the former Marxist, has "got (evangelical) religion" and is calling for individual salvation rather than political efforts to change the world.[38] Ironically, his views also seem, in part, to converge with Samuel Huntington's claim that Western values are too unique and precious for us Westerners to expect or promote global collaborations based on them or their Eastern cousins![39]

Reading further, one finds Habermas to be a cautious modernist, but not a defeatist: if modernity "no longer comes with a promise of happiness," "a meaning that is foolproof against all misunderstanding" it associates humanity with more independence—but not automatically more happiness. In critically discussing German unification's normative deficits, he appeals to emancipatory standards defined from a "political and constitutional point of view," "to principles that were achieved only over the course of centuries of struggles, and of the collective experience of social recognition that were finally assimilated into our political culture."[40] In defending an emancipatory standard with considerable cosmopolitan appeal, he nonetheless grounds it in Western history and culture.

The Challenge of Non-Western, Postcolonial, Feminist, and Postmodern Emancipatory Concerns

Having discussed how security might be better understood, we now turn to clarifying emancipation in ways allowing more adequately for the critical study and promotion of their linkage. I would suggest that we still need to achieve the fuller inclusion of multiple Western *and* non-Western perspectives on the meanings of freedom, without giving up the distinctive and attractive appeal to human improvement and emancipatory development that is so central to the ethical/global concerns of the critical security studies project. I mention West and non-West together because the West/non-West opposition has become more prominent in post–Cold War times, especially since September 11, 2001, and because there is an overlap between postmodern, post-Westphalian, and postcolonial ways of thinking that doesn't support dangerous, dichotomous reductions of identification and perspective on security issues. What about those many individuals who can be considered simultaneously to live in both worlds, or those seen as traveling between them or within their overlapping parts? The valid point of references to the non-Western is that it is often worthwhile to reinclude geoculturally excluded non-Westerners in globally oriented policy discussions wherever they live. But it should be said, as well, that the United States (which has the UN's headquarters in its midst), Canada, and the United Kingdom are still to be judged relatively open on such issues, compared with many other states or societies.

If we indeed find widely recognized existential threats to liberty in primarily non-Western contexts, we have to allow that there may be metaphysical, religious, or more general cultural differences in how these notions are defined, applied, and responded to. If the rootedness of most versions of the critical security studies project in Rooseveltean visions is granted, the character of that project as a hegemonic contender must be acknowledged, and its appeal must be rethought. Indeed, the partial convergence of criticisms I want seriously to address combines both Western late modern, postmodern, and non-Western contemporary perspectives.

Of the several relevant sources on this subject that I can recommend, the most exciting for me has been Fred Dallmayr's exploration of new Western and non-Western voices from Islam and Buddhism, which appeared well before the Islamically rationalized attack of Mohammed Atta and others on the World Trade Center on September 11.[41]

The good news suggested by Dallmayr's review is that there are non–terror prone social movements in Islamic, Buddhist, and other non-Western societies that are pressing for changes under banners that can clearly be recognized as emancipation-oriented. But the bad news for cosmopolitan utopian realists is that from an Islamic or Buddhist perspective—and there are various of these—liberty does not always mean the same thing that secular, modern Westerners take it to mean. A problem with critical security studies literature and critical social theorists is that they usually cite primarily or exclusively Western writers like Kant, Marx, Cox, Habermas, or Bhaskar as their specialists on emancipation. One could do worse! But these are all secular rationalist thinkers, identified positively with key aspects of modernity that some non-Western or postcolonial writers (and some postmodernists) reject. An impressive contribution of Dallmayr's cited chapter is the exploration of Buddhist and Islamic self-transcending meanings of freedom, emancipation, and redemption that Western writers must deal with if a globalizing search for intersubjective, discursive agreements concerning existential survival threats is to proceed.[42]

Isaiah Berlin may have offered the best antihistoricist aphorism for opera lovers—history does not have a libretto—but postcolonial, postmodern, and feminist thinkers are more generally identified with the rejection of liberal, progressive, or emancipatory metanarratives as adequate for telling world historical stories about mankind.[43] They have problematized as well the subject-object, public-private, and self-other logocentric dichotomies in terms of which these accounts have been authored.[44] The significant if partial convergence of thematics between feminist/postmodern Western critics of Enlightenment-inspired emancipation projects and the views of several of the Buddhist and Islamic writers in Dallmayr's chapter is sufficient cause for taking both groups of critics more seriously. Happily, the emancipatory and redemptive language of the non-Westerners suggests that an appropriately cross-cultural or multicultural approach to security and emancipation may still be possible in such contexts. But one should expect partial convergences on needs, not agreement on foundations.

In this regard, remarks by a leading postmodernist, Jacques Derrida, are particularly gratifying. They occurred in an exchange with Ernesto

Laclau, Richard Rorty, and Simon Critchley on remarkable overlaps between postmodern deconstruction and late-modern pragmatism. In response to remarks by Critchley and Rorty that his earlier writings falsely presented Derrida as much more of a "private ironist" than a Rortyan "public liberal," Derrida reiterated and enlarged upon a commitment to "the great classical discourse of emancipation."

> I believe that there is an enormous amount to do today for emancipation, in all domains and all the areas of the world and society. Even if I would not wish to inscribe the discourse of emancipation into a teleology, a metaphysics, an eschatology, or even a classical messianism, I nonetheless believe that there is no ethicopolitical decision or gesture without what I would call a "Yes" to emancipation, to the discourse of emancipation, and even, I would add, to some messianicity.[45]

Although Derrida doesn't think his messianism could easily be translated into Judeo-Christian or Islamic terms, his explication sounds remarkably Habermasian, referring to a "messianic structure that belongs to all language [and to] the performative dimension of the promise." Speaking for or against truth, even lying, invokes such a messianic, a priori "believe me" as soon as one opens one's mouth. And "I do not see how one can pose the question of ethics if one renounces the motifs of emancipation and the messianic."

From these quotations, I find Derrida true to the postmodern critique of grand metanarratives, in a way that any Egyptian, Turk, Iranian, Aztec, or Indian (in both meanings) could share. As contemporary feminists have similarly argued about their gender biases, such a person would note suspiciously that the great, global, emancipatory, and cosmopolitan movements—from Alexander's philosophical brotherhood of man, to Augustus's Stoic Roman rule, to late Roman and medieval and modern Christianity, Islam, Buddhism, liberalism, and Marxism—have all been used to justify or obscure imperialistic or quasi-colonial practices. A Derridean postmodernist would obviously be allergic to neorealist essentialism, but she would be readier than most pragmatically, nonfoundationally, to engage in the situation-specific discourse of emancipation, of freedom from oppression and other possibly existential threats to which the discursive concern with "securitization speech acts" is also oriented. Derrida recognizes as well both an emancipatory, self-transcending, potentially dramatic, pervasive redemption motif, not unlike those articulated by Dallmayr's Islamic and Buddhist thinkers.

My own hermeneutic explorations of Judeo-Christian and other retellings of hero/liberator/salvation stories[46] similarly found transreligiously or cross-culturally valid forms of highly motivating narrative accounts, whose "truths" could vary with the different individual readings of them, and that could be differentiated on just such a "world-changing" versus "self-situation transcending" axis. Self-transcending orientations were an important part of Anwar Sadat's going to Jerusalem in the name of peace; they should make many Jews and Christians resonate when they reinterpret such actions performatively in the terms of vocabularies and motivational appeals they are more familiar with. Pragmatically, Bartolomé de Las Casas was, arguably, more of a success in Machiavellian power terms than was Machiavelli himself, even though by the end of his life he was widely recognized as an originator of opposition to New World imperial conquests by Christian European powers on what we would now take to be human rights grounds. Similarly, contrary to the rationalistic, secular Cold War practice in much of the West that opposed Weberian to Marxian social science, Weber's "iron cage" critique of modern bureaucratic society reads a lot like a combination of Marx and the Hebrew prophets! A Habermasian reformulation of the Weberian perspective, in terms of Wittgensteinian language games, or truth discourses, sounds like Marx, but is methodologically quite close to the Derrida we have been discussing.

Hence I conclude this section with the thought that even though globalizing emancipatory discourses—whether they be due to Woodrow Wilson,[47] Franklin Roosevelt, or George W. Bush and associates—have to be looked upon with a certain skepticism, and partial, performative, pragmatic convergences are possible on concrete security issues, convergences that can reasonably be said to preserve or augment emancipatory concerns. These must not be overlooked in an era characterized by George W. Bush in terms of the global war on terror. Although I cannot predict where the most productive domains for such discussions will be, perhaps they will include racially or religiously based repressions of distinctive minorities living in several countries, conquest-oriented military invasions across recognized boundaries, movements toward gender equality, and the rights of organized but underpriviledged peoples to provide more of their own economic sustenance.

Emancipatory Restructurings of
Collective Memories and Futures

I suppose that it is my Enlightenment ancestry as an educator that excites me when I come across historically pregnant quotes like the following from Milan Kundera's *The Book of Laughter and Forgetting:*

> The struggle of man against power is the
> Struggle of memory against forgetting.[48]

I certainly agree with the emancipatory import—concerning a potentially vital "apology issue" in contemporary Japanese retellings of their

World War II involvement—of William Howell's criticisms of particularistic, self-flattering, Japanese governmental and societal conduct on this point.[49] And I agree with Joshua Foa Dienstag's partial explanation for the success of the Eastern European 1989 revolutions: "As much as the virtues of capitalism, it was the memory of 1956 that threatened, and ultimately overwhelmed, communist rule [in Hungary]."[50] As an important piece of evidence for this claim, Dienstag recalls the early 1989 debate in Hungary occasioned by a governmental historical commission's redescribing the 1956 revolt as a "popular uprising" rather than a "counterrevolutionary" protest. Without such relegitimation efforts, the nationally emancipatory policy of withdrawal from the Warsaw Pact and the antiauthoritarian and hence emancipatory move toward a multiparty system in Hungary would similarly be considered counterrevolutionary.

But as a respectful gesture toward the many advocates for the views of Friedrich Nietzsche, Derrida, and Michel Foucault on such challenging subjects as power, truth, and enlightenment, I want here briefly to explore some of the more complex aspects of memories concerning Japan, the rest of East Asia, and the United States during the World War II period. In Dienstag's suggestive reading of Nietzsche, (re)writing human histories can—not surprisingly to the reader who has followed my story line so far— create collective identity transformations, existential *redemptions* from the violence of the past.

Dienstag's performative, Nietzschean title—"Dancing in Chains"— connotes the Homer-like overcoming of the cognitive and causal constraints of a painful past as creatively as possible. His next-to-last footnote conveys his attitude toward freedom even better; he cites Hannah Arendt's rather anti-Heidiggerian account in her *Between Past and Future,* "of *freedom as 'the capacity to begin something new'* [which account] captures as well as any I know the sense in which a concern for freedom and a concern for the future must coincide, as Nietzsche suggested."[51] Perhaps contra Milan Kundera, he has argued that "simply telling stories will not make us free; an inability to narrate, however, is an impediment that must be overcome on the path to freedom. It is a failure of imagination in the face of a singularly powerful memory [that has subordinated us]."[52] He recognizes too that "human beings fight over history because they conceive their pasts to be an essential part of who they are. And they are right."[53] After a suggestive treatment of the ways human lives are defined in terms of their actions—whose constitutive intentions are importantly shaped by their characters and relevant cultural narratives—he has earlier introduced this Arendtian theme. The plan of his book is comparatively to review and assess the contributions of Locke, Hegel, and Nietzsche as political theorists attempting "to design new plots for history"[54] where both the dramatic and the interventionist sense of plotting is intended.

The link to redemption is a bit more complicated. As articulated in a powerful chapter entitled "The Future of Pain," according to Nietzsche both society and the permanence of forms in memory are established by acts of violence. Bodily understood, consciousness, interpretations, morality, contracts, conscience, and Christian meekness are all results of a continuing history of violence and cruelty. In this terrible world, where memories and identities are fused, character transformations are possible:

> A new future is created by a rewriting of the past. It is a redemption of that past. It is the reshaping of the past to make a new value. Columbus, who had to reinterpret the globe before he could discover a new continent, is our modern-day Homer. [I]f we enter this future of disciplined creativity, the past will stand redeemed as its necessary prehistory. The attraction is that of a "multi-stringed culture" in place of the monotonous life of the Last Man.[55]

The different ways that we can rewrite our pasts allows a multiplicity of related, possible, less violent futures. It is this redemptive possibility "that the philosophy of Nietzsche awakens us to in its audacious attempt to remake the future and redeem the past by retelling our history."[56]

I want briefly to explore these notions, and extend them to recent and contemporary U.S. security policies, within the context of a beautifully nuanced but profoundly critical account of Hiroshima's efforts at urban renewal by Lisa Yoneyama. Her account occurs in a book full of such "TimeSpace" remappings.[57] Briefly, she argues that Hiroshima's publicly accented history is being rewritten by its urban planners and business leaders to emphasize "brightness, comfort, and cleanliness." Unlike some other thought-provoking reminders, the beautiful Peace Memorial Park is being preserved. But in Yoneyama's eyes, the partly destroyed Atomic Bomb Dome is becoming museumized, in a history-cleansing fashion, almost like a Disney theme park! An imperial castle actually destroyed by the atomic bomb has been reconstructed and is presented as a cultural site, emphasizing its romantic possibilities rather than its military past.

Having revisited the associated museum myself in the late 1990s, I, too, was struck by the ways the horror of the human suffering associated with the 1945 bombing had been less graphically displayed compared to what I had seen on my previous visit there. The history of its destruction, and its role as an imperial command post from which Japanese armies were being shipped off toward the Asian theater of war, were not obviously documented. As with the earlier, revisionist account of why the United States proceeded to drop the bomb, no effort was made to treat the suffering of the Japanese civilians in Hiroshima as in any way related to the war they started in Asia with Japanese mainland invasions, the anticivilian atrocities of the Rape of Nanking, and so on. No sense of the emancipatory concerns of the Rooseveltean coalition, as reviewed above, is presented. Even though Japanese ontological particularism may help explain their failure to make some—to many Westerners obvious—comparisons, one must ask, in light of the painful accounts that Yoneyama evokes from Hiroshima's war-impacted citizens: Are the business goals of the "renewers" consonant with these victims' need for recognition and renewal themselves? Is this truncated representation of Japanese history broadly contributive to a new era of trust-based international relations in East Asia? Without implying that U.S. histories of World War II do not also deserve critical revisions, I must agree that Howell's previously cited suggestion that more realistic public accounts of Japanese past debts vis-à-vis its neighbors would help improve its continuing relations with its neighbors. That way the further militarization of regional international relations could be at least partly neutralized.

In the interests of critical reciprocity, these remarks on Japanese memorial practices lead me to reflect on those of my own country and its allies. I do so in light of the previously established rootedness of the critical security project in the Rooseveltean hegemonic project, as revealed by a rereading of a U.S. memorial for their national leader during the Depression and World War II. I am compelled to ask: Are we living up to the ideals that so many of our fellow countrymen died for? Is the hatred of war emphasized in the FDR Memorial a clear principal of contemporary U.S. foreign policy? It is agreed that we do not like body bags, and our military tactics are calculated to minimize them, but do we not like the high-tech killing of others just a little too much, especially if it produces good videos?

Are we as committed to multilateralism and human rights universalism as Franklin and Eleanor Roosevelt were? Neither the two-party governance of the Bill Clinton era nor the one-party rule of George W. Bush have an unblemished record in this respect. Even before the era-redefining impact of the September 11 attacks, our national sense of existential security threats was changing away from widely appreciated New Deal ideals toward more internationally criticized, self-righteous demands and new, destabilizing doctrines of preemptive war initiation. With the open-ended war on terror and unsubstantiated claims of the imminent threat of weapons of mass destruction used to justify the preemptive 2003 U.S.-British attack against Iraq, endless U.S. supremacy has become the dominant U.S. goal.

In the current era of the U.S. strategy of "full spectrum dominance," or the "Command of the Commons,"[58] what has happened to the Rooseveltean commitment to eventual disarmament and to economic development for the peoples of the world—not just their major investors and bankers—in our national budgets or planning priorities? Why were Saddam Hussein and others blamed for the failure of the Cold War peace dividend to materialize even before September 11? Why do post-2001 military budgets seem to increase across the board, with increases in expenditures that cannot be justified as antiterrorist?[59] When senators talk about "special interests," why do they ever so rarely talk about defense industries and war profiteers, as Roosevelt used to do during peacetime, but much less often during the actual war period?

Where is the call for budget savings that might result from a more multilateralist reconsideration of the occluded parts of the past contribution of our allies? Why do U.S. politicians support calls for U.S. hegemony and extraordinarily low U.S. casualties at the same time? Is it because of our hollow hegemonic pretensions, which we don't like to fully admit unto ourselves, and which would be more sharply debated were they more fully and explicitly costed out?[60]

Why do so few of us train our students in defense budgeting skills necessary for sustained civilian control over defense spending? Although dollars are not adequate ways of measuring capabilities or threats, we may still ask: Why does the United States spend more than five times its closest competitor in contemporary military budgets? Where is the discussion of the substantial savings that would result if the United States were to reorient its forces in a defensive posture and efficiently try to strengthen, rather than weaken, UN multilateral peacekeeping and peace enforcement forces?

Are we seriously planning for a less armed, more multipolar, reasonably just and peaceful world order of the future, or are Americans and their British ally thinking that we shall remain preeminent forever, like the gods of Mount Olympus? Are we tending more to memorialize the good old days of World War II and the Cold War without being reminded of the extreme violence they contained? Ought not we critically oriented academic security scholars involve ourselves and our students in at least some of the difficult but challenging research programs mentioned earlier in this chapter? Do not scholars in Western countries need better to understand what other peoples and societies want—and what their possibly multiple civilizational identities mean? What should be the international, transnational, and (sub)national components of more collaborative efforts minimally to achieve the security components of such goals? In the interest of building a more stable and just world order that will ameliorate and survive the eventual decline in U.S. hegemony, it would be good to start preparing its intellectual foundations now, by recalling more accurately the roots of Anglo-American and NATO security priorities.

Conclusion

This chapter reflects on the crucial role that emancipation plays in the critical security studies project, one where security and emancipation are closely joined. In attempting to suggest a broad, focused, constructively critical framework for such inquiries, I recognize the possible positive connections of security and emancipation but nonetheless argue that claims as to actual co-occurrences must be critically investigated. The problem that alternative linkages of these desired conditions are suggested by different, globally oriented hegemonic projects—such as Roosevelt's Four Freedoms and the George W. Bush administration's call for perpetual superiority—has been recognized. Following Fred Dallmayr's pioneering work, I have suggested that culturally sensitive concepts of emancipation should be linked in a posthegemonic way to similarly culturally sensitive, concretely researchable conceptions of existential security. This approach has important historical dimensions as well: reunderstanding the past can help us and others better understand our own past as well as reimagine the future in more genuinely liberating ways.[61]

Epistemologically, this has meant engaging not only with postmodernist orientations familiar from French-, German-, and English-language literatures but also with more traditional, religious, postcolonial, and/or non-Western views on the meaning and practice of emancipation and redemption. Looking for convergent, pragmatic compromises helps find multiple moorings for human improvement, even if it is not always common ground. East and West are taking on new, overlapping, and interpenetrating meanings as we try to transcend geopolitical, geoeconomic, and geocultural cleavages in today's world. Even Derrida recognizes the importance in serious scholarly contexts "where . . . a certain type of propositional form . . . governs . . . [and] argumentation is clearly essential," without however eliminating our sensitivity to language's effects in such a process.[62] The ironical return of what Stephen Toulmin would describe as early modern, skeptical, humane, context-sensitive standards of reasonableness for scientific and practical inquiry on international security questions is surely postmodern irony, as well as a good, multicivilizational basis on which to recommence this inquiry![63]

Notes

Contributors to my thinking in this chapter are Ken Booth, Ann Tickner, Neta Crawford, Randall Forsberg, Kimberly Nolan, Thomas Schmalberger, and Colin Wight; none should be held responsible for what I made of their suggestions and ideas, for which nonetheless I am most grateful.

1. Inscription, Franklin Delano Roosevelt Memorial, Washington, D.C. See Roosevelt's 1941 "Annual Message" and his "Address at the Annual Dinner of the White House Correspondents Association," for the context in which these phrases first occurred.

2. Derrida, "Remarks," at p. 82.

3. Booth, "Security and Self," p. 113.

4. Looking back at Johan Galtung's pioneering *The True Worlds* suggests a much earlier date for full engagement with these issues, plus a critical determination to transcend differences between Cold War antagonists self-labeled as "The Free World" (fighting totalitarian "Communism") versus "Socialism" (fighting "imperialism"). In that respect, it is interesting to note that "freedom" and "liberation" are used sparingly in that volume, pointed more toward enhanced diversity and unrepressed political participation, and against structural violence or domination; and violence is conceived as "any avoidable impediment to self-realization." *The True Worlds,* pp. xxiv, 1, 48f., and 66–69. Galtung's was a perspective that few scholars in either of the first "Two Worlds" were willing or able to embrace or emulate at that time.

5. Booth, "Security and Emancipation," pp. 313–316. This article has been said by Devetak, "Critical Theory," in Burchill et al., *Theories,* p. 167, "to inaugurate critical security studies."

6. The locus classicus for Gramscians and many others is Robert Cox's essay "Social Forces, States, and World Orders," originally published in 1981, and included in Cox, with Sinclair, *Appproaches.* Along with many other Americans and Western Europeans, I found Jürgen Habermas's discussions of the emancipatory knowledge interest most provocative. In a 1988/1996 essay on "Emancipatory Empiricism," I cited Habermas's 1986 conception of that knowledge interest as "something profoundly ingrained in certain of our social structures, the calling into question, and deep-seated wish to throw off, relations which repress without necessity," quoted from his *Autonomy and Solidarity,* p. 198, and Herbert Marcuse's incisive, beautifully crafted account of surplus repression in his *Eros and Civilization.*

The labeling of a tradition of "'Reflective' or 'Critical' historiography" goes back at least to the beginning of the previous century, and is doubtless connected to Kantian and even broader intellectual currents; see my "Rescuing 'Reason' from the 'Rationalists,'" in *Rediscoveries and Reformulations,* pp. 207–237, esp. p. 220.

7. The quotations are, respectively, from Cox with Sinclair, *Approaches,* p. 89, and Booth, "Security and Emancipation," p. 318. See also Booth, "Security and Self."

8. The quoted remarks in this paragraph are from Booth, "Security and Emancipation," esp. pp. 318–323.

9. For those interested in counting the millions involved, and attempting either quantitative analyses of intergroup violence or preventively oriented forecasts of related state failures, Ted Gurr's ongoing work is especially significant. See both Gurr, "Peoples Against States"; and Davies and Gurr (eds.), *Preventive Measures.*

10. In the terminology of Galtung's peace research (see Galtung, *The True Worlds*), "human self-realization" would be the more appropriate term at this point than "security as a process" or "human emancipation," but Galtung would describe the diminution of such obstacles as "violence" reduction.

11. Krause and Williams (eds.), *Critical Security Studies,* p. xiff.

12. This is the objection to alternative or comprehensive security approaches offered in Walt, "The Renaissance of Security Studies."

13. Krause and Williams (eds.), *Critical Studies Studies,* p. 39.

14. This theme has been previously well developed in Barry Buzan, *People, States, and Fear: An Agenda,* and by many of the contributors to the Krause and Williams volume.

15. Pateman, *The Sexual Contract*; Tickner, *Gender in International Relations.*

16. For example, Mische, "Ecological Security and the Need to Reconceptualize Sovereignty"; and Homer-Dixon, "On the Threshold."

17. This phrase comes from Booth, "Security in Anarchy."

18. Besides Booth, relevant citations include Linklater, *Transformation*, and Campbell and Dillon (eds.), *The Political Subject of Violence*.

19. In the U.S. security studies context, the rediscovery of social constructivism is nicely reviewed by Ted Hopf, "The Promise of Constructivism in International Relations Theory"; he distinguishes the "conventional constructivist" writings of Nicholas Onuf, Peter Katzenstein, Yosef Lapid, and Friedrich Kratochwil from the "critical constructivist" writings of many poststructuralist and postmodernist writers, such as Michael Dillon, James Der Derian and Cynthia Weber. Drawing on earlier classical European, Middle Eastern, and Asian traditions, Galtung, *The True Worlds*, p. 30, prophetically suggested the dialectical (or "post-positivist") argument that equates science with "Empiricism + Criticism + Constructivism."

20. This line of thought is well developed in Linklater's writings, especially Linkater, *Transformation*. I was also struck by the way community-building, or international integration (in the sense of Karl Deutsch or Ernst Haas) links and transforms the connections of security-seeking and emancipatory overcomings while hearing Jef Huysmans 1998 ISA-ECPR paper "The Question of the Limit."

21. Roosevelt, "Annual Message to Congress," his "Address at the Annual Dinner of White House Correspondents' Association," and his "Letter Accepting the Annual Award of the Churchman." All reprinted in "Room Four: Freedom of Speech" of *FDR Speaks*.

22. See especially Forsberg, "Confining the Military to Defense"; also her "Toward the End of War," "Defense Cuts," "Cooperative Security—The Military Problem," and "Force Without Reason," *Boston Review* online, www.polisci.mit.edu/BostonReview/. Indeed Booth at one point cites the World War II origins of his emancipatory orientation, and acknowledges the influence of Forsberg's Institute for Defense and Disarmament Studies in his work; in a personal communication he says he has never consciously been a disciple of Roosevelt. I too have been associated with Forsberg's institute, and didn't fully realize the connections to Roosevelt suggested here before the development of this chapter.

23. See the sources cited in footnote 21 above. The Churchman letter has the most succinct formulation: "freedom of worship and utterance, freedom from want and fear" (boldface omitted).

24. Roosevelt, "Annual Message to Congress," p. 15f. Emphasis in original in boldface; changed to italics here.

25. Ibid., p. 16.

26. Roosevelt, "Address at the Annual Dinner of the White House Correspondents Association," p. 28.

27. Buzan, Wæver, and de Wilde, *Security*. An update of this approach is given in Buzan and Wæver, *Regions and Powers*.

28. Buzan, Wæver, and de Wilde, *Security*, pp. 21–29. In the next several paragraphs, these pages are the principal source of direct quotations.

29. In the above list, perhaps the most difficult entity to conceptualize in securitization terms is a "technology," which I think of as embedded within specific social practices. Buzan, Wæver, and de Wilde convincingly suggest that the "dikes" in Holland are a nonstate object/technology-in-place of clear existential importance.

30. See especially Dalby, "Contesting an Essential Concept," in Krause and Williams, eds., *Critical Security Studies*, pp. 3–31.

31. Galtung, *Peace by Peaceful Means*. See also Ackerman and Kruegler, *Strategic Nonviolent Conflict*.

32. See Linklater's discussion of "Political Community and Human Security" elsewhere in this volume. The discussion below of Habermasian linkages between community, society, and emancipation has been stimulated by that chapter as well.

33. Alker, "Emancipatory Empiricism," p. 333.

34. Ibid., p. 354, italics and ellipses omitted. An excellent study elaborating upon and exemplifying such an approach is Patomaki, "How to Tell Better Stories About World Politics." See also Bhaskar, *Dialectic*, and his *Plato*. Together they represent an extraordinarily impressive attempt philosophically to map out the multiple dimensions of human freedom.

35. One productive way to do this for international relations scholars would be to further engage with Isaiah Berlin, *Four Essays on Liberty*, including his critical discussion of E. H. Carr's influential historiographic views. Another would be to sympathetically engage with feminist critiques of critical theory, such as Marie Fleming, *Emancipation and Illusion*. "Heterological historians" grappling ethically with the impossibility of doing precise and accurate justice to the "mass exterminations" of the twentieth century are also worth reading; see Edith Wyschogrod, *An Ethics of Remembering*.

36. In a Linklater-like fashion, I have taken these (and subsequent Habermasian quotations) from his conversation with Michael Haller on "What Theories Can Accomplish."

37. Somewhat similar views have been expressed by Ernst B. Haas, Russell Hardin, Eric J. Hobsbawm, and Patrick Moynihan. In the concluding chapter of a two-volume study, Haas concludes: "The studies of the older nation-states showed an undeniable affinity between nationalism, progress, and peace. . . . Our optimistic hypothesis is not born out by events [in the newer nations of the present study]." Haas, *Nationalism, Liberalism, and Progress, Volume 2: The Dismal Fate of New Nations*, pp. 424–426. Similarly, discussing the future of ethnic nationalism, Hardin notes: "Hobsbawm thinks nationalism is no longer a main agent for global progress and emancipation as it once arguably was. Moynihan thinks it [the problematical fruits of the newer nationalisms] the dominant issue of our era. . . . Nationalism and ethnic mobilization today bring more degradation and ruin than emancipation and progress, but they nevertheless dominate politics in much of the world." Hardin, *One for All*, p. 226.

38. See Alker, *Rediscoveries*, p. 140f. and p. 250ff. for relevant elaborations and citations.

39. Huntington, *The Clash of Civilizations and the Remaking of World Order*, pt. 5.

40. Habermas, "What Theories Can Accomplish," pp. 106–107.

41. Chapter 3 of Dallmayr's particularly impressive *Alternative Visions* is relevantly entitled "Liberation Perspectives East and West." Among others, he crucially engages with "Laclau, *Emancipation(s)*; Pieterse, "Emancipations, Modern and Postmodern," pp. 6–7, 19, 23–24; Queen and King (eds.), *Engaged Buddhism*; and Shari'arti, *On the Sociology of Islam*. See also the various contributions on the liberation in East and West theme of Ayoob, Dalby, Fierke, Acharya, and Klein in Krause and Williams (eds.), *Critical Security Studies;* and Dallmayr, Connolly, and Rengger, "Global Conversation."

42. Neumann, *Russia*, p. 170, presents a remarkably similar Solzhenitsyn quote: "The [spritually racked and dejected] West has supped more than its fill of every kind of freedom, including intellectual freedom. And has this saved it?

Unlimited external freedom in itself is quite inadequate to save us. Intellectual freedom is a very desirable gift, but of conditional, not intrinsic, worth, only a means by which we can attain another and higher goal."

43. Metaphorically, in my view, world history has many imperfect librettos, making the problem of coherently presenting several of them especially challenging. Methodologically, the most helpful suggestions on how to do so that I have seen are Campbell, "Political Prosaics, Transversal Politics, and the Anarchical World," chap. 1 in Shapiro and Alker (eds.), *Challenging Boundaries*; and Duara, *Rescuing History from the Nation*. See also Ling's stimulating, feminist *Postcolonial International Relations*. For the alternative, more conservative argument that an overarching emancipatory narrative of world history is rationally/spiritually possible, and strengthened by the investigation of non-Western sources, see Butler, *History as the Story of Freedom,* and Liftin, "Towards an Integral Perspective on World Politics." For a more general discussion of such metaphorical understandings of world politics see the Special Issue "Images and Narratives in World Politics," *Millennium* 30, no. 3 (2001).

44. The Devetak and True chapters on "Postmodernism" and "Feminism," respectively, in Burchill et al., *Theories*, are especially accessible treatments in this regard, without overhomogenizing these clusters of viewpoints.

45. Derrida, "Remarks," p. 82. The quotation in the next paragraph is also from this source.

46. Relevant discussions supporting the arguments of this paragraph are contained in Alker, *Rediscoveries*, pp. 134–143, 172–183, 231–237. For an independent, but somewhat similar analysis, see Wierzbicka, *What Did Jesus Mean? Explaining the Sermon on the Mount and the Parables in Simple and Universal Human Concepts.*

47. The Wilsonian version of the U.S. emancipatory mission in world affairs is in the United States now being cited by both defenders and critics of George W. Bush's hegemonic/supremacy-maintaining practices. For a superb review of recent books on Wilson's diplomacy, see Steel, "The Missionary."

48. Cited as the initial quote of Howell, "The Inheritance of War."

49. Ibid., passim.

50. Dienstag, *Dancing in Chains*, p. 205.

51. Footnote 15 in the final chapter, entitled "The Politics of Memory," in ibid., p. 249 (emphasis added).

52. Ibid., p. 196f.

53. Ibid., p. 206.

54. Ibid., p. 19.

55. Ibid., p. 135f.

56. Ibid., p. 189.

57. Yoneyama, "Taming the Memoryscape," in Boyarin (ed.), *Remapping Memory.*

58. See Posen, "Command of the Commons."

59. See Randall C. Forsberg's articles and the Boston Review MIT website, cited above, and Carl Conetta and Charles Knight's similar publications from the Project on Defense Alternatives, 186 Hampshire St., Cambridge, MA 02139. Some of these critical publications, as well as a good selection of official Defense Posture and National Strategy documents, are available at www.comw.org/, followed either by pda or qdr.

60. See Steel, *Temptations of a Hegemon*, especially chapters 5 and 7; and Zakaria, "Our Hollow Hegemony"; Goldstein, *The Real Price of War.*

61. My own favorite text on the humbling need for better Western understanding of Islam comes from a book written well before September 11, 2001:

> Western audiences, out of ignorance, yield too easily to fundamentalist Muslim claims that Islam is prescriptive in simple ways. To argue otherwise requires knowledge of Islamic hermeneutics, dialectics, and dialogics. This knowledge is difficult for those who have lost contact with their own Christian and Jewish traditions . . . or with those of ancient Greece which too often are nostalgically idealized and hypostasized into paragons of virtue no longer viable. (Fischer and Abedi, *Debating Muslims*, p. 147)

62. Derrida, "Remarks," p. 78.
63. Toulmin, *Cosmopolis*. Related discussions of epistemological standards associated with practical reasoning occur in Alker, *Rediscoveries,* chaps. 1, 2, 12.

9

On Emancipation: Necessity, Capacity, and Concrete Utopias

Richard Wyn Jones

There are currently two rather different conceptualizations of critical security studies (CSS) in evidence. For some, it represents a distinct project in its own right: CSS is regarded as an attempt to develop an emancipation-oriented understanding of the theory and practice of security. This is certainly my own view of the enterprise.[1] The alternative view is of CSS as a typological device; as a useful label under which to group all those contemporary approaches to the study of security that do not share the narrow metatheoretical assumptions of traditional security studies.[2]

This distinction between CSS as a distinct project and CSS as a generic label may be further clarified with reference to the so-called postpositivist turn in international relations.[3] According to the CSS-as-label view, CSS may be understood as the specific security studies manifestation of the postpositivist turn in international relations. Thus, in his influential analysis of postpositivism, Steve Smith has identified five distinct postpositivist epistemologies (potentially or actually) influencing the study of international relations (IR): scientific (or critical) realism, hermeneutics, critical theory, feminist standpoint, and postmodernism.[4] According to the broad view, the term "CSS" describes the whole constellation of different—and even contradictory—approaches to the study of security generated from these different positions, even if it should also perhaps be noted that, in reality, the so-called postmodernist influences have been by far the strongest.[5] In contrast, the CSS-as-project view draws largely, although not exclusively, on one of these five approaches—namely, critical theory—to provide its metatheoretical underpinnings.[6]

Thus far, some of the most apparently profound and seemingly intractable differences between both versions of CSS have revolved around the question of emancipation. For those of us who adhere to the more specific version, or perhaps vision, of CSS, a notion of emancipation is central.

It is the starting point of analysis in that after Booth security is conceptualized in terms of emancipation[7]; and in an important sense it is the point of the whole exercise inasmuch as Marx's injunction to understand the world in order to change it shapes the whole enterprise. Those influenced by postmodernist or poststructuralist thinkers tend, however, to be much more skeptical or even absolutely opposed.

Emancipation stems from the Latin *emancipare*, meaning "the action of setting free from slavery or tutelage," and is a concept that has been associated with some of the great progressive struggles in modern history. Nevertheless, in the view of many poststructuralist critics, emancipation has become indelibly tainted by association with the metanarratives of modernity, especially Marxism and liberalism. As such, it has become complicit in the suffering engendered by the practices and pathologies of modernism (broadly defined). The result is that even for some putative radicals emancipation has come to be seen as "part of the problem and not part of the solution."[8]

However, this distinction between a specific, emancipation-oriented, critical theory–based CSS and a more general, emancipation-skeptic, poststructuralist-influenced CSS can be overplayed. In the first section of this chapter I will contend that, whatever the rhetoric, a notion of emancipation is implicit in the work of those scholars who are proponents of the broader "label" version of CSS; indeed, I will argue that some concept of emancipation is a *necessary* element of *any* form of analysis that attempts to problematize and criticize the status quo. This in turn means that all those seeking to develop CSS need to take emancipation more seriously. This entails thinking-through in far greater depth what emancipation might mean in terms of social practices and institutions, as well as how it might be brought about. The remainder will seek to stimulate a discussion around the first of these questions by focusing on the ideas of the Frankfurt School of critical theory.[9]

Frankfurt School critical theory has been defined by one of its most eloquent contemporary interpreters, Stephen Eric Bronner, as "a *cluster of themes* inspired by an emancipatory intent."[10] It represents one of the most serious, sophisticated, and sustained attempts to delineate the meaning(s) of emancipation in the contemporary world. In the second section of this chapter I will seek to explicate and evaluate the different—indeed, contradictory—ways in which the Frankfurt School tradition of critical theory has conceptualized humanity's *capacity* for emancipatory transformation. The final section of the chapter moves then from the abstract to the more specific and focuses on the ways in which various critical theorists have attempted to transpose metalevel understandings of emancipatory potential into visions of *concrete utopias*.

Necessity

The thesis that *all* proponents of CSS depend on some notion of the existence of possibilities for progressive alternatives—that is, emancipation—can be demonstrated by a textual analysis of the work of those scholars who have attempted to develop an approach to security on the basis of some form of poststructuralism. Consider the work, for example, of R. B. J. Walker and Ole Wæver—both prominent writers on security who have been heavily influenced by elements of poststructuralist thought and hence falling into the broader definition of CSS (even if this characterization is explicitly rejected by Wæver—see below).

In Walker's discussion of "The Subject of Security," we find the following revealing passage:

> If the subject of security is the *subject* of security, it is necessary to ask, first and foremost, how the modern subject is being reconstituted and then ask what security could possibly mean in relation to it. It is in this context that it is possible to envisage a critical discourse about security, a discourse that engages with contemporary transformations of political life, with emerging accounts of who we might become, and the conditions under which we might become other than we are now without destroying others, ourselves or the planet on which we all live.[11]

Implicit in all this is some notion of "improving" on the present and, however contingently and tentatively, the possibility of moving toward a "better world"; in other words, some notion of emancipation. Indeed, it is this that gives the work its whole political-ethical direction.

A close reading of Wæver's now influential "securitization" approach also reveals similar concerns. Take, for example, the following slightly opaque footnote in which he discusses the merits and demerits of "securitizing" and "desecuritizing" issues as part of what seems to be, in the broadest sense of the word, a "progressive" political project.

> For understandable but contingent institutional reasons, poststructuralists have emerged on the academic scene with the political program of tearing down "givens," of opening up, making possible, freeing. This invites the reasonable question: opening up for what? Neo-nazis? War? How can the poststructuralist be sure that "liberating minds" and "transcending limits" will necessarily lead to more peaceful conditions, unless one makes an incredible enlightenment-indebted "harmony of interests" assumption? For someone working in the negatively-driven field of security, a poststructuralist politics of responsibility must turn out differently, with more will to power and less de-naturalization.[12]

Again, Wæver seems to be hinting at some notion of emancipation—or, at the very least, this formulation requires a search for some means beyond the purely arbitrary to allow the observer to decide whether, and how, some forms of society are more acceptable (or emancipated) than others.

Wæver's deeply ambiguous position is well illustrated in his collaborative work with Barry Buzan and Jaap de Wilde, *Security: A New Framework for Analysis*.[13] In that work, the authors strive to differentiate themselves from CSS—which, when they are not assembling some strawman caricature, they seem to conceptualize in the narrower of the two senses discussed in this chapter. They certainly make great play of their refusal to "define some emancipatory ideal."[14] However, in the very same paragraph, they also proclaim the need "to understand the dynamics of security *and thereby maneuver them*."[15] They even claim that one of the benefits of the approach they champion in the book is that it "becomes possible to evaluate whether one finds it good or bad to securitize a certain issue."[16] Thus, despite the explicit disavowal, it is clear that there is some kind of emancipatory impulse at work here: the authors wish to establish a normative framework with which to evaluate the "goodness" and "badness" of certain practices and promote the former while disavowing the latter.

As this brief discussion demonstrates, it is clear that the *critical* edge of the work of these authors depends on the possibility of progressive alternatives to the status quo—that is, what is generally understood as some notion of emancipation. What is equally clear, however, is that none of the authors mentioned actually engage with the nature of these alternatives in any serious way. Rather their discussion of emancipation—what it means at either the abstract or concrete levels—is left either implicit or always deferred. This, in turn, has rather serious implications for the coherence of their work. So, for example, in the case of Buzan, Wæver, and de Wilde, their failure to seriously engage with the question of why some outcomes are to be preferred to others means that their own preference for "desecuritization" receives precious little theoretical support in their work. (It is therefore ironic, given their hostility to CSS, that Habermasian discourse ethics may provide just the buttress that their position requires!)

Why have writers on security that have been influenced by poststructuralism been so loath to engage seriously with emancipation? Why, indeed, do they seem to lack the necessary theoretical and political vocabulary with which to do this? We may speculate that this lacuna is a reflection of the fact that, generally speaking, few poststructuralist IR scholars have followed the "ethical turn" now so apparent in the work of those key figures who supply so much of their inspiration. For as Axel Honneth notes:

> If the philosophical movement of postmodernism was, in its beginnings, apparently directed against every kind of normative theory, then this initial reticence has since given way to a dramatically changed attitude.

> Writers like Derrida and Lyotard, at first primarily concerned with a radi-
> cal perpetuation of the critique of reason, turn today to questions of
> ethics. . . . The field of moral theory, which until recently had constituted
> for all representatives of poststructuralism a particularly salient example
> of modernity's compulsive universalism, has now become the true medi-
> um for the further development of postmodern theories.[17]

One inevitable corollary of this engagement with political-ethical
issues is that the question of plausible and desirable alternatives—that is, of
emancipation—is inevitably broached. To challenge and question the status
quo it is necessary to have some notion what would constitute an improvement upon it; it is precisely that which provides critical purchase on the
object of inquiry. It is not surprising, therefore, that Jacques Derrida, for
example, has moved to associate himself with the "great classical discourse
of emancipation."[18]

There are already signs that this engagement is being echoed in the
study of politics. In his essay "Beyond Emancipation," the political theorist
Ernesto Laclau rejects understandings of emancipation based on "religious
and modern secularised eschatologies" but nevertheless embraces a politics
orientated toward liberation and freedom.[19] Jan Neverdeen Pieterese has
usefully characterized this position as one that, while rejecting the ideal of
Emancipation (with a capital E)—that is, emancipation as part of a totalizing metanarrative—still finds it necessary to uphold a more circumscribed
notion of emancipation.[20] As will become apparent in the next two sections
of this chapter, this is a position that contemporary critical theorists wholeheartedly endorse.

In the study of IR and security, the work of David Campbell is another
clear example of the "ethical turn" in poststructuralism.[21] Here we find
deconstruction giving way to a type of political and ethical reconstruction;
that is, to a concern with emancipation—if by another name.

At this point it may not be entirely fanciful to suggest that, despite
their very real differences, a concern with understanding and, where possible, providing support for emancipatory struggles may eventually form a
point of contact—even of common ground—between the various postpositivist approaches to IR. Critical theorists will, of course, need little per-
suading of the validity of this concern. Nor will those influenced by critical
realism. Alex Wendt, for example, has recently described his own position
as one that "combines emancipation, which can only occur by deep transformation of the existing order over the long run, with the positivist willingness to think scientifically about that task."[22] But the growing willingness of poststructuralist-inspired thinkers to articulate and examine the
notions of progressive transformation and betterment already (and
inevitably) present in their work indicates that emancipation will become a
central concern in these circles as well. Thus, far from being the point of

division between the two versions of CSS highlighted at the start of this chapter, emancipation may become the common concern that unites them. Lest there be any misunderstanding, this is not to suggest that all proponents of critical security studies could or should alight on some facile, lowest-common-denominator consensus on the issue(s) of emancipation. As the remainder of this chapter will demonstrate, the trajectory of the Frankfurt School tradition itself is evidence enough that any such agreement is highly unlikely. Rather, my hope is that, like advocates of critical theory, all those committed to developing critical security studies will come to believe that debates about what might constitute the contours of a more emancipated order, and the routes by which this may be approached, are a central and inescapable part of their endeavors.

This is, of course, speculation. What is less open to doubt is that for those who already conceive of CSS as an emancipation-oriented project, the work of the Frankfurt School of critical theory provides an invaluable resource, representing as it does the most serious and, to my mind, sophisticated theoretical engagement with the concept. The next section will focus on the often contradictory but always stimulating ways in which that tradition has understood humanity's capacity for emancipatory transformation.

Capacity

The starting point in any discussion of Frankfurt School critical theory is Max Horkheimer's programmatic essay "Traditional and Critical Theory," written in 1937.[23] The understanding of emancipation contained within it is very recognizably Marxist in character and inspiration. Horkheimer equates emancipation with the increased domination of nature. Humans, he argues, are freer the less prone they are to the vicissitudes of nature. Furthermore, the possibilities for this better life are seen as already present in the existing forces of production. The problem is that their potential is squandered because of the way in which they are currently utilized for the benefit of capital rather than that of humanity as a whole. This potential could be unlocked, however, in a society based on some form of socialist planning.[24] Horkheimer thus makes regular reference to the possibility of developing a "rational society," "the right kind of society," one that is "self-determined," regulated according to "planful decision" and inhabited by a new "self-aware mankind."[25]

It is important to note that the particular understanding of emancipation presented in the essay plays a vital role in critical theory. It provides the standpoint for the critique of the status quo. Rather than criticize the prevailing order in terms of some blueprint for an ideal society, critical theory criticizes it on the basis of the unfulfilled potential that already exists within it—that is, through a form of *immanent* critique. The ability to identify immanent, unrealized, or unfulfilled possibilities within the reality of any given order is therefore vital in order to allow this approach critical purchase on its object of study.

When he wrote "Traditional and Critical Theory," Horkheimer was still relatively sanguine about the existence of such emancipatory possibilities. He was also convinced, again in orthodox Marxist fashion, that a class existed within society—the proletariat—that had the potential to realize those potentialities. The proletariat, he argued, experienced the disjuncture between humanity's potential to control nature (i.e., the emancipatory possibilities) provided by the ever more powerful forces of production at its disposal and the use to which that potential is actually put under capitalist relations of production.[26]

However, Horkheimer was less confident that the proletariat would actually set about exercising the power "to change society" that "objectively considered" it enjoys.[27] Two sets of reasons are advanced to explain this pessimism: the first sits full-square within the Marxist tradition; the second heralds the genesis of the argument that, when fully developed in the book *Dialectic of Enlightenment* (discussed below), not only leads to a thoroughgoing revision of critical theory's relationship to that tradition but also to radically different understanding of emancipation.

The main argument advanced in "Traditional and Critical Theory" to explain the proletariat's quiescence was a familiar one in many intellectual, left-wing circles in the 1930s. Horkheimer refers to the divisions within the working class and notes also the failure of the working class to recognize its real position and its real interests. The lessons he draws are that critical theorists must avoid "canonising" the proletariat but rather retain their independence and integrity and act as a "critical promotive factor . . . to stimulate change."[28]

In the essay, however, Horkheimer also begins to develop another, far bleaker analysis. This contends that the proletariat's submission in the face of the prevailing order is not merely a form of "false consciousness" that even if stubborn is potentially erasable. Rather, he attributes the working class's quiescence to a far more serious, and intractable, malaise. Modern capitalism, Horkheimer argues, has extinguished the individual's potential for autonomous activity. Mechanisms such as the state's bureaucratic apparatus and the mass media have effectively undermined human subjectivity and left humanity (the proletariat included) acting as "mere functions of the economic machine."[29] At this stage, however, the deeply pessimistic implications of this line of argument are not pursued. Rather, the overall thrust of "Traditional and Critical Theory" is that progressive change is possible, even if it is unlikely to occur in the short run.

Horkheimer's subsequent collaboration with Theodor Adorno, which led in 1947 to the publication of their masterpiece *Dialectic of*

Enlightenment, does develop this second line of argument to its logical conclusion.[30] In doing so they initiate a radical departure from the vision of critical theory developed in "Traditional and Critical Theory."

Recasting the whole history of human civilization, Adorno and Horkheimer claim that the very process whereby humanity has gained control over nature—far from being emancipatory, as Horkheimer had previously held—actually leads to domination and oppression. Or to put the argument at its starkest, anti-Semitism and the depravity of the concentration camps did not represent the reemergence of a long-buried, atavistic impulse. Rather, these developments were the inevitable and inescapable consequences of civilization itself. This is because during the process of civilization instrumental rationality—the form of rationality necessary to domesticate and control the natural world—takes on an ever greater role and status until other forms of rationality—those concerned with ends as well as means—become totally marginalized and redundant. This atrophy of reason leaves humanity prey to all kinds of inhumanity. Thus, the inexorable rise of instrumental rationality as a necessary corollary to civilization leads to ever greater barbarism in human relations—also as a necessary corollary.[31]

As even this brief discussion indicates, the implications of their analysis are far-reaching. If human history is conceived as the inexorable march of instrumental rationality from mythic prehistory to the gas chambers, then any form of progressive development (emancipation) ceases to be an immanent, intramundane possibility. Adorno even argues, in one of his deliberately shocking turns of phrase, that "nothing complicitous with this world can have any truth."[32] Where does this leave critical theory?

Adorno and Horkheimer did tentatively suggest the development of a different relationship between humankind and nature. This envisaged emancipation as involving "reconciliation" with nature[33]; a realization that humanity is "of" nature, rather than "above" nature, and the concomitant development of a noninstrumental relationship with it.[34] But given that the critique of instrumental rationality advanced in *Dialectic of Enlightenment* is itself based on totalizing assumptions about humankind—in effect, a set of anthropological claims about humanity's relations with its material surroundings, as well as intraspecies relationships—all such depiction must remain at the level of hypothesis. Adorno and Horkheimer cannot point to any concrete examples of what types of institutions and relationships might characterize a more emancipated society. They have never existed, and given the all-pervading effects of instrumental rationality, it is clear that they never could.

So the radically revised notion of emancipation advanced in *Dialectic of Enlightenment* is utopian in the negative sense: it has no relationship to the real world. It is literally unimaginable. To be sure, emancipation remained a kind of "regulative ideal" for Adorno and Horkheimer. Indeed, epistemologically, it is only this possibility that gives critical theory coherence and, indeed, purpose. Without keeping some notion of emancipation in play, critical theory cannot demur from the stress on repetition, calculability, and predictability characteristic of traditional theory (or positivism, as it has become known—somewhat loosely, it has to be said—in IR circles). Thus in his subsequent work, Horkheimer, for example, attempted to develop what amounts to a godless theology that located emancipatory impulses in what he argued was an anthropologically based propensity for pity and human solidarity. But the type of critique that could be built on these foundations was immanent only in the loosest, and most tenuous, sense and certainly has not satisfied subsequent generations of critical theorists.

Jürgen Habermas is by far the best-known contemporary critical theorist. His attempts to revivify the Frankfurt School tradition have, paradoxically perhaps, led him to reject many of the central arguments of its most famous early protagonists. Nowhere is this more apparent than in his reading of humanity's emancipatory capacity.

Habermas's crucial move in his recasting of critical theory was to distinguish between production, work, or labor, on the one hand, and interaction or communication on the other.[35] Habermas argues that these "realms" of social activity are characterized by two distinct types of human behavior: the realm of work or production is characterized by instrumental action, and the realm of interaction is characterized by communicative action. He further argues that the earlier generation of critical theorists was mistaken in locating the capacity for emancipation in the realm of production: "to set free the technical forces of production . . . is not identical with . . . liberation from servitude and degradation."[36] In contrast, Habermas has argued that the locus of emancipatory potential is to be found in the realm of interaction or communication: an argument most fully elaborated in the two-volume study *Theory of Communicative Action*.[37]

Habermas's output has been enormous. Yet his central claim concerning communication, and indeed his basic argument concerning the locus of emancipatory capacity, is simple. It is summarized in *Knowledge and Human Interests*:

> The human interest in autonomy and responsibility is not mere fancy, for it can be apprehended a priori. What raises us out of nature is the only thing whose nature we can know: language. Through its structure, autonomy and responsibility are posited for us. Our first sentence expresses unequivocally the intention of a universal and unconstrained consensus.[38]

Although the theoretical underpinnings of this claim may have changed, Habermas has nevertheless maintained the same fundamental line of argument. He argues that there is something inherent in speech that acts, in effect, as a promissory note for the possibility of a better world. The nature of this "something" is delineated via his theory of universal (or, more recently, formal) pragmatics.

Reducing consideration of communication to the analysis of speech, Habermas argues that speech acts necessarily involve a series of presuppositions if they are to be valid. Specifically, four "validity-claims" are identified: if a speech-act is to be valid then this presupposes that the utterance is *meaningful, true, justified,* and *sincere.* These validity-claims are presupposed in *all* speech-acts—lying, for example, relies on these presuppositions. The possibility of unforced understanding is therefore inherent in speech—indeed, speech depends upon it. The implications of this argument, if correct, are far-reaching. On the Habermasian reading, speech is the location of emancipatory promise and capacity. It generates an immanent, nonmetaphysical form of rationality against which individual and social behavior may be measured. Those institutions and practices that hinder the realization of the potential for unconstrained communication and unforced understanding inherent in speech are to be regarded as unacceptable and hence ripe for transformation; those developments that help realize this potential are considered emancipatory.[39]

Habermas's work has generated a vast critical literature. A number of commentators have focused in particular on his claim that the "communicative turn" that he initiated in critical theory does indeed provide a persuasive account of emancipatory capacity.

One major question mark is whether Habermas's theory of communicative action can bear the normative weight that he wishes to rest upon it.[40] Even more fundamentally, doubt has been cast on the basic categories upon which Habermas has constructed his theory of society. In particular, the differentiation between work and interaction, and the identification of the former with instrumental action, and the latter with communicative action, seem to set up a series of unnecessarily antinomic dualisms. How useful is it to imply that instrumental and communicative activity are somehow governed by separate logics and practices? Rather than viewing them as distinct, is it not better to recognize, and reflect on, the fact that discourse oriented toward success (characteristic of "work") and discourse oriented toward understanding (characteristic of "interaction") are invariably mutually implicated?

Such mutual implication underlines the problematic implications of Habermas's tendency simply to ignore "work"—the sphere of production and labor—and concentrate his theoretical attention solely on interaction. For one need not make grandiose claims about the "dignity of labor" to recognize that the realm of work cannot simply be reduced to simple relations of instrumentality. One need not be an economic reductionist to accept that a person's position in the realm of production has major implications for their role and status within society; and one need not posit that the proletariat is a "universal class" uniquely placed to emancipate humanity, to argue that emancipatory politics can be generated through people's experience in the realm of work.

Interaction does not occur in a vacuum. Rather it occurs within a context that is at least partly structured by people's economic activities—and, importantly, by their relationship with nature. Thus to refuse to engage seriously with "economic" relationships—as if these relationships do not also embody social, political, moral, and even aesthetic elements—is to constrain the critical edge of critical theory. Even in terms of Habermas's own theory, it is clear that inequalities inherent in the structures of economic accumulation have major distorting effects on the pursual of mutual understanding. Simply to decry those effects without attempting to expose their causes or search for remedies—effectively Habermas's position—seems to cast doubt on the whole theoretical enterprise. This is all the more so because Habermas himself, in standard Marxist fashion, is candid in his recognition of the primacy of productive relationships.[41]

Craig Calhoun argues that the theory of communicative action is so abstract as to render Habermas's theory unable to account for particular sociocultural identities.[42] Such is Habermas's concern with the general and universal that he fails to give sufficient or due weight to the specific identity-contexts in which communicative action takes place. This unease is given more concrete form in the work of perhaps the most creative of the latest generation of German critical theorists, Axel Honneth.

While Honneth certainly concurs with the broad thrust of Habermas's communicative turn—that is, the attempt to locate emancipatory potential and politics in the realm of interaction rather than work—he dissembles from Habermas's stress on language. Honneth's worry is that in understanding communication solely in terms of speech (viewed generically and abstractly) Habermas fails to meet what he regards as the "unrenounceable premise" of critical theory, which is that it must be able to ground its critique in real-world experience.[43] To diagnose the ills of the modern world in terms of the theory of communicative action is not, according to Honneth, to grasp those real-world, pretheoretical experiences that generate emancipatory impulses and emancipatory politics. This leads him to try to reconstruct the communicative turn in terms of a theory of recognition.

Honneth contends that human beings have "intuitive notions of justice" premised on respect for their "dignity, honour, or integrity" and that they "encounter each other within the parameters of the reciprocal expectation that they receive recognition as moral persons and for their social achievements."[44] When these expectations are not met this has serious consequences because the experience of social recognition presents a condition on which the development of the identity of human beings depends, its denial, that is, disrespect, is necessarily accompanied by the sense of a threatening loss of personality . . . [and resulting] shame, anger, or indignation.[45]

By shifting the communicative paradigm from a theory of language to a theory of recognition, Honneth argues that he can demonstrate which real-world or intramundane experiences generate emancipatory political action, thereby—he believes—providing a more convincing underpinning for the critical theory project itself. Or in his own words, "Those feelings of injustice which accompany structural forms of disrespect represent a pretheoretical fact on the basis of which a critique of the relations of recognition can identify its own theoretical perspective in social reality."[46] The sociological presumption of recognition of identity becomes, for Honneth, the locus of emancipatory promise and potential.

Of course, Honneth is aware that "the struggle for recognition"—the title of his 1995 book—is an extremely ambivalent source of political inspiration. It can give rise not only to the pacifistic internationalist sentiment that, for example, overwhelmingly characterizes Welsh nationalism but also, as Honneth himself points out, to the neo-Nazi groups that have developed in Germany. Thus, a crucial question that critical theorists must address is "how a moral culture could be so constituted as to give those affected, disrespected and ostracized, the individual strength to articulate their experiences in the democratic public sphere, rather than living them out in the countercultures of violence."[47]

The importance of this question need hardly be underlined in a world convulsed by some of the barbaric manifestations of identity politics such as ethnic cleansing, and Honneth's theoretical model certainly provides an innovative means by which it might be framed.

Honneth's work is not without its problematic aspects, however. Two can be briefly mentioned here. First, although Honneth aims to uncover and analyze the *struggle* for recognition, his argument seems to be based on the assumption of an essential harmony between the identity-claims of individual subjects. That is, his argument is premised on the notion that the full development of an individual's identity can take place without impinging upon the identity of another. But is this really the case? Isn't it rather that in some instances, at least, the "successful development" of the identity of one group can take place only at the expense of another? And if this is so, does it not fundamentally call into question Honneth's presumption of an essential—or at least potential—harmony between identity-claims? Second, it is not clear that Honneth is sufficiently cognizant of the extent to which interests and identities are entwined and, indeed, the extent to which the latter are often expressions of the former. To conceive conflicts solely in terms of (narrowly understood) identity is to ignore some of the most basic sources, and dynamics, of tension and contention.

As Honneth's project is still in its formative stages, it is too early to judge whether his account of emancipatory capacity will supersede that of Habermas. There are clearly major problems that will have to be overcome if this is to transpire. More generally, although the attempt to identify the locus of emancipatory potential in the realm of communication may well represent a distinct improvement on those that sought to locate immanent, unfulfilled potential in the realm of production, there is clearly much work still to be done. The Frankfurt School may have clarified the issues, and focused on key questions, but they remain a long way from providing the answers. This in turn may well lead some observers to ask, Why does this matter? Should we be concerned by the inability of critical theorists to provide a fully satisfactory account of the intramundane basis for the belief that emancipatory transformation is possible? Do we really require the complex intellectual constructions of the Frankfurt School tradition in order to make claims about emancipation?

Bronner, for one, is doubtful whether the expenditure of intellectual effort involved is worthwhile. His argument is that a simple review of the historical record is sufficient to justify certain institutions and practices over others:

> It is enough to look back at *real systems* and see that, with few historical exceptions, the extent to which the liberal rule of law is employed is the extent to which grievances are open to consistent forms of equitable redress. It is enough to note that the extent to which reciprocity is denied is the extent to which popular sovereignty is subverted, inequality is legitimated, and the subject's security is lost. It is enough to know from the past that the arbitrary exercise of power is grounded in terror.[48]

Furthermore, in a statement that resonates with the sentiments of the "early" critical theory of "Traditional and Critical Theory," Bronner argues that "the interests of critical theory in justice and happiness are validated by those who suffer from their denial."[49] The starting point for critical theory should not be some abstracted notion of emancipation and human potential but rather the corporeal, material existence and experiences of individual human beings.

Bronner's comments are well taken. They are a salutary warning against the persistent tendency of critical theory to collapse into "nothing more than an academic exercise."[50] While metatheory *is* important, as Bronner recognizes, its importance must be measured in terms of its contribution to the generation of theory that is oriented toward real-world social transformation. Put another way, providing a persuasive account of humanity's capacity is one thing, but it is the realization of that potential that must be the ultimate concern. It is this social transformation that is the *point* of critical theory, and it is according to its adequacy for this task that critical theory must be judged. As Nancy Fraser argues, "It is in the crucible of political practice that critical theories meet the ultimate test of vitality."[51] Furthermore, in good dialectical fashion, it is important that those critical theorists who choose to concentrate their efforts on metatheoretical activity habitually remind themselves that practical struggle offers insights for theory-building just as surely as vice versa.

Nevertheless, Bronner's argument that the historical record in effect speaks for itself on issues of grounding is too complacent. Consider, for example, his short account, quoted above, of what history "proves." Bronner argues that history demonstrates that the liberal rule of law and accountability (democracy) are demonstrably superior to any previous or present alternative. This would seem to be not only plausible but also irrefutable. But note his subsequent comment "that the extent to which reciprocity is denied is the extent to which popular sovereignty is subverted, inequality is legitimated, and the subject's security is lost." What Bronner seems to be suggesting is that, contra Habermas and Honneth, there is no need to worry unduly about the source(s) of expectations concerning reciprocity; rather it is enough to recognize that popular sovereignty, equality, and security are the necessary prerequisites for reciprocity in the real world.

Bronner's argument should be considered in light of the Marxian critique of capitalism of which critical theory is an intellectual heir. Marxist political economy argues that capitalism generates inequality and insecurity and that the reified separation of economics and politics into separate spheres—a move so characteristic of capitalism—undermines the claim of liberal democracies to be polities based on popular sovereignty. The important point to note is that none of this critique is based on pointing to historical, or contemporary, examples of an actually existing, alternative order. History certainly does not prove the superiority of an alternative mode of production to that of capitalism. Neither can the Marxian critique of capitalism be *reduced* to an immanent critique in the sense of juxtaposing the present order to the justifications that are supplied for it—that is, an argument along the lines of the following: *this is a society that claims to be based on equality and yet this principle is not enacted in relation to this particular group (women/linguistic minority, etc.) within it.* Rather, as Norman Geras has persuasively argued, Marx and his adherents have also relied on another form of immanent critique, a critique that—often implicitly—measures the present on the basis of a conception of actually existing, but not yet actualized, human potential.[52] The debate over emancipatory capacity is in essence a debate about delineating both the source and character of this potential. By abandoning the latter form of critique and concentrating solely on the former—a move that is implicit in Bronner's position—critical theory would be narrowing the basis of its critique in an unwarranted and unhelpful fashion. As the Marxian critique of capitalist political-economy illustrates, accounts of human potential form an important part of the critical theorist's theoretical armory.

If this argument is correct, there is certainly justification for critical theorists pursuing the question of emancipatory capacity. Moreover, students of CSS—of whatever metatheoretical hue—have much to learn from them. The work of critical theorists is also useful in thinking through another key question in the politics of emancipation, namely, what emancipation means in terms of actual institutions and forms of life.

Concrete Utopias

In the 1960s, radical German students came into conflict with the founders of critical theory.[53] One of the many sources of discord was the students' frustration with the unwillingness of Adorno and Horkheimer to move beyond very generalized exhortations concerning emancipation, empowerment, freedom, and happiness to provide descriptions of the characteristics of a more emancipated society. It was high time, in their view, that critical theorists outlined positive visions of *concrete utopias*.[54]

It is not difficult to understand the source of the students' frustration. Politics involves making choices: choices between different visions of the ends pursued, and choices between different means of pursuing them. But choices are seldom clear-cut. Means and ends may conflict, short-term goals may contradict longer-term objectives, and actions often have unintended consequences. Part of the task of theory that is committed to emancipatory transformation is thus surely to delineate and clarify the choices being faced in the practical realm and to examine and illuminate conflicts and contradictions between them. In this way, theory can give direction to action; theory and practice can be consciously unified in praxis.

Adorno and Horkheimer, for their part, justified their refusal to engage with the task of delineating the possible contours of a more emancipated order in terms of the Judaic prohibition on the portrayal of Jehovah.[55] But as we have seen, it is clear that the major theoretical stumbling block for them was their analysis of instrumental rationality as an all-pervading, all-encompassing, and wholly negative force within contemporary society. This led them to believe that they had no grounds for considering that any form of progressive development was possible.

Even if we set that argument to one side, there are clearly difficulties and dangers involved in any attempt to sketch concrete utopias: the dangers of dogmatism and utopianism (again, in the negative sense). However, a reading informed by both the spirit and method of critical theory suggests that these dangers are minimized if three provisos are heeded. First, and most obviously given the discussion in the previous section, visions of concrete utopias must be consistent with the deeper notions of emancipatory capacity. Thus, for example, if the possibility of emancipation is grounded in the economic realm, then, logically, depictions of a more emancipated order cannot simply concentrate on (narrowly defined) political institutions. Second, descriptions—indeed, prescriptions—of a more emancipated order must focus on *realizable* utopias. Critical theorists must not lose sight of the fact that the coherence of their project is dependent on their utilization of the critical potential of immanence. If they succumb to the temptation of suggesting a blueprint for an emancipated order that is unrelated to the possibilities inherent in the present—a tendency that Marx argued was characteristic of "utopian socialists" such as Robert Owen—then critical theorists have no way of justifying their arguments epistemologically. Furthermore, it is highly unlikely that a vision of an emancipated order that is not based on immanent potential will be politically efficacious.

Finally, in addition to basing their visions of concrete utopias on realizable, immanent possibilities, critical theorists must also restate their understanding of emancipation as a "process" rather than an "endpoint," a direction rather than a destination.[56] Such an understanding is, of course, inherent in a dialectical approach that regards each order or condition as the bearer of its own negation. Thus even if a more emancipated order is brought into existence, the process of emancipation remains incomplete. There is always room for improvement; there is always unfinished business in the task of emancipation.

Moving beyond these extrapolations from the principles and precepts of critical theory, what else can be gleaned from the work of contemporary critical theorists about the broad contours of concrete utopias? The answer is: a great deal. This is because the ideas of critical theory have had a major impact on theories of deliberative and cosmopolitan democracy. This influence can be clearly seen in the work of individuals such as David Held, Kenneth Baynes, and Andrew Arato—thinkers who have all written extensively about critical theory and are also significant figures in contemporary debates concerning how democracy can be broadened and deepened.[57] Through their work the ideas of critical theory—and especially its Habermasian reformulation—are informing concrete proposals for institutional reform. Not only this, but Habermas himself has attempted to explore the political and legal implications of his ideas, most systematically in the book *Between Facts and Norms*.[58]

His book serves to underline both the strengths and weaknesses of these critical theory–inspired attempts to explore the contours of concrete utopias. Viewed positively, the proceduralist view of democracy developed by Habermas seems to offer the genuine possibility of incorporating the strengths, and transcending the weaknesses, of the competing liberal and civic republican conceptions of democratic politics. And fittingly given the strictures alluded to above, Habermas's stress is consistently on outlining appropriate processes rather than on setting out rigid visions of *the* good life. That being said, read from a perspective animated by a concern with world politics, the book is also notable for the fact that its focus is almost exclusively internal. Habermas has very little to say about the possibilities for change at the international level. Notwithstanding its undisputed importance, *Between Facts and Norms* is basically a book about—and for— developed Western liberal democracies.

Granted, Habermas does ponder the future of the nation-state, arguing the case for the development of world citizenship.[59] But compared to the sophistication of his discussions of the inside, the treatment of the outside is somewhat superficial and perfunctory. His comments center on how the development of transnational civil society might eventually presage the development of a "global welfare regime," arrived at, he speculates, through an intermediate stage of regional consolidation along the lines of the European Union.[60] But to my mind at least, by far the most thoughtful and thought-provoking attempt to come to grips with world politics from a recognizably Habermasian perspective is to be found not in Habermas's own work but in that of international relations theorist Andrew Linklater.[61] However, I would also argue that despite the suggestiveness of Habermas's treatment of the inside, and despite the many virtues of Linklater's work, attempts to utilize a Habermasian frame of reference to global politics are destined to remain ultimately unconvincing because of the way in which Habermas identifies humanity's emancipatory capacity.

By drawing the distinction between work and interaction, and arguing that the locus for emancipatory possibilities is to be found in the latter and not the former, Habermas tends to marginalize theoretical consideration of issues relating to political economy—at least as it pertains to the consideration of the conditions for and possibilities of emancipatory transformation. Indeed, a key supposition underpinning Habermas's attempts to work through the implications of his ideas for politics is that the economic realm should remain a relatively autonomous subsystem in which activity is mediated and steered via money and not, for example, economic democracy or some form of democratically controlled planning. Habermas wants to deepen democracy in the political realm; he wants also to resist encroachments on the realm of politics by the economic realm. However, he does not want to roll back the market, having abandoned the old-left dream of extending democracy into the realm of economic production and exchange as a dangerous and self-defeating illusion.

But in considering contemporary world politics, and in particular the vast (and rapidly growing) socioeconomic inequalities and their appalling human costs, the tendency to pass over issues of economic governance at the global level leaves Habermasian theory naked before many of the forces that generate suffering and insecurity and hinder emancipatory change. A cursory consideration of the abject material state of a large proportion of the world's population renders as uncharacteristically complacent even Habermas's carefully qualified declaration that "state citizenship and world citizenship form a continuum whose contours, at least, are already becoming visible."[62]

The contours are not visible precisely because Habermas, and the left in general at this point in history, have no credible alternative political economic vision for the future. Contemporary critical theorists like Habermas and his followers may attempt to make a virtue out of necessity by arguing that this does not really matter; or, in any case, while there is no alternative to it, the market does work if it is confined to the economic realm. But the numbing statistics detailing poverty, suffering, and death outside the core of the current world system suggest another reading: while there may indeed be no alternative at present, the market system does not work. This in turn suggests that a key priority for any contemporary critical theory that seeks seriously to explore the possibilities of concrete utopias should be to reengage with issues of political economy. Some strands within the contemporary critical theory may offer assistance in this process, in particular the work of Moishe Postone and Axel Honneth.[63] But intellectual resources will also need to be sought from well beyond the bounds of critical theory and even postpositivist thought more generally.[64]

Conclusion

This chapter has sought to demonstrate that a concern with emancipation is necessarily central to any form of CSS. Ultimately, it is only some concept of emancipation that gives critical purchase on the object of inquiry. This being so, it is important to subject the (usually implicit) assumptions as to what constitutes enhanced human freedom to critical discussion and assessment. Here I have sought to explore some of the issues at stake by evaluating some of the debates within the critical theory tradition on both the locus of humanity's emancipatory capacity, as well as the contours of a more emancipated society. Although I have identified significant flaws in critical theory's treatments of these key themes, I wish to conclude by stressing that whatever faults have been highlighted, this does not diminish the potential usefulness of this tradition for those developing CSS—quite the opposite, in fact. Even if the ideas are not wholly convincing, the writing of successive generations of the Frankfurt School represent a sustained and sophisticated treatment of the issues that arise from taking emancipation seriously. As such they represent an invaluable source of ideas, suggesting not only possibilities but also potential pitfalls.

Michel Foucault once lamented that he would have "saved useful time" and "avoided certain errors" had he encountered the work of the Frankfurt School earlier on his own extraordinary intellectual journey.[65] His words should stand as a salutary warning to all of us engaged in the development of CSS: petty sectarianism wherein overly rigid adherence to a particular strand of thought is allowed to stand in the way of proper engagement with the resources provided by other traditions will inevitably hinder intellectual development. This in turn can only harm attempts to influence, in however mediated a form, the development of a more just and peaceful world—a world, in Adorno's words, "of distinctiveness without domination, with the distinct participating in each other."[66]

Notes

I would like to thank Eli Stamnes, Michael Williams, and Ken Booth for their comments on earlier drafts of this chapter.

1. Wyn Jones, *Security*.

2. See, for example, Krause, "Critical Theory and Security Studies," pp. 298–333. It is also clear that this is the view of the approach that underpins Krause and Williams, *Critical Security Studies*, inasmuch as that contributors to that book are drawn from a very wide range of metatheoretical positions.

3. For an overview see Smith, Booth, and Zalewski, *International Theory*.

4. Steve Smith, "Positivism and Beyond," in ibid., pp. 35–38.

5. The terms "postmodernism" and "poststructuralism" will be used interchangeably in this chapter.

6. This formulation of the differences between the CSS-as-project and the CSS-as-label approaches is meant to be illustrative rather than definitive or exhaustive. Nevertheless it is important to state categorically that the former's links to critical theory necessarily mean an overlap in concerns—if not always in approach—with other postpositivist strands. So, for example, the critical approach is concerned with transcending all forms of unjust social marginalization, be they based on class, gender, language, or other markers of difference. On critical theory see the essays collected in Wyn Jones, *Critical Theory*.

7. Booth, "Security and Emancipation."

8. These were the words used to me by a senior IR scholar whose work is one of the foundation stones of the poststructuralist approach to the field.

9. The second question is explored in Wyn Jones, *Security*, pp. 145–163.

10. Bronner, *Of Critical Theory*, p. 3. Emphasis in the original.

11. Walker, "The Subject of Security," in Krause and Williams, *Critical Security Studies*, p. 78.

12. Wæver, "Securitization and Desecuritization," in Lipschutz (ed.), *On Security*, p. 86.

13. Buzan, Wæver, and de Wilde, *Security*.

14. Ibid., p. 35.

15. Ibid. My emphasis.

16. Ibid., p. 34.

17. Honneth, "The Other of Justice," in White, *The Cambridge Companion to Habermas,* p. 289. This chapter provides an illuminating—and sympathetic—discussion of the "ethical turn" in postmodernism as exemplified by the work of Lyotard, Levinas, and Derrida. It also usefully compares and contrasts their work to the discourse ethics of Habermas and Apel.

18. Derrida, "Remarks on Deconstruction and Pragmatism," in Mouffe (ed.), *Deconstruction and Pragmatism,* p. 82.

19. Laclau, "Beyond Emancipation," in *Emacipation(s),* pp. 1–19.

20. Pieterese (ed.), *Emancipations, Modern and Postmodern,* special issue of *Development and Change,* p. 322.

21. Campbell, *National Deconstruction.*

22. Wendt, "What Is International Relations For? Notes Towards a Post-critical View," in Wyn Jones (ed.), *Critical Theory,* pp. 205–224.

23. Horkheimer, "Traditional and Critical Theory," in *Critical Theory,* pp. 188–243. See also Wyn Jones, *Security,* pp. 9–28.

24. A distinction needs to be made between socialist and Soviet-style planning. Helmut Dubiel demonstrates that members of the Frankfurt School had few illusions about the latter. See his *Theory and Politics,* pp. 15–20, 41–44, 73–76.

25. Horkheimer, "Traditional and Critical Theory," pp. 229, 241.

26. Ibid., p. 213.

27. Ibid., p. 214.

28. Ibid., pp. 217, 215.

29. Ibid., p. 237.

30. Adorno and Horkheimer, *Dialectic.*

31. Clearly this is a complex argument and space precludes an in-depth discussion here. For an explanation and critique see Wyn Jones, *Security,* pp. 29–52.

32. Cited in Jameson, *Late Marxism,* pp. 177–178.

33. Adorno and Horkheimer, *Dialectic,* p. 54.

34. Dubiel, *Theory and Politics,* p. 96.

35. In addition to Habermas's own writing, the following provide stimulating overviews: Honneth, "Work and Instrumental Action"; Honneth, "Social Dynamics"; Outhwaite, *Habermas.*

36. Habermas, *Knowledge and Human Interests,* p. 169.

37. Habermas, *Theory of Communicative Action, Volume 1: Reason and the Rationalization of Society*; and *Theory of Communicative Action, Volume 2: Lifeworld and System.*

38. Habermas, *Knowledge and Human Interests,* p. 314.

39. For a more detailed discussion of Habermas's argument see Wyn Jones, *Security,* pp. 56–64.

40. See Bronner, *Of Critical Theory,* p. 305.

41. Habermas, *The Past as Future,* interview by Michael Haller, translated by Max Pensky, p. 117.

42. Calhoun, *Critical Social Theory,* pp. 193–230.

43. Honneth, "Social Dynamics," p. 255.

44. Ibid., p. 262.

45. Ibid., p. 263.

46. Ibid., p. 264.

47. Ibid., p. 269.

48. Bronner, *Of Critical Theory,* p. 325.

49. Ibid., p. 326.

50. Ibid., p. 325.

51. Fraser, *Unruly Practices*, p. 2.

52. Geras, *Marx and Human Nature*.

53. See Wiggershaus, *Frankfurt School*, pp. 431–655; also Hohendahl, *Reappraisals*.

54. Wiggershaus, *Frankfurt School*, p. 623.

55. See Jay, *Adorno*, p. 20.

56. On the distinction between process and end-point utopias see Nye, "The Long-Term Future of Deterrence," in Kolkowicz (ed.), *The Logic of Nuclear Terror*, pp. 245–247. Its relevance to security has been repeatedly stressed by Booth, for example his "The Three Tyrannies," in Dunne and Wheeler (eds.), *Human Rights and Human Wrongs*, pp. 31–70.

57. See, for example, Held, *Democracy and the Global Order*; Kenneth Baynes, "Deliberative Politics, the Public Sphere, and Global Democracy," in Wyn Jones (ed.), *Critical Theory*, pp. 161–170; Cohen and Arato, *Civil Society and Political Theory*.

58. Habermas, *Facts and Norms*.

59. Ibid., pp. 491–515.

60. Habermas, "Beyond the Nation-State?" in Erikssen and Fossum (eds.), *Democracy in the European Union*, pp. 29–41.

61. See in particular, Linklater, *The Political Transformation of Community*.

62. Habermas, *Facts and Norms*, p. 515.

63. See Postone, *Time, Labour, and Social Domination*, and Honneth, *Recognition*.

64. The argument in the preceding paragraph is further developed in Wyn Jones, "Introduction," in Wyn Jones, *Critical Theory*, pp. 1–19.

65. Foucault, *Remarks on Marx*, p. 119.

66. Adorno, *Aesthetic Theory*, p. 48.

10

Communal Conflict
and Emancipation:
The Case of Northern Ireland

Joseph Ruane and Jennifer Todd

The values and principles of the Enlightenment have been more contested since the 1980s than at any time in the past two centuries. Those who remain committed to them have to contend with the failure of past attempts to give them practical expression, particularly Marxist socialism, and postmodernist claims that the project as a whole is redundant, even destructive.[1] The lessons of the past and the strictures of postmodernism have to be heeded, but in a critical manner, to ensure that those principles and themes that have continuing value are retained. The concept of emancipation is one of these. Emancipation is seen by many as an idealistic and nebulous notion, irrelevant to practical affairs. This is far from the case. Now, as in the past, the emancipatory aim of dismantling the conditions that give rise to conflict, and in the process changing aims, identities, and aspirations, remains urgent and practical. In this chapter we show the relevance of the concept to the resolution of the conflict in Northern Ireland.

Communal conflict in Northern Ireland has taken an overt, and often violent, form since the late 1960s. During this period, the search for a settlement has proceeded. For the most part it has taken a realist form: the situation has been viewed as inherently conflictual, and the only solution thought to lie in some form of deal or compromise whereby each side agrees to put aside some of its interests while satisfying others. This realist approach dominates the academic literature on Northern Ireland.[2] It informed the policy goals of the British and Irish governments through the 1970s and 1980s. However, there has been increasing openness to emancipatory ideas. From the joint Downing Street Declaration of 1993 to the Belfast Agreement of 1998, the British and Irish governments and many of the political parties in Northern Ireland have allied emancipatory aims and rhetoric with realist strategies. We show how this has been made possible by changes in (but not yet transformations of) the conditions of conflict.

The Belfast Agreement of April 10, 1998, was a product of these changes, and it has given hope of a long-term peaceful settlement in Northern Ireland. At its core, it gives an institutional framework within which conflict can be managed over the short to middle terms. An emancipatory approach, however, aims not simply to manage conflict but to resolve it: its goal is to undermine the conditions of conflict so as to diffuse the focused communal opposition and disperse the intense communal conflict that has so long existed. It identifies the social and cultural bases of existing conflictual interests and identities and the conditions under which those brought into conflict by them can act upon and change them.

The concept of emancipation used here is not one in which an oppressed group frees itself from its oppressors. When conflicts are viewed in such terms, the result is often bloody and persistent struggle that reproduces rather than dismantles the conditions of conflict. Emancipation is rather "a process by which the participants in a system which determines, distorts and limits their potentialities come together actively to transform it, and in the process transform themselves."[3] The system in question is the historical system of conflictual relationships that emerged during the sixteenth and seventeenth centuries. It survives today, but some of the crucial interests that underpinned it have faded. It is now possible to dismantle what remains through the combined action of governments, political parties, communities, classes, and individuals. In what follows, we trace the origins of the Northern Ireland conflict, theorize its underlying causes, and chart its development over time. We identify the conditions from which the Belfast Agreement emerged and the tensions and contradictions in the current settlement. We argue that these can be addressed only by strengthening the emancipatory elements in the process.

The Constitution of the Conditions of Conflict

The historical roots of the Northern Irish conflict lie in the mode of Ireland's integration into the English/British state in the sixteenth and seventeenth centuries. This was accomplished by conquest followed by colonization; it left a deeply conflictual legacy.[4] By the end of the seventeenth century, settlers or their descendants represented up to 27 percent of the total population. They were culturally and religiously distinct from the rest of the population—English or Scottish in identity and attachment, religiously Anglican or Presbyterian—and they controlled the resources of the country and the machinery of state. Agricultural capitalism and state centralization created an integrated society with a cohesive ruling class of settler stock, which had secured its position by conquest in recent memory and was religiously different from the majority of the population at a time when, everywhere in Europe, religion was a source of political conflict and struggle. Irish society was deeply divided along communal lines, and the security of the settlers depended on the external support of the English crown.

The sources of conflict may be theorized as a system of relationships with three interlocking elements: a set of overlapping cultural differences, a structure of dominance, dependence, and inequality, and a tendency toward communal polarization. The first element refers to the presence in the society of a set of binary distinctions: religious (Protestant versus Catholic), ethnic (English and Scottish versus Old English and Gaelic Irish), settler-native, and cultural-ideological (civility versus barbarism, modernity versus backwardness). Crucially, these distinctions overlapped: to be Protestant was to be of settler stock, English or Scottish (as opposed to Gaelic Irish) in ethnic identity, and to view one's role in society as a civilizing one; to be Catholic was to be of Gaelic Irish or Old English stock, indigenous to the island or long settled in it, and to feel cast in the role of a barbarous or backward people.

The second element in the system refers to the triangular relations of power and control that existed between the British government and Protestants and Catholics in Ireland. By the end of the seventeenth century, economic and political power lay overwhelmingly in the hands of the Protestant settler community and its British supporters. The British government exercised control over Ireland, directly through its ability to legislate for Ireland and its appointment of the Irish executive, indirectly through the Irish Protestant ruling class. Irish Protestants exercised power within Ireland, but as a minority they depended for their security on British support. Catholic inequality was, therefore, an integral part of a more complex structure of dominance and dependence.

The third element in the system of relationships is the tendency toward communal polarization. Both Catholics and Protestants were divided among themselves. Those Protestants who settled in the north of Ireland were predominantly Presbyterian of Scottish extraction; those who settled elsewhere were Anglican of English extraction. Anglicanism was the established religion, and for a time Presbyterians were subjected to penal restrictions. But from the beginning the two Protestant communities were conscious of a shared political interest in the face of a possible Catholic resurgence. Catholics were divided on class, regional, and linguistic lines, but they also had a common interest in defending or advancing their position. The result was a tendency for the society to divide into just two communities, each internally divided but united in its opposition to the other.

Continuity and Change in the System of Relationships
The three elements of the system of relationships powerfully reinforced each other and, once set in place, showed remarkable resilience, surviving

transformations in the economy, in the class structure, in the form of the state, and in the public culture. There was also change. The system was renewed and reinforced in the nineteenth century by the addition of a further "totalizing" dimension of difference—mutually exclusive "Irish" versus "British" national identities and allegiances—and by the establishment of ever more solidaristic and oppositional communities. There was change as well in the relations of dominance, dependence, and inequality and in particular in the balance of power.

The Catholic defeat at the end of the seventeenth century was total, but a Catholic recovery soon began and with it an ability to press for reform.[5] Protestants, concerned for their security and position, resisted such pressure. The British government was committed to maintaining the Protestant position in Ireland as essential to its own control over Ireland, but it also recognized the need for reform. It backed concessions to Catholics, but of a gradual kind so as not to threaten the Protestant position. In Catholic eyes, such concessions were always too little, too late, and they had little effect on Catholic loyalty or acceptance of the new order. In consequence, the gradual Catholic recovery of power provoked intensifying conflict.

Subsequent centuries saw political and economic upheaval: the joint Catholic and Protestant revolutionary organization, the United Irishmen in the 1790s, the Act of Union (1800) between Ireland and Britain, industrialization in the North-East, and the Great Famine of 1845–1849.[6] The purpose of the Act of Union was to firmly fix British political and military control over Ireland. Ireland was also expected to benefit economically and politically: union would give access to British and imperial markets and to British investment; since Protestants were the large majority in the British Isles as a whole, it would be possible to make concessions to Catholics without endangering Protestant interests.

Union did not, however, fulfill the religious, political, or economic hopes Catholics placed in it. The right to sit in parliament (promised at the time of union) was not granted until the 1820s, when Catholics formed a mass movement to demand it with the threat of force. The union brought economic benefits to the Protestant-dominated northeast of the island; the Catholic-dominated parts of the island suffered severe crises of adjustment. Economic decline, a sense of political impotence, and cultural Anglicization produced in response a nationalism that was simultaneously economic, political, and cultural. It appealed primarily—though not exclusively—to Catholics, for whom resentment at the central British government coincided with bitterness at continuing Protestant advantage. Protestants countered by stressing the benefits of union and their own identification with Britain and the empire. Both communities were acutely aware that—with the extension of the franchise—Catholics were becoming the dominant political force on the island.

The demand for Irish home rule began in 1870, and support for it was overwhelmingly Catholic. The issue soon divided the British establishment and led to armed Ulster Protestant resistance. After World War I, both nationalist and unionist demands increased, leading first to Anglo-Irish war, which ended with the British concession of dominion status to twenty-six out of the thirty-two counties, then to civil war in the new Irish state. The six northern counties were granted devolved government in a reconstituted union of Great Britain and Northern Ireland. There, too, force was needed to establish the new state: nationalist and republican resistance was countered by harsh security measures and sectarian attacks on the Catholic population.[7]

From the Settlement of 1921 to the Crisis of 1969–1972

The settlement of 1921 did not dissolve the system of relationships or its conflictual effects. Both north and south of the border, Catholics and Protestants constructed their differences as before—in terms of religion, ethnicity, settler-native status, culture, national identity, and allegiance. Britain now underwrote the position of Protestants in Northern Ireland rather than in Ireland as a whole; Protestant dominance of Catholics ended elsewhere on the island but was renewed in intensified form within Northern Ireland. Northern Protestants were a demographic majority in Northern Ireland but a minority on the island as a whole. They felt threatened by the Catholic and Gaelic ethos of the Southern state and by its aspiration and claim to jurisdiction over the whole island.[8] They responded by tightening their grip on power in Northern Ireland and by policies of exclusion and discrimination against Catholics. The effect was to intensify Catholic hostility to the Northern state and nationalist demands for reunification.

There was continuity in another respect as well—in the continued Catholic recovery of power at the level of the island as a whole. Northern Catholics were initially divided, demoralized, and in disarray; over time they developed a common identity and sense of purpose and an enhanced political capacity. This was paralleled by developments in the Southern state. In the 1920s, divided and impoverished by the civil war, it had struggled to survive. By the 1960s it was a stable, liberal democracy with an expanding economy and international standing. Meanwhile, the economic and political capacities of Northern Protestants were declining. The Northern economy grew more rapidly than the Southern one in the years after World War II, but due to foreign rather than native industry as well as to increased funding from the British exchequer. Greater economic dependence left Northern Protestants more vulnerable to external criticism and political pressure from London. The United Kingdom itself had lost ground internationally from the height of its economic and political preeminence and imperial power in the early part of the century. By the 1960s the empire was gone, the economy was lagging behind its international competitors, dependence on the United States was growing, and the outlook in Europe was uncertain following Charles de Gaulle's veto of Britain's application for membership in the European Common Market in 1963.

Taken together, these changes represented a significant shift in the triangular balance of power between nationalists (North and South), Ulster unionists, and the British state and created a structural opening for a Catholic/nationalist challenge to the settlement of 1921. The civil rights movement—unified only by a commitment to improving the conditions of Catholics within Northern Ireland—provided that challenge.[9] Police and loyalists responded with attacks on civil rights marchers, discrediting the state in international opinion and provoking British pressure for reform. As Catholic demands and Protestant resistance increased, mounting intercommunal tension finally exploded in violence in August 1969.

The British army intervened in support of the Unionist government but failed to restore order. Instead, the Catholic and nationalist challenge to the structures of government, and Protestant resistance to that challenge, intensified. As violence escalated, the British government defined the problem as one of security, but the effect of increasingly harsh security policies was to alienate further the Catholic community. When British paratroopers shot dead thirteen unarmed demonstrators in Derry in January 1972, outrage and protest throughout the island of Ireland demonstrated the failure to restore stability and international legitimacy to Northern Ireland. The system of government that had operated in Northern Ireland between 1921 and 1972—one in which Protestants controlled Catholics—had ceased to be viable. In March 1972, the British government prorogued the Northern parliament and introduced direct rule from London as a temporary measure. The search for a new system of government for Northern Ireland had begun.

The Search for a Settlement:
From Direct Rule to the Anglo-Irish Agreement (1985)

The British government faced enormous difficulties in finding a new system of government. Northern Ireland was composed of two religiously and culturally distinct, and now also armed, communities locked in a power struggle. Their interests and identities were sharply opposed, and they were divided not only on how power should be exercised in Northern Ireland but also on whether Northern Ireland should exist at all.

Moreover, the British state was internal as well as external to the conflict. It had set up Northern Ireland and had facilitated Protestants in establishing control over it; it was committed to the union; it underpinned the Northern economy financially; and it had laid down the principle that the constitutional position of Northern Ireland would be determined by a majority of its people. But it was also committed to reform, and as such it was the best hope Catholics had of achieving equality within Northern Ireland.

Two factors further complicated the situation. First, violence increased the oppositional character of the two communities. From 1969, unionists cut their ties to the South and deepened their identification with Britain; the numbers willing to define their identity as Irish fell sharply. Northern Catholics affirmed much more strongly their islandwide identity and interest in Irish culture and opposed expressions of unionist culture they perceived as dominatory. Internally the communities were as divided as ever—perhaps more so—but their members clung to each other for protection or support. In working-class areas large-scale movements of population created religiously homogeneous neighborhoods.

Second, the balance of power was very difficult to read. The British government insisted that any new form of government had to have the support of both communities. But what if unionists refused to cooperate? The British government insisted that it would not withdraw from Northern Ireland unless this was the will of the majority of its population, but could the Irish Republican Army (IRA) force it to? The government declared its commitment to achieving greater equality between Catholic and Protestant, but could Protestants block reform, and if the impetus for reform slowed, could Catholics revive it? How long could republicans maintain a campaign of violence, and could they be defeated? How far was the government in the South—itself fearful of republicanism—committed to supporting Northern nationalists? Could the U.S. government be brought into the picture on the side of nationalism?

While these questions remained open, each community had an incentive to hold out for as much as it could and to resist compromise. Successive initiatives failed to meet the criterion of cross-community support. The first and most hopeful, in 1973, put in place a power-sharing executive and the Council of Ireland with representatives from North and South; the Council never met, and the executive was brought down after six months by a combined loyalist-unionist industrial strike.[10] Subsequent initiatives had less success and violence continued. This was the context for a redirection of policy by the British and Irish governments. The Anglo-Irish Agreement (AIA) of 1985 granted the republic a "more than consultative" role in the government of Northern Ireland.[11] It was an attempt, on the one hand, to bring the Irish government formally into the process of seeking a settlement and, on the other hand, to buttress constitutional nationalism against the growing challenge of republicanism's political wing, Sinn Fein.[12]

The AIA aroused the intense anger of unionists, who were not consulted in the negotiations and who felt deeply threatened by the role now granted to the Irish government in the affairs of Northern Ireland. The unionist parties sought unsuccessfully to bring it down, and loyalist paramilitary violence intensified. For their part, republicans rejected the agreement as a firmly fixed partition. But for each of these parties, the AIA served as a goad and incentive toward negotiating a more inclusive agreement that would better address their interests.

The Peace Process and the Belfast Agreement (1998)

Having failed to bring down the AIA, the unionist parties attempted to renegotiate it. Between 1989 and 1992 a series of talks were initiated by the British government, now working more closely with the Irish government, with the unionist parties and the constitutional nationalist party—the Social Democratic and Labour Party (SDLP).[13] Agreement was not reached, and the divisions between nationalist and unionist remained stark. At the same time, the republican leadership had initiated another process in which they explored alternative strategies to armed struggle. The SDLP leadership and (later) the Irish government worked with them to that end. The goal was to create the conditions whereby Sinn Fein would enter the political process and participate in the search for an agreement: their long-term aim remained a united Ireland, but they now foresaw a more gradualist and peaceful path toward it. In return for the opening of political opportunities to Sinn Fein, the IRA would end its campaign of violence.

The governments responded cautiously but positively and in December 1993 issued a joint statement (the Downing Street Declaration) setting out the principles on which a comprehensive settlement might be reached. They included recognition of the Irish right to self-determination, of the right of a majority in Northern Ireland to withhold its consent to Irish unity, and of the need to ensure civil, social, and economic rights for members of both communities. The IRA declared an indefinite cease-fire in August 1994; the loyalist paramilitaries followed six weeks later. At that point progress slowed. The joint British-Irish Framework Document published in March 1995 was strongly rejected by unionists. The British government, constrained by its dependence on Ulster Unionist Party (UUP) votes in the House of Parliament, insisted on decommissioning of weapons before Sinn Fein could be included in any negotiations. Meanwhile, despite the peace, communal tensions on both sides were rising. Impatient with the pace of progress, the IRA abandoned its cease-fire in February 1996.

Breakthrough did not come until June of the following year, when general elections returned the Labour Party to power in Britain with an overwhelming majority and a Fianna Fail–led coalition in the Irish republic. The governments removed the demand for decommissioning of arms prior to negotiations and set a definite date for talks, the IRA renewed its cease-fire in July, and interparty talks began in September. Two unionist parties—the United Kingdom Unionist Party (UKUP) and the Democratic Unionist Party (DUP), which represented between them less than half the unionist electorate, refused to negotiate with Sinn Fein without the decommissioning of IRA weapons.

There was strong pressure on the parties to reach agreement from the British, Irish, and U.S. governments and from the international chairmen of the talks. Eventually, on April 10, 1998, against the expectations of most observers, with the British and Irish prime ministers present and with telephone calls to the main participants by President Bill Clinton, an agreement was concluded. It was ratified in referenda, North and South, six weeks later.

This represents a settlement of one of the most enduring communal conflicts in modern times. The details of the negotiations have never been made public, and the form of implementation of the agreement is still subject to political struggle.[14] Here, we focus on three broad, and urgent, questions raised by the Belfast Agreement. What made agreement possible? Have the systemic conditions of conflict changed? How can the settlement be sustained? We argue that the agreement was made possible by contextual changes that did not, however, affect the underlying conditions of conflict; indeed, they were assimilated as new elements within the system of relations. The result was endemic instability in the institutions of the agreement that can be overcome only by prioritizing the emancipatory aspects of the agreement.

The Context of Agreement

At the level of strategy and policy, agreement became possible because two parties to the conflict altered their position in an important way. Republicans replaced their goal of forcing a British withdrawal by armed struggle with one of achieving Irish unity by peaceful and more gradual means, beginning with full equality within Northern Ireland and increasing North-South linkages. Mainstream unionists accepted the principle of power-sharing in Northern Ireland and formal linkages with the Republic of Ireland in return for an IRA cease-fire and disarmament and nationalist acceptance of the principle of consent.

These revisions in strategy were made in a changing structural context that was in varying degrees motivating, enabling, and pressurizing. First, there was a reduction in the degree of ambiguity and indeterminacy surrounding the relations of power. By the mid-1980s it was clear to the IRA that the British government would not withdraw in response to its campaign and to unionists that it would not return Northern Ireland to majority rule. It was also clear that the Southern government would not turn its back on Northern nationalists or weaken its pressure on republicanism and that the British and Irish security forces would not defeat the IRA militarily or wean communal support for them in Northern Ireland. The potential role of the United States was also evident, both in terms of direct presidential involvement and Irish Americans' support for the Catholic community, particularly in relation to fair employment. It was clear, too, that the Catholic recovery evident in the 1921–1969 period was continuing. Catholic numbers were growing as a proportion of the total population; their position at the middle levels of the economy was strengthening; their political position had been greatly strengthened by the AIA. Each side now had a more realistic appreciation of its situation, the options open, and the dangers.

Second, there were changes in the wider context of the conflict. The common membership of Britain and the Irish Republic in the European Union and the end of the Cold War removed any remaining strategic interest that Britain might have in Northern Ireland and, by extension, any interest in buttressing the position of the loyal Protestant majority. The improvement in relations between the United Kingdom and the Irish Republic were part of this picture. The long-term pattern of improvement in British-Irish relations evident from the 1960s was slowed by conflicts over Northern Ireland, but it was renewed in the mid-1980s and given solid foundations by the AIA. The peace process brought the two government still closer, though Conservative Party dependence on UUP votes in the House of Commons cut across this until the return of the Labour Party to power in June 1997 with a large majority.[15] Meanwhile, in Britain, Labour's program of constitutional reform—in particular devolution in Scotland and Wales— introduced more regional variation in the character of the union and made possible new "variable geometry" relationships between the two parts of Ireland and between each and the constituent parts of Great Britain. Finally, the new prime minister, Tony Blair, made a deep personal commitment to the peace process at a time when his personal and political standing and moral authority were very high.

Changes in the Republic of Ireland were also important. The 1990s were a watershed in the history of the republic. There was exceptional growth in the economy, substantial erosion in the moral authority of the Catholic Church, stronger commitment to the principles of political and cultural pluralism, improved standing in Europe, increased prominence of Irish culture internationally, a conviction that the old colonial relationship with Britain had now run its course, and, in consequence, a greater willingness to allow a blurring of the boundaries between the two countries, particularly—though not solely—if this would facilitate a solution to the conflict. For unionists, these changes made the republic seem culturally less alien and pointed to the financial benefits that could flow from closer relations with the South. To republicans they suggested that there really was a dynamic in the situation that could bring unity in the longer term; it had been much more difficult to believe this during the late 1970s and 1980s, when the republic's economy was stagnant and national self-confidence was low. To the Irish government the changes gave a new weight and self-assurance in relations with unionists and the British government.

The worldwide ideological transformations of the 1980s and 1990s also contributed. The discourses of globalization, economic neoliberalism, the "end of history," and postmodernism all conveyed the impression that the world was living through "new times" in which new approaches could now be found to address long-established problems. The transformation of South Africa and the evidence of progress in Israel and Palestine—both situations to which Northern Ireland had been compared—encouraged the view that a similar breakthrough was possible in Northern Ireland. The notion of a new world order characterized by local conflicts to be managed by the leading powers, especially the United States, enabled the intervention of the U.S. president in Northern Ireland and gave it greater legitimacy in British and unionist eyes.

Third, there was now available to all the parties an analysis of the conflict to which a majority in both communities could give public assent. Traditionally, the language of political conflict in Northern Ireland had been absolutist and zero-sum. Thus Sinn Fein argued that the conflict was a colonial one that could be resolved only by British withdrawal, whereas unionists argued that power-sharing and closer links with the republic were a slippery slope to Irish unity. Agreement required moving away from such polarized assumptions, but without abandoning the concerns, motivations, and aspirations on which the earlier perspective was based. This meant an analysis that allowed for radically different, but equally plausible, scenarios for the future.

The analysis came from John Hume, leader of the SDLP.[16] For some time he had argued that the basis for the historic British-Irish conflict was over, in that Britain no longer had a strategic interest in remaining in Ireland. But the past had left a difficult legacy in relations between the communities in Northern Ireland, between North and South in Ireland, and between Britain and Ireland. This was manifested in continuing inequality and violence, but its root cause was the failure to build legitimate political institutions that could win the allegiance of all. This had now to be addressed. The political goal of Irish nationalism should not be Irish unity but an agreed Ireland in which difference is accepted and respected, in which coercion and threat are ruled out and the inequalities of the past are overcome. In the construction of that new order, the British government could play a positive and facilitative role.

Hume's analysis was taken up in the peace process and gained clearer emancipatory resonances. For example, for the two governments "the most urgent and important task facing the people of Ireland, North and South and the British and Irish governments together, is to remove the causes of conflict, to overcome the legacy of history and to heal the divisions that have resulted."[17] The ideal of making a new future by overcoming the causes of conflict proved capable of uniting all parties and provided a shared discursive paradigm for negotiation. At the same time, the different parties had very different ends in view.

In Hume's view peaceful cooperation between the traditions would lay the foundations for some form of Irish unity in the future. Yet unionists could argue that if an agreed settlement could be reached with the union still intact, Northern Ireland would have overcome the crisis of the 1969 period and the union would be secure for the future. For their part, republicans could use Hume's analysis to identify a peaceful road to a united Ireland: an end to unionist dominance in Northern Ireland would remove one of the key motivations unionists had to protect the union. In short, each group could draw very different conclusions from a shared commitment to undoing the causes of the conflict. The shared paradigm made possible agreement on institutions while investing these with opposed meanings, expectations, and strategic plans.

Finally, the agreement was in part the product of the specific form of the peace process, in particular the way in which those who engaged became locked into it. In previous negotiations, in particular those of 1989–1992, the parties were pressured by the governments to negotiate and felt that they would lose credibility and international allies if they were seen to cause a breakdown. These pressures and incentives increased dramatically in 1997–1998, with intergovernmental threats (for unionists, threats of imposed North-South structures, and for republicans, threats of marginalization) magnified by the increasing U.S. interest and influence on all parties. Moreover, this time the cease-fires and permanent peace were themselves in the balance, and public and political tolerance of the possibility of a return to violence had decreased. All parties were under pressure to participate in the negotiations and to stay there until agreement was reached. Each was fearful that if it withdrew it would leave the field to its opponents and would be held responsible if the process as a whole collapsed.

An Emancipatory Approach:
Dismantling the Systemic Conditions of Conflict

The results of the Belfast Agreement have been mixed. Rather than stability and renewed moderation, there have been recurrent crises and intensified divisions between nationalist and unionist and among unionists. In the November 2003 assembly elections, the more extreme unionist and nationalist parties (respectively the Democratic Unionist Party and Sinn Fein) became the majority parties in their respective blocs. By 2004, not all of the provisions of the Belfast Agreement were as yet fully implemented, although movement on all parts was under way.[18]

The most serious set of implementation problems has centered on the decommissioning of IRA weapons and conflicting interpretations about the provision made for this in the Belfast Agreement. This lay at the root of the UUP refusal to form an executive with Sinn Fein and led to major delays in achieving the full and stable functioning of the Northern Ireland Assembly and North-South bodies. Even after the IRA commenced decommissioning in autumn 2001, however, crises continued; the UUP refused to accept the bona fides of the republican movement. Other conflicts centered on the reform of the police and symbolic politics, in particular the right of Protestant Orangemen to march through Catholic areas.

In one sense this is a typical security dilemma where neither side is ready to move to a compromise until assured that it will not thereby lose position or resources.[19] Republicans have been unwilling to give up their guns until they know that the agreement will be fully implemented and that unionists will not be permitted to stall or stop that implementation. Unionists have been unwilling to implement the agreement until they know that they are not thereby giving new resources to republicans who remain committed to overthrowing the state—by violent means, if necessary. Much effort by the two governments has been put into choreographing simultaneous movement by both parties, so that a win-win settlement may be presented and each side can enter wholeheartedly into the new institutions. The 2003 election results put paid to that governmental strategy: the unionist public clearly declared its dissatisfaction with the situation and voted in the more extreme Unionist Party who wanted not to implement but to renegotiate the agreement; the nationalist public, in turn, voted for the party that was driving unionists to a bargain they were unwilling to meet.

Why has the security dilemma been so difficult to resolve? In our view it is not because of a lack of external guarantors, or checks and balances, or even the will of the parties involved.[20] It is rather because there has been no consensus on what the Belfast Agreement actually committed the parties to, and thus no agreement on what would constitute implementation of those commitments.[21] The Belfast Agreement has not resolved the underlying conflict, nor indeed did its architects expect it to do so.[22] It promises a framework for resolution, whereby formal sovereignty (which remains British) is balanced against institutional and structural change (to increase equality in Northern Ireland and islandwide integration). But there is no agreement on what constitutes the proper balance. At present, not so much the fact of the union but its nature is the focus of conflict; but all parties know that change in the latter may speed or delay a change in the former. Conflict therefore is reproduced within the institutions of the agreement in an attempt to shape them in opposing directions. Moreover, in the middle term, when and if the demographic balance changes, the result is likely to be intense political crisis.

Here one can see the limits of the realist approach to conflict management. Because it addresses the symptoms of the conflict rather than its underlying causes, the stability of the political institutions it puts in place is not assured. Minor changes in those institutions, however desirable in themselves, will not resolve the basic problem: no checks or balances or guarantees will make changes in the balance of power more palatable to the community that loses, and without change in the conditions of conflict individuals still define themselves as members of one or the other opposed community.

Underlying the multiple crises faced in the process of implementing the Belfast Agreement are the old systemic conditions of conflict. Despite changes in the elements, the system remains. First, while wider developments have given some opportunities to question the oppositional dimensions of difference, these binary oppositions remain core cultural categories in Northern Ireland. Most important of all, local conditions still tend to confirm them in everyday social practice.

Second, the structure of dominance, dependence, and inequality has changed but has not yet been dismantled. Reforms have decreased but not yet removed the inequality between Protestant and Catholic, and it remains to be seen if the promised reforms in the Belfast Agreement will be fully implemented so as to remove the remaining aspects of communal inequality.[23] The British government's stance has changed in important ways, particularly its statement that it "has no selfish strategic or economic interest in Northern Ireland."[24] However, interests sedimented in long-established institutions and practices of statecraft, and embodied in dispositions and habits of thought, work against change. In particular, the state has been slow to implement all the provisions of the agreement and even slower to distance itself from support for the Ulster Unionist Party. The reasons for the British state–Ulster Unionist alliance are different than they were in the past—between 1998 and 2003 the British government attempted to back up the supporters of the agreement within the UUP against their detractors. But whatever the intent, the structural relations remained the same and fed oppositional cultural understandings and communal expectations and strategies.

Third, the communities themselves have changed—in their attitudes to the state and in their internal structure. This is most evident in the internal fracturing among unionists and Protestants. Yet they have not splintered, much less formed an overarching Northern Irish community. And there has been least change of all in the tendencies toward communal polarization. Despite increasing divisions among unionists, the relationship between the communities remains one of mistrust and antagonism.[25] This is in part the legacy of years of bitter conflict, reinforced by the perception that communal understandings, identities, and interests remain objectively opposed, that power remains a crucial resource, and that each is likely to use the new institutions to advance its position.

Systemic feedback patterns have therefore remained, even though elements of the system have changed, and these feedback patterns ensure that the new elements are assimilated within an older conflictual structure. Yet the contingency of the system is much more apparent now than ever in the past. Its elements are now clearly in process of change. For the first time one can begin to imagine relations on the island of Ireland and between Britain and Ireland taking a radically different form than they did in the past. However, this process has only begun, and relations as they exist, particularly on the island of Ireland, retain considerable capacity to generate conflict. This is most likely to happen if the balance of nationalist-unionist power in the North and on the island shifts more rapidly than the improvement in nationalist-unionist relations made possible (in theory at least) by the Belfast Agreement. At current levels of communal conflict a rapid shift in the balance of communal power is likely to provoke a renewed and prolonged political crisis.

It is here that the relevance of an emancipatory approach to the conflict becomes clear. It directly addresses the underlying conditions of conflict. As it weakens them, even in the short term, it diffuses conflict, stabilizes the agreed political institutions, and allows them to function optimally. In the longer term, it brings the historic communal conflict to an end by dismantling the system of relationships. As the causal feedback patterns that reproduce each level of the system, and thus regenerate communal polarization and conflict, are loosened and finally broken, conflict and opposition become dispersed among a multiplicity of actors rather than focused in one enduring communal conflict. Such an emancipatory approach would be multistranded, weakening the oppositional and self-reproductive tendencies at each level of the system by moderating and differentiating the dimensions of difference; undoing the structure of dominance, dependence, and inequality and weakening the forces producing communal polarization; and breaking the feedback loops and causal patterns between the levels, which allow change at one level to be assimilated within the conflict-generating system.

In practical terms, insofar as the conflict rests on sharp and converging oppositions in respect of religion, ethnicity, settler-native status, notions of progressiveness and backwardness, national identity, and allegiance, then one strand of the emancipatory process involves reducing the extent of opposition on each of the dimensions, distancing the dimensions one from another, as well as from the social institutions and power relations dominant in the society. Culturally, this approach would have various manifestations: reducing the degree of religious opposition and hostility; reinterpretations and reconstructions of Irish history that reduce the starkness of the settler-native and British-Irish opposition; and the publicization and official valorization of new combinations of concepts and oppositions that subvert the older oppositions. Socially, the aim is to ensure that these oppositions, with their valuation of one side and devaluation of the other, no longer inform the norms and practices of the social institutions in which individuals live, learn, and work; not just equality of opportunity but "parity of esteem" is necessary to ensure that key social institutions no longer reproduce the oppositions or valorize the cultural capital identified with one side of the opposition. Politically, the task is to reduce the salience and oppositional quality of these distinctions within public institutions in both jurisdictions—for example, the role of the churches in education and medicine in the Irish state and the British/Irish opposition in national practices, symbols, and institutions. These are tasks for ecumenists, intellectuals, educationists, and reconciliation groups, as well as for the Equality and Human Rights Commissions and political leaders and policymakers in both jurisdictions.

Second, insofar as conflict has been maintained by interests and alliances built into a structure of dominance, dependence, and inequality, that also needs to be changed. The British state no longer relies on the Protestant community to protect its interests in Ireland. But its political repositioning has been much less clear and decisive than its strategic. It must fulfill the promise of the agreement by clearly repositioning itself; rather than backing any party or community, it must assert the ground rules given in the agreement itself. The legacy of the past also remains powerful in the remaining communal inequality, in unionist resistance to a relationship of equality, and in nationalist identification of unionists—and to some degree the entire Northern Protestant community—as an alien presence on the island. Here the goal must be reform toward equality in a context where the right to self-determination of any one community respects the equal right of the other. At issue here is not only the equalization of power resources but also the diminution of the relevance of communal power as a resource and of the changing balance of power as a force for conflict. The task is to develop institutions throughout the island of Ireland where an egalitarian culture and ethos prevail so that the self-interest of each community (in strengthening minority rights and opportunities for participation) coincides with the self-interest of all. The Belfast Agreement sketches a way forward.[26] Such institutions would create an islandwide egalitarian civic (not necessarily political) community that would further erode the relevance of communal power.

Finally, the conflict is maintained by tendencies toward communal polarization that limit individuals' capacity for empathy and sense of moral responsibility across communal boundaries. Emancipation involves a reduction in the intensity of communal identification. This requires greater individualization—greater willingness by individuals and subgroups to explore and give expression to their own needs and desires, even if this brings them into conflict with wider communal loyalties and identities—a process that can be strengthened by institutionalizing a strong rights culture in both parts of the island. Here the Human Rights Commissions in Northern Ireland and the Irish state have key roles. A bill of rights for Northern Ireland that translates matters of vital communal interest into universalistic rights would go far toward the goal; to date, however, the political will to back such a bill of rights has been weak. It also requires the building of cross-community networks based on overlapping interests and concerns and, ultimately, the forging of new forms of community, whether in Northern Ireland or on the island (or archipelago) as a whole. Some of these networks are envisaged in the Belfast Agreement, particularly the proposed North-South bodies. The task is to develop and expand such networks, both as envisaged in the Belfast Agreement and more generally in the public sphere, the culture, and the media.

Conclusion

The emancipatory approach to conflict resolution as outlined above directly addresses the historic and contemporary conditions of conflict. It points to a clear and attainable set of policy priorities and goals that will address the conflict at its source. It goes beyond the realist project of brokering political compromise, but it does not reject this concern. Rather, an emancipatory approach can build on, sustain, and develop the settlement already achieved in Northern Ireland. It builds on the momentum of change that is implicit in the Belfast Agreement, it develops the ideals that have been embodied in public discourse since the peace process, and thus it sustains the political institutions that the Belfast Agreement sets in place. As the necessary changes are implemented, so short-term communal interests, identities, and oppositions will no longer dominate motivation, and all parties and social groups can find new paths to pursue their interests and will gain an interest in preventing a resurgence of communal identification and conflict. In this, an emancipatory approach is at once practical and necessary. Despite the gains made by the Belfast Agreement, the potential for continuing conflict and for renewed and prolonged crisis at some stage in the future remains considerable. Given the implications of a rapid shift in the balance of power, there is no room for delay in implementing such a process.

Notes

1. Lyotard, *The Postmodern Condition*; Bauman, *Modernity and Ambivalence*.
2. For reviews of the literature see McGarry and O'Leary, *Explaining Northern Ireland*; Whyte, *Interpreting Northern Ireland*. Ruane and Todd, *Dynamics of Conflict,* gives a detailed analysis of the historical and contemporary causes of conflict on which we draw in the remainder of this chapter.
3. Ruane and Todd, *Dynamics of Conflict*, p. 15.
4. Brady and Gillespie (eds.), *Natives and Newcomers*; Canny, *Making Ireland British, 1580–1650*.
5. Bartlett, *The Fall and Rise of the Irish Nation*.
6. Foster, *Modern Ireland, 1600–1972*.
7. Hepburn, *A Past Apart*; Bardon, *History of Ulster*, pp. 494, 537–538, 540–541, 600–601.
8. Kennedy, *The Widening Gulf*.
9. Purdie, *Politics in the Streets*.
10. Bardon, *History of Ulster*, pp. 706–711.
11. FitzGerald, *All in a Life*, pp. 494–575.
12. See O'Leary and McGarry, *The Politics of Antagonism*. For a unionist view, see Aughey, *Under Siege*.
13. Bloomfield, *Political Dialogue in Northern Ireland*; Bloomfield, *Developing Dialogue in Northern Ireland*.
14. For analyses of the agreement see O'Leary, "The Nature of the British-Irish Agreement," *New Left Review* 233, pp. 66–96; Ruane and Todd (eds.), *After the Good Friday Agreement*; Wilford (ed.), *Aspects of the Belfast Agreement; Cox, Guelke, and Stephen (eds.), *A Farewell to Arms*; Ruane and Todd, "Politics of Transition."
15. Patterson, "From Insulation to Appeasement," in Wilford (ed.), *Aspects of the Belfast Agreement*.
16. See Todd, "The Reorientation of Constitutional Nationalism," in Coakley (ed.), *Beyond Orange and Green*.
17. *The Joint Declaration for Peace*, statement made by the British and Irish governments at Downing Street, December 15, 1993, article 1.
18. For an analysis of the social and political situation up until the end of 2003, see Ruane and Todd, *The Dynamics of Conflict and Transition in Northern Ireland*.
19. Posen, "The Security Dilemma and Ethnic Conflict," in Brown (ed.), *Ethnic Conflict and International Security; Walter, "Designing Transitions."
20. Walter, "Designing Transitions," points to external guarantors as a central condition of overcoming the security dilemma. Such guarantors exist in Northern Ireland.
21. See Ruane and Todd, "Politics of Transition," on the radically different interpretations of the parties.
22. Mansergh, "The Challenges of the Good Friday Agreement and the Consolidation of Peace."

23. *Agreement Reached in the Multi-Party Negotiations*, section on "Rights, Safeguards, and Equality of Opportunity."

24. *The Joint Declaration for Peace,* article 4.

25. Hughes and Donnelly, "Ten Years of Social Attitudes to Community Relations in Northern Ireland."

26. *Agreement Reached in the Multi-Party Negotiations*, section on "Rights, Safeguards, and Equality of Opportunity."

Part 4

CONCLUSION

11

Beyond Critical Security Studies

Ken Booth

In the first chapter I introduced critical security studies as the study of an issue area, more specifically as a body of critical knowledge concerned with security, community, and emancipation. These latter three concepts were then elaborated in each of the main sections of the book. In this final chapter I want to move beyond CSS as *a body of critical knowledge* and outline a specific *critical theory of security*. The challenges faced by humans at all levels demand a more effective theory of security: our times are too complex and the world too varied for the reductionisms, parsimony, simplicities, regressive implications, silences, and normative assumptions of political realism in its various manifestations.

The critical theory of security to be discussed in this chapter, for reasons of space, is in outline form only.[1] I do not expect—or want—every student of security to embrace the whole package on offer. I doubt whether all the contributors to this volume would agree with every word below, and in any case slavish adherence to any theoretical package would be irrational for students properly committed to critical theory, because its intellectual spirit is to challenge all orthodoxies, including its own. In true counterorthodoxy fashion, I hope that students will critique the framework below and reassemble the parts in their own ways. This is how it should be. Reflexivity ("strategic monitoring"), which involves the application of a theory back on its own ideas and practices, is a basic feature of critical theory true to itself.[2] Chapter 3 by Graeme Cheeseman illustrated such reflexivity in relation to what had become the orthodoxies of alternative thinking about military force(s) resulting from the changing landscapes of technology and international politics since the late 1980s.

Toward and Then Beyond

If critical theorizing about security is to advance as an academic project, it needs to go not only beyond political realism, but also beyond CSS. This is because the latter is a body of knowledge and not a *theory* of security as such. It does not tell us which referents to prioritize in world politics, or which threats to watch, or who might be the agents for change, or even how security should be defined. Moving "toward critical security studies"[3]— that is, developing a body of knowledge that exposes the weaknesses of prevailing ideas and at the same time opens our minds to different ways of thinking and doing—is an important step in itself, but it does not go far enough. The next stage is to move beyond studying this body of knowledge to developing a distinctive *theory* of security.

CSS is an issue area for the study of a variety of critical approaches beyond the realist mainstream, as Steve Smith explained in Chapter 2. One approach he identifies is represented in the book *Critical Security Studies: Concepts and Cases,* edited by Keith Krause and Michael C. Williams.[4] That book does not offer a theory of security; nor does it claim to. The editors deliberately did not attempt to define a "critical" approach of their own. Indeed, they chose not to define a precise meaning for the term "critical," or even "security," for fear of invoking "a new orthodoxy."[5] Their book is an extended rejection, with illustrations, of neorealist security studies. As such, it gives space to a wide range of theoretical orientations. As it happens, the differences between some of these approaches are at least as significant as the differences they have with neorealism. The approaches chosen by Krause and Williams included subaltern realism, poststructuralism, and contributions "that lean on" Wittgenstein. The ambition of the editors was to move *toward* CSS, and to some extent they were successful.[6] But some of the approaches given voice were not critical in the Coxian sense discussed in Chapter 1, and the Frankfurt School critical theory to be advanced below was minimally represented.[7] More important still, it is impossible to base a research strategy or political activities on an eclectic collection of perspectives that share little except rejecting neorealism.

There are times when definite lines have to be drawn. The spirit informing the theoretical framework to be outlined in this chapter is therefore very different to that of Krause and Williams. It will attract attacks from some ostensibly critical quarters, as well as from traditional realists. But research strategies and political projects require a focus and a sense of direction, and these are not offered by eclectic rejectionism. For a start, we need a clear understanding of what we mean both by "critical" and "security" if we want to develop a coherent critical theory of security. I do not share at this point the worry of Krause and Williams about invoking "a new orthodoxy"; I do however fear the consequences of perpetuating old orthodoxies in a fast-moving political landscape. The price for old thinking about world security is paid, daily, in the death, disease, poverty, and oppression of millions.

The Highway of Critical Security Theory

The framework of ideas developed below might be visualized in the Kantian metaphor of a highway. In my adaptation of it, the image to keep in mind is of two major roads, themselves the product of a series of feeder roads, converging and widening into a single highway.[8] The two major roads are the *critical theory tradition in social theory,* and the *radical tradition in international relations theory.* The highway that is produced is *critical security theory.*

The Critical Theory Tradition

The critical theory tradition goes back to Kant.[9] Of most immediate relevance for current purposes, however, is the work of the Frankfurt School, whose origins lay in the establishment of the Institute for Social Research at the University of Frankfurt in 1923. During the Nazi period and World War II, the school was exiled in the United States before being reestablished in Germany in 1950.[10] Key scholars in the school's work over some eighty-plus years have been Max Horkheimer, Theodor Adorno, and Jürgen Habermas.

The most thorough exposition to date bringing together the work of the Frankfurt School and the problematique of security is Richard Wyn Jones's book *Security, Strategy, and Critical Theory.*[11] He describes his approach to thinking about security as developing "in the light" of the Frankfurt School,[12] and I am happy to endorse this formulation. I also share his view that not all critical theories are equally useful when thinking about security and that the use of the word "critical" in the label CSS should signal the special helpfulness of the Frankfurt School. Not all critics of realist-derived security studies would share this view, of course, particularly postmodernists and poststructuralists hostile to metanarratives (other than their own), or those peace researchers committed to positivism.

In addition to the Frankfurt School, there are three other feeder roads into the critical theory tradition:

- The body of ideas identified with Antonio Gramsci, together with those of his interpreters in international studies (the neo-Gramscians). They have contributed with considerable insight to thinking about hegemony, civil society, and the different roles of intellectuals in politics.
- The Marxian tradition offers a deep mine of ideas that are especially useful for thinking about ideology, class, and structural power.
- An embryonic school of critical international relations theory has developed. It has begun to examine cosmopolitan ideas and practices relating to community, democracy, force, and law.[13]

In what follows, seeking to bring together the main themes of the critical theory tradition, I am conscious of synthesizing an enormous amount of sometimes complex theorizing. Purists might squeal, but the risk is worth taking in the interests of shaping a coherent and accessible body of ideas relevant to a critical theory of security. Four core themes emerge:[14]

Theme one: all knowledge is a social process. Knowledge does not simply exist, waiting to be discovered like a glacier. Social and political theories, and the concepts and conceptualizations that derive from them, are the products of social processes. To a greater or lesser degree, theorists both write and are written by the theories of their time and circumstances. In this sense, all knowledge about human society is historical knowledge, emerging as it does from concrete contexts. Social and political theories are not therefore neutral or objective; they contain "nontheoretical interests." They exist in real worlds, not some imagined world of decontextualized theory; their findings, concerns, and implications are not those that might be understood by a disinterested and omniscient god (if she existed), standing apart from earthly context. Theories are, to repeat Robert Cox's famous formulation, "*for* some one or *for* some purpose." One aim of critical theory, then, is to seek to reveal the "interests of knowledge" as a factor in social and political enquiry. Knowledge here includes what is often described as "common sense." From a Gramscian perspective, common sense is equally "*for* some one or *for* some purpose." All political theorizing has some ethical dimensions, whether it is at the level of sophisticated programmatic planning or down-to-earth common sense. The political realm is necessarily a realm of ethics and morality. If all positions, including the claim to have none, have some nontheoretical (normative) implications, objectivity is a false idol in the study of human society. The most that can be attained is a degree of (subjective) critical distance from the object of enquiry.

Theme two: traditional theory promotes the flaws of naturalism and reductionism. In a famous essay published in 1937, Max Horkheimer, a key figure in the Frankfurt School, gave the label "traditional theory" to the flawed theorizing that his critical theory would seek to overcome.[15] In particular, he criticized the way traditional theory's commitment to the scientific method had spread uncritically and powerfully into all fields. The fallacy of naturalism, which I discuss in Chapter 1, is the idea that human beings and societies belong to the same world of nature as everything else and so should be capable of being explained by the same scientific method. In particular, when it comes to explaining human society, the characteristic reductionism of the scientific method is flawed and needs to be replaced by a more holistic perspective. Theorists can therefore be divided between those who see themselves primarily as *scientists* seeking objective truth about society and

Frankfurt School critical theorists who accept they are part of a social process (seeking to promote emancipation). The former (falsely) consider that they are working apart from the world they seek to explain, whereas the latter understand they are embedded in society, and that theorizing is a social act. Gramsci made the important distinction, respectively, between *traditional* and *organic* intellectuals.

Theme three: critical theory offers a basis for political and social progress. Critical theory stands outside and questions the social and political phenomena it is examining, as was explained in Chapter 1. It avoids, as far as possible, the negative consequences of *problem-solving* theories, particularly the legitimizing and replicating of the regressive aspects of prevailing situations. Problem-solving theories such as political realism leave power where it is, whereas critical theory attempts to bring about structural changes in the human interest, that is, reordering power in emancipatory ways. Power, in its manifold varieties, cannot be escaped, but it can be reordered in a more benign direction. In the strategic action undertaken to attempt to bring change about, there is no sounder basis than *immanent critique*—the discovery of the latent potentials in situations on which to build political and social progress. This means building with one's feet firmly on the ground, not constructing castles in the air.

Theme four: the test of theory is emancipation. Human society in global perspective is shaped by ideas that are dangerous to its collective health. The evidence for the latter is widespread. It is revealed in the extent of structural oppression suffered on account of gender, class, or race; it is apparent in the threats to the very environment that sustains all life; it is seen in the risks arising out of the unintended consequences from developments in technology; and, as ever, it is experienced in the regular recourse to violence to settle political differences. A more just society in global perspective would be one that progressively limits the power of regressive structures and processes, steadily squeezing the space for violent behavior in all its direct and indirect manifestations; in this process, new opportunities would open up for the exploration of what it might mean to be human. This exploration, in the spirit of emancipation, begins with critique. A radical rethinking of the theories and practices that have shaped political life is an essential foundation for the reinvention of human society. Such rethinking, to be true to the spirit of emancipation, requires students to embrace a global perspective. The smaller social units of universal human society will not be predictably secure until the whole is systematically secured; this is one reason why what is called political studies (or even science) should be logically regarded as a subfield of the study of world politics or international relations (broadly defined) and not the other way around. Emancipation for critical theorists is both a critical device for judging theory and the continuing goal of practice; its politics seeks to denaturalize and overcome oppressive social divisions in human society at all levels. The only transhistorical and permanent fixture in human society is the individual physical being, and so this must naturally be the ultimate referent in the security problematique. Such reverence for the person—the singular body—should be understood as synonymous with the idea that people exist collectively, in some social context or other. A notion of community remains the best way of expressing how this can be translated into living a good life. The search for multilevel emancipatory communities, locally and globally, is the biggest institutional challenge faced by a critical theory of security. In the pursuit of this objective, *discourse ethics*—wherein communication (the basis for community) rather than traditional politico-military strategizing (the medium of conflict)—must therefore be a priority. Some of the key linkages between community and security were explained in Andrew Linklater's chapter (Chapter 5), in which he underlined how so much hinges on the way in which political community is constructed.

The Radical International Relations Tradition

The critical theory tradition is mainly (though not wholly) important in relation to how we might think about what is reliable knowledge (epistemology), and what should be done (emancipatory praxis). What I am calling the radical international relations tradition relates more to what is real in world politics (ontology), and what values might inform the praxis of global politics in the human interest.[16]

All social and political theories have normative implications, to a lesser or greater extent, either implicitly or explicitly. The feeder roads of the radical international theory tradition are explicitly value-laden, and the normative thrust is *progressive*. The latter is a word I use deliberately, fully aware of its problems and reputation. The concept of progress is unfashionable in some circles. To postmodernists, for example, the idea of progress is almost synonymous with all that has gone wrong with the world in the past 200 years; it is part of the modernity that, according to some, led to the Holocaust.[17] Such views underline the need to reconsider the concept of progress. This will become easier as progress ceases to be identified as strongly as it has been with the hubris of nineteenth-century liberalism or twentieth-century totalitarianism (hardly the complete story of the idea of progress), and as the wave of postmodernism and poststructuralism weakens in Western intellectual life. In any case, an idea of progress informs poststructuralist arguments more so than is generally recognized. The inconsistencies and confusions of poststructuralist writers on emancipation— together with the possibility for a more constructive engagement with

Frankfurt School critical theorists—was one of the themes of Richard Wyn Jones's chapter (Chapter 9).

Despite all the assaults on the idea of progress, it remains necessary, globally manifested, and (now) is almost universally hard-wired. By "progressive" I mean simply a belief in the importance of having ideals in society and trying to shape law, politics, and institutions accordingly. The idea of progress derives from the laudable refusal of some people to believe that this is the best of all possible worlds. Without rational ideals to challenge power, it remains where it is, to be countered only by countervailing power or unreason.

Five main schools of thought in the radical international relations tradition are relevant to the development of a critical theory of security:

• The philosophical tradition of social idealism, in which human society is conceived as self-constituted and international politics regarded as just another aspect of human-made reality.

• The Peace Research and Peace Studies School, which since the 1950s has explicitly promoted the value of peace. In the 1960s this project expanded from concentrating on the problem of war into addressing the study of all forms of violence, from direct to structural.

• The World Society or World Order School, which offers inspiration because of the way its proponents developed an explicitly value-framed and progressive approach to the study of global issues.

• Feminist theorizing, whose contribution has been the uncovering of the gender interests served by political and social theories, as well as the exposure of the role(s) played by gender in the workings of world politics in practice.

• Historical sociology, which has a place in this body of ideas because its starting point opens up the state and so challenges the ahistorical biases and inherent conservatism and statism of political realism. Historical sociology therefore interrogates what realism takes as given and so has radical implications for students of international politics.[18]

Together, these feeder roads add the following core themes to those identified earlier:

Theme five: human society is its own invention. If this is true in part, it must be so in whole. What we call "international relations," therefore, is one aspect of human-made reality—"facts by human agreement" on a global scale, in other words. The social idealism represented by Philip Allott's writing about the role of law, and of the "self-forged chains" that exist nowhere but in the mind, is of a similar inspiration to that in peace research arguing that political violence is a learned behavior, not an inevitable feature of human social interaction.[19] Social learning can and does take place, but what has been learned historically has often not been benign. To the contrary, regressive attitudes have been internalized. Central to what Allott calls these "deformed ideas" has been the way humans have internalized conflict as a foundational myth. This has been nowhere stronger than on what he calls the "grandest stage of all," the "tragi-comedy of the state-system." According to this line of thought about the openness of history, human society became what it need not have been. Humans could have chosen different directions and could yet choose a different future. This injunction refers not only to reinventing international politics but also to the need for a new international political economy. This is a dimension of world politics usually ignored or taken for granted by realist security studies. Such an outcome must be resisted by CSS, as was argued in Chapter 6 by Roger Tooze; critical perspectives on security must be informed by a critical political economy.

Theme six: regressive theories have dominated politics among nations. Theory constitutes behavior, and some of the key theories that have formed human society on a global scale have not been calculated to produce a more civilized, peaceful, or just system of international relations. Examples of such thinking include ethnocentric and masculinist ideas, as well as the negative images of humanity cultivated by prevailing notions about human nature or the human condition.[20] Sandra Whitworth's chapter (Chapter 4) revealed some of the regressive ideas and social dangers in masculinist and racist thinking. Ethnocentrism is a particular obstacle to creating a just global society and so must be challenged by more systematic knowledge about the ideas and feelings, and the hopes and fears, of people(s) with different thoughtways. One feature of regressive (noninclusive) theories about humanity is the way they make important sections of society invisible. As a result, gender, race, and class, for example, are frequently downplayed as categorical structures of humanity. The gendered character of how societies and economies work was invisible in the academic study of international relations until feminist theorizing opened the eyes of those who were prepared to see. Above all, the ideology of statism corrupts all it touches. The concept of *human security*, for example, which originally encouraged the idea of a different and more important referent than the sovereign state, has been co-opted and incorporated into statist discourses, reviving old ideas about high and low politics.

Theme seven: the state and other institutions must be denaturalized. Human institutions like the state are historical phenomena, not biological necessities. Inquiry into the growth of state formations in different parts of the world will help the process of problematizing all institutional identifiers that divide humanity and that get in the way of recognizing and implementing the view that every person, in principle, has equal moral worth. The temporality of all institutions should lead us to focus on the individual as the ultimate referent for security; the corollary of this is that we should also consider as central to our concerns the ultimate collectivity of individuals, common humanity. Hedley Bull, best known for being one of the leading exponents of the "international society" approach, described "world order" as being "more fundamental and primordial" than international order, because the "ultimate units" of human society are not states or other sociopolitical groupings but individual human beings. The latter are "permanent and indestructible in a sense in which groupings of them of this or that sort are not."[21] The fluidity of political identity was one of the themes of Jan Jindy Pettman's chapter (Chapter 7). She argued that identities were sites of contention and the outcomes of power struggles, and that in a world where state practices are shaped so much by ideas of elite security and privilege the interests of the rest tend to be marginalized. What is more, echoing the sixth theme above, is the view that elite attitudes are prone to racialized and militarized understandings of international situations.

Theme eight: progressive world order values should inform the means and ends of an international politics committed to enhancing world security. In today's circumstances, when the world is not working for the vast majority of its inhabitants, the agenda for progressive change is huge. For students of security, the exploration of conflict resolution and conflict management is a major departure from realism's fatalistic assumption of violence in human affairs and, hence, the belief that force can only be met by force. The neatest and most comprehensive formulation of the ideas that should inform progressive global change grew out of the work of the World Order School, with its advocacy of values such as the delegitimation of violence, the promotion of economic justice, the pursuit of human rights, the spread of humane governance, and the development of environmental sustainability.[22] It is my belief that these normative goals should be pursued in a nondualistic fashion in order to avoid the dangers of *instrumental reason*, that is, the threat of bringing about a perversion of humanity, society, or nature by concentrating entirely on functional processes even in the rational pursuit of a desirable goal.[23] Nuclear strategy is an illustration of the danger of instrumental reason. Its evolution shows how a belief in the absolute priority of national defense, and the subsequent immersion in its processes and goals, perverts intuitions and ideas about humanity, society, and nature and so opens up the possibility of war crimes, environmental disaster, genetic damage, and untold human catastrophe. Instrumental reason is a dimension in what Robert Lifton and E. Markusen have called "the genocidal mentality"[24]; the instrumentalist dynamic shows how even good men (and women) can rationalize their activities and become the instruments of profound human wrongs. One counter to the dualistic ends-justify-the-means rationality, as was discussed earlier, is the Gandhian conception of conceiving ends and means as amounting to the same thing: a concrete end might be out of reach, but the means that are its equivalent are not.[25]

The eight core themes just identified point in the direction of the intellectual highway of a critical theory of security. In summary:

- All knowledge is a social process.
- Traditional theory promotes the flaws of naturalism and reductionism.
- Critical theory offers a basis for political and social progress.
- The test of theory is emancipation.
- Human society is its own invention.
- Regressive theories have dominated politics among nations.
- The state and other institutions must be denaturalized.
- Progressive world order values should inform the means and ends of an international politics committed to enhancing world security.

From this sense of direction, I now propose a definition of a distinct theory of security from a Frankfurt School critical theory perspective: *Critical security theory is both a theoretical commitment and a political orientation. As a theoretical commitment it embraces a set of ideas engaging in a critical and permanent exploration of the ontology, epistemology, and praxis of security, community, and emancipation in world politics. As a political orientation it is informed by the aim of enhancing security through emancipatory politics and networks of community at all levels, including the potential community of communities—common humanity.*

This chapter began by distinguishing CSS as a body of knowledge from a *theory* of security with a critical perspective. It then offered a framework and definition of a particular critical theory of security. This particular framework and definition can guide us in our explorations in relation to three fundamental (philosophical-theoretical-political) questions.

- What is real? A critical theory of security seeks to denaturalize and historicize all human-made political referents, recognizing only the primordial entity of the socially embedded individual. The exploration of referents is seen through the lens of emancipatory interests, not predefined ideas about the nature of the political world. Whereas other theories of security narrow the agenda because of their singular, privileged referents, critical theory is open to the exploration of all referents, historical and future-imagined, and therefore must consider the range of different threats associated with them. Imagined referents, the potential of new identities, are particularly significant for critical theory, because herein lies the possibility of the future reality of security, community, and emancipation in world politics.

• What is knowledge? Critical security theory questions the reliability of much of what passes for knowledge about world politics. The reliability of this traditional knowledge is under question because of the political and epistemological assumptions of those who have the status of fact makers in contemporary society. In particular, critical theory challenges the ideal of objectivity in traditional theory and instead settles for the more realistic goal of critical distance between theorist and subject. In this way, the presumptions and assumptions of structurally powerful contemporary knowledge are interrogated, while critical theory pursues its own "knowledge-interests" against the test of an inclusive conception of human emancipation. Given the different starting point of critical theory from other theories, the conceptualization of security is different, and this informs what is thought to be relevant and reliable knowledge.

• What might be done? While the spirit of critical theory is forward-looking, guided by emancipatory interests, the understanding of knowledge as a historical process involves rethinking the past as a basis for inventing a better future. History, after all, is not what happened but how it has been interpreted; historiography is partly about discovery, but more about invention. Consequently, what has been done, and might be done, looks very different depending on how one tells the story of the past. It can be done with regressive assumptions or an emancipatory interest. Similarly, one's conception of practice and problem-solving will vary. On the one side is the traditional theorist who sees practice as separate from theory and conceives problem-solving within a predefined world. On the other side is the Frankfurt School critical theorist who conceives a constitutive relationship between theorizing and practice and who prioritizes solving the (macro) problem of the existing situation rather than the (micro) problems within that situation. For the traditional theorist, what might be done takes place within the parameters of replicating the world; for the Frankfurt School critical theorist what might be done is inspired by the hope of changing the world, not for theory's sake but for improving the lives of real people in real places.

Contending Approaches

Before elaborating critical security theory as just defined, I want briefly to look at several other approaches that might or should find themselves on a CSS syllabus but that I do not believe offer the basis for a convincing theory of security. Space forbids an extensive discussion of these contending approaches, and so the remarks below only summarize key criticisms.

Postmodernism/Poststructuralism

Postmodern/poststructural engagement with the subject of security in international relations has been characterized by some of the general problems of the genre, notably obscurantism, relativism, and faux radicalism.[26] What has particularly troubled critics of the postmodern sensibility has been the latter's underlying conception of politics.[27]

Terry Eagleton, for one, has praised the "rich body of work" by postmodern writers in some areas but at the same time has contested the genre's "cultural relativism and moral conventionalism, its scepticism, pragmatism and localism, its distaste for ideas of solidarity and disciplined organization, [and] its lack of any adequate theory of political agency."[28] Eagleton made these comments as part of a general critique of the postmodern sensibility, but I would argue that specific writing on security in international relations from postmodern and poststructuralist perspectives has generally done nothing to ease such concerns. Eagleton's fundamental worry was how postmodernism would "shape up" to the test of fascism as a serious political challenge. Other writers, studying particular political contexts, such as postapartheid South Africa, have shown similar worries; they have questioned the lack of concrete or specific resources that such theories can add to the repertoire of reconstruction strategies.[29] Richard A. Wilson, an anthropologist interested in human rights, has generalized exactly the same concern, namely, that the postmodernist rejection of metanarratives and universal solidarities does not deliver a helpful politics to people in trouble. As he puts it, "Rights without a metanarrative are like a car without seat-belts; on hitting the first moral bump with ontological implications, the passenger's safety is jeopardised."[30] The struggle within South Africa to bring down the institutionalized racism of apartheid benefited greatly from the growing strength of universal human rights values (which delegitimized racism and legitimized equality) and their advocacy by groups in different countries and cultures showing their political solidarity in material and other ways.

Anxiety about the politics of postmodernism and poststructuralism is provoked, in part, by the negative conceptualization of security projected by their exponents. The poststructuralist approach seems to assume that security cannot be common or positive-sum but must always be zero-sum, with somebody's security always being at the cost of the insecurity of others. At the same time, security itself is questioned as a desirable goal for societies because of the assumption of poststructuralist writers that the search for security is necessarily conservative and will result in negative consequences for somebody. They tend also to celebrate insecurity, which I regard as a middle-class affront to the truly insecure.[31] In the shadow of such views, it is not surprising that the postmodern/poststructuralist genre is sometimes seen as having affinities with realism. Political realists and poststructuralists seem to share a fatalistic view that humans are doomed to insecurity; regard the search for emancipation as both futile and dangerous; believe in a notion of the human condition; and relativize norms. Both leave power where it is in the world: deconstruction and deterrence are equally static theories.

Securitization Studies

Securitization studies is the approach advocated by what has become known as the Copenhagen School.[32] It is only marginally "critical" in theoretical orientation as the term is being used here. Even so, the approach is sometimes seen as standing significantly outside mainstream security studies because of its work on identity and societal security, together with its occasional poststructural flourishes. Claims have been made that securitization studies should be the next phase in the study of the theory and practice of security, but this would be mistaken, for the Copenhagen School is a curious combination of liberal, poststructural, and neorealist approaches. Not surprisingly a bundle of conceptual problems and political issues is piled up by this curious theoretical mixture. The conceptualizations of the central themes of securitization and desecuritization are state-centric, discourse-dominated, and conservative.

Feminism

Security has been a significant theme for some feminist theorists. But feminist theorizing is a broad church, embracing multiple perspectives, and to the extent there is a feminist school of security studies, it is as theoretically varied as feminist theorizing as a whole. This means that feminist security studies includes perspectives extending from radical feminism (believing in the unique qualities—nurturing and peacefulness—of women), to poststructural approaches (deconstructing the very concept of woman). This said, all feminist theorists share a focus on gender, and gender must also be a central theme of any critical theory of security. Issues relating to gender and security/insecurity should not be ghettoized within feminist theorizing, and critical perspectives should play whatever part they can in avoiding this outcome. The agenda of feminist politics, therefore, insofar as it concerns security, must be integral to a critical theory of security.[33] Important concerns are shared, such as exposing how power works, uncovering the role of gender, giving voice to the silenced in world politics, seeking to understand the general from the particular, and having a political orientation toward emancipation. But clearly, some forms of feminist theorizing—that which essentializes or that which opposes universalizing—are not congenial.

Constructivism

Constructivism is an immensely diffuse set of approaches to studying world politics. Who, including Kenneth Waltz and his conception of neorealism, is not a constructivist in some sense?[34] The most clearly constructivist school of international relations today is the curiously labeled English School, with its emphasis on norms and rules within a supposed society of states.[35]

Although constructivism offers important insights into the dynamics of world politics,[36] it does not in itself constitute a *theory* of international relations, comparable with realism, for example, with its distinctive set of ideas about the centrality of states, the causal significance of the distribution of power, and the logic of balance-of-power policies. Constructivism is a metatheoretical orientation, seeking to offer richer explanations of how the world works[37]; it does not in itself give us a politically relevant ontology or praxiological orientation. It offers little or no guidance as to whether globalization is desirable or whether the U.S.-UK invasion of Iraq in 2003 was sensible. Constructivism is not a theory of security; what it does is act as a counter to those theories claiming that life, including politics among nations, is determined (by biology, for example). It reinforces the idea, to paraphrase Alexander Wendt, that security is what we make it.[38]

Real People in Real Places

While criticizing various contending theories, and outlining the case for a specific critical theory of security, I want to emphasize the desirability of *pluralism*. Any project aimed at rethinking security from the bottom up must not be closed to the ideas and questions raised by different theoretical perspectives. That being said, the drawing of theoretical lines is essential for an effective research strategy, not to mention any political orientation. At the same time, whatever one's theoretical preference, regular engagement with other theoretical perspectives, including political realism, will help keep everybody honest. There should be no synthesis of critical approaches around the lowest common denominator or any misinformed ignoring of the tradition of political realism.

Students of security these days seem to be condemned to a lifetime of theoretical dialectic, but the typical student will not be interested in theory for its own sake but rather for what it can do in helping us to understand what is happening around us ("theory explains the world"), then in engaging with world politics more effectively ("there is nothing more practical than a good theory"). In other words, most of us are interested in theory because we are interested in real people in real places. So, for example, the concept of emancipation should not be allowed to be characterized, as it sometimes is by critics, as abstract or unrelated to real conflicts. In Chapter 10, Joseph Ruane and Jennifer Todd showed in the all too concrete conflict in Northern Ireland that emancipatory notions played a significant part in helping to shift the three decades of Troubles there to a situation in which peace could finally be envisaged.

Being directly relevant to real situations—being a set of guidelines for action—has supposed to have been the particular strength of political realism (as was discussed in Chapter 1). Unlike most political realists, one of its founding figures, E. H. Carr, questioned what he called "pure realism" or "consistent realism." He argued that sound political thought and sound political life were synonymous with finding a place for both utopianism and realism. Although he struggled to bring together the planes of utopianism and realism, he was sure that it was an "unreal kind of realism" that ignored the element of morality in any world order. He therefore concluded that the "essential ingredients of all effective political thinking" were "a finite goal, an emotional appeal, a right of moral judgement and a ground for action."[39] I believe the framework for a critical theory of security mapped out earlier—albeit in a preliminary way—contains those essential ingredients and in doing so helps to point in the direction of a *utopian realist* theory of security. Carr would have rejected such a possibility (he thought it impossible to bring together the planes of realism and utopianism), but he would have been sympathetic with the attempt. Utopian realism attempts to bring together the theoretical and the empirical, as well as the *where we are* (globally and locally) and the *where we want to go* (a harmonious human community with enhanced world security).[40] It attempts to do so in a nondualistic manner, fusing ends and means in a manner whereby one's ideals are evident in how one acts, not only in what one hopes to achieve.

Old thinking about world politics guarantees old practices; the means recommended by traditional theories will ensure that the end will be the same old world with the same old dangers—and perhaps worse, given the predictable tinderbox of the decades ahead. By this I mean that states with weapons of mass destruction (WMD) will not persuade others to give them up (except by coercion) if those very WMD states themselves continue to develop the weapons and implicitly if not explicitly declare their possession to have political and strategic utility. Likewise, when powerful states use violence, even if it is claimed to be a last resort for humanitarian purposes, they are not acting in a manner calculated to make violence less likely; if they achieve success in their own terms, they do so only by proving to others that strategic violence can have political utility. Consistency requires that those who propose that world politics is run by laws behave lawfully themselves and that those powerful states that proclaim democracy should be willing themselves to live with being outvoted. The strategic challenge for emancipatory politics is to develop ideas for dealing with today's security threats (to whatever referents we are studying) in ways sensitive to the view expressed by Albert Camus that the means one uses today shapes the ends one might perhaps reach tomorrow.[41]

If a critical theory of security is to reverse the "escape from the real" that has characterized so much academic writing about international relations,[42] then it is essential to ask what it means for real people in real places. What, for example, does one's theorizing mean for the people(s) of the Balkans, women in east Africa, the prospects for the poorest classes in some region, the war on terror, the future of the Middle East, the likelihood of resource wars, or the possibility of nuclear weapons being used somewhere? It has only been constraints on space that have prevented more case studies being offered in this volume, to illustrate what critically informed empirical studies might look like. Such an engagement with the real should be the heart of the next stage in the growth of critically informed security studies.[43]

Another central task is that of trying to learn lessons, in the hope of contributing to the prevention of oppressive structures and situations developing in the first place. In this respect, the U.S.-led war on Iraq in 2003 will provide fertile ground for lessons. While President George W. Bush and his allies, notably Prime Minister Tony Blair, argued that the war made the world a safer place, critics argue that U.S. and UK leaders and policies over the years contributed significantly to creating the dangerous regional situation in the first place, while their policies in 2002–2004 made the situation less rather than more secure. In light of this record, critics maintain that nobody could have confidence that U.S.-UK policies in Iraq would create postconflict harmony in the region. Critics point out that different attitudes to building up local strongmen, supplying arms to human rights abusers, pursuing nuclear disarmament, strengthening the UN, and the more vigorous (and less partisan) search for a just and lasting peace between Palestine and Israel—to mention only headline items—would have helped create a different relationship between Iraq and the West. The war against Iraq in 2003, according to this argument, has made the world a more dangerous place, not only by exacerbating the situation in the Middle East but also by replicating policies that legitimize violence and that reject multilateral international bodies. Meanwhile, as leaders of many states focus on the war on terror, more important long-term threats to human security and regional order—poverty, disease, environmental decay—remain marginal or ignored. Remembering Camus, we should understand that human society will never achieve tomorrow what its most powerful do not choose to begin to practice today.

There are, however, resources for benevolent change. *Immanent critique* points to the growing voice of global civil society, for example, though the obstacles to benign change should not be underestimated.[44] Where one stands on these matters is a scholarly responsibility to be considered with utmost seriousness because somewhere, some people, as these very words are being read, are being starved, oppressed, threatened, or killed in the name of some theory of international politics or economics—or security.

The framework of critical security theory outlined above is policy-relevant, concerned with improving the conditions of political possibility in the issue area of security. One familiar difficulty from any critical perspective in this respect is the fact that current crises are the symptoms of particular structural wrongs and so are deeply embedded in the workings of society. In order to deal with such difficulties, as the old saying goes, one would not want to start from here. When one is already embroiled in a crisis, realistic options are massively reduced. The main contribution of critical approaches must therefore be precrisis, to help us think more constructively about ethical commitments, policies, agents, and sites of change, to help humankind, in whole and in part, to move away from the structural wrongs that ensure that crises, like earthquakes, will periodically rent the political landscape.

The critical theory project in security studies—committed to the development of scholarship relating to the in/security of real people in real places—can be translated into the two tasks of critique and reconstruction. Critique entails critical explorations of what is real (ontology), what is reliable knowledge (epistemology), and what can be done (praxis). Reconstruction requires engagement with concrete issues in world politics, with the aim of maximizing the opportunities for enhancing security, community, and emancipation in the human interest. Hayward Alker in Chapter 8 showed why, despite everything, there is reason for rational hope. Not only is there Kenneth Boulding's argument about the possibilities revealed by historical actualities, but also Alker's suggestion about the scope for pragmatic concrete projects that are possible across cultures and political theories (what he calls "existential *redemptions* from the violence of the past").

The one world in which we all live is getting smaller, more overheated, and increasingly overcrowded. Meanwhile, the realities of security are becoming more complex as politico-economic and technocultural globalization interacts with traditional conflicts arising out of international competition and mistrust. Runaway science, irrationalities and extremisms of one sort or another, and growing pressures on resources threaten to add more combustible fuel to the already dangerous global situation. Human society in the decades to come is threatened by a future of complex insecurity. The outcome for world society is as uncertain as it has ever been—perhaps even more so, given current and future destructive capabilities. Confronted by the threat of complex insecurity, human society needs a theory of world security that is ontologically inclusive, epistemologically sophisticated, and praxeologically varied. Old thinking is guaranteed to replicate: Can a critical theory move beyond this and help to emancipate? Security studies will contribute—however remotely or indirectly—to replicating or changing peoples' conditions of existence. As students of security, whether one is new to the subject or has been studying it for decades, we have a choice: we can decide to study in ways that replicate a world politics that does not work for countless millions of our fellow human beings; or we can decide to study in ways that seek to help to lift the strains of life-determining insecurity from the bodies and minds of people in real villages and cities, regions and states. The stakes could not be higher.

Notes

1. It will be elaborated in Booth, *Theory of World Security*.
2. This is discussed with sophistication in McSweeney, *Security, Identity, and Interests*, pp. 140–142. The discussion contains a criticism of the tendency of international relations scholars to use the term "reflexive" and "reflective" synonymously.
3. This is the title of the preface to Krause and Williams, *Critical*, p. vii.
4. Ibid.
5. Ibid., p. viii.
6. Note their aim, ibid., p. vii.
7. The only version of the approach to be outlined in the present chapter is my "Security and Self," pp. 83–119.
8. This elaboration of the metaphor borrows from Hannah Arendt's borrowing. See Young-Bruehl, *Hannah Arendt*, p. 213.
9. For an accessible summary of the ideas of Kant as applied to international relations, see Williams and Booth, "Kant."
10. Overviews of the work of the Frankfurt School are Held, *Introduction to Critical Theory*; Bernstein, *Recovering Ethical Life*; Stirk, *Critical Theory, Politics, and Society*; and Bottomore, *The Frankfurt School and Its Critics*
11. Wyn Jones, *Security, Strategy, and Critical Theory*.
12. Ibid., p. ix.
13. For Gramsci's work see his *Selections from the Prison Notebooks*, and Fiori, *Antonio Gramsci*. For an introduction to Cox's work, see Cox, "Social Forces," and "Gramsci, Hegemony, and International Relations," and Cox and Sinclair, *Approaches to World Order*. For an introduction, with useful references, see Smith, "Marxism and International Relations Theory," in Groom and Light, *Contemporary International Relations*, and Linklater, "Marxism," in Burchill et al., *Theories of International Relations*. Critical international relations theory was launched, in practice if not name, by Linklater: *Men and Citizens in the Theory of International Relations*; *Beyond Realism and Marxism*; *Transformation of Political Community*; see also "The Question of the Next Stage in International Relations Theory." On cosmopolitan democracy, see Held, *Democracy and Global Order*, and Held et al., *Global Transformations*. I would add the school of critical realism to this list, although it has not (so far) produced work directly on security. See Patomaki and Wight, "After Postpositivism." A useful collection of essays discussing most of the approaches above is Wyn Jones (ed.), *Critical Theory and World Politics*.

14. Helpful insights for students of security are Wyn Jones, *Security*, and Hofffman, "Critical Theory and the Inter-Paradigm Debate"; and Linklater, "The Achievements of Critical Theory," in Smith et al., *International Theory*. The indispensable starting point is Horkheimer's seminal essay, "Traditional and Critical Theory," in Horkheimer, *Critical Theory*.

15. Horkheimer, "Traditional and Critical Theory."

16. Note Johansen, *The National Interest and the Human*, and Mel Gurtov, *Global Politics in the Human Interest*.

17. See in particular Bauman, *Modernity and the Holocaust*. A very different perspective on the Enlightenment is captured in Porter, *Enlightenment*.

18. Examples of a key work in each of the schools just mentioned are, respectively: Allott, *Eunomia*; Galtung, *There Are Alternatives*; Falk, *Human Rights Horizons*; Enloe, *Bananas, Beaches, and Bases*; and Tilley, *Coercion, Capital, and European States*.

19. Falk and Kim (eds.), *The War System*, contains an important selection of relevant literature. Also, Allott, "The Future of the Human Past," in Booth (ed.), *Statecraft and Security*.

20. On these notions and human history, see Allott, "The Future of the Human Past."

21. Bull, *The Anarchical Society*, p. 22.

22. This school of thought has been preeminently represented in the work of Falk. See, inter alia, *A Study of Future Worlds*, *The Promise of World Order*, and *Human Rights Horizons*.

23. See Horkheimer, *Critique of Instrumental Reason;* and Adorno and Horkheimer, *Dialectic of Enlightenment*.

24. Lifton and Markusen, *The Genocidal Mentality*.

25. This is briefly explained in Richards, *The Philosophy of Gandhi*, pp. 31–32. See also Parekh, *Gandhi's Political Philosophy*, pp. 142–170. I have elaborated the argument in "Two Terrors, One Problem."

26. Proponents of the genre attempt to resist being labeled, though they form a clearly identifiable school of thought. In what follows I will use the terms more or less interchangeably, and call the shared outlooks a "sensibility." For a taste of the intellectual battlefield, see the now famous/infamous attack on French postmodernism and some of its alleged pretensions in Sokol and Bricmont, *Intellectual Impostures*. The book is an account of the way a notorious academic trick uncovered the abuse of scientific concepts by iconic French postmodernists: see p. ix.

27. A sympathetic survey is Richard Devetek, "Postmodernism," in Burchill et al., *Theories*. Another, more explicitly for students of security, is Smith, "Epistemology, Postmodernism, and International Relations Theory," pp. 330–336. A strong critique of the postmodernist genre is Eagleton, *The Illusions of Postmodernism*.

28. Eagleton, *The Illusions*, pp. 134–135.

29. For example, Glaser, *Politics and Society in South Africa*, esp. p. 68.

30. Wilson (ed.), *Human Rights, Culture, and Context*, p. 8.

31. Examples of the approach are Dillon, *The Politics of Security*; and Der Derian, "The Value of Security," in Lipschutz (ed.), *On Security*.

32. The key text of the Copenhagen School is probably Buzan et al., *Security*.

33. The first comprehensive explicitly feminist reading of security was Tickner, *Gender in International Relation*.

34. See Waltz, *Theory*, p. 48; see Wight, "Philosophy," p. 38.

35. For a recent set of essays on the English School, see the special issue of *International Relations* 17, no. 3 (December 2003).

36. Sympathetic overviews of constructivism are: Reus-Smit, "Constructivism," in Burchill et al., *Theories*; and Adler, "Constructivism and International Relations," in Carlsneas et al., *Handbook*.

37. The most prominent, but controversial text, is Wendt, *Social Theory*.

38. The reference is to Wendt's article, "Anarchy Is What States Make of It," pp. 391–425.

39. Carr, *The Twenty Years' Crisis, 1919–1939*, pp. 10, 89.

40. I attempted to challenge the conventional interpretation of Carr as simply a realist in "Security and Anarchy," pp. 527–545.

41. See Hoffmann, *Duties Beyond Borders*, p. 197.

42. This is elaborated in Booth, "Human Wrongs"; the phrase is Clement Rosset's.

43. See the special issue of *International Relations* 18, no. 3 (September 2004). A range of articles looks at specific empirical cases through critical lenses.

44. For a selection of perspectives see Lechner and Boli (eds.), *The Globalization Reader*, 2nd ed., pts. 6–10.

List of Acronyms

AIA	Anglo-Irish Agreement
CBMs	confidence-building measures
CFE	Conventional Forces in Europe (Treaty)
CSBMs	confidence- and security-building measures
CSCE	Conference for Security and Cooperation in Europe
CSCM	Conference on Security and Cooperation in the [Western] Mediterranean
CSS	critical security studies
DUP	Democratic Unionist Party
IMF	International Monetary Fund
IPE	international political economy
IR	international relations
IRA	Irish Republican Army
NGOs	nongovernmental organizations
NOD	nonoffensive defense
OECD	Organization for Economic Cooperation and Development
OPEC	Organization of Petroleum Exporting Countries
RMA	revolution in military affairs
SDLP	Social Democratic and Labour Party
SPD	Social Democratic Party
SS	security studies
UKUP	United Kingdom Unionist Party
UNDP	United Nations Development Programme
UUP	Ulster Unionist Party
WMD	weapons of mass destruction

Bibliography

Acharya, Amitav, and Arabinda Acharya. "Human Security in the Asia Pacific: Puzzle, Panacea, or Peril?" CANCAPS Bulletin, no. 27 (November 2000). Available online at www.iir.ubc.ca/cancaps/cbul27.html#husec.

Ackerman, Peter, and Christopher Kruegler. *Strategic Nonviolent Conflict: The Dynamics of People Power in the Twentieth Century* (Westport, Conn.: Praeger, 1994).

Adler, Emmanuel. "Constructivism and International Relations," pp. 95–118 in Walter Carlsneas et al., *Handbook of International Relations* (London: Sage, 2002).

Adler, Emmanuel, and Michael Barnett (eds.). *Security Communities* (Cambridge, UK: Cambridge University Press, 1998).

Adorno, Theodor. *Aesthetic Theory*. Trans. C. Lenhardt, ed. Gretel Adorno and Rolf Tiedemann (London: Routledge and Keegan Paul, 1984).

Adorno, Theodor W., and Max Horkheimer. *Dialectic of Enlightenment*. Transl. John Cumming (London: Verso, 1979).

Agnew, John, and Stuart Corbridge. *Mastering Space: Hegemony, Territory, and International Political Economy* (London: Routledge, 1995).

Agreement Reached in the Multi-Party Negotiations (Dublin: Government Publications, 1998).

Albelda, R., et al. (eds.). *Alternatives to Economic Orthodoxy* (Armonk, N.Y.: M. E. Sharpe, 1987).

Alford, Jonathon. "Confidence-Building Measures in Europe: The Military Aspects." *Adelphi Paper No. 149* (London: IISS, 1979).

Alker, Hayward R. "Emancipatory Empiricism: Toward the Renewal of Empirical Peace Research." Pp. 332–354 in Hayward R. Alker (ed.), *Rediscoveries and Reformulations: Humanist Methodologies for International Studies* (Cambridge: Cambridge University Press, 1996).

——— (ed.). *Rediscoveries and Reformulations: Humanist Methodologies for International Studies* (Cambridge: Cambridge University Press, 1996).

Allott, Philip. *Eunomia: New Order for a New World* (Oxford, UK: Oxford University Press, 1990 and 2001).

———. "The Future of the Human Past." Pp. 323–337 in Ken Booth (ed.), *Statecraft and Security: The Cold War and Beyond* (Cambridge, UK: Cambridge University Press, 1999).

———. "Globalization from Above: Actualizing the Ideal Through Law." Pp.

61–79 in Ken Booth, Tim Dunne, and Michael Cox (eds.), *How Might We Live? Global Ethics in the New Century* (Cambridge, UK: Cambridge University Press, 2001).

———. *The Health of Nations: Society and Law Beyond the State* (Cambridge, UK: Cambridge University Press, 2002).

Alting von Geusau, Frans A. M., and Jacques Pelkmans (eds.). *National Economic Security: Perceptions, Threats, and Policies* (Tilburg, The Netherlands: John F. Kennedy Institute, 1982).

Anderson, Benedict. *Imagined Communities* (London: Verso, rev. ed., 1991).

Ang, Ien, and Jon Stratton. "Asianing Australia: Notes Towards a Critical Transnationalism in Cultural Studies," *Cultural Studies* 10, no. 1 (1996): 16–31.

Apel, Karl-Otto. "The Conflicts of Our Time and the Problem of Political Ethics." In F. Dallmayr (ed.), *From Contract to Community* (New York: Marcel Dekker, 1979).

Appy, Christian G. *Working-Class War: American Combat Soldiers and Vietnam* (Chapel Hill and London: University of North Carolina Press, 1993).

———. *Towards a Transformation of Philosophy* (London: Routledge and Kegan Paul, 1980).

Arkin, William, and Lyne R. Dobrofsky. "Military Socialization and Masculinity," *Journal of Social Issues* 34, no. 1 (1978): 151–168.

Armengol, Viçenc Fisas. "NOD and the Western Mediterranean." Pp. 166–175 in Bjørn Møller and Håkan Wiberg (eds.), *Non-Offensive Defence for the Twenty-First Century* (Boulder: Westview Press, 1994).

Armstrong, Major Barry. Testimony to the Commission of Inquiry into the Deployment of Canadian Forces to Somalia, 12 March 1997.

"Army Commander Probes Report of Lepine Dinner," *Ottawa Citizen,* November 10, 1995, p. A3.

Art, Robert J. "To What Ends Military Power?" *International Security* 4 (Spring 1980): 4–35.

Art, Robert J., and Kenneth N. Waltz (eds.). *The Use of Force: Military Power and International Politics*, 4th ed. (Lanham, Md.: University Press of America, 1993).

Ashley, Richard K. "The Poverty of Neorealism," *International Organization* 38, no. 2 (1984): 225–286.

———. "Three Modes of Economism," *International Studies Quarterly* 27 (1983): 463–496.

Augelli, Enrico, and Craig N. Murphy. *America's Quest for Supremacy and the Third World* (London: Pinter Publishers, 1988).

Aughey, A. *Under Siege: Ulster Unionism and the Anglo-Irish Agreement* (Belfast: Blackstaff, 1989).

Axworthy, Lloyd. "Canada and Human Security: The Need for Leadership," *International Journal* 52, no. 2 (1997): 183–196.

Ayoob, Mohammed. "Defining Security: A Subaltern Realist Perspective." Pp. 121–146 in K. Krause and M. Williams (eds.), *Critical Security Studies: Concepts and Cases* (Minneapolis: University of Minnesota Press, 1997).

Baldwin, David. "The Concept of Security," *Review of International Studies* 23, no. 1 (1997): 5–26.

Ball, Desmond, "Building Confidence and Security in the Asia-Pacific Region." Pp. 245–261 in Gary Klintworth (ed.), *Asia-Pacific Security: Less Uncertainty, New Opportunities?* (New York: Longman/St. Martin's, 1996).

Bardon, J. *A History of Ulster* (Belfast: Blackstaff, 1992).

Barnett, Jon. *The Meaning of Environmental Security: Ecological Politics and*

Policy in the New Security Era (London and New York: Zed Books, 2001).

Bartlett, Thomas. *The Fall and Rise of the Irish Nation: The Catholic Question 1690–1830* (Dublin: Gill and Macmillan, 1992).

Bauman, Zygmunt. *Modernity and Ambivalence* (Cambridge, UK: Polity, 1991).

———. *Modernity and the Holocaust* (Cambridge, UK: Polity, 1995).

Beck, Ulrich. "Risk Society Revisited: Theory, Politics, and Research Programmes." In Barbara Adam, Ulrich Beck, and Joost Van Loon, *The Risk Society and Beyond: Critcal Issues for Social Theory* (London: Sage, 2000).

Behnke, Andreas. "The Message or the Messenger? Reflections on the Role of Security Experts and the Securitization of Political Issues," *Cooperation and Conflict* 35, no. 1 (2000): 89–105.

Bello, Walden. "East Asia: On the Eve of the Great Transformation," *Review of International Political Economy* 5, no. 3 (1998): 424–444.

Benhabib, Seyla. *Situating the Self: Gender, Community and Postmodernism in Contemporary Ethics* (Cambridge, UK: Polity, 1993).

Benhabib, Seyla, and Drucilla Cornell (eds.). *Feminism as Critique: Essays on the Politics of Gender in Late-Capitalist Societies* (Cambridge, UK: Polity, 1987).

Bercuson, David. *Significant Incident: Canada's Army, the Airborne, and the Murder in Somalia* (Toronto: McClelland and Stewart, 1996).

Berger, Mark. "Yellow Mythologies: The East Asian Miracle and Post–Cold War Capitalism," *Positions* 4, no. 1 (1999): 92.

Berlin, Isaiah. *Four Essays on Liberty* (New York: Oxford University Press, 1969).

Bernstein, J. M. *Recovering Ethical Life. Jurgen Habermas and the Future of Critical Theory* (London: Routledge, 1995).

Berry, Chris. *A Bit on the Side: East-West Topographies of Desire* (Sydney: EMPress, 1994).

Bhaskar, Roy. *Dialectic: The Pulse of Freedom* (London: Verso, 1993).

———. *Plato, Etc.* (London: Verso, 1994).

Bhikhu, Parekh. *Gandhi's Political Philosophy: A Critical Examination* (London: Macmillan, 1989).

Biddle, Stephen. "Victory Misunderstood: What the Gulf War Tells Us About the Future of Conflict," *International Security* 21, no. 2 (Fall 1996): 139–179.

Bilgin, Pinar, Ken Booth, and Richard Wyn Jones. "Security Studies: The Next Stage?" *Nacao E Defesa* 84, no. 2 (1998): 131–157.

Bloomfield, D. *Developing Dialogue in Northern Ireland: The Mayhew Talks 1992* (London: Palgrave, 2001).

———. *Political Dialogue in Northern Ireland: The Brooke Initiative, 1989–1992* (London: Macmillan, 1998).

Booth, Ken. "Conclusion: Security Within Global Transformation?" Pp. 338–355 in Ken Booth (ed.), *Statecraft and Security: The Cold War and Beyond* (Cambridge, UK: Cambridge University Press, 1998).

———. "Dare Not to Know: International Relations Theory Versus the Future." Pp. 328–350 in Ken Booth and Steve Smith (eds.), *International Relations Theory Today* (Cambridge, UK: Polity, 1995).

———. "Human Wrongs and International Relations," *International Affairs* 71, no. 1 (1995): 103–126.

———. "A New Security Concept for Europe." Pp. 1–7 in Paul Eavis (ed.), *European Security: The New Agenda* (Bristol: Saferworld, November 1990).

———. "A Reply to Wallace," *Review of International Studies* 23 (1997): 371–377.

———. "Security and Emancipation," *Review of International Studies* 17, no. 4 (1991): 313–326.

———. "Security and Self: Reflections of a Fallen Realist." Pp. 83–119 in Keith Krause and Michael C. Williams (eds.), *Critical Security Studies: Concepts and Cases* (Minneapolis: University of Minnesota Press, 1997).

———. "Security in Anarchy: Utopian Realism in Theory and Practice," *International Affairs* 67, no. 3 (1991): 527–545.

———. "Strategy." Pp. 109–127 in A. J. R. Groom and Margot Light (eds.), *Contemporary International Relations: A Guide to Theory* (London: Pinter, 1994).

———. *Theory of World Security* (Cambridge, UK: Cambridge University Press, forthcoming).

———. "Three Tyrannies." Pp. 31–70 in Tim Dunne and Nick Wheeler (eds.), *Human Rights in Global Politics* (Cambridge, UK: Cambridge University Press, 1999).

———. "Two Terrors, One Problem." In J. N. Rosenau and E. Aydinli (eds.), *Globalization, Security, and the Nation State* (New York: SUNY Press, forthcoming).

Booth, Ken (ed.). *New Thinking About Strategy and International Security* (London: HarperCollins, 1991).

———. *Statecraft and Security: The Cold War and Beyond* (Cambridge, UK: Cambridge University Press, 1999).

Booth, Ken, and Tim Dunne (eds.). *Worlds in Collision: Terror and the Future of Global Order* (Houndmills, UK: Palgrave Macmillan, 2002).

Booth, Ken, and Eric Herring. *Keyguide to Information Sources in Strategic Studies* (London: Mansell, 1994).

Booth, Ken, and Peter Vale. "Security in Southern Africa: After Apartheid, Beyond Realism," *International Affairs* 71, no. 2 (1995): 285–304.

———. "Critical Security Studies and Regional Insecurity: The Case of South Africa." Pp. 349–352 in K. Krause and M. Williams (eds.), *Critical Security Studies: Concepts and Cases* (Minneapolis: University of Minnesota Press, 1997).

Booth, Ken, and Russell Trood (eds.). *Strategic Culture in the Asia-Pacific* (London: Macmillan, 1999).

Boserup, Anders, and Robert Neild (eds.). *The Foundations of Defensive Defence* (London: Macmillan, 1990).

Botsman, Peter. and Mark Latham (eds.). *The Enabling State: People Before Bureaucracy* (Annandale: Pluto, 2001).

Bottomore, Tom. *The Frankfurt School and Its Critics* (London: Routledge, 2002 [1984]).

Bourdieu, Pierre. *Acts of Resistance* (Cambridge, UK: Polity Press, 1998).

———. *Outline of a Theory of Practice*. Transl. R. Nice (Cambridge, UK: Cambridge University Press, 1997).

———. *Practical Reason* (Cambridge, UK: Polity Press, 1998).

Bracken, Paul. "The Military After the Next," *Washington Quarterly* 16, no. 4 (1993): 157–174.

Brady, Ciaran, and Raymond Gillespie (eds.). *Natives and Newcomers: The Making of Irish Colonial Society, 1534–1641* (Dublin: Irish Academic Press, 1986).

Brock-Unte, Birgit. *Educating for Peace: A Feminist Perspective* (Oxford, UK: Pergamon Press, 1985).

Bronner, Stephen Eric. *Of Critical Theory and Its Theorists* (Oxford, UK: Blackwell, 1994).

Brooks, Doug. "Messiahs or Mercenaries? The Future of Private Military Services," *International Peacekeeping* 7, no. 4 (Winter 2000): 129–144.

Brown, Chris. "'Turtles All the Way Down': Antifoundationalism, Critical Theory, and International Relations," *Millennium* 23, no. 2 (1994): 213–236.

Builder, Carl H. *The Icarus Syndrome: The Role of Air Power Theory in the Evolution and Fate of the U.S. Air Force* (New Brunswick, N.J., and London: Transaction Publishers, 1994).

Bull, Hedley. *The Anarchical Society: A Study of Order in World Politics* (London: Macmillan, 1977).

Burch, Kurt, and Robert Denemark (eds.). *Constituting International Political Economy* (London: Lynne Rienner Publishers, 1997).

Burchill, Scott, et al. *Theories of International Relations* (London and New York: Macmillan and St. Martin's, 1996).

Burk, James (ed.). *The Military in New Times: Adapting Armed Forces to a Turbulent World* (Boulder: Westview Press, 1994).

Burke, Anthony. *In Fear of Security: Australia's Asian Anxiety* (Sydney: Pluto, 2001).

———. "The Political Philosophy of Security and Antipodean Echoes." Research Paper, Department of Political Science, Australian National University, Canberra, August 1997.

Burton, J. W. *Peace Theory* (New York: Knopf, 1962).

Butfoy, Andrew. *Common Security and Strategic Reform: A Critical Analysis* (Basingstoke, UK: Macmillan, 1997).

———. "Critical Reflections on Non-Offensive Defence," *Working Paper No. 14* (Clayton: Centre for International Relations, Monash University, May 1995).

Butler, Clark. *History as the Story of Freedom: Philosophy in Intercultural Context* (Amsterdam and Atlanta: Rodopi, 1997).

Buzan, Barry. *An Introduction to Strategic Studies: Military Technology and International Relations* (London: Macmillan, 1987).

———. *People, States, and Fear* (Boulder: Lynne Rienner, 1983).

———. *People, States and Fear: An Agenda for International Security Studies in the Post–Cold War Era*, 2nd edition (Boulder: Lynne Rienner, 1991).

———. "The Present as a Historic Turning Point," *Journal of Peace Research* 30, no. 4 (1995): 385–398.

Buzan, Barry, et al. *The European Security Order Recast: Scenarios for the Post-Cold War Era* (London: Pinter, 1990).

Buzan, Barry, and Ole Wæver. *Regions and Powers: The Structure of International Security* (Cambridge, UK: Cambridge University Press, 2003).

———. "Slippery? Contradictory? Sociologically Untenable? The Copenhagen School Replies," *Review of International Studies* 23, no. 2 (1997): 241–250.

Buzan, Barry, Ole Wæver, and Jaap de Wilde. *Security: A New Framework for Analysis* (Boulder: Lynne Rienner Publishers, 1998).

Calhoun, Craig. *Critical Social Theory: Culture, History, and the Challenge of Difference* (Oxford: Blackwell, 1995).

Callahan, David. *Unwinnable Wars: American Power and Ethnic Conflict* (New York: Hill & Wang, 1997).

Camilleri, Joseph, and Jim Falk. *The End of Sovereignty? The Politics of a Shrinking and Fragmenting World* (Aldershot, UK: Edward Elgar, 1992).

Campbell, David. "The Deterritorialisation of Responsibility: Levinas, Derrida, and Ethics After the End of Philosophy," *Alternatives* 19 (1994): 455–484.

———. *National Deconstruction: Violence, Identity, and Justice in Bosnia* (Minneapolis: University of Minnesota Press, 1998).

———. "Political Prosaics, Transversal Politics, and the Anarchical World." Chap. 1 in M. J. Shapiro and H. R. Alker (eds.), *Challenging Boundaries: Global Flows, Territorial Identities* (Minneapolis: University of Minnesota Press,

1996).

———. *Writing Security: United States Foreign Policy and the Politics of Identity* (Manchester, UK: Manchester University Press, 1992).

Campbell, David, and Michael Dillon (eds.). *The Political Subject of Violence* (Manchester, UK: Manchester University Press, 1993).

Canny, Nicholas. *Making Ireland British 1580–1650* (Oxford, UK: Oxford University Press, 2001).

Carey, John (ed.). *The Faber Book of Utopias* (London: Faber and Faber, 1999).

Carr, E. H. *Nationalism and After* (London: MacMillan, 1945).

———. *The Twenty Years' Crisis, 1919–1939: An Introduction to the Study of International Relations* (London: Macmillan, 1946).

Carrithers, Michael, *Why Humans Have Cultures: Explaining Anthropology and Social Diversity* (Oxford, UK: Oxford University Press, 1992).

———. *The Twenty Years' Crisis 1919–1939: An Introduction to the Study of International Relations* (London: Macmillan, 1st edition 1939; 2nd edition 1946).

Castells, Manuel. *End of Millennium* (Oxford, UK: Blackwell, 1998).

Chalmers, Malcolm. *Confidence-Building in South-East Asia* (Bradford: Department of Peace Studies, University of Bradford/Westview Press, 1996).

Chalmers, Malcolm, Owen Greene, Edward J. Laurance, and Herbert Wulf (eds.). *Developing the UN Register of Conventional Arms* (Bradford: University of Bradford Arms Register Studies No. 4, 1994).

Chatterjee, Partha. "A Response to Taylor's 'Modes of Civil Society,'" *Public Culture* 3, no. 1 (1990): 119–132.

Cheeseman, Graeme. "The Application of the Principles of Non-Offensive Defence Beyond Europe: Some Preliminary Observations." *Working Paper No. 78* (Canberra: Peace Research Centre, Australian National University, April 1990).

———. *The Search for Self-Reliance: Australian Defence Since Vietnam* (Melbourne: Longman Cheshire, 1993).

Cheeseman, Graeme, and Robert Bruce (eds.). *Discourses of Danger and Dread: Australian Defence and Security Thinking After the Cold War* (St. Leonards, UK: Allen & Unwin, 1996).

Cheney, Peter. "Canada . . . Canada." *Toronto Star*, July 10, 1994, p. F1.

Chomsky, Noam. *World Orders, Old and New* (London: Pluto, 1994).

Chow, Rey. *Writing Diaspora* (Bloomington: Indiana University Press, 1993).

Christensen, Thomas. *Useful Adversaries: Grand Strategy, Domestic Mobilization, and Sino-American Conflict, 1947–1958* (Princeton, N.J.: Princeton University Press, 1996).

von Clausewitz, Karl. *On War.* Ed. and trans. M. Howard and P. Paret (Princeton, N.J.: Princeton University Press, 1976).

Cohen, Jean, and Andrew Arato. *Civil Society and Political Theory* (Cambridge, Mass.: MIT Press, 1992).

Cohn, Carol. "Sex, Death, and the Rational World of Defense Intellectuals," *Signs* 12, no. 4 (1987): 687–718.

Commission of Inquiry into the Deployment of Canadian Forces to Somalia. *Document Book No. 1, Hewson Report* (Ottawa: Canada, 1995).

———. *Document Book No. 8, Racism* (Ottawa: Canada, 1995).

Commission on Human Security. *Human Security Now* (New York: United Nations, 2003). Executive Summary available online at www.humansecurity-chs.org/finalreport/outline.html.

Connell, R. W. *Masculinities* (Berkeley: University of California Press, 1995).

Cooke, Miriam, and Angela Woollacott (eds.). *Gendering War Talk* (Princeton, N.J.: Princeton University Press, 1993).

Cooper, Andrew F. *Canadian Foreign Policy: Old Habits and New Directions* (Scarborough, UK: Prentice Hall, Allyn and Bacon, 1997).

Cooper, Robert. "Security and the Energy Crisis." *Adelphi Paper* 115 (London: IISS, 1975).

Corbridge, Stuart, Ron Martin, and Nigel Thrift. *Money, Power and Space* (Oxford, UK: Blackwell, 1994).

Cotton, James, and John Ravenhill (eds.). *Seeking Asian Engagement: Australia in World Affairs, 1991–1995* (Melbourne: Oxford University Press, 1997).

Coulon, Jocelyn. *Soldiers of Diplomacy: The United Nations, Peacekeeping, and the New World Order* (Toronto: University of Toronto Press, 1998).

Cox, Michael, Ken Booth, and Tim Dunne (eds.). *The Interregnum: Controversies in World Politics, 1989–1999* (Cambridge, UK: Cambridge University Press, 1999).

Cox, M., A. Guelke, and F. Stephen (eds.). *A Farewell to Arms: From "Long War" to Long Peace in Northern Ireland* (Manchester, UK: Manchester University Press, 2000).

Cox, Robert W. "Gramsci, Hegemony, and International Relations: An Essay in Method," *Millennium* 12, no. 2 (1983): 162–175.

———. "Social Forces, States, and World Orders: Beyond International Relations Theory," *Millennium: Journal of International Studies* 10, no. 2 (1981): 126–155.

———. "Towards a Post-Hegemonic Conceptualization of World Order: Reflections on the Relevancy of Ibn Khaldun." In James N. Rosenau and Ernst-Otto Czempiel (eds.), *Governance Without Government: Order and Change in World Politics* (Cambridge, UK: Cambridge University Press, 1992).

Cox, Robert W., with Timothy J. Sinclair. *Approaches to World Order* (Cambridge: Cambridge University Press, 1996).

Crane, George. "Imagining the Economic Nation: Chinese Responses to Globalization." ISA conference paper, Minneapolis, 1998.

Crawford, Beverly. *Economic Vulnerability in International Relations* (New York: Columbia University Press, 1993).

van Creveld, Martin. *The Transformation of War* (New York: Free Press, 1991).

Croft, Stuart, and Terry Terriff (eds.). *Critical Reflections on Security and Change* (London: Frank Cass, 2000).

Crystal, Jonathan. "The Politics of Capital Flight: Exit and Exchange Rates in Latin America," *Review of International Studies* 20, no.2 (1994): 131–148.

Curthoys, Ann. "Feminism, Citizenship, and National Identity," *Feminist Review* 44 (1993): 19–38.

Curthoys, Ann, and Carol Johnson. "Articulating the Future and the Past: Gender, Race, and Globalisation in One Nation Discourse," *Hecate* 24, no. 2 (1998): 92–111.

Dalby, Simon. "Contesting an Essential Concept: Reading the Dilemmas in Contemporary Security Discourse." Pp. 3–32 in Keith Krause and Michael Williams (eds.), *Critical Security Studies: Concepts and Cases* (Minneapolis: University of Minnesota Press, 1997).

———. *Geopolitical Change and Contemporary Security Studies: Contextualizing the Human Security Agenda* (Institute of International Relations, University of British Columbia, Vancouver, Working Paper No. 30, April 2000).

Dallmayr, Fred. *Alternative Visions: Paths in the Global Village* (Lanham, Md.: Rowman and Littlefield, 1998).

Dallmayr, Fred, William E. Connolly, and Nicholas Rengger. "Global Conversation," *Millennium* 30, no. 2 (2001): 331–364.

Daniel, Donald C., and Brad C. Hayes (eds.). *Beyond Traditional Peacekeeping* (London, Macmillan, 1995).

Darby, Phillip (ed.). *On the Edge of International Relations: Postcolonialism, Gender, and Dependency* (London: Pinter, 1997).

Davies, John L., and Ted Robert Gurr (eds.). *Preventive Measures: Building Risk Assessment and Crisis Early Warning Systems* (Lanham, Md.: Rowman and Littlefield, 1998).

Davis, James R. *The Sharp End: A Canadian Soldier's Story* (Vancouver: Douglas and McIntyre, 1997).

Department of Foreign Affairs and International Trade, Government of Canada. *Human Security: Safety for People in a Changing World* (Ottawa, April 1999). Available online at www.dfait-maeci.gc.ca/foreignp/HumanSecurity/menue.html.

Der Derian, J. "The Value of Security: Hobbes, Marx, and Baudrillard." In R. D. Lipschutz (ed.), *On Security* (New York: Columbia University Press, 1995).

Derrida, Jacques. "Remarks on Deconstruction and Pragmatism." Transl. Simon Critchley. Pp. 77–88 in Chantal Mouffe, *Deconstruction and Pragmatism* (London and New York: Routledge, 1996).

Desbarats, Peter. *Somalia Cover-Up: A Commissioner's Journal* (Toronto: McClelland and Stewart, 1997).

Desch, Michael. "Culture Clash: Assessing the Importance of Ideas in Security Studies," *International Security* 23, no. 1 (1998): 141–170.

Desjardins, Marie-France. *Rethinking Confidence-Building Measures* (Oxford, UK: IISS Adelphi Paper No. 307/Oxford University Press, 1996).

Deutsch, Karl. *Political Community at the International Level* (New York: Archon Books, 1970).

Devetak, Richard, and Richard Higgott. "Justice Unbound: Globalization, States and the Transformation of the Social Bond," *International Affairs* 75, no. 3 (1999): 483–489.

Dibb, Paul. *Towards a New Balance of Power in Asia.* Adelphi Paper No. 295 (Oxford, UK: Oxford University Press/IISS, 1995).

Dienstag, Joshua Foa. *"Dancing in Chains": Narrative and Memory in Political Theory* (Stanford: Stanford University Press, 1997).

Dillon, Michael. *The Politics of Security: Towards a Political Philosophy of Continental Thought* (London: Routledge, 1996).

Dion, Stéphane. "Canada Is Going to Make It After All!" Notes for an address by the Honourable Dion, President of the Privy Council and Minister of Intergovernmental Affairs at the biennial conference of the Association for Canadian Studies in the United States, Minneapolis, Minnesota, November 21, 1997, p. 1, cited from Wayne Cox and Claire Turenne Sjolander, "Damage Control: The Politics of National Defence," in Leslie Pal (ed.), *How Ottawa Spends 1998–99: Balancing Act: The Post-Deficit Mandate* (Toronto: Oxford University Press, 1998), pp. 217–242.

Dirlik, Arif. "Critical Reflections on 'Chinese Capitalism' as Paradigm," *Identities* 3, no. 3 (1997): 303–330.

Donnelly, Jack. *Realism and International Relations* (Cambridge, UK: Cambridge University Press, 2000).

Dornan, Christopher. "Scenes from a Scandal." *Globe and Mail,* 21 January 1995, p. D1.

Doty, Roxanne Lynn. "Immigration and National Identity: Constructing the Nation," *Review of International Studies* 22 (1996): 235–255.

————. *Imperial Encounters: The Politics of Representation in North-South Relations* (Minneapolis: University of Minnesota Press, 1996).

Doyle, Michael. "Liberalism and World Politics," *American Political Science Review* 80 (1983): 1151–1168.

Drucker, Peter. "The Global Economy and the Nation-State," *Foreign Affairs* 76, no. 5 (September/October 1997): 159–171.

Duara, Prasenjit. *Rescuing History from the Nation: Questioning Narratives of Modern China* (Chicago: University of Chicago Press, Chicago, 1995).

Dubiel, Helmut. *Theory and Politics: Studies in the Development of Critical Theory.* Transl. Benjamin Gregg (Cambridge, Mass.: MIT Press, 1985).

Dudink, Stefan. "The Unheroic Men of a Moral Nation: Masculinity and Nation in Modern Dutch History." Pp. 146–151 in Cynthia Cockburn and Dubravka Zarkov (eds.), *The Postwar Moment: Militaries, Masculinities and International Peacekeeping* (London: Lawrence and Wishart, 2002).

Duedney, Daniel, and Richard Mathews (eds.). *Contested Grounds: Security and Conflict in the New Environmental Politics* (Albany: State University of New York Press, 1999).

Dunant, Sarah, and Roy Porter (eds.). *The Age of Anxiety* (London: Virago, 1997).

Dunn, David J. "Peace Research." In Trevor Taylor (ed.), *Approaches and Theory in International Relations* (London: Longman, 1978).

Dunne, Timothy. *Inventing International Society: A History of the English School* (London: MacMillan, 1998).

Eagleton, Terry. *The Illusions of Postmodernism* (Oxford, UK: Blackwell, 1996).

The East Asian Miracle: Economic Growth and Public Policy (Washington, D.C.: World Bank, 1993).

Ehrenreich, Barbara. *Blood Rites: Origins and History of the Passions of War* (New York: Metropolitan Books, 1997).

————. "Fukuyama's Follies: So What If Women Ruled the World?" *Foreign Affairs* (January/February 1999): 118.

Elliott, Larry, and Dan Atkinson. *The Age of Insecurity* (London: Verso, 1998).

Elliott, Lorraine. "Environmental Conflict: Reviewing the Arguments," *Journal of Environment and Development* 5, no. 2 (June 1996): 149–167.

Elliott, Lorraine, and Graeme Cheeseman (eds.). *Forces for Good? Cosmopolitan Militaries in the 21st Century* (Manchester, UK: Manchester University Press, forthcoming 2004).

Elshtain, Jean. *Women and War* (New York: Basic Books, 1987).

Enloe, Cynthia. *Bananas, Beaches, and Bases: Making Feminist Sense of International Politics* (Berkeley: University of California Press, 1990).

————. *Does Khaki Become You? The Militarization of Women's Lives* (London: Pluto Press, 1983).

————. *Maneuvers: The International Politics of Militarizing Women's Lives* (Berkeley: University of California Press, 2000).

————. *The Morning After: Sexual Politics at the End of the Cold War* (Berkeley: University of California Press, 1993).

————. "Silicon Tricks and the Two Dollar Woman," *New Internationalist,* no. 227 (January 1991): 14–16.

Eriksson, Johan. "Observers or Advocates? On the Political Role of Security Analysts," *Cooperation and Conflict* 34, no. 3 (1999): 311–330.

Evans, Gareth. "The Asia-Pacific and Global Change," *The Monthly Record* (April 1991): 126.

————. *Australia's Regional Security* (Canberra: Department of Foreign Affairs and Trade, 1989).

van Evera, Stephen. *Causes of War: Power and the Roots of Conflict* (Ithaca: Cornell University Press, 1999).

Falk, Richard A. *Human Rights Horizons: The Pursuit of Justice in a Globalizing World* (New York: Routledge, 2000).

———. *On Humane Governance: Toward a New Global Politics* (Cambridge, UK: Polity Press, 1995).

———. *The Promise of World Order* (Philadelphia: Temple University Press, 1987).

———. *A Study of Future Worlds* (New York, Free Press, 1975).

Falk, Richard A., and Samuel S. Kim (eds.). *The War System: An Interdisciplinary Approach* (Boulder: Westview, 1980).

Fawn, Rick, and Jeremy Larkins (eds.). *International Society After the Cold War: Anarchy and Order Reconsidered* (Houndsmills, UK: Macmillan, 1996).

Findlay, Trevor. "The New Peacekeepers and the New Peacekeeping." Pp. 1–31 in Trevor Findlay (ed.), *Challenges for the New Peacekeepers: SIPRI Research Report No. 12* (Oxford, UK: Oxford University Press/SIPRI, 1996).

Fiori, Giuseppe. *Antonio Gramsci: Life of a Revolutionary.* Trans. Tom Nairn (London: Verso, 1990).

Fischer, Michael M. J., and Mehdi Abedi. *Debating Muslims: Cultural Dialogues in Postmodernity and Tradition* (Madison: University of Wisconsin Press, 1990).

FitzGerald, Garret. *All in a Life: An Autobiography* (Dublin: Gill and Macmillan, 1991).

Fleming, Marie. *Emancipation and Illusion: Rationality and Gender in Habermas's Theory of Modernity* (University Park: Pennsylvania State University, 1997).

Forsberg, Randall. "Toward the End of War," *Boston Review* 22, no. 5 (1997): 4–9.

Foster, R. F. *Modern Ireland 1600–1972* (London: Allen Lane and Penguin Press, 1988).

Foucault, Michel. "Governmentality." Trans. P. Pasquino. In G. Burchell, et al. (eds.), *The Foucault Effect: Studies in Governmentality* (London: Harvester Wheatsheaf, 1991).

———. *Remarks on Marx: Conversations with Duccio Trombadori.* Transl. R. James Goldstein and James Casciato (New York: Semiotext(e), 1981).

Francis, Daniel. *National Dreams: Myth, Memory and Canadian History* (Vancouver: Arsenal Pulp, 1997).

Francke, Linda Bird. *Ground Zero: The Gender Wars in the Military* (New York: Simon and Schuster, 1997).

Fraser, Nancy. *Unruly Practices: Power, Discourse and Gender in Contemporary Social Theory* (Cambridge, UK: Polity, 1989).

Freedman, Lawrence. "The Changing Forms of Military Conflict," *Survival* 40, no. 4 (1998–1999).

Fry, Greg, and Jacinta O'Hagan (eds.). *Contending Images of World Politics* (Basingstoke: Macmillan, 2000).

Gallagher, Winifred. *The Power of Place* (New York: Harper Collins, 1994).

Gallie, W. B. "Essentially Contested Concepts," *Proceedings of the Aristotelian Society* 56 (1955–1956): 167–198.

Galtung, Johan. *Peace by Peaceful Means: Peace and Conflict, Development and Civilization* (London and Thousand Oaks, Calif.: PRIO and Sage, 1996).

———. *There Are Alternatives: Four Roads to Peace and Security* (Nottingham: Spokesman, 1984).

———. *The True Worlds: A Transnational Perspective* (New York: Free Press, 1980).

———. "Violence, Peace, and Peace Research," *Journal of Peace Research* 6, no. 3 (1969): 167–192.

Ganguly, Sumit, and Ted Greenwood (eds.). *Mending Fences: Confidence- and Security-Building Measures in South Asia* (Boulder: Westview, 1996).

Gates, David. "Air Power and the Theory and Practice of Coercion," *Defense Analysis* 13, no. 3 (1997): 239–254.

———. *Non-Offensive Defense: A Strategic Contradiction?* (London: Institue for European Defence and Strategic Studies, 1987).

General Court Martial Transcripts of Private Brocklebank, 1994, vol. 3, entry 19, in *Information Legacy: A Compendium of Source Material from the Commission of Inquiry into the Deployment of Canadian Forces to Somalia* (Ottawa: Government of Canada, 1997).

Geras, Norman. *Marx and Human Nature* (London: Verso, 1983).

Ghai, Yash. "The Politics of Human Rights in Asia, the United Nations: Between Sovereignty and Global Governance?" Conference, LaTrobe University, Melbourne, 1995.

Giddens, Anthony. "Affluence, Poverty and the Idea of a Post-Scarcity Society." In Ken Booth (ed.), *Security and Statecraft: The Cold War and Beyond* (Cambridge, UK: Cambridge University Press, 1998).

———. *The Nation-State and Violence: Volume Two of a Contemporary Critique of Historical Materialism* (Cambridge, UK: Polity, 1985).

———. *Runaway World: How Globalisation Is Reshaping Our Lives* (London: Profile Books, 1999).

Gill, Lesley. "Creating Citizens, Making Men: The Military and Masculinity in Bolivia," *Cultural Anthropology* 12, no. 4 (1997): 527–550.

Gill, Steven. *American Hegemony and the Trilateral Commission* (Cambridge, UK: Cambridge University Press, 1990).

Gill, Steven (ed.). *Gramsci, Historical Materialism and International Relations* (Cambridge, UK: Cambridge University Press, 1993).

Gilpin, Robert, with J. Gilpin. *The Political Economy of International Relations* (Princeton, N.J.: Princeton University Press, 1987).

Glaser, Daryl. *Politics and Society in South Africa: A Critical Introduction* (Thousand Oaks, Calif.: Sage, 2001).

Goldstein, Joshua. *The Real Price of War: What You're Paying for the War on Terror* (New York: New York University Press, 2004).

———. *War and Gender* (Cambridge, UK: Cambridge University Press, 2001).

Goldsworthy, David, "An Overview." In James Cotton and John Ravenhill (eds.), *Seeking Asian Engagement: Australia in World Affairs, 1991–1995* (Melbourne: Oxford University Press, 1997).

Gongora, Thierry, Michel Fortmann, and Stephane Lefebvre. "Modern Land Warfare Doctrines and Non-Offensive Defense: 'An Interesting Idea,'" *Defense Analysis* 11, no. 1 (1995).

Gopinath, Gayatri. "Nostalgia, Desire, and Diaspora: South Asia Sexualities in Motion," *Positions* 5, no. 2 (1997): 467–489.

Government of Canada. *Canada in the World, Government Statement* (Ottawa: Government of Canada, 1995).

———. *Canada's Foreign Policy: Principles and Priorities for the Future Report of the Special Joint Commitee Reviewing Canadian Foreign Policy* (Ottawa: Government of Canada, 1994).

———. *Dishonoured Legacy: The Lessons of the Somalia Affair* (Ottawa: Minister of Public Works and Government Services Canada, 1997).

———. *Information Legacy: A Compendium of Source Material from the Commission of Inquiry into the Deployment of Canadian Forces to Somalia* (Ottawa: Government of Canada, 1997).

————. *Security in a Changing World, 1994*. Report of the Special Joint Committee on Canada's Defence Policy (Ottawa: Government of Canada, 1994).

Gramsci, Antonio. *Selections from the Prison Notebooks*. Transl. Quintin Hoare and Geoffrey Nowell Smith (London: Lawrence and Wishart, 1971).

Gray, Colin. "World Politics as Usual After September 11: Realism Vindicated." Pp. 226–234 in Ken Booth and Tim Dunne (eds.), *Worlds in Collision: Terror and the Future of Global Order* (Houndmills, UK: Palgrave Macmillan, 2002).

Gray, John. *False Dawn: The Delusion of Global Capitalism* (London: Granta, 1998).

Gurr, Ted R. "Peoples Against States: Ethnopolitical Conflict and the Changing World System," *International Studies Quarterly* 38 (1994): 347–378.

Gurtov, Mel. *Global Politics in the Human Interest*, 2nd ed. (Boulder and London: Lynne Rienner Publishers, 1991).

Haas, Ernst B. *Nationalism, Liberalism, and Progress, Volume 2: The Dismal Fate of New Nations* (Ithaca: Cornell University Press, 2000).

Habermas, Jürgen. *Between Facts and Norms: Contributions to a Discourse Theory of Law and Democracy*. Transl. William Rehg (Cambridge, Mass.: MIT Press, 1996).

————. "Beyond the Nation-State? On Some Consequences of Economic Globalization." In Erik O. Erikssen and John E. Fossum (eds.), *Democracy in the European Union: Integration Through Deliberation?* (London: Routledge, 2000).

————. *Justification and Application: Remarks on Discourse Ethics* (Cambridge, UK: Polity, 1993).

————. *Knowledge and Human Interests*. Transl. Jeremy J. Shapiro (Cambridge, UK: Polity, 1986).

————. *The Past as Future* (Cambridge, UK: Polity, 1994).

————. *Theory of Communicative Action, Volume 1: Reason and the Rationalization of Society*. Transl. Thomas McCarthy (London: Heinemann, 1984).

————. *Theory of Communicative Action, Volume 2: Lifeworld and System: A Critique of Functionalist Reason*. Transl. Thomas McCarthy (London: Heinemann, 1987).

————. "What Theories Can Accomplish—and What They Can't." Pp. 99–120 in Jürgen Habermas (interviewed by Michale Haller), *The Past as Future* (Lincoln: University of Nebraska Press, 1994).

Halperin, David. "Review: A Bit on the Side." *UTS Review* 1, no. 1 (1995): 140.

Hamilton, Annette. "Fear and Desire: Aborigines, Asians, and the National Imaginary," *Australian Cultural Studies* 9 (1990): 14–35.

Hampson, Fen Osler. *Madness in the Multitude: Human Security and World Disorder* (Ottawa: Oxford University Press, 2001).

Hansen, Lene. "A Case for Seduction: Evaluating the Poststructuralist Conceptualization of Security," *Cooperation and Conflict* 32, no. 4 (1997): 369–397.

————. "The Little Mermaid's Silent Security Dilemma and the Absence of Gender in the Copenhagen School," *Millennium* 29, no. 2 (2000): 285–306.

Hardin, Russell. *One for All: The Logic of Group Conflict* (Princeton, N.J.: Princeton University Press, 1995).

Harkavy, Robert. "Images of the Coming International System," *Orbis* 41, no. 4 (1997): 569–590.

Harrison, Deborah, and Lucie Laliberté. *No Life Like It: Military Wives in Canada* (Toronto: James Lorimer, 1994).

Hartsock, Nancy. "The Barracks Community in Western Political Thought," *Women's Studies International Forum* 5, no. 4 (1982): 283–286.

Heilbroner, Robert. *Twenty-First Century Capitalism* (New York: Norton, 1993).

Heilbroner, Robert, and William Milberg. *Crisis of Vision in Modern Economic Thought* (Cambridge, UK: Cambridge University Press, 1995).

Heininger, Janet E. *Peacekeeping in Transition: The United Nations in Cambodia* (New York: The Twentieth Century Fund Press, 1994).

Held, David. *Democracy and Global Order: From the Modern State to Global Governance* (Cambridge, UK: Polity, 1995).

————. *Introduction to Critical Theory: Horkheimer to Habermas* (Cambridge, UK: Polity, 1980).

Held, David, et al. *Global Transformations: Politics, Economics, and Culture* (Cambridge, UK: Cambridge University Press, 1999).

Hepburn, A. C. *A Past Apart: Studies in the History of Catholic Belfast 1850–1950* (Belfast: Ulster Historical Foundation, 1996).

Higgott, Richard. "International Political Economy." In A. J. R. Groom and Margot Light (eds.), *Contemporary International Relations: A Guide to Theory* (London: Pinter Publishers, 1994).

Hills, Jill, "Dependency Theory and Its Relevance Today: Telecommunications and Structural Power," *Review of International Studies* 20, no.2 (1994): 169–186.

Hirst, Paul, and Grahame Thompson. *Globalization in Question* (Oxford: Polity, 1996).

Hoffman, Mark. "Critical Theory and the Inter-Paradigm Debate," *Millennium* 16, no. 2 (1987): 231–249.

Hoffmann, Stanley. *Duties Beyond Borders: On the Limits and Possibilities of Ethical International Politics* (Syracuse N.Y.: Syracuse University Press, 1981).

Hohendahl, Uwe. *Reappraisals: Shifting Alignments in Postwar Critical Theory* (Ithaca: Cornell University Press, 1991).

Hollis, Martin. "The Last Post?" Pp. 301–308 in Steve Smith, Ken Booth, and Marysia Zalewski (eds.), *International Theory: Positivism and Beyond* (Cambridge, UK: Cambridge University Press, 1996).

Hollis, Martin, and Steve Smith. *Explaining and Understanding International Relations* (Oxford, UK: Clarendon, 1990).

Holsti, K. J. "The Coming Chaos? Armed Conflict in the World's Periphery." Pp. 283–310 in T. V. Paul and John A. Hall (eds.), *International Order and the Future of World Politics* (Cambridge, UK: Cambridge University Press, 1999).

————. *The State, War, and the State of War* (Cambridge, UK: Cambridge University Press, 1996).

Homer-Dixon, Thomas F. "On the Threshold: Environmental Changes as Causes of Acute Conflict," *International Security* 16 (1991): 76–116.

Honneth, Axel. "The Other of Justice: Habermas and the Ethical Challenge of Postmodernism." In Stephen K. White, *The Cambridge Companion to Habermas* (Cambridge, UK: Cambridge University Press, 1995).

————. "The Social Dynamics of Disrespect: On the Location of Critical Theory Today" (translated by John Farrell), *Constellations* 16, no. 2 (1994): 255–269.

————. *The Struggle for Recognition. The Moral Grammar of Social Conflicts* (Cambridge: Polity Press, 1995).

————. "Work and Instrumental Action," *New German Critique* 25 (1982): 31–54.

Hooper, Charlotte. *Manly States: Masculinities, International Relations, and Gender Politics* (New York: Columbia University Press, 2001).

Hopf, Ted. "The Promise of Constructivism in International Relations Theory," *International Security* 23 (1998).

Horkheimer, Max. *Critical Theory: Selected Essays*. Transl. Matthew J. O'Connell et al. (New York: Seabury Press, 1972).

———. *Critique of Instrumental Reason: Lectures and Essays Since the End of World War II*. Transl. M. J. O'Connell et al. (New York: Seabury, 1974).

Howell, William. "The Inheritance of War: Japan's Domestic Politics and International Ambitions." In Gerritt W. Gong (ed.), *Remembering and Forgetting: The Legacy of War in East Asia* (Washington, D.C.: Center for Strategic and International Studies, 1996).

Hughes, Joanne, and Caitlin Donnelly. "Ten Years of Social Attitudes to Community Relations in Northern Ireland." Northern Ireland Life and Times Occasional Paper no. 1, August 2001. Available online at www.ark.ac.uk.

Huntington, Samuel. *The Clash of Civilizations and the Remaking of World Order* (New York: Simon and Schuster, 1996).

Hutton, Will, and Anthony Giddens (eds.). *On the Edge: Living with Global Capitalism* (London: Vintage, 2001).

Huysmans, Jef. "Revisiting Copenhagen: Or, on the Creative Development of a Security Studies Agenda in Europe," *European Journal of International Relations* 4, no. 4 (1998): 447–477.

———. "Security! What Do You Mean? From Concept to Thick Signifier," *European Journal of International Relations* 4, no. 2 (1998): 226–255.

Hyan Yi Kang, Laura. "Si(gh)ting Asian/American Women as Transnational Labour," *Positions* 5, no. 2 (1997).

Independent Commission on Disarmament. *Common Security: A Programme for Disarmament. The Report of the Independent Commission on Disarmament and Security Issues Under the Chairmanship of Olaf Palme* (London: Pan Books, 1982).

Jameson, Frederic. *Late Marxism: Adorno, or, the Persistence of the Dialectic* (London: Verso, 1990).

Jay, Martin. *Adorno* (London: Fontana, 1984).

Jepperson, Ronald, Alexander Wendt, and Peter Katzenstein. "Norms, Identity, and Culture in National Security." Pp. 33–75 in P. Katzenstein, *The Culture of National Security: Norms and Identity in World Politics* (New York: Columbia University Press, 1996).

Jervis, Robert. "Cooperation Under the Security Dilemma," *World Politics* 30, no. 2 (January 1978): 167–214.

Jockel, Joseph T. *Canada and International Peacekeeping* (Washington, D.C.: Center for Strategic and International Studies, 1994).

Johansen, Robert C. *The National Interest and the Human Interest. An Analysis of U.S. Foreign Policy* (Princeton, N.J.: Princeton University Press, 1980).

———. "Radical Islam and Nonviolence: A Case Study of Religious Empowerment and Constraint." In Fred Dallymayr (ed.), *Border Crossings: Toward a Comparative Political Theory* (Lanham, Md.: Lexington Books, 1999).

Johnson, Chalmers. *Blowback: The Costs and Consequences of American Empire* (New York: Henry Holt, 2002).

Johnson, James. "Habermas on Strategic and Communicative Action," *Political Theory* 19 (1991): 181–201.

Johnston, Alastair Iain. *Cultural Realism: Strategic Culture and Grand Strategy in Chinese History* (Princeton, N.J.: Princeton University Press, 1995).

Jones, Deiniol. *Cosmopolitan Mediation? Conflict Resolution and the Oslo Accords* (Manchester, UK: Manchester University Press: 1999).

Kahn, Joel S. "Malaysian Modem or Anti–Anti Asian Values," *Thesis Eleven* 50 (1997): 15–33.

Kaldor, Mary. "Introduction." Pp. 1–15 in Mary Kaldor and Basker Vashee (eds.), *Restructuring the Global Military Sector: New Wars* (London and Washington, D.C.: Pinter, 1997).

———. *New and Old Wars: Organized Violence in a Global Era* (Oxford, UK: Polity, 1999).

Kaldor, Mary (ed.). *Global Insecurity* (London and New York: Pinter Press, 2000).

Kaldor, Mary, and Basker Vashee (eds.). *Restructuring the Global Military Sector: New Wars* (London and Washington, D.C.: Pinter, 1997).

Kant, Immanuel. "Idea for a Universal History with a Cosmopolitan Purpose." In H. Reiss (ed.), *Kant's Political Writings* (Cambridge, UK: Cambridge University Press, 1970).

Kaplan, Robert. "The Coming Anarchy," *Atlantic Monthly* 273, no. 2 (1994): 44–81.

Kapstein, E. *The Political Economy of National Security* (London: McGraw Hill, 1992).

Katzenstein, Peter (ed.). *The Culture of National Security: Norms and Identity in World Politics* (New York: Columbia University Press, 1996).

Kennedy, Dennis. *The Widening Gulf: Northern Attitudes to the Independent Irish State, 1919–1949* (Belfast: Blackstaff, 1988).

Kenny, Anthony. *The Logic of Deterrence* (London: Firestone Press, 1985).

Kier, Elizabeth. *Imagining War: French Military Doctrine Between the Wars* (Princeton, N.J.: Princeton University Press, 1997).

Kissinger, Henry. *The White House Years* (London: Weidenfeld and Nicholson, 1979).

Klare, Michael. "An Avalanche of Guns: Light Weapons Trafficking and Armed Conflict in the Post–Cold War Era." Pp. 55–77 in Mary Kaldor and Basker Vashee (eds.), *Restructuring the Global Military Sector: New Wars* (London and Washington, D.C.: Pinter, 1997).

Klein, Bradley. "How the West Was Won: The Representational Policies of NATO," *International Studies Quarterly* 34, no. 3 (September 1990): 311–325.

———. *Strategic Studies and World Order: The Global Politics of Deterrence* (Cambridge, UK: Cambridge University Press, 1994).

Knorr, Klaus. *Power and Wealth: The Political Economy of International Power* (New York: Basic Books, 1973).

Knorr, Klaus, and Frank Trager (eds.). *Economic Issues and National Security* (Lawrence, Kan.: Regents Press for the National Security Education Program, 1977).

Knudsen, Tonny Brems. "Humanitarian Intervention Revisited: Post–Cold War Responses to Classical Problems," *International Peacekeeping* 3, no. 4 (Winter) 1996: 146–165.

Kolodziej, Edward. "Security Studies for the Next Millennium: Quo Vadis?" Pp. 18–38 in S. Croft and T. Terriff (eds.), *Critical Reflections on Security and Change* (London: Frank Cass, 2000).

Korten, David C. *When Corporations Rule the World* (London: Kumarian, 1995).

———. "Your Mortal Enemy," *Guardian*, October 21, 1998, p. 5.

Kowert, Paul, and Jeffrey Legro. "Norms, Identity, and Their Limits: A Theoretical Reprise." Pp. 451–497 in P. Katzenstein, *The Culture of National Security: Norms and Identity in World Politics* (New York: Columbia University Press, 1996).

Krasner, Stephen D. "The Accomplishments of International Political Economy." In Steve Smith, Ken Booth, and Marysia Zalewski (eds.), *International Theory:*

Positivism and Beyond (Cambridge, UK: Cambridge University Press, 1996).

———. *Defending the National Interest: Raw Materials Investment and American Foreign Policy* (Princeton, N.J.: Princeton University Press, 1978).

———. "International Political Economy: Abiding Discord," *Review of International Political Economy* 1, no. 1 (1994): 13–20.

Krause, Jill, and Neil Renwick (eds.). *Identities in International Relations* (Basingstoke, UK: Macmillan, 1996).

Krause, Keith. "Critical Theory and Security Studies: The Research Programme of 'Critical Security Studies,'" *Cooperation and Conflict* 33, no. 3 (1998): 298–333.

Krause, Keith, and Michael Williams. "Broadening the Agenda of Security Studies: Politics and Methods," *Mershon International Studies Review* 40, supp. 2 (1996): 229–254.

———. "From Strategy to Security: Foundations of Critical Security Studies: Concepts and Cases." Pp. 33–59 in Keith Krause and Michael Williams (eds.), *Critical Security Studies: Concepts and Cases* (Minneapolis: University of Minnesota Press, 1997).

———. "Preface: Towards Critical Security Studies." Pp. vii–xxi in K. Krause and M. Williams (eds.), *Critical Security Studies: Concepts and Cases* (Minneapolis: University of Minnesota Press, 1997).

Krause, Keith, and Michael C. Williams (eds.). *Critical Security Studies: Concepts and Cases* (Minneapolis: University of Minnesota Press, 1997).

Kymlicka, Will. *Liberalism, Community, and Culture* (Oxford: Clarendon Press, 1989).

Laclau, Ernesto. *Emacipation(s)* (London: Verso: 1996).

Lafitte, Gabriel. "ReOrientations," *Arena Magazine* (September 1994): 14.

Lake, Marilyn. "Mission Impossible: How Men Gave Birth to the Australian Nation," *Gender and History* 4, no. 3 (1992): 305–322.

Lambeth, Benjamin S. "Technology Trends in Air Warfare." Pp. 131–163 in Alan Stephens (ed.), *New Era Security: The RAAF in the Next Twenty-Five Years* (Canberra: Air Power Studies Centre, 1996).

Landay, Jonathan S. "Hazing Rituals in Military Are Common—and Abusive," *Christian Science Monitor*, February 11, 1997, p. 1.

Latham, Robin. "Thinking About Security After the Cold War," *International Studies Notes* 20, no. 3 (1995): 9–16.

Laurance, Edward J., Siemon T. Wezeman, and Herbert Wulf. *Arms Watch: SIPRI Report on the First Year of the UN Register of Conventional Arms* (Oxford, UK: Oxford University Press/Stockholm International Peace Research Institute Report No. 6, 1993).

Lawler, Peter. *A Question of Values: Johan Galtung's Peace Research* (Boulder: Lynne Reinner Publishers, 1996).

Lawson, Tony. *Economics and Reality* (London: Routledge, 1997).

Lechner Frank J., and John Boli (eds.). *The Globalization Reader*, 2nd ed. (Malde, Mass.: Blackwell, 2004).

Legro, Jeffrey. *Cooperation Under Fire: Anglo-German Restraint During World War II* (Ithaca: Cornell University Press, 1995).

Levite Ariel E.. and Emily B. Landau. "Confidence and Security Building Measures in the Middle East," *Journal of Strategic Studies* 20, no. 1 (March 1997): 143–171.

Liftin, Karen. "Towards an Integral Perspective on World Politics: Sovereignty and the Challenge of Global Ecology," *Millennium* 32, no. 1 (2003): 2003.

Lifton, R. J., and E. Markusen. *The Genocidal Mentality: The Nazi Holocaust and the Nuclear Threat* (New York: Basic Books, 1990).

Ling, L. H. M. *Postcolonial International Relations: Conquest and Desire Between Asia and the West* (London: Palgrave, 2002).

Ling, Lily. "Hegemony and the Internationalizing State: A Postcolonial Analysis of China's Integration into Asian Corporatism," *Review of International Political Economy* 3, no. 1 (1996): 1–26.

Linklater, Andrew. *Beyond Realism and Marxism: Critical Theory and International Relations* (London: Macmillan, 1990).

———. "Citizenship and Sovereignty in the Post-Westphalian State," *European Journal of International Relations* 2 (1996):77–103.

———. "Citizenship, Humanity and Cosmopolitan Harm Conventions," *International Political Science Review* 22 (2001): 261–278.

———. "Marxism." Pp. 129–154 in Scott Burchill et al., *Theories of International Relations* (London and New York: Macmillan and St. Martin's, 1996).

———. *Men and Citizens in the Theory of International Relations* (London: Macmillan, 1982; 2nd ed. 1990).

———. "The Question of the Next Stage in International Relations Theory: A Critical-Theoretical Point of View," *Millennium* 21, no. 1 (1992): 92–97.

———. "The Transformation of Political Community," *Review of International Studies* 23 (1997): 321–338.

———. *The Transformation of Political Community: Ethical Foundations of the Post-Westphalian Era* (Cambridge, UK: Polity, 1998).

———. *The Transformation of Political Community* (Oxford: Blackwell Publishers, 1998).

———. "Unnecessary Suffering." In Ken Booth and Tim Dunne (eds.), *Worlds in Collision: Terror and the Future of Global Order* (Basingstoke, UK: Palgrave Macmillan, 2002).

———. "What Is a Good International Citizen?" Pp. 21–43 in Paul Keal (ed.), *Ethics and Foreign Policy* (St. Leonards, UK: Allen & Unwin, 1992).

Lipshutz, Ronnie (ed.). *On Security* (New York: Columbia University Press, 1995).

Little, Richard. "Ideology and Change." Pp. 30–45 in Barry Buzan and R. J. Barry Jones (eds.), *Change and the Study of International Relations* (London: Pinter, 1981).

Lukes, Stephen. *Power: A Radical View* (London: Macmillan, 1974).

Luttwak, Edward N. *Strategy and History: Collected Essays*, vol. 2 (New Brunswick, N.J.: Transaction Books, 1985).

Lyotard, Jean-François. *The Postmodern Condition: A Report on Knowledge* (Manchester, UK: Manchester University Press, 1984).

———. "The Other's Rights." In S. Shute and S. Hurley (eds.), *On Human Rights: The Oxford Amnesty Lectures* (New York: Basic Books, 1993).

Macintosh, James. "Confidence- and Security-Building Measures: A Skeptical Look." *Working Paper No. 85* (Canberra: Peace Research Centre, Australian National University, July 1990).

———. "Confidence Building and the Arms Control Process: A Transformation View." *Arms Control and Disarmament Studies No. 2* (Ottawa: Canadian Department of Foreign Affairs and International Trade, 1996).

Mack, Andrew. *Peace Research Around the World* (Canberra: Strategic and Defence Studies Centre, Australian National University, 1985).

Mackinlay, John (ed.). *A Guide to Peace Support Operations* (Providence, R.I.: Institute for International Studies, Brown University, 1996).

MacMillan, John. "A Kantian Protest Against the Peculiar Discourse of Inter-Liberal State Peace," *Millennium*, 24 (1995): 549–562.

———. *On Liberal Peace: Democracy, War and the International Order* (London: Tauris Academic Studies, 1998).

Malcolm, Ian. *Does the Blue Helmet Fit? The Canadian Forces and Peacekeeping* (Ottawa: The Norman Paterson School of International Affairs Occasional Paper No. 3, Carleton University, 1993).

Malmgren, Harald. "Coming Trade Wars," *Foreign Policy* 1 (Winter 1970–1971).

Mandel, Robert. *Armies Without States: The Privatization of Security* (Boulder: Lynne Rienner Publishers, 2002).

Mander, Jerry, and Edward Goldsmith (eds.). *The Case Against the Global Economy* (San Francisco: Sierra Club Books, 1996).

Mann, Michael. "Has Globalization Ended the Rise and Rise of the Nation-State?" *Review of International Political Economy* 4, no. 3 (1997).

Mansergh, Martin. "The Challenges of the Good Friday Agreement and the Consolidation of Peace," *Ceide: A Review from the Margins* 2, no. 3 (1999): 5–8.

Manson, General Paul D. "Peacekeeping in a Changing World." Address to the Empire Club of Canada, Toronto, November 17, 1988, in *Canadian Speeches* 2, no. 8 (December 1988): 35–41.

McClintock, Ann. *Imperial Leather: Race, Gender, and Sexuality in the Colonial Conquest* (New York: Routledge, 1995).

McCoy, Alfred. "Ram Boys: Changing Images of the Masculine in the Philippine Military." Paper presented at the International Studies Association Annual Meetings, Toronto, Canada, March 18–22, 1997.

———. "'Same Banana': Hazing and Honor at the Philippine Military Academy," *Journal of Asian Studies* 54, no. 3 (August 1995): 689–726.

McGarry, John, and Brendan O'Leary. *Explaining Northern Ireland: Broken Images* (Oxford, UK: Basil Blackwell, 1995).

McGibbon, Rodd. "Engaging with the Asia-Pacific: Australian Foreign Policy in the Pacific Century." Ph.D. diss., Australian National University, 1997.

McGillivray, Mark, and Gary Smith (eds.). *Australia and Asia* (Melbourne: Oxford University Press, 1997).

McInnes, Colin. "Alternative Defence." Pp. 126–144 in Colin McInnes (ed.), *Security and Strategy in the New Europe* (London: Routledge, 1992).

McSweeney, Bill. "Durkheim and the Copenhagen School: A Response to Buzan and Waever," *Review of International Studies* 24, no. 1 (1998): 137–140.

———. "Identity and Security: Buzan and the Copenhagen School," *Review of International Studies* 22, no. 1 (1996): 81–93.

———. *Security, Identity and Interests: A Sociology of International Relations* (Cambridge, UK: Cambridge University Press, 1999).

Mearsheimer, John. *The Tragedy of Great Power Politics* (New York: W. W. Norton, 2001).

Metz, Steven. *Strategic Horizons: The Military Implications of Alternative Futures* (Carlisle Barracks, Penn.: U.S. Army War College, Strategic Studies Institute, 1997).

Metz, Steven, and James Kievet. *The Revolution in Military Affairs and Conflict Short of War* (Carlisle Barracks, Penn.: U.S. Army War College Strategic Studies Institute, 1995).

Midgley, E. Brian *The Natural Law Tradition and the Theory of International Relations* (London: Paul Elek, 1974).

Milner, Anthony. "The Rhetoric of Asia." In James Cotton and John Ravenhill (eds.), *Seeking Asian Engagement: Australia in World Affairs, 1991–1995* (Melbourne: Oxford University Press, 1997).

Mische, Patricia. "Ecological Security and the Need to Reconceptualize Sovereignty," *Alternatives* 14 (1989).

Mittelman James H. (ed.). *Globalization: Critical Reflections* (London: Lynne Rienner Publishers, 1996).

Moghadam, Valentine. *Identity Politics and Women: Cultural Reassertions and Feminisms in International Perspective* (Boulder: Westview, 1994).

Møller, Bjorn. "A Common Security and NOD Regime for the Asia-Pacific?" *Pacifica Review* 9, no. 1 (1997): 23–43.

———. *Common Security and Nonoffensive Defense: A Neorealist Perspective* (Boulder: Lynne Rienner Publishers, 1992).

———. *Dictionary of Alternative Defense* (Boulder: Lynne Rienner Publishers, 1995).

———. *Resolving the Security Dilemma in Europe: The German Debate on Non-offensive Defence* (London: Brassey's, 1991).

———. "Small States, Non-Offensive Defence, and Collective Security." Pp. 127–154 in Efraim Inbar and Gabriel Sheffer (eds.), *The National Security of Small States in a Changing World* (London: Frank Cass, 1997).

Møller, Bjørn, and Håkan Wiberg (eds.). *Non-Offensive Defence for the Twenty-First Century* (Boulder: Westview, 1994).

Moon, Katherine. "East Versus West: Sex Industries in East Asia." International Studies Association conference paper (Toronto, 1997).

Moran, Theodore H. "The Globalization of America's Defense Industries: Managing the Threat of Foreign Dependence," *International Security* 15, no. 1 (1990).

Morgan, David H. J. "Theater of War: Combat, the Military, and Masculinities." In Harry Brod and Michael Kaufman (eds.), *Theorizing Masculinities* (London: Sage Publications, 1994).

Morgan, Patrick. "Liberalist and Realist Security Studies at 2000: Two Decades of Progress?" Pp. 39–71 in Stuart Croft and Terry Terriff (eds.), *Critical Reflections on Security and Change* (London: Frank Cass, 2000).

Morgenthau, Hans J. *Politics Among Nations: The Struggle for Power and Peace*, 2nd ed. (New York: Knopf, 1948).

Morrison, Alex, and Suzanne M. Plain. "Canada: The Seasoned Veteran," Paper presented at the International Studies Association Annual Meeting, Washington, D.C., March 28–April 1, 1994.

Moskos, Charles C., John Allen Williams, and David R. Segal. "Armed Forces After the Cold War." Pp. 1–15 in Charles C. Moskos, John Allen Williams, and David R. Segal (eds.), *The Postmodern Military: Armed Forces After the Cold War* (Oxford, UK: Oxford University Press, 1999).

Mueller, John. *Retreat From Doomsday: The Obsolescence of Major War* (New York: Basic Books, 1989).

Murithi, Tim. *Moral Development, Discourse Ethics, and Ethnic Conflict*. PhD diss., Keele University, 1998.

Murphy, Craig N., and Roger Tooze (eds.). *The New International Political Economy* (Boulder: Lynne Rienner Publishers, 1991).

Murray, Alistair J. H. *Reconstructing Realism: Between Power Politics and Cosmopolitan Ethics* (Keele, UK: Keele University Press, 1997).

Mutimer, David. "Beyond Strategy: Critical Thinking in the New Security Studies." Pp. 77–101 in Craig Snyder (ed.), *Contemporary Security Studies* (London: Macmillan, 1999).

Nef, Jorge. *Human Security and Mutual Vulnerability: The Global Political Economy of Development and Underdevelopment,* 2nd ed. (Ottawa: International Development Research Centre, 1999).

Newmann, Iver B. *Russia and the Idea of Europe* (London: Routledge, 1996).

Noordin, Sopiee. "The Development of an East Asian Consciousness." Pp. 180–193 in Greg Sheridan (ed.), *Living with Dragons: Australia Confronts Its Asian Destiny* (St. Leonards, Sydney: Allen & Unwin, 1995).

Nye, Joseph. "Collective Economic Security," *International Affairs* 50, no. 4 (1974): 584–598.

———. "The Long-Term Future of Deterrence." Pp. 245–247 in Roman Kolkowicz (ed.), *The Logic of Nuclear Terror* (Boston: Allen & Unwin, 1987).

———. *Nuclear Ethics* (New York: Free Press, 1986).

———. "The Three Tyrannies." Pp. 31–70 in Tim Dunne and Nicholas J. Wheeler (eds.), *Human Rights and Human Wrongs* (Cambridge, UK: Cambridge University Press, 1999).

Off, Carol. *The Lion, the Fox, and the Eagle: A Story of Generals and Justice in Yugoslavia and Rwanda* (Toronto: Random House Canada, 2000).

O'Leary, Brendan. "The Nature of the British-Irish Agreement," *New Left Review* 233 (1999): 66–96.

O'Leary, Brendan, and John McGarry. *The Politics of Antagonism: Understanding Northern Ireland* (London: Athlone, 1993).

Ong, Aihwa. "A Momentary Glow of Fraternity: Narratives of Chinese Nationalism and Capitalism," *Identities* 3, no. 3 (1997): 331–366.

Ong, Aihwa, and Donald Nonini (eds.). *Underground Empires: The Cultural Politics of Modern Chinese Transnationalism* (New York: Routledge, 1997).

Ormerod, Paul. *The Death of Economics* (New York: Wiley, 1997).

Ostry, Silvia, and R. R. Nelson. *Techno-Nationalism and Techno-Globalism: Conflict and Cooperation* (Washington, D.C.: Brookings Institution, 1995).

Outhwaite, William. *Habermas: A Critical Introduction* (Stanford: Stanford University Press, 1994).

Pape, Robert A. *Bombing to Win: Air Power and Coercion in War* (Ithica: Cornell University Press, 1996).

Parekh, Bhikhu. *Gandhi's Political Philosophy. A Critical Examination* (London: Macmillan, 1989).

Pateman, Carole. *The Sexual Contract* (Stanford: Stanford University Press, 1988).

Patomaki, Heikki. "How to Tell Better Stories About World Politics," *European Journal of International Relations* 2 (1996): 105–133.

Patomaki, Heikki, and Colin Wight. "After Postpositivism? The Promises of Critical Realism," *International Studies Quarterly* 44, no. 2 (2000): 213–237.

Patterson, H. "From Insulation to Appeasement: The Major and Blair Governments Reconsidered." Pp. 166–183 in Colin Wilford (ed.), *Aspects of the Belfast Agreement* (Oxford, UK: Oxford University Press, 2001).

Pederson, M. Susan, and Stanley Weeks. "A Survey of Confidence and Security Building Measures." Pp. 81–100 in Ralph A. Cossa (ed.), *Asia Pacific Confidence and Security Building Measures* (Washington, D.C.: Center for Strategic & International Studies, 1995).

Perkin, Howard. *The Third Revolution: Professional Elites in the Modern World* (London: Routledge, 1996).

Pettit, Philip. *Republicanism: A Theory of Freedom and Government* (Oxford: Clarendon Press, 1997).

Pettman, Jan Jindy. "Border Crossings/Shifting Identities." Pp. 261–284 in M.

Shapiro and H. Alker (eds.), *Territorial Identities and Global Flows* (Minneapolis: University of Minnesota Press, 1995).

———. "Gender, Ethnicity, Race, and Class in Australia." Pp. 65–94 in S. Stasiulis and N. Yuval-Davis (eds.), *Unsettling Settler Societies* (London: Sage, 1995).

———. "Gender in Australian Foreign Policy." In W. Tow and M. Hanson (eds.), *Issues in International Relations for the Twenty First Century: An Australian Perspective* (Sydney: Oxford University Press, 2001).

———. "Feminist International Relations After 9/11," *Brown Journal of World Affairs* 10, no. 2 (2004): 85–96.

———. "A Feminist Perspective on 'Australia in Asia.'" In J. Docker and G. Fischer (eds.), *Race, Colour, and Identity in Australia and New Zealand* (UNSW Press: Sydney, 2000).

———. "Nationalism and After," *Review of National Studies* 24, no. 5 (1998): 149–164.

———. "Women on the Move: Globalisation, Gender and the Changing Division of Labour," *Global Society* 12, no. 3 (1998): 389–403.

———. *Worlding Women: A Feminist International Politics* (London: Routledge, 1996).

Pieterese, Jan Neverdeen (ed.). *Emancipations, Modern and Postmodern*, special issue of *Development and Change* (London: Sage Publications, 1992).

Polanyi, Karl *The Great Transformation: The Political and Economic Origins of Our Time* (Boston: Beacon Press, 1957).

Porter, Bruce D. *War and the Rise of the State: The Military Foundations of Modern Politics* (New York: Free Press, 1994).

Porter, Roy. *Enlightenment: Britain and the Creation of the Modern World* (London: Allen Lane, 2000).

Posen, Barry R. "Command of the Commons: The Military Foundation of U.S. Hegemony," *International Security* 28, no. 1 (2003): 5–46.

———. "The Security Dilemma and Ethnic Conflict." In Michael E. Brown (ed.), *Ethnic Conflict and International Security* (Princeton, N.J.: Princeton University Press, 1993).

Postone, Moishe. *Time, Labour, and Social Domination: A Reinterpretation of Marx's Critical Theory* (Cambridge, UK: Cambridge University Press).

Price, Richard *The Chemical Weapons Taboo* (Ithaca: Cornell University Press, 1997).

Prins, Gwyn (ed.). *Threats Without Enemies* (London: Earthscan, 1993).

Project Ploughshares. *Report to Donors* (Waterloo, Ontario: Project Ploughshares, February 1996).

Prouse, Robert. "The Dark Side that Emerged in Somalia is Inside all Canadians," *Ottawa Citizen,* July 15, 2000, pp. A4–A6.

Pugliese, David. "Almost 20% of '85 Airborne Unit Had Police Record, Report Found." *Ottawa Citizen,* October 4, 1995, p. A4.

———. "Military Brass Let Racist Skinheads Go to Somalia." *Ottawa Citizen,* October 13, 1995, p. A1.

———. "Somalia: What Went So Wrong?" *Ottawa Citizen,* October 1, 1995, p. A6.

Purdie, Bob. *Politics in the Streets: The Origins of the Civil Rights Movement in Northern Ireland* (Belfast: Blackstaff, 1990).

Queen, Christopher S., and Sallie B. King (eds.). *Engaged Buddhism: Buddhist Liberation Movements in Asia* (Albany: State University of New York Press, 1996).

Rapoport, Anatole. "Critique of Strategic Thinking." Pp. 201–227 in Naomi

Rosembaum (ed.), *Readings in the International Political System* (Englewood Cliffs, N.J.: Prentice-Hall, 1970).

Ratner, Steven. *The New UN Peacekeeping* (London: Macmillan, 1995).

Razack, Sherene. "From the 'Clean Snows of Petawawa': The Violence of Canadian Peacekeepers in Somalia," *Cultural Anthropology* 15, no. 1 (2000): 127–163.

Reich, Robert. *The Work of Nations* (New York: Alfred A. Knopf, 1991).

Reid, Tony. "The Ides of May for Two Sino–Southeast Asian Minorities" (APMRN workshop: ANU, October 1998).

Rengger, Nick. "The Ethics of Trust in World Politics," *International Affairs* 73 (1997): 469–487.

Report of the Special Joint Committee Reviewing Canadian Foreign Policy (Ottawa: Government of Canada, 1994).

Reus-Smit, Christian. "Constructivism." Pp. 209–230 in Scott Burchill et al., *Theories of International Relations* (London and New York: Macmillan and St. Martin's, 1996).

Reynolds, Henry. "Catching Up with Our Geography," *Australian Society* (April 1999).

Richards, Glyn. *The Philosophy of Gandhi* (Richmond: Curzon Press, 1995).

Robin, Corporal Christopher. Testimony to the Commission of Inquiry into the Deployment of Canadian Forces to Somalia, October 12, 1995, Ottawa, Canada.

Roosevelt, Franklin D. "Address at the Annual Dinner of the White House Correspondents Association, March 15, 1941." In "Room Four: 'Freedom of Speech, Freedom of Worship, Freedom from Want, Freedom from Fear.'" Pp 17–29, in *FDR Speaks: The FDR Memorial Collection*. A collection of twelve pamphlets (Washington, D.C.: Parks & History Association, 1997).

———. "Annual Message to Congress, January 6, 1941." In "Room Four: 'Freedom of Speech, Freedom of Worship, Freedom from Want, Freedom from Fear.'" Pp. 3–16, in *FDR Speaks: The FDR Memorial Collection*. A collection of twelve pamphlets (Washington, D.C.: Parks & History Association, 1997).

———. *FDR Speaks: The FDR Memorial Collection*. A collection of twelve pamphlets (Washington, D.C.: Parks & History Association, 1997).

Rorty, Richard. *Contigency, Irony, and Solidarity* (Cambridge: Cambridge University Press, 1989).

Rose, Gideon. "Neoclassical Realism and Theories of Foreign Policy," *World Politics* 51, no. 1 (1998): 144–172.

Rosecrance, Richard. *The Rise of the Trading State: Commerce and Conquest in the Modern World* (New York: Basic Books, 1986).

Rosenau, James. *Along the Domestic-Foreign Frontier: Exploring Governance in a Turbulent World* (Cambridge, UK: Cambridge University Press, 1997).

———. "Armed Force and Armed Forces in a Turbulent World." Pp. 25–62 in James Burk (ed.), *The Military in New Times: Adapting Armed Forces to a Turbulent World* (Boulder: Westview Press, 1994).

Rothgeb, John M. Jr. *Defining Power: Influence and Force in the Contemporary International System* (New York: St. Martin's, 1993).

Rothschild, Emma. "What Is Security?" *Daedalus* 124, no. 3 (1995): 53–98.

Rowse, Tim. *After Mabo* (Melbourne: Melbourne University Press, 1993).

Ruane, Joseph, and Jennifer Todd. *The Dynamics of Conflict in Northern Ireland: Power, Conflict, and Emancipation* (Cambridge, UK: Cambridge University Press, 1996).

———. *The Dynamics of Conflict and Transition in Northern Ireland* (Cambridge, UK: Cambridge University Press, forthcoming 2004).

———. "The Politics of Transition? Explaining Political Crises in the

Implementation of the Belfast (Good Friday) Agreement," *Political Studies* 49 (2001): 923–940.

Ruane, Joseph, and Jennifer Todd (eds.). *After the Good Friday Agreement: Analysing Political Change in Northern Ireland* (Dublin: University College Dublin Press, 1999).

Rubinstein, Robert A. "Cultural Aspects of Peacekeeping: Notes on the Substance of Symbols," *Millennium* 22, no. 3 (1993): 548.

Ruggie, John G. *Constructing the World Polity* (London: Routledge, 1998).

Russett, Bruce. *Controlling the Sword: The Democratic Convergence of National Security* (Cambridge, Mass.: Harvard University Press, 1990).

Sassen, Saskia. "Globalization of Denationalization," *Review of International Political Economy* 10, no. 1 (2003): 1–22.

Schell, Jonathon. *The Fate of the Earth* (London: Picador, 1982).

Scholte, Jan Aart. *Globalization: A Critical Introduction* (Basingstoke, UK: Macmillan, 2000).

Schweller, Randall. *Deadly Imbalances: Tripolarity and Hitler's Strategy of World Conquest* (New York: Columbia University Press, 1998).

Searle, John. *The Construction of Social Reality* (London: Allen Lane, 1995).

Sens, Allen G. *Somalia and the Changing Nature of Peacekeeping: The Implications for Canada.* A study prepared for the Commission of Inquiry into the Deployment of Canadian Forces to Somalia (Ottawa: Minister of Public Works and Government Services Canada, 1997).

Shapcott, Richard. *Justice, Community and Dialogue in International Relations* (Cambridge, UK: Cambridge University Press, 2001).

Shari'arti, Ali. *On the Sociology of Islam.* Transl. by Hamid Algar (Berkeley: Mizan, 1979).

Shaw, Martin. *Post-Military Society: Militarism, Demilitarization, and War at the End of the Twentieth Century* (Cambridge, UK: Polity, 1991).

———. "There Is No Such Thing as Society: Beyond Individualism and Statism in International Security Studies," *Review of International Studies* 19, no. 2 (1993): 159–175.

Singer, Max, and Aaron Wildavsky. *The Real World Order: Zones of Peace, Zones of Turmoil* (Chatham, N.J.: Chatham House, 1993).

Singh, Jasit, and Vatroslav Vekaric (eds.). *Non-Provocative Defence: The Search for Equal Security* (New Delhi: Lancer, 1989).

Sivard, Ruth Leger. *World Military and Social Expenditures* (Leesburg, Va.: WMSE Publications, various years).

Slaughter, Anne-Marie. "The Real New World Order," *Foreign Affairs* 76, no. 5 (September/October 1997): 183–197.

Smith, Gary. "Australia's Political Relationship with Asia." Pp. 100–122 in Mark McGillivray and Gary Smith (eds.), *Australia and Asia* (Melbourne: Oxford University Press, 1997).

Smith, Gary, and St. John Kettle (eds.). *Threats Without Enemies: Rethinking Australia's Security* (Sydney: Pluto, 1992).

Smith, Hazel. "Marxism and International Relations Theory." Pp. 142–155 in A. G. R. Groom and Margot Light (eds.), *Contemporary International Relations: A Guide to Theory* (London: Pinter Publishers, 1994).

Smith, Michael. *Realist Thought from Weber to Kissinger* (Baton Rouge: Louisiana State University Press, 1986).

Smith, Steve. "Epistemology, Postmodernism, and International Relations Theory: A Reply to Osterud," *Journal of Peace Research* 34, no. 3 (1997): 330–336.

———. "The Increasing Insecurity of Security Studies: Conceptualizing Security in the Last Twenty Years." Pp. 72–101 in Stuart Croft and Terry Terriff (eds.), *Critical Reflections on Security and Change* (London: Frank Cass, 2000).

———. "Mature Anarchy, Strong States and Security," *Arms Control* 12, no. 2 (1991): 325–339.

———. "Power and Truth: A Reply to William Wallace," *Review of International Studies* 23 (1997): 507–515.

Smith, Steve, Ken Booth, and Marysia Zalewski (eds.). *International Theory: Positivism and Beyond* (Cambridge, UK: Cambridge University Press, 1996).

Snow, Donald. *National Security: Defense Policy for a New International Order*, 3rd ed. (New York: St. Martin's, 1995).

———. *Uncivil Wars: International Security and the New Internal Conflicts* (Boulder: Lynne Rienner, 1996).

Sokol, Alan, and Jean Bricmont. *Intellectual Impostures: Postmodern Philosophers' Abuse of Science* (London: Profile Books, 1999).

Sokolsky, Joel J. "Great Ideals and Uneasy Compromises: The United States Approach to Peacekeeping," *International Journal* 50, no. 2 (Spring 1995): 266–293.

"Soldier Confirms Airborne Held Massacre Party," *Ottawa Citizen*, November 9, 1995, p. A3.

Sopiee, Noordin. "The Development of an East Asian Consciousness." Pp. 180–193 in Greg Sheridan (ed.), *Living with Dragons: Australia Confronts Its Asian Destiny* (Sydney: Allen & Unwin, 1995).

Soros, George. "The Capitalist Threat," *Atlantic Monthly*, February 1997, pp. 45–58.

Sperling, Jonathan, and Emile Kirchner. "Economic Security and the Problem of Cooperation in Post–Cold War Europe," *Review of International Studies* 24, no. 2 (1998): 221–237.

Spero, Joan E. *The Politics of International Economic Relations* (London: George Allen & Unwin, 1977).

Steans, Jill. *Gender and International Relations: An Introduction* (Cambridge, UK: Polity, 1998).

Steel, Ronald. "The Missionary," *New Review of Books,* November 20, 2003, p. 6ff.

———. *Temptations of a Hegemon* (Cambridge, Mass.: Harvard University Press, 1996).

van Steenbergen, Bart (ed.). *The Condition of Citizenship* (London: Sage Publications, 1994).

Stiehm, Judith Hicks. *Arms and the Enlisted Woman* (Philadelphia: Temple University Press, 1989).

Stiglitz, Joseph. *Globalization and Its Discontents* (London: Penguin, 2002).

Stirk, M. R. *Critical Theory, Politics, and Society: An Introduction* (London: Pinter, 2000).

Stoler, Ann. *Race and the Education of Desire* (Durham, N.C.: Duke University Press, 1995).

Strange, Susan. "International Economics and International Relations: A Case of Mutual Neglect," *International Affairs* 46, no. 2 (1970): 304–315.

———. "International Political Economy: Beyond Economics and International Relations," *Economies Et Societes, Relations Economiques Internationales,* Serie P, 4/1998 (1998): 5–26.

———. *The Retreat of the State: The Diffusion of Power in the World Economy* (Cambridge, UK: Cambridge University Press, 1996).

———. "Towards a Theory of Transnational Empire." In Ernst-Otto Czempiel and

James N. Rosenau (eds.), *Global Changes and Theoretical Challenges* (Lexington, Mass.: Lexington Books, 1989).

———. "Wake Up, Krasner! The World Has Changed," *Review of International Political Economy* 1, no. 2 (1994): 209–220.

Suhrke, Astri. "Human Security and the Interests of States," *Security Dialogue* 29, no. 3 (1998): 218–292.

Sullivan, David. "Sipping a Thin Gruel," in Graeme Cheeseman and Robert Bruce (eds.), *Discourses of Danger and Dread: Australian Defence and Security Thinking After the Cold War* (St. Leonards, UK: Allen & Unwin, 1996).

Takasu, Yukio (Director General of the Foreign Ministry of Japan). "Statement by Director General Yukio Takasu at the International Conference on Human Security in a Globalized World," Ulan-Bator, May 8, 2000. Available online at www.mofa.go.jp/policy/human_secu/index.html.

Ter Borg, Marlies, and Wim A. Smit (eds.). *Non-Provocative Defence as a Principle of Arms Reduction* (Amsterdam: Free University Press, 1989).

Terriff, Terry, Stuart Croft, Lucy James, and Patrick M. Morgan. *Security Studies Today* (Cambridge, UK: Polity, 1999).

Thomas, Caroline. *Global Governance, Development, and Human Security: The Challenge of Poverty and Inequality* (London: Pluto, 2000).

———. *In Search of Security: The Third World in International Relations* (Brighton, UK: Harvester Wheatsheaf, 1987).

Thomas, Caroline, and Peter Wilkin (eds.). *Globalization, Human Security, and the African Experience* (Boulder: Lynne Rienner Publishers, 1999).

Thomas, Keith (ed.). *The Revolution in Military Affairs: Warfare in the Information Age* (Canberra: Australian Defence Studies Centre, Australian Defence Force Academy, 1997).

Thompson, William R. "The Future of Transitional Warfare." Pp. 63–92 in James Burk (ed.), *The Military in New Times: Adapting Armed Forces to a Turbulent World* (Boulder: Westview Press, 1994).

Thucydides. *History of the Peloponnesian War.* Transl. R. Warner (London: Penguin, 1954).

Tickner, Ann. *Gender in International Relations: Feminist Perspectives on Achieving Global Security* (New York: Columbia University Press, 1992).

———. *Gendering World Politics* (New York: Columbia University Press, 2001).

———. "Re-Visioning Security." Pp. 175–197 in K. Booth and S. Smith. *International Relations Theory Today* (Cambridge, UK: Polity, 1995).

Tilley, Charles. *Coercion, Capital and European States, AD 990–1990* (Oxford: Blackwell, 1990).

Todd, Jennifer. "The Reorientation of Constitutional Nationalism." Pp. 71–83 in J. Coakley (ed.), *Beyond Orange and Green: Redefining the Union and the Nation in Contemporary Ireland* (Dublin: University College Dublin Press, 2002).

Toffler, Alvin, and Heidi Toffler. *Wars and Anti-Wars: Survival at the Dawn of the 21st Century* (Boston: Little, Brown, 1993).

Tooze, Roger. "International Political Economy." In S. Smith (ed.), *International Relations: British and American Approaches* (Oxford, UK: Blackwell, 1985).

———. "The Unwritten Preface: International Political Economy and Epistemology," *Millennium: Journal of International Studies* 17, no. 2 (1988): 285–293.

Tooze, Roger, and Craig N. Murphy. "The Epistemology of Poverty and the Poverty of Epistemology in IPE: Mystery, Blindness, and Invisibility," *Millennium: Journal of International Studies* 25, no. 3 (1996): 681–707.

Toulmin, Stephen. *Cosmopolis: The Hidden Agenda of Modernity* (New York: Free Press/Macmillan, 1990).

Transformation Moment: A Canadian Vision of Common Security. The Report of the Citizens' Inquiry into Peace and Security (Waterloo, Ontario: March 1992).

Tyson, Laura D. *Who's Bashing Whom? Trade Conflicts in High Technology Industries* (Washington, D.C.: Institute for International Economics, 1992).

United Nations Development Programme (UNDP). *Human Development Report 1994* (New York: Oxford University Press, 1994). Citations from a reprint of sections of the report, "Redefining Security: The Human Dimension," *Current History* (May 1995): 229–236.

―――. *Human Development Report* (New York: Oxford University Press, annual).

United Nations Institute for Disarmament Research. *Nonoffensive Defense: A Global Perspective* (New York: Taylor & Francis, 1990).

Van den Berge, Maarten. "Culture as Ideology in the Conquest of Modernity: Japan's Regional Regulation Strategies," *Review of International Political Economy* 2, no. 3 (1995).

Vayrynen, Tarja. "Phenomenology and Conflict Analysis: The Implications of the Work of Alfred Schutz." Ph.D. diss., University of Kent, 1995.

Viner, Jacob. *The Long View and the Short: Studies in Economic Theory and Policy* (New York: Free Press, 1958).

Viviani, Nancy. "Australia and Southeast Asia." In James Cotton and John Ravenhill (eds.), *Seeking Asian Engagement: Australia in World Affairs, 1991–1995* (Melbourne: Oxford University Press, 1997).

Volcker, Paul. "Can We Bounce Back?" *Financial Times.* October 7, 1998.

Wæver, Ole. "Securitization and Desecuritization." Pp. 46–86 in Ronnie Lipschutz (ed.), *On Security* (New York: Columbia University Press, 1995).

―――. "Securitizing Sectors? Reply to Eriksson," *Cooperation and Conflict* 34, no. 3 (1999): 334–340.

Wæver, Ole, et al. *Identity, Migration, and the New Security Agenda in Europe* (London: Pinter, 1993).

Wæver, Ole, Pierre Lemaitre, and Elzbieta Tromer. *European Polyphony: Perspectives Beyond East-West Confrontation* (London: Macmillan, 1990).

Walker, R. B. J. *One World, Many Worlds: Struggles for a Just World Peace* (Boulder: Lynne Rienner Publishers, 1988).

―――. "The Subject of Security." Pp. 61–81 in Keith Krause and Michael C. Williams (eds.), *Critical Security Studies: Concepts and Cases* (Minneapolis: University of Minnesota Press, 1997).

Wallace, William. "Truth and Power, Monks and Technocrats: Theory and Practice in International Relations," *Review of International Studies* 22 (1996): 301–321.

Walt, Stephen. "International Relations: One World, Many Theories," *Foreign Policy* 110 (1998): 29–46.

―――. "The Renaissance of Security Studies," *International Studies Quarterly* 35, no.2 (1991): 211–239.

―――. "Rigor or Rigor Mortis? Rational Choice and Security Studies," *International Security* 23, no. 4 (1999): 5–48.

Walter, Barbara F. "Designing Transitions from Civil War: Demobilization, Democratization, and Commitment to Peace." Pp. 415–443 in Michael Brown,

Owen R. Coté Jr., Sean M. Lynn-Jones, and Steven E. Miller (eds.), *Nationalism and Ethnic Conflict* (Cambridge, Mass.: MIT Press, 2001).

Waltz, Kenneth. "America as a Model for the World? A Foreign Policy Perspective," *PS: Political Science and Politics* (December 1991): 667–670.

———. "The Continuity of International Politics." Pp. 348–353 in Ken Booth and Tim Dunne (eds.), *Worlds in Collision: Terror and the Future of Global Order* (Houndmills, UK: Palgrave Macmillan, 2002).

———. "Kant, Liberalism and War," *American Political Science Review* 56 (1962): 331–340.

———. *Theory of International Politics* (Reading, Mass: Addison-Wesley, 1979).

Walzer, Michael. "Notes on the New Tribalism." In C. Brown (ed.), *Political Restructuring in Europe: Ethical Perspectives* (London: Routledge, 1994).

———. *Spheres of Justice: A Defence of Pluralism and Equality* (Oxford, UK: Blackwell, 1995).

Weart, Stephen. *Never at War: Why Democracies Will Never Fight One Another* (New Haven, Conn.: Yale University Press, 1998).

Weiss, Linda. "Globalization and the Myth of the Powerless State," *New Left Review* 225 (1997): 3–27.

Wendt, Alexander. "Anarchy Is What States Make of It: The Social Construction of Power Politics," *International Organization* 46, no. 2 (1992): 391–425.

———. *Social Theory of International Politics* (Cambridge, UK: Cambridge University Press, 1999).

———. "What Is International Relations For? Notes Towards a Post-Critical View." Pp. 205–224 in Richard Wyn Jones (ed.), *Critical Theory and World Politics* (Boulder: Lynne Rienner Publishers, 2001).

Wenek, Major R. W. J. *The Assessment of Psychological Fitness: Some Options for the Canadian Forces.* Technical Note 1/84, Ottawa: Directorate of Personnel Selection, Research on Second Careers, July 1984.

Wheeler, Nicholas J., and Ken Booth. "The Security Dilemma." In J. Baylis and N. J. Rengger (eds.), *Dilemmas of World Politics* (Oxford, UK: Oxford University Press, 1992).

Whitworth, Sandra. "Gender, Race and the Politics of Peacekeeping." Pp. 176–191 in Edward Moxon-Browne, (ed.), *A Future for Peacekeeping?* (London: Macmillan, 1998).

———. *Men, Militarism, and UN Peacekeeping: A Gendered Analysis* (Boulder: Lynne Rienner Publishers, 2004).

———. "The Ugly Unasked Questions About Somalia," *Globe and Mail*, February 14, 1997, p. A27.

———. "Women, and Gender, in the Foreign Policy Review Process." Pp. 83–98 in M. A. Cameron and Maureen Appel Molot, *Canada Among Nations 1995: Democracy and Foreign Policy* (Ottawa: Carleton University Press, 1995).

Whyte, John. *Interpreting Northern Ireland* (Oxford, UK: Clarendon, 1990).

Wierzbicka, Anna. *What Did Jesus Mean? Explaining the Sermon on the Mount and the Parables in Simple and Universal Human Concepts* (New York: Oxford University Press, 2001).

Wiggershaus, Rolf. *The Frankfurt School: Its History, Theories, and Political Significance.* Transl. Michael Robertson (Cambridge, UK: Polity, 1994).

Wight, Colin. "Philosophy of the Social Sciences." Pp. 23–52 in Walter Carlsnaes, Thomas Risse, and Beth A. Simmons (eds.), *Handbook of International Relations* (London: Sage, 2002).

Wilford, R. (ed.). *Aspects of the Belfast Agreement* (Oxford, UK: Oxford University Press, 2001).

Williams, Howard, and Ken Booth. "Kant: Theorist Beyond Limits." Pp. 71–98 in Ian Clark and Iver B. Newmann (eds.), *Classical Theories of International Relations* (Houndmills, UK: Macmillan, 1996).

Williams, Michael. "The Practices of Security: Critical Contributions," *Cooperation and Conflict* 34, no. 3 (1999): 341–344.

Williams, Raymond. *Keywords: A Vocabulary of Culture and Society* (Glasgow: Fontana, 1976).

Wilson, Richard A. (ed.). *Human Rights, Culture, and Context: Anthropological Perspectives* (London: Pluto, 1987).

Wing, Ian. *Refocusing Concepts of Security: The Convergence of Military and Non-military Tasks* (Canberra: Land Warfare Studies Centre Working Paper No. 111, November 2000).

Winslow, Donna. *The Canadian Airborne Regiment in Somalia: A Socio-Cultural Inquiry*. A study prepared for the Commission of Inquiry into the Deployment of Canadian Forces to Somalia (Ottawa: Government Services Canada, 1997).

———. "Rites of Passage and Group Bonding in the Canadian Airborne," *Armed Forces and Society* 25, no. 3 (Spring 1999): 440.

Wiseman, Geoffrey. *Common Security and Non-Provocative Defence: Alternative Approaches to the Security Dilemma* (Canberra: Peace Research Centre Monograph No. 7, Australian National University, 1989).

Wohlforth, William. *The Elusive Balance: Power and Perceptions During the Cold War* (Ithaca: Cornell University Press, 1993).

Wood, Ellen Meiksins. "The Separation of the Economic and the Political in Capitalism," *New Left Review* 127 (1981).

Worthington, Peter, and Kyle Brown. *Scapegoat: How the Army Betrayed Kyle Brown* (Toronto: McClelland Bantam, 1997).

Wyn Jones, Richard. "'Message in a Bottle'? Theory and Praxis in Critical Security Studies," *Contemporary Security Policy* 16, no. 3 (1995): 299–319.

———. "The Nuclear Revolution." Pp. 90–109 in Alex Danchev (ed.), *Fin De Siecle: The Meaning of the Twentieth Century* (London: I. B. Taurus, 1995).

———. *Security, Strategy, and Critical Theory* (Boulder: Lynne Rienner Publishers, 1999).

———. "'Travel Without Maps': Thinking About Security After the Cold War." Pp. 196–218 in Jane Davis (ed.), *Security Issues in the Post–Cold War World* (Cheltenham, UK: Edward Elgar, 1996).

Wyn Jones, Richard (ed.). *Critical Theory and World Politics* (Boulder: Lynne Rienner Publishers, 2001).

Wyschogrod, Edith. *An Ethics of Remembering: History, Heterology, and the Nameless Others* (Chicago: University of Chicago Press, 1998).

Yoneyama, Lisa. "Taming the Memoryscape: Hiroshima's Urban Renewal." In Jonathan Boyarin (ed.), *Remapping Memory: The Politics of TimeSpace* (Minneapolis: University of Minnesota Press, 1994).

Young-Bruehl, Elisabeth. *Hannah Arendt: For Love of the World* (New Haven, Conn.: Yale University Press, 1982).

Youngs, Gillian. "From Realism to Neorealism: Theoretical Transition as Discourse, State-Centrism and Beyond" (PhD Thesis, Nottingham Trent University, June 1996).

Yuval-Davis, Nira. *Gender and Nation* (London: Sage, 1997).

Zakaria, Fareed. *From Wealth to Power* (Princeton, N.J.: Princeton University Press, 1998).

———. "Our Hollow Hegemony," *New York Times Magazine*, November 1, 1998.

The Contributors

Hayward Alker is John A. McCone Professor of International Relations in the School of International Relations at the University of Southern California.

Ken Booth is E. H. Carr Professor and head of department in the Department of International Politics, University of Wales, Aberystwyth.

Graeme Cheeseman is visiting fellow in the School of Politics at the University College, University of New South Wales, Canberra, Australia.

Andrew Linklater is Woodrow Wilson Professor in the Department of International Politics, University of Wales, Aberystwyth.

Jan Jindy Pettman is professor of women's studies, Australian National University, Canberra.

Joseph Ruane is senior lecturer in the Sociology Department, University College, Cork, Ireland.

Steve Smith is vice chancellor of the University of Exeter.

Jennifer Todd is senior lecturer, Department of Politics, University College, Dublin, Ireland.

Roger Tooze is visiting professor of global political economy, Bristol Business School, University of Western England, and acting director of the International Centre for Journalism and Society, City University, London.

Sandra Whitworth is associate professor of political science and women's studies at York University in Toronto, Canada, and a faculty associate at the Centre for International and Security Studies.

Richard Wyn Jones is senior lecturer in the Department of International Politics, University of Wales, Aberystwyth.

Index

About the Book

Realist assumptions of security studies increasingly have been challenged by an approach that places the human being, rather than the state, at the center of security concerns. This text is an indispensable statement of the ideas of this critical security project, written by some of its leading exponents.

The book is structured around three concepts—security, community, and emancipation—that arguably are central to the future shape of world politics. Each of its three parts begins with a survey of key theoretical issues, followed by an investigation of current case material. The authors emphasize that critical security is about the problems of real people in real places, and about linking theory and practice. Throughout, they address the fundamental questions at the heart of critical thinking about security.

Ken Booth is E. H. Carr Professor and head of the Department of International Politics, University of Wales, Aberystwyth. His numerous publications include *Strategy and Ethnocentrism, International Theory: Positivism and Beyond,* and *Worlds in Collision: Terror and the Future of Global Order.*